GENDERED
ENCOUNTERS

GENDERED
ENCOUNTERS

CHALLENGING CULTURAL BOUNDARIES
AND SOCIAL HIERARCHIES IN AFRICA

Maria Grosz-Ngaté and
Omari H. Kokole, editors

Routledge
New York & London

Published in 1997 by
Routledge
29 West 35th Street
New York, NY 10001

Published in Great Britain by
Routledge
11 New Fetter Lane
London EC4P 4EE

Library of Congress Cataloging–in–Publication Data

Gendered encounters: challenging cultural boundaries and social
   hierarchies in Africa/Maria Grosz-Ngaté and Omari H. Kokole. editors.
     p. cm.
   Includes bibliographical references and index.
   ISBN 0-415-91642-9. — ISBN 0-415-91643-7 (pbk.)
   1. Women—Africa. 2. Sex role—Africa. 3. Africa—Civilization.
I. Grosz-Ngaté, Maria Luise.   II. Kokole, Omari H.
HZ1787.G45   1996
306' .096—dc20   96–28338
                                               CIP

In memory of Omari H. Kokole, colleague and friend, who died suddenly after work on this volume had been completed.

CONTENTS

ACKNOWLEDGMENTS

This volume took shape while Maria Grosz-Ngaté was post-doctoral associate at the Institute of Global Cultural Studies (IGCS) at the State University of New York, Binghamton, from 1993–1995. We thank Professor Ali A. Mazrui, IGCS director, for encouraging the project and for making available the resources of the Institute. We also extend our gratitude to Jay Keith, and especially to Ruzima C. Sebuharara and Lauren Berk, for providing valuable support in the preparation of the manuscript.

The editors

CONTRIBUTORS

Victoria Bernal is Associate Professor of anthropology at the University of California, Irvine.

Paulla Ebron is Assistant Professor of anthropology at Stanford University.

Gillian Feeley-Harnik is Professor of anthropology at the Johns Hopkins University.

Charles Didier Gondola is Research Associate at the "Laboratoire dynamique des sociétés en développement," URA-CNRS 363, Université Paris-VII.

Sandra E. Greene is Associate Professor of history at Cornell University.

Maria Grosz-Ngaté is an anthropologist who lives in Ithaca, NY.

Dorothy Hodgson is Assistant Professor of anthropology at Rutgers University.

Omari H. Kokole is Associate Director of the Institute of Global Cultural Studies and Assistant Professor of political science and of Africana studies at the State University of New York, Binghamton.

Obiagele Lake is Assistant Professor of anthropology at the University of Iowa.

Barbara A. Moss is Assistant Professor of history at the University of Georgia.

Helen Nabasuta Mugambi is Associate Professor of comparative literature at the California State University, Fullerton.

Judy Rosenthal is Assistant Professor of anthropology at the University of Michigan, Flint.

INTRODUCTION

Maria Grosz-Ngaté

In a recent travel essay on Mali, Roberta Allen (1995) described a fifteen-day journey whose highlights were Timbuktu and the Dogon country. The photographs accompanying the article included portraits of three women of varying ages, two elder men, and a young boy. With the exception of the boy, these individuals were represented as generic types with a singular identity—"a Bambara woman," "a nomadic woman," "a Muslim elder," "a Dogon woman," and "a Dogon elder"—even though their appearance did not make these categories self-evident. In support of the differences thus established, the caption went on to explain that "Mali is home to several distinct tribal groups and religions" (1995:24), thereby reifying cultural identity and making religion a marker of difference on a par with ethnicity.

I start with this by no means unusual example of "othering" to emphasize the persistent identification of Africa with clearly distinguishable and separate "tribes." Consequently, the irruption of violent conflict on the continent is seen as the logical outcome of "natural" divisions and serves to further reinforce these widely held preconceptions. The identification of Africa with distinct peoples and primordial loyalties is not confined to the popular imagination but extends to thinking in government and academic circles as well. Even anthropology departments still frequently list introductory courses on Africa as "Peoples and Cultures of Africa," a title that evokes multiplicity but also separation and boundedness. Certain versions of Afrocentricity, on the other hand, reify and essentialize cultural particularity, then elevate it to an "African" universal. These examples could be multiplied. They are baffling in view of the long-standing debate on ethnicity in Africa and especially the considerable amount of Africanist research and writing in recent years that has emphasized the interplay of culture and history and the permeability of boundaries. One of the objectives of this volume is to continue to undermine the notion of homogeneous and bounded cultural wholes by shifting the spotlight to the historical dynamics and cultural creativity which have characterized the continent over time. More specifically, the essays here explore the interplay between global historical forces and local social relations and cultural configurations through the prism of gender.

Though focusing on Africa and motivated by a concern with representations of Africa and Africans, this volume is also inspired by current efforts in the human sciences more generally to question established truths about cultural difference and associated boundaries between "self" and "other." As a member of a discipline whose very origin was predicated on European preoccupations with the "other," I would like to begin with an outline of the recent debate on "culture" in anthropology.[1]

Interestingly, this debate coincides with the embracing of "culture" by other human science disciplines and its insertion into their analytical toolkit. Challenged by members of groups who had previously been defined as "other" and by changing political realities, anthropologists have had to reflect anew on the culture concept and its epistemological foundations. During the 1980s we began to focus on the role our discipline had played in establishing "cultures" as distinct and cohesive entities through our ethnographies. Exploring how the contingent encounters of ethnographic research are transformed into authoritative texts, some (Clifford and Marcus 1986; Clifford 1988; Rosaldo 1989; Stoler 1989) called for textual experimentation as a way of making ethnographic writing reflect more closely the interactions and power relations between the researcher and her/his interlocutors.

In arguing that the fieldwork encounter is also overdetermined by the researcher's engagement with earlier texts that influence both the formulation of research problems and the research process, Appadurai (1988:17) went one step further. He drew attention to the twin issues of "place" and "voice": rather than unproblematically assuming a unity of people and place, anthropologists ought to make the location of the ethnographer and the way certain places come to be identified with particular theoretical constructs an integral part of the analysis. Other anthropologists have reexamined the culture concept from different perspectives and agree that the notion of culture as a bounded entity is no longer tenable. Kahn (1989:15), who, like Appadurai, focuses on the location of the ethnographer, has argued that "culture" is produced through the "ethnographic dialogue," that is to say, it is "new knowledge, rather than a simple appropriation in (our) thought of an already existing phenomenon already present out there in the world." For him, the notion of *a* culture is similar to the notion of race as a biological construct in that it is impossible to identify valid criteria for unambiguously demarcating groups of people. Nonetheless, drawing on his own research in Malaysia, he proposes that, rather than discarding the culture concept altogether in the absence of a better alternative, anthropologists should analyze their own constructions alongside and in relation to those of indigenous hegemonic groups who valorize "tradition":

> In asking about the conditions (social and ideological) under which images of Malay tradition are generated, and their impact on, for example, political processes in contemporary Malaysia, I stand not as an outsider observing and describing an amusing folk conception, but as an insider who individually, but also as part of a group of urban dwelling, middle class anthropologists, who is for better or worse a participant in this particular culture industry [sic]. (Kahn 1989:23)

Dirks (1990) traces the historicization of the culture concept in anthropology as well as its migrations into cultural studies and history and concludes that it retains some of its weaknesses in all of these reappropriations. Yet he, too, is not ready to cast it out. Instead, he contends that "culture" and "history" are both useful categories when they inform each other without being taken as having self-evident meaning. Finally, Abu-Lughod (1991, 1993a) has argued that the culture concept both makes a focus on cultural distinctiveness inevitable and, in stressing coherence, also glosses over internal variation and difference.[2]

> As a professional discourse that elaborates on the meaning of culture in order to account for, explain, and understand cultural difference, anthropology [therefore] ends up also constructing, producing, and maintaining difference. Anthropological discourse helps give cultural difference (and the separation between groups of people that it implies) the air of the self-evident. (1993a:12)

Abu-Lughod does not consider the possibility of a less reifying concept but advocates "writing against culture." She proposes several strategies toward that end, including a reorientation from culture to practice and discourse, a focus on the interconnections (historical and/or contemporary) between the locations of the researcher and those who are the subjects of research, and a shift away from collective subjects to "ethnographies of the particular" (1991:147–157). She demonstrates the latter admirably in *Writing Women's Worlds* (1993a).[3]

FROM THE LOCAL TO THE GLOBAL AND BACK

Implicit in the notion of a "culture" is the idea that culture is a purely local construction and is tied to a specific territory. Current challenges to this conceptualization, as exemplified by Abu-Lughod's critique, are informed by a heightened awareness of global interconnectedness spurred by late-twentieth-century movements of people, knowledge, and commodities and by a growing body of crossdisciplinary work on "globalization." The idea of an interconnected world first received widespread attention through the work of Wallerstein (1974) on the emergence of the "modern world system." Wallerstein's model was widely debated and some of its details were challenged, but the underlying ideas generated a considerable number of studies on various dimensions of capitalist expansion. Wolf (1982) and Mintz (1985) demonstrated how anthropological studies might benefit from a perspective that emphasized connection rather than isolation. Other scholars (Appadurai 1990, 1991; Featherstone 1990; Friedman 1994; Giddens 1990; Hannerz 1989, 1991, 1992; Harvey 1989; King 1991; Pred and Watts 1992; Robertson 1992) turned their attention to the social and cultural implications of "globalization," the most recent phase in the making of the modern world. Strategies of flexible accumulation, global capital markets, and movements of labor linked to globalization are accompanied by a variety of effects, such as an altered experience of time and space, multiple linkages that transcend national boundaries, and repercussions for individuals and communities who may be far removed from the points where decisions are made or events take place. The rapid dissemination of cultural products has raised concerns about cultural homogenization. In the face of U.S. hegemony during the post-WWII era, cultural homogenization often became synonymous with "Americanization" or the "Coca-Colaization" of the world. Yet research thus far has shown that transnational cultural products do not simply replace local ones but are often refashioned and given new meaning.[4] Hall (1991:28) has referred to this as a "peculiar form of homogenization" that "does not work for completeness." He and others (e.g., Pred and Watts 1992) have argued that the failure to eliminate specificity is integral to contemporary capitalism: Rather than sweeping up everything in its wake, capitalism absorbs and works through difference, resulting in multiple capitalisms and multiple modernities. For Hall, global mass culture nonetheless remains "centered in the West," because its motivating forces are the technologies, capital, and advanced labor concentrated in the West, as well as the imageries of the West.

Hannerz (1991), while recognizing local specificities, similarly points to the dominant role played by the West, contending that cultural exchanges are overwhelmingly unidirectional as a result of the existing asymmetry between center and periphery. Appadurai (1990:16), for his part, is less concerned with directionality than with effect, noting that even the absorption of "instruments of homogenization" (e.g., armaments, language hegemonies, clothing styles) into local political and cultural economies leads to unexpected outcomes. He also rejects all forms of center-periphery models for their inability to capture the complexities of global cultural economies. And whereas Hannerz (1991:112–116) stays closer to conventional categories by positing market, state, form of life, and movement as frameworks through which cultural processes occur, Appadurai proposes five overlapping but not iso-morphic constructs—ethnoscapes, mediascapes, technoscapes, finanscapes, and ideoscapes—for apprehending processes and relationships in the current global order. It is worth quoting Appadurai here at length:

> The suffix -scape allows us to point to the fluid, irregular shapes of these landscapes, shapes which characterize international capital as deeply as they do international clothing styles. These terms with the common suffix -scape also indicate that these are not objectively given relations which look the same from every angle of vision, but rather that they are deeply perspectival constructs, inflected by the historical, linguistic and political situatedness of different sorts of actors: nation-states, multinationals, diasporic communities, as well as sub-national groupings and movements (whether religious, political or economic), and even intimate face-to-face groups, such as villages, neighborhoods and families. Indeed, the individual actor is the last

locus of this perspectival set of landscapes, for these landscapes are eventually navigated by agents who both experience and constitute larger formations, in part by their own sense of what these landscapes have to offer. (1990:7)

The challenge of this vision lies in translating it into concrete research projects that elucidate specific issues.[5] Rather than abandoning the focus on the local in favor of the global, those concerned with the ways in which global historical forces affect people's lives will have to examine how the global and the local intersect at specific points within these nexi, the power relationships at work in these processes, and how social agents in different locations apprehend, negotiate, and act upon these forces. It is therefore well worth heeding Watts (1992:122), who, drawing on Scott, reminds us that "it is important to recall . . . that the experience of the large abstraction we choose to call capitalism always arrives . . . in quite personal, concrete, localized and mediated forms."

Reconceptualizing the "local" also requires thinking afresh about the connection between "culture" and "place." For a long time, anthropologists conflated "a culture," or "a people," and place; "tribes" were identified with specific territories to the point where the "tribal" designation often came to stand for a locale (e.g., "in Hausa"). This too has been thrown into question by globalization: not because the identification of community and place has been "natural" and unmediated in the past, but because of an acute awareness that "the viability of actual places has been powerfully threatened through changing material practices of production, consumption, information flow and communication coupled with the radical reorganization of space relations and of time horizons within capitalist development" (Harvey 1993:40). Furthermore, recent work by geographers has made it clear that place and space stand in a dialectical relationship.[6] Anthropologists have turned to this new geography for inspiration in reconsidering the relationship between culture and place. In a seminal article, Gupta and Ferguson (1992) noted that representations of space have generally entailed borders, rupture, and disjunctions mapped onto social entities such as "cultures" or nation-states. They also pointed out that taking the link between culture and place for granted has had the effect of making invisible people at the margins (e.g., nomads, migrants, immigrants), differences within a locale, hybridity facilitated by the colonial encounter, and the hierarchical interconnection of spaces. Only by prising apart culture and place and by introducing space and power as salient dimensions is it possible to conceptualize global/local intersections in new ways:

The presumption that spaces are autonomous has enabled the power of topography to conceal successfully the topography of power. . . . If one begins with the premise that spaces have *always* been hierarchically interconnected, instead of naturally disconnected, then cultural and social change becomes

not a matter of cultural contact and articulation but one of rethinking difference *through* connection. (Gupta and Ferguson 1992:8)

Taking space and power to be constitutive of culture makes it impossible to conceive
of culture as the production of a territorially bounded group of people and opens the
way for making the external integral to the internal and the global to the local.

AFRICA AND GLOBAL CULTURAL ECONOMIES

Africa has been largely absent in the emerging body of scholarship on global cultural
economies. This has been due in part to scholars' preoccupation with configurations
of and responses to transnational capitalism, on the one hand, and with U.S.-domi-
nated "mass culture" as a homogenizing force on the other. While Africa is not outside of these circuits, declining terms of trade since the 1970s and reverse flows of
capital have entailed economic stagnation.[7] Not only have infrastructures—from
roads to schools and means of communication—deteriorated, the introduction and
use of new information technologies have lagged behind those of other parts of the
world. Multinationals have therefore avoided locating manufacturing enterprises on
the continent—South Africa being one of the few exceptions—favoring instead regions of the world where the need for investment in infrastructure is minimal. For
many African countries, the agricultural sector continues to be the mainstay of the
economy even though it has been beset by serious problems. Needless to say, the
economic problems of the continent are part and parcel of uneven globalization. As a
result, much social science research over the past fifteen years has concentrated
on identifying the sources of economic decline and faltering agricultural production,
analyzing their different dimensions, and charting possibilities for change.

In spite of economic decline and a concomitant research concentration on
African livelihoods, urban and rural Africans are firmly tied into global cultural
economies. Gandoulou's pioneering work (1989a, b) on Congolese youths who emigrate to Paris to acquire the trappings of high fashion in order to return home as "elegant persons" is only one illustration of this. Africans also express their conception of
the wider world and their position in it through new cultural forms, as evidenced by
thriving popular arts.[8] Studies have pointed to the energy visual, verbal, and musical
genres derive from social change and influences of multiple origins. The most prominent of these studies have concentrated on popular music, tracing the innovative appropriation of Western musical styles and of music from the African diaspora in the
Americas as well as the dissemination of new musics within the continent (Bemba
1984; Coplan 1985; Erlmann 1991; Konaté 1987; Waterman 1990). These and
other works on popular arts have highlighted cultural creativity and social context,
yet much remains to be done in analyzing the connections between local cultural
economies and the global movement of technologies, commodities, and capital.

There is evidence that the spread of Rastafarianism from Jamaica to North America, Europe, and sub-Saharan Africa has been greatly facilitated by the music and fashion with which it is associated (Savishinsky 1994). The introduction and widespread use of audio cassettes more generally, the circulation of films ranging from kung fu to Indian melodramas and indigenous African productions, and the distribution and consumption of European wax prints and damask adapted to African tastes are but a few areas that merit such multidimensional inquiry. Research of such scope is currently being conducted on used clothing in Zambia: It combines an examination of the local economic significance of used garments imported from North America and Europe, their transformation into fashionable ware, and the meanings they take on in marking class and gender with a study of the transcontinental commodity circuits in which they are embedded (Hansen 1994).

In view of prevailing images of African "cultures" as discrete and isolated, it is important to note that involvement in translocal networks on the continent is not uniquely tied to globalization. Connections within and across regions predate not only the twentieth century but also the arrival of Europeans on African shores. Trade between Sahelian West Africa, North and Northeast Africa, and Mediterranean Europe across the Sahara Desert flourished by the eighth century A.D., as did trade across the Indian Ocean between the East African coast, the Arabian peninsula, and India. Within the continent communities were linked through trade across ecological zones. These "travels of culture" have generally been seen as involving only a relatively small number of people (e.g., merchants) and as more important in providing the sumptuary goods that helped set apart and legitimate elites than in affecting local, everyday social interaction and culture. Yet to suggest that durable cross-societal bonds did not develop until the emergence of overlapping ecumenes after about 1500 (Appadurai 1990:1–2) makes developments linked to the expansion of capitalism in Europe more unique than they really are. The diffusion of Islam, initially linked with long-distance trade, created connections across vast spaces, and the concomitant insertion of Muslim ancestors into local genealogies shows how some social groups repositioned themselves in light of wider spatial links and networks of power (Devisse 1989).

The Mali empire, the most prominent early state formation in West Africa, was at its height during the fourteenth century, linking people from the Atlantic coast to the desert edge and the savannas of the interior. Its linguistic and sociocultural imprint on the populations of the region remains in evidence to date. In Southern Africa, the click sounds in Nguni languages are evidence of historical relations between Nguni-speaking immigrants and Zhu speakers indigenous to the region. Wilmsen (1989, 1991) has made a strong case for viewing the San (Zhu speakers) not as a pristine people who have preserved a harmonious way of life untouched by "the outside world" but as people who have been integrated at the bottom of a social hierarchy over the course of centuries. Wilmsen (1991) shows how, rather than having remained outside regional social networks, they have participated in shifting but enduring connections that have become increasingly unequal. Long-distance trade and various forms of migration have historically influenced and helped reshape local practices and ideologies. Moreover, the development, expansion, and contraction of centralized polities in various parts of the continent, the trans-Atlantic slave trade, and the settlement of Portuguese in the Zambezi valley and of other Europeans in the Cape, all involved the modification or even transformation of social practices and, often, the emergence of new identities. Speaking from a vantage point shaped by research in West Africa but taking into account developments in other parts of the continent, Amselle (1985:24) proposed analyzing local formations in the context of a series of overlapping "social spaces which structured the African continent in the precolonial era." These would take account of interactions in different domains across broad areas and of the power relations these entailed, thus showing how particular "societies" and "cultures" are produced in relationship with others.

I dwell on precolonial interconnections in Africa not to counter Appadurai's contention that contemporary interactions are of a different nature and scale but to insist that African "cultures" have always been shaped within a wider social field. Following European conquest, colonial rule established "infrastructures" that promoted the North-South movement of cultural flows between the European metropoles and their colonies overseas at the same time as it created and reified new boundaries within the continent.

INTERSECTIONS OF THE LOCAL AND THE GLOBAL IN AFRICA: GENDERED PERSPECTIVES

If early theorizing of globalization and global cultural economies was concerned with developing models and conceptual constructs, more recent work has begun to take into account how these forces engage markers of difference such as race, ethnicity, gender, class, and religion. This volume focuses specifically on gender, examining how the encounter between local and translocal/global cultural currents reshapes social practices and cultural configurations. By placing gender at the center of analysis, we seek to show both that translocal and transnational cultural flows are inherently gendered and that gender is a crucial site of intersection between "inside" and "outside." Furthermore, to the extent that gender is linked to actual persons, a focus on gender helps us avoid the risk of treating global forces and currents of culture as though they were imbued with agency. Together, the essays should complement the work of literary scholars (e.g., Ogundipe-Leslie and Boyce Davies, 1994) to advance African gender theory.

There is by now a voluminous social science literature on women and gender in Africa. However, much of it has so far concentrated on the socioeconomic dimensions of capitalist expansion and globalization rather than on the gendered nature of cultural flows across social and national boundaries or the ways in which such flows are mediated by local gender constructs and relations. In the 1970s, feminist scholars doing research in Africa sought to determine women's position in different social domains and how it varied in relation to social organization, a preoccupation that grew directly out of North American feminist concerns. These studies provided a basis for examining changes in gender relations and in women's spheres of activity and access to resources as a result of colonialism and incorporation into a capitalist world economy. In contrast with the studies conducted in the 1970s, the literature of the last decade has examined gender as a complex of socioeconomic relations and has emphasized historical process. Culture remained nonetheless largely implicit in this work and was given attention only to the extent that socioeconomic relations are always culturally shaped.

We build on this work but shift our emphasis to the cultural dimension of globalization and socioeconomic transformation in their interrelationship with gender. While most of the studies in this volume focus on contemporary phenomena, some do deal with earlier historical periods and thus extend the evidence for translocal/global connections back in time. Those that focus on the present are historically grounded and all bring together culture, power, and economy in their analyses, thus following the recent tendency to bridge the culturalist-materialist dichotomy.

The first three essays show that women frequently act as cultural mediators, bridging what is perceived as inside and outside and creatively seizing new opportunities. They confirm previous critiques of the Lévi-Straussian postulate that women are merely passive objects of exchange between men as well as critiques of feminist work that views culture as a primarily male preserve. Greene's essay undermines the notion of precolonial societies as bounded wholes and demonstrates the value of viewing culture as a process rather than as a monolithic whole. Her focus on female slaves, male strangers, and their descendants in southeastern Ghana also makes clear how integral socially marginal individuals are to social reproduction and collective identity construction. While slave women were incorporated into the Anlo-Ewe polity as subordinates and dependents of a particular kind, their very presence served as a constant reminder of the power relationships that linked Anlo with its neighbors and the wider hinterland. It is possible to surmise that female slaves incorporated as wives influenced local practices even if the available data make it difficult to do more than speculate in what ways this might have happened. Slave daughters of prominent Anlo men who were given in marriage to male strangers engaged in the trans-Atlantic trade further extended Anlo connections. Like their mothers, they acted as cultural mediators through their persons and their bodies, allowing their fathers and other "insiders" to maintain a unitary Anlo Ewe identity. At the same time, they took advantage of their position by accumulating wealth on their own account and becoming respected members of the polity. This provided the basis for their descendants to claim an identity as Anlo insiders. The interplay between gender and cultural identity is not unique to this period, for Anlo practices and identity have emerged in interaction with a wider social field at least since the seventeenth century (Greene 1996).

The women discussed by Lake still mediate "inside" and "outside," though the "inside" here is not the Anlo polity of the nineteenth century but the Ghanaian nation-state in the latter part of the twentieth century. Daughters of Africans forcibly removed from the continent during the trans-Atlantic slave trade, they have returned to the motherland from the African diaspora in the Americas. Their experience of reintegration points to the complexities of "inside" and "outside," of being both the same and different, an issue creatively explored by Aidoo (1965) in her play *The Dilemma of a Ghost.* Unlike the (im)migrants who are at the center of most diaspora studies and who reimagine their homeland from a minority location after leaving it, women returnees to Ghana come to a home they have only known in the imagination. Those from the United States have left a powerful nation-state for one that stands in a dependent relationship within the global political economy, yet they feel empowered by their move because they have escaped the status of a stigmatized and dominated minority. Those from the Caribbean are in a more ambiguous position: though coming from nations where they are part of the majority, their countries' geographical proximity to the United States and historical ties to Britain serve as a constant reminder of their political and economic marginality.[9] For both groups, Ghana is highly significant as an African territory, that is, as a material location, not only an imaginatively and discursively constructed "place." It is important to stress this point in view of the current, often celebratory, emphasis on deterritorialization and fragmentation as a phenomenon linked with globalization in the late twentieth century. The fact that many of Lake's interviewees indicated that they had integrated socially but not culturally suggests that they might have taken common historical origin, experience of oppression, and racial solidarity to be synonymous with common culture when first coming to Ghana. Since they learned otherwise upon settling there, they have been developing new identities founded on their experience in Ghana *and* in the diaspora. These women act as mediators with the motherland for their relatives in the diaspora and, though not discussed by Lake, most likely also for Ghanaians with African and non-African communities in the Americas.

The paper by Gondola focuses on an African city as a crucible of change. It deals with women in colonial Kinshasa (Zaire) and illustrates how a focus on popular culture might provide perspectives on gender relations not captured by examination of the political and economic spheres alone. It also adds to the fine studies of African musical cultures that have appeared in recent years, the major domain in which the cultural dimensions of globalization have been explored. Gondola shows that, once permitted by the colonial authorities to migrate to the city, women did not confine themselves to the activities officially open to them—housekeeping, gardening, and small-scale trade—but seized new opportunities as they presented themselves. One such sphere of action was opened by the emergent popular music, a fusion of gendered musics unique to the urban milieu. While it remained male dominated, much as the genres on which it drew, it became an arena in which women were able to pursue their interests and even transgress established social norms. In the context of the time, this meant remaining single and more autonomous with respect to men, having multiple partners and a greater opportunity to accumulate wealth, and networking with other women. Gondola argues that women used this space to renegotiate gender relations in ways that would not have been possible in everyday life and that these women paved the way for contemporary female entrepreneurs. At the same time, his analysis of one contemporary song illustrates the ambivalence this shift has held for men.

Scholars working on Southern Africa have been at the forefront of the recent attention given to culture and gender, examining colonialism in the region as a cultural project as much as a politicoeconomic one.[10] Studies in this vein (e.g., Comaroff and Comaroff 1991; Hansen 1989, 1992; Schmidt 1992) have explored the reconfiguration of gender ideologies and relations and their intersection with race and class in conjunction with missionary activities, European domesticity, and the patriarchal policies of the colonial state. Rather than treating culture as received tradition, these scholars have viewed it as fluid, contingent, and processual, focusing on the ways it is made and remade by ordinary people in everyday life:

> Colonialism was a transforming encounter in which African women and men played active but different parts in shaping new spatial boundaries and experimenting with the many meanings of domesticity, in the process constructing and apportioning on their own terms boundaries between home and work, male and female, labor and leisure. (Hansen 1992:5)

Moss's paper in this volume expands the existing literature on missionary efforts to "civilize" Africans by remaking them in the European image. These efforts involved the creation of "new needs" linked to the consumption of European products (Burke 1993). Women and children were considered the most impressionable and were the first to be targeted for conversion by the missions. Drawing on Victorian notions of domesticity and women's role in social reproduction, missionaries sought to teach Shona women homemaking and "mothercraft." Yet, as Comaroff and Comaroff (1992:39) have noted, we should not assume

> that a full-grown, stable model of 'home life' was taken from Europe to the colonies. . . . In Africa and Europe alike the construction of the domestic world was a highly specific cultural and social project, invariably shaped by—and, in turn, itself influencing—the political worlds in which it occurred.

Moss, like Hunt (1992) in Zaire, found that in transmitting certain European notions, missionaries also departed from them in ways that served to maintain race and class boundaries. For example, women's aprons were made of coarse brown material, and European dishes like boiled puddings were prepared with mealie meal, the local staple. Moreover, the shift from locally produced products to European commodities was often constrained by economic realities.

If the process of commoditization discussed by Moss appeared to be relatively smooth, impeded primarily by economic constraints, Hodgson's discussion in this volume of possession among Maasai women in Tanzania makes it clear that "modernity" has come at a price. The phenomenon of possession (*orpeko*) seems to have appeared among Maasai women as their access to resources diminished and power relations increasingly shifted in favor of men in the wake of monetization, commoditization, and "development." Significantly, the problems women face and seem powerless to resolve manifest themselves in ills that take hold of a woman's body. Experienced by each woman individually, they are "cured" at the individual level. But the "cure" inserts women into a collectivity that, while not directly addressing the problems, at least provides a network of support. Hodgson's study confirms Boddy's (1994:421) point that possession, though shaped by local specifics, is "never only local and . . . always complex." One might add to this, as Hodgson notes perceptively, that gender relations and ideologies are never only local but are constituted "in interaction with translocal material, social and cultural processes." While possession among Maasai women does not constitute a "cult," it, and the actions it makes possible,

> provide ways of understanding, trying out, coming to terms with, and contesting modernity, colonialism, capitalism, and religious and other hegemonies [and] allow the implicit synthesis of the foreign with the local and historically relevant while reshaping all in the process. (Boddy 1994:421)

Everywhere on the continent Africans engage with cultural currents as they move between rural and urban areas and across national and regional boundaries. This phenomenon is not confined to intellectual and political elites but extends to men and women in all walks of life. More recent scholarly attention has concentrated on migrants to the North—migrant laborers in France, vendors of tourist art in Europe and North America, women merchants who regularly travel to Milan or London—while migrants across national boundaries within the continent and to other regions of the South have received far less consideration. Bernal's essay in this volume illustrates the valuable insights to be gained from research on migration within the South. Her paper provides a salutary counterpoint to the common assumption that modernity is predicated on "Westernization" and that Islamic fundamentalism is a return to tradition in the face of "Westernization." She discusses how a particular village in Sudan has become enmeshed in global cultural economies as men migrate to urban Sudan and, more importantly, to Saudi Arabia. As a regional center of economic and political power, Saudi Arabia is also a source of ideological and cultural influence (Bernal 1994:41). Male migrants return with consumer goods that are not primarily associated with Europe or the U.S. but with what is considered to be a superior form of Islam. In short, Saudi material wealth and Saudi Islam are closely identified with each other. More than the pilgrims who have long traveled to Saudi Arabia, migrants bring back cosmopolitan knowledge, including knowledge of more "correct" religious practices. The less scripturalist form of Islam practiced locally comes to be associated with ignorance, material poverty, and women. Yet these seemingly clear dichotomies are disrupted by other currents and do not inevitably lead to greater domination of women by men who are purveyors of goods and of knowledge: Sudanese men are well aware of their subordinate status in Saudi Arabia in spite of the religion they share with their employers, and the women, though they might adopt new forms of Islamic dress, also receive more support in obtaining a formal education. Bernal concludes that

> even as women become the symbolic focus of fundamentalist reform and of local tradition, women are gaining greater control over their marital destiny, obtaining education, and, in a few cases, even garnering their own incomes through formal employment. Increasing Islamic "orthodoxy" and expanding horizons for women are not so much opposing processes as two facets of the larger transformation of the village resulting from capitalist expansion and incorporation into global cultural circuits.

Bernal's paper illustrates how the meaning of "local" is transformed as particular places are drawn into new nexi of culture, power, and economy, but it also makes clear that these shifts are fraught with ambiguities. Along with the papers by Hodgson and Moss, it highlights the differential implications global forces have for women and men. It goes without saying that the women and men in question occupy specific social locations and that the implications are likely to vary for those in other locations.

The last set of essays is concerned with the gendered nature of cultural flows. Feeley-Harnik's essay dissects European and African political theories and notions of rule. It does precisely what Roberts (1992:240) argues is missing in Appadurai's model of global culture, namely to treat the circulation of knowledge, of theoretical discourses, as a kind of cultural flow. Nineteenth-century Madagascar, where both Sakalava and Merina shifted to female rule, is at the center of Feeley-Harnik's analysis. She starts with an overview of the gendered nature of European political theology to show how it informed the discursive construction of African political hierarchy and ultimately the strategies employed by the colonizing powers. But her analysis does not end there, for she discusses how Europeans and Africans interacted through their competing theories and practices. By drawing on indigenous theories of human reproduction as models of social and political reproduction, she is able to demonstrate that the European emphasis on rulers as unitary individuals systematically effaced the "polybodied" nature of political hierarchy. Taking African female rulers to be mere figureheads provided Europeans with a rationale for conquest on the one hand, but on the other it also gave Malagasy rulers "hidden sources of new political autonomy" under the guise of feminine leadership dismissed by the same Europeans.

Rosenthal's contribution, like that of Hodgson in the previous section, focuses on possession, though across the continent in coastal Togo and in the context of religious orders rather than as an individual phenomenon. The spirits, which may possess adherents of the orders (primarily, but not exclusively, women), are considered to be the spirits of "northern" slaves who had been captured or bought and integrated into coastal society. Although it was generally women who were retained locally while men were sold into the trans-Atlantic trade, the spirits are male and female yet stand as "husbands" to the "wives," female or male, they possess. Geographic and cultural boundaries are transcended as the "North" is celebrated as integral to the "South." Hence, as Matory (personal communication) has observed, the Gorovodu and Mama Tchamba orders are "constructively imagining and re-shaping relations within nation-states that are often antagonistically divided between north and south." In addition, social categories—male and female, master and slave—are turned topsy-turvy. Rosenthal's suggestion that we view gender "as a traveling sort of trope rather than a reality stuck to the bodies of real women and men" is well worth exploring in other African contexts. Her work, like Feeley-Harnik's on polyarchy and that of Matory (1993, 1994) on Oyo Yoruba religion, points gender studies in Africa in a new direction. It shows very clearly that gender in Africa is a more complex phenomenon than much of the existing literature leads us to believe, with its emphasis on the gender division of labor and on sex segregation. Though valuable for its analyses of socioeconomic organization and change, most earlier studies have taken the categories male and female to be self-evident (Grosz-Ngaté 1989). "Male daughters" and "female husbands,"[11] for example, have been seen as evidence of the greater flexibility of female gender roles and the economic autonomy of certain women prior to European colonization, but have not been explored for what they might reveal about notions of gender. In the conflation of gender and sexuality "male" and "female" have been assumed to be fixed and unambiguous categories.

Mugambi's essay puts the spotlight on media, specifically the radio songs popular in Uganda, and how these contribute to the discourse on gender and nation. Media products like movies, videos, and television serials are ubiquitous at least in urban Africa and, although considered homogenizing forces par excellence, are only now beginning to be studied (e.g., Abu-Lughod 1993b; Fuglesang 1994). Their diverse origins in the United States, former colonial metropoles, India, neighboring African countries, and national capitals raise questions about relative import, interpretation, and construction of identities and communities, among others. Even radio, though available for much longer than the visual media, has received little attention so far. Yet given its reach into remote rural areas, it has been instrumental in the circulation of knowledge and the dissemination of national ideologies, as well as in processes of language standardization and the establishment of language hierarchies (Spitulnik 1994). Mugambi discusses how Kiganda radio songs critique shifting gender relations and contribute to the construction of a national community. Of particular interest is her discussion of the rhetorical strategies song artists use to establish their authority. By borrowing "migratory texts"—formulaic openings and the trickster motif—from oral narrative, song artists anchor their pronouncements in tradition, thus giving them a weight they might otherwise not have. Moreover, the strategic deployment of widely recognized elements from the storytelling tradition enables the artists to reach people across ethnic, gender, age, class, rural, and urban boundaries. The effectiveness of new means of communication is therefore directly linked to the authorizing power of earlier modes of speech.

Mugambi's essay represents one effort to examine how cultural currents enter into the gendered construction of nationhood in Africa. In this, she is one of the growing number of literary and cultural studies scholars to explore a topic Africanist social scientists have been slow to address. African writers and filmmakers, by contrast, have probed the place of gender and sexuality in the construction of nationhood and the nation-state for some time. Particularly noteworthy here are the works of Ousmane Sembène (1973), V. Y. Mudimbe (1976), and Nuruddin Farah (1986). Cobham's (1992:57) assessment of Farah can be extended to Mudimbe and Sembène as well:

> Farah's destabilization of national and sexual boundaries forces a remapping of the terrain that would take more fully into account the complexity of the modern nation-state in Africa. In the process, the evocation of "traditional" truths as the paradoxically static yet organic point of departure for the nation state is replaced by a sense of the dynamic interaction and internal contradictions of both the traditional and the modern in today's African nation.

It bears stressing that Mudimbe's and Sembène's novels (and the superb film Sembène made of his novel) appeared when studies of African women were still in their infancy and certainly well before postmodernist perspectives began to influence the formulation of issues on a wide scale in the North American academy.

The last chapter in this volume by Paulla Ebron, probes nation, sexuality, and narrative, though from a somewhat different angle than the three novels just mentioned. At issue is tourism in The Gambia in which the desires of European women for satisfying sexual relationships and the desires of young Gambian men for economic success lead to relationships that are vilified by elder men and the state. This constellation calls for a reconsideration of sex tourism and of tourism more generally as a global cultural force. Whereas during the European conquest and colonization white men took possession both of the continent and of African women, now "unruly" European women threaten the health and viability of the postcolonial nation-state by "corrupting" its male youths. On the face of it, there seems to be merely a gender inversion in the continuing unequal power relationships between Europe and Africa, though perhaps more dangerous because of its implications for patriarchy. By listening to the tales about these sexual adventures rather than giving attention only to the "facts," Ebron is able to show that agency is not exclusively located in the economically powerful "West." Young Gambian men style themselves as tricksters in the tales they tell about their encounters with European women and thus assume agency while rejecting the position of powerless victim. Ebron's analysis offers rich insights into the dynamics of gender, sexuality, power, desire, and difference that characterize the encounters between the local and the global that are its focus. It also underlines the need "to attend to the localizing processes in which particular male and female sexualities are discursively and institutionally created" rather than assuming a homogeneous global sphere of circulation.

While Ebron's paper deals explicitly with travel, the themes of mobility and movement—of gendered persons, things, ideas, knowledge, and symbols—run through the other papers as well. At one level, they help dispel any notion of timeless cultural practices either historically or in a present characterized by economic stagnation. Rather than promoting a retreat into the past, politico-economic difficulties appear to be fertile ground for change and a creative reworking of "tradition." Culture clearly emerges as a site where translocal and transnational processes are actively mediated and negotiated in Africa, much as anywhere else. More important, by turning the spotlight on gender, the contributors to this volume are able to elucidate how these processes engage and interact with one particular form of difference. Together they show that the study of women and, especially, of gender remains a productive field of inquiry in spite of the already voluminous literature.

At another level, the essays demonstrate the value of grounding discussion of global processes (in the broadest sense) in local realities, hence the continued need for fine-grained ethnographic research. Only by attending to the varied local ramifications of global processes is it possible to apprehend their meanings and appreciate their materiality; otherwise they remain mere abstractions. The shift from taking the "local" (however defined) to be *the* social totality to analyzing it as it is constituted in interaction with social forces that extend both in space and in time, represents an important step forward in the human sciences.

Finally, the contributions to this volume and the theoretical shifts that made them possible invite reflection on the conditions that circumscribe social science theorizing in and about Africa. The issues addressed here have been articulated in African literature at least since the 1960s, and in various ways, by writers ranging from Ama Ata Aidoo to Yambo Ouologuem, Buchi Emecheta and Ngugi wa Thiongo to V. Y. Mudimbe. Assuming, then, that the conceptualization of these issues has been singularly enabled by the space created by postmodernism would be yet another instance of the view of a North-South flow of knowledge in which Africa is no more than a passive and silent recipient. Anthropologists (and other social scientists) might examine the conditions of possibility in social science production that have prevented us from turning to African writers for inspiration in directing and framing our inquiries and which continue to stand in the way of South-North flows of theory, even in the context of "globalization."

NOTES

My thanks to Lemuel Johnson, Fouad Makki, Jonathan Ngaté, Maxwell Owusu, and Judy Rosenthal for their reading of earlier drafts of this introduction. I am grateful for their comments even if I have been unable to make effective use of all of them.

1. I refer here specifically to U.S. anthropology where "culture" has been more central than in other national traditions. Nonetheless, British anthropology too has been concerned with distinct and singular societies even though it has privileged social structure, i.e., "society" over "culture." The anthropological propensity to highlight coherence (*between* rather than *within* societies) must be seen in the broader context of post-Enlightenment science, a science that strives to find order and eliminate ambiguity.

2. Abu-Lughod refers broadly to "anthropology" though her polemic clearly grows out of her engagement with U.S. cultural anthropology.

    Thornton (1988) has attributed the anthropological tendency to posit social entities as discrete social wholes to its rhetorical strategies and textual mode: "A text, to be convincing as a description of reality, must convey some sense of closure. For the ethnography, this closure is achieved by the textual play of object-reference and self-reference that the classificatory imagination permits. The discreteness of social entities, it appears, is chiefly an artifact of textual description that classifies them and substitutes the logic of classification for the experience of the 'everyday.' . . . The sense of a discrete social or cultural entity that is conveyed by an ethnography is founded on the sense of closure or completeness of both the physical text and its rhetorical format" (299). Amselle (1990), on the other hand, holds that the notion of autonomous cultures is an artifact of the comparative method which operates on the assumption of a preexisting matrix from which particular features can be abstracted. For him, the very production of "culture" is the result of a shifting field of power relations.

3. Although the final chapter in that volume focuses on cultural identity, her theoretical discussion preceding the text ignores the connection between self-representations that emphasize cultural distinctiveness and the anthropological stress on cultural difference.

4. Hannerz (1989, 1991) and Appadurai (1990) discuss this issue in a general way and a growing number of case studies deal with it in specific contexts.

5. Roberts (1992) provides an insightful discussion of Appadurai's model in relation to "world music," highlighting both its potential and its complexity.

6. Or, as Harvey (1993:23) has put it: "What goes on in a place cannot be understood outside of the space relations which support that place any more than the space relations can be understood independently of what goes on in particular places."

7. Adedeji (1993) has referred to the economic decline of the past two decades as the "growing marginalization" of Africa. The part played by international terms of trade

in this process is not likely to change significantly in the near future since Africa is the one region of the world that emerged as a publicly acknowledged loser from the 1994 GATT agreement concluded at the end of the Uruguay round of negotiations.

8. The September 1987 issue of **The African Studies Review** was devoted entirely to an overview of the popular arts and a discussion of terminology. The lead article by Karin Barber was followed by commentaries from several scholars. See Barber (1987).

9. The repatriates in Lake's study were from the English-speaking Caribbean. Issues from the perspective of women from the Francophone islands have, to my knowledge, only been dealt with in the fiction of Francophone women writers.

10. The work of Ann L. Stoler (1989), concentrating on Southeast Asia, but also extending to Africa, has been seminal in this regard.

11. Though I borrow these terms from Amadiume (1987), the phenomenon of "female husbands," more widely known in the anthropological literature as "woman-woman marriage," has been shown to have existed also in eastern and southern Africa.

BIBLIOGRAPHY

Abu-Lughod, Lila. 1991. "Writing Against Culture." In **Recapturing Anthropology**: **Working in the Present**, pp.137–162, Richard G. Fox, ed. Santa Fe, NM: School of American Research Press.

———. 1993a. **Writing Women's Worlds**: **Bedouin Stories**. Berkeley: University of California Press.

———. 1993b. "Finding a Place for Islam: Egyptian Television Serials and the National Interest." **Public Culture** 5(3):493–513.

Adedeji, Adebayo. 1993. "Marginalisation and Marginality: Context, Issues and Viewpoints." In **Africa Within the World**, p.xx, Adebayo Adedeji, ed. London & New Jersey: Zed Books.

Aidoo, Ama Ata. 1965. **The Dilemma of a Ghost**. Burnt Mill, Harlow, UK: Longman.

Allen, Roberta. 1995. "Mali Adventure, From Timbuktu to Dogon Country." **The Sophisticated Traveler**, **The New York Times Magazine**, Part 2, September 17.

Amadiume, Ifi. 1987. **Male Daughters, Female Husbands**: **Gender and Sex in an African Society**. London and New Jersey: Zed Books Ltd.

Amselle, Jean-Loup. 1985. "Ethnies et espaces: pour une anthropologie topologique." In **Au coeur de l'éthnie**, pp. 11–48, Jean-Loup Amselle et Elikia M'Bokolo, eds. Paris: Editions de la Découverte.

———. 1990. **Logiques métisses: Anthropologie de l'identité en Afrique et ailleurs**. Paris: Editions Payot.

———. and et Elikia M'Bokolo, eds. 1985. **Au coeur de l'éthnie**: **Ethnies, tribalisme et état en afrique**. Paris: Editions de la Découverte.

Appadurai, Arjun. 1988. "Introduction: Place and Voice in Anthropological Theory." **Cultural Anthropology** 3(1):16–20.

———. 1990. "Disjuncture and Difference in the Global Cultural Economy." **Public Culture** 2(2):1–24.

———. 1991. "Global Ethnoscapes: Notes and Queries for a Transnational Anthropology." In **Recapturing Anthropology**: **Working in the Present**, pp. 191–210, Richard G. Fox, ed. Santa Fe, NM: School of American Research Press.

Barber, Karin. 1987. "Popular Arts in Africa." **African Studies Review** 30(3):1–78.

Bemba, Sylvain. 1984. **50 ans de musique du Congo-Zaire**. Paris & Dakar: Présence Africaine.

Bernal, Victoria. 1994. "Gender, Culture, and Capitalism: Women and the Remaking of Islamic 'Tradition' in a Sudanese Village." *Comparative Studies in Society and History* 36(1):36–67.

Boddy, Janice. 1994. "Spirit Possession Revisited: Beyond Instrumentality." *Annual Review of Anthropology* 23:407–434.

Burke, Timothy J. 1993. "Lifebuoy Men, Lux Women: Commodification, Consumption and Cleanliness in Colonial Zimbabwe." Unpublished Ph.D. dissertation: Johns Hopkins University.

Chrétien, Jean-Pierre et Gérard Prunier, eds. 1989. *Les éthnies ont une histoire*. Paris: Editions Karthala et ACCT.

Clifford, James. 1988. *The Predicament of Culture*. Cambridge, MA: Harvard University Press.

———. and George Marcus, eds. 1986. *Writing Culture: The Poetics and Politics of Ethnography*. Berkeley: University of California Press.

Cobham, Rhonda. 1992. "Misgendering the Nation: African Nationalist Fictions and Nuruddin Farah's Maps." In *Nationalisms & Sexualities*, pp. 42–59. Andrew Parker, Mary Russo, Doris Sommer, and Patricia Yaeger, eds. New York and London: Routledge.

Comaroff, Jean and John. 1991. *Of Revelation and Revolution: Christianity, Colonialism, and Consciousness in South Africa*. Chicago: University of Chicago Press.

———. 1992. "Home-Made Hegemony: Modernity, Domesticity, and Colonialism in South Africa." In *African Encounters with Domesticity*, pp. 37–74. Karen T. Hansen, ed. New Brunswick, NJ: Rutgers University Press.

Coplan, David B. 1985. *In Township Tonight!: South Africa's Black City Music and Theatre*. London and New York: Longman.

Devisse, Jean. 1989. "Islam et éthnies en Afrique." In *Les éthnies ont une histoire*, pp. 103–115. Jean-Pierre Chrétien et Gérard Prunier, eds. Paris: Editions Karthala et ACCT.

Dirks, Nicholas B. 1990. "Is Vice Versa? Historical Anthropologies and Anthropological Histories." Paper (30 pp.) presented at CSST Conference on The Historic Turn in the Human Sciences, University of Michigan, Ann Arbor, October.

Erlmann, Veit. 1991. *African Stars: Studies in Black South African Performance*. Chicago: University of Chicago Press.

Farah, Nuruddin. 1986. *Maps*. New York: Pantheon Books.

Featherstone, Mike, ed. 1990. *Global Culture*. London: Sage Publications.

Friedman, Jonathan. 1994. *Cultural Identity and Global Process*. London: Sage Publications.

Fuglesang, Minou. 1994. "Islamic Reform and Romantic Melodrama in a Global Corner: Viewing Video and TV in a Lamu Town, Kenya." Paper presented in the conference on "Media, Popular Culture, and 'the Public' in Africa," Northwestern University, April 29 and May 1.

Gandoulou, Justin-Daniel. 1989a. *Au coeur de la sape: Moeurs et aventures de Congolais à Paris*. Paris: L'Harmattan.

———. 1989b. *Dandies à Bacongo: Le culte de l'élégance dans la société congolaise contemporaine*. Paris: L'Harmattan.

Giddens, Anthony. 1990. *The Consequences of Modernity*. Cambridge: Polity Press.

Greene, Sandra E. 1996. *Gender and Ethnicity among the Anlo Ewe*. Portsmouth: Heinemann.

Grosz-Ngaté, Maria. 1989. "Hidden Meanings: Explorations into a Bamanan Construction of Gender." *Ethnology* XXVIII(2): 167–183.

Gupta, Akhil and James Ferguson. 1992. "Beyond 'Culture': Space, Identity, and the Politics of Difference." *Cultural Anthropology* 7(1):6–23.

Hall, Stuart. 1991. "The Local and the Global: Globalization and Ethnicity." In *Culture, Globalization and the World-System*, pp. 19–39. Anthony D. King, ed. Binghamton, NY: Dept. of Art and Art History, State University of New York.

Hannerz, Ulf. 1989. "Notes on the Global Ecumene." *Public Culture* 1(2):66–75.

———. 1991. "Scenarios for Peripheral Cultures." In *Culture, Globalization and the World-System*, pp. 107–128. Anthony D. King, ed. Binghamton, NY: Dept. of Art and Art History, State University of New York.

———. 1992. *Cultural Complexity: Studies in the Social Organization of Meaning*. New York: Columbia University Press.

Hansen, Karen T. 1989. *Distant Companions: Servants and Employers in Zambia, 1900–1985*. Ithaca: Cornell University Press.

———. 1992. "Introduction: Domesticity in Africa." In *African Encounters with Domesticity*, pp. 1–33. Karen T. Hansen, ed. New Brunswick, NJ: Rutgers University Press.

———. 1994. "Dealing with Used Clothing: Salaula and the Construction of Identity in Zambia's Third Republic." *Public Culture* 6:503–523.

Harvey, David. 1989. *The Condition of Postmodernity*. Oxford, UK: Basil Blackwell.

———. 1993. "From Space to Place and Back Again: Reflections of Postmodernity." In *Mapping the Futures: Local Cultures, Global Change*. J. Bird et al., eds. London: Routledge.

Hunt, Nancy R. 1992. "Colonial Fairy Tales and the Knife and Fork Doctrine in the Heart of Africa." In *African Encounters with Domesticity*, pp. 143–171. Karen T. Hansen, ed. New Brunswick, NJ: Rutgers University Press.

Kahn, Joel S. 1989. "Culture: Demise or Resurrection?" *Critique of Anthropology* 9(2):5–25.

King, Anthony D., ed. 1991. *Culture, Globalization and the World-System*. Binghamton, NY: Dept. of Art and Art History, State University of New York.

Konaté, Yacouba. 1987. *Alpha Blondy: Reggae et société en Afrique Noire*. Abidjan: CEDA & Paris: Karthala.

Matory, J. Lorand. 1993. "Government by Seduction: History and the Tropes of 'Mounting' in Oyo-Yoruba Religion." In *Modernity and its Malcontents*, pp. 58–85. Jean & John Comaroff, eds. Chicago: University of Chicago Press.

———. 1994. *Sex and the Empire that Is No More: Gender and the Politics of Metaphor in Oyo Yoruba Religion*. Minneapolis: University of Minnesota Press.

Mintz, Sidney W. 1985. *Sweetness and Power: The Place of Sugar in Modern History*. New York: Viking Penguin.

Mudimbe, V. Y. 1976. *Le bel immonde*. Paris: Présence Africaine.

Ogundipe-Leslie, Molara and Carole Boyce Davies, eds. 1994. "Women as Oral Artists." (Special Issue) *Research in African Literatures*. 25(3), Fall 1994.

Pred, Allan and Michael J. Watts. 1992. *Reworking Modernity: Capitalisms and Symbolic Discontent*. New Brunswick, NJ: Rutgers University Press.

Roberts, Martin. 1992. "'World Music' and the Global Cultural Economy." *Diaspora* 2(2):229–242.

Robertson, Roland. 1992. *Globalization: Social Theory and Global Culture*. London: Sage Publications.

Rosaldo, Renato. 1989. *Culture and Truth: The Remaking of Social Analysis*. Boston: Beacon Press.

Savishinsky, Neil J. 1994. "Rastafari in the Promised Land: The Spread of a Jamaican Socioreligious Movement Among the Youth of West Africa." *African Studies Review* 37(3):19–50.

Schmidt, Elizabeth. 1992. *Peasants, Traders, and Wives: Shona Women in the History of Zimbabwe, 1870–1939*. Portsmouth, NH: Heinemann.

Sembène, Ousmane. 1973. *Xala*. Paris: Présence Africaine.

Spitulnik, Debra A. 1994. "Radio Culture in Zambia: Audiences, Public Words, and the Nation-State." Unpublished Ph.D. dissertation, University of Chicago.

Stoler, Ann L. 1989. "Making Empire Respectable: The Politics of Race and Sexual Morality." *American Ethnologist* 16(4):634–660.

Stoller, Paul. 1989. *The Taste of Ethnographic Things: The Senses in Anthropology*. Philadelphia: University of Pennsylvania Press.

Thornton, Robert J. 1988. "The Rhetoric of Ethnographic Holism." *Cultural Anthropology* 3(3):285–303.

Wallerstein, Immanuel. 1974. *The Modern World System*. New York: Academic Press.

Waterman, Christopher. 1990. *Jujy: A Social History and Ethnography of an African Popular Music*. Chicago: University of Chicago Press.

Watts, Michael J. 1992. "Space for Everything (A Commentary)." *Cultural Anthropology* 7(1):115–129.

Wilmsen, Edwin N. 1989. *Land Filled with Flies: A Political Economy of the Kalahari*. Chicago: The University of Chicago Press.

———. 1991. "Pastoro-Foragers to 'Bushmen': Transformations in Kalahari Relations of Property, Production and Labor." In *Herders, Warriors, and Traders: Pastoralism in Africa*, pp. 248–263. John G. Galaty and Pierre Bonte, eds. Boulder, CO: Westview Press.

Wolf, Eric. 1982. *Europe and the People Without History*. Berkeley: University of California Press.

CROSSING BOUNDARIES/ CHANGING IDENTITIES:
FEMALE SLAVES, MALE STRANGERS, AND THEIR DESCENDANTS IN NINETEENTH- AND TWENTIETH-CENTURY ANLO

SANDRA E. GREENE

In the last twenty years, scholars interested in the social history of precolonial Africa have generated an impressive body of studies on gender relations in various parts of the continent. These studies have emphasized that women assumed a number of roles in the religious, political, economic, and social institutions of the societies in which they lived, but that their roles and activities did not have the same prestige as those of men. Women had political authority, but their power was limited in comparison with their male counterparts. Women held important religious offices and could gain significant social and economic prestige within their communities, but the majority of women had fewer opportunities than men to obtain such positions because of their gender (Alpers 1984a; Guy 1990; Musisi 1991). Some of these same studies also emphasize the fact that women in precolonial Africa attempted to defy their marginalization. Some joined religious orders, in part, to gain greater control over their lives. Others formed gender-based organizations which they then used as a basis of support when they faced difficulties within their husbands' households (Alpers 1984b; Eldredge 1991; Greene 1996).

More recently, scholars have also begun to extend the study of gender to social groups that have traditionally not been the subject of this kind of analysis. These groups include those who were socially marginalized because of their ethnicity or their slave status. In my own work on the Anlo-Ewe, for example, I document the fact that there existed in this society a number of ethnic outsider groups who were denied the opportunity to obtain prestigious positions within the Anlo political, religious, and social institutions of the society because of their foreign origins. Such groups worked hard to redefine themselves as ethnic insiders throughout the eighteenth and nineteenth centuries, but they also frequently did so in ways that explicitly disadvantaged the young women rather than the young men in their families (Greene 1996). Robertson and Klein (1983) have described a similar pattern of disadvantage based on gender in their study of African slave systems. They note that the majority of individuals enslaved in Africa were women and that from this slave population, more was frequently demanded of women than of men. Both studies also document the fact that women from ethnic outsider families and enslaved women resisted the disadvantaged positions into which they were placed by their family elders and masters, respectively. All took advantage of whatever opportunities came their way to improve their situation.

Despite these findings, many questions remain. We know, for example, that when nineteenth-century ethnic outsider women in Anlo successfully challenged their marginalization, they altered not only their own social status, but also helped change the very character of gender and ethnic relations in that society (Greene 1996). Did enslaved women effect similar societal changes as they too challenged their status? Evidence from the history of the Anlo suggests that they did. We know, for example, that in nineteenth- and early twentieth-century Anlo, marriages between enslaved women and stranger men were common and that these unions became for both parties the means to improve their own social positions. Enslaved women used these marriages to acquire substantial wealth, and their stranger husbands used them to establish linkages with prominent Anlo families in the areas in which they lived. While the men and women involved in these unions were rarely able to use the benefits they derived from their marriages to redefine their own or their children's social positions during the nineteenth century, I argue that the wealth and social connections they established did provide a foundation for their twentieth-century descendants to effect major changes not only in their own identities as outsiders and the descendants of enslaved women, but also in the very character of twentieth-century Anlo gender relations.

I begin by examining briefly the nature of slavery and stranger/host relations in Anlo in the period between the late seventeenth and the late nineteenth centuries. I then discuss the ways in which stranger men, slave masters, and enslaved women manipulated for their own advantage the prevailing eighteenth- and nineteenth-century cultural practice of arranging and/or supporting marriages between stranger men and enslaved women by focusing on the history of a select number of individuals and their families. In discussing these histories and the impact of British colonial rule on the social boundaries that distinguished slaves and strangers from the rest of the Anlo population, I prove not only that the descendants of stranger men and enslaved women altered their own identities as well as gender relations in twentieth-century Anlo; I also illustrate the pivotal role that enslaved women (as intermediaries between insiders and outsiders within Anlo and between this polity and the larger world) have played in the changing character of Anlo gender and ethnic relations as the Anlo have adjusted to greater involvement in the colonial and post-colonial world.

SLAVERY IN PRECOLONIAL ANLO

According to a number of European travelers' accounts, Anlo involvement in the sale of slaves for export began in the late 1680s or early 1690s when a number of

European merchants, especially those of Portuguese origin, began to frequent the Anlo littoral in order to purchase the prisoners of war made available by the residents in the area because of their conflicts with the polity of Anexo (Bosman 1705: 330, 331; Law 1982: 158). European interests in the area and Anlo's exports of slaves continued thereafter as the Anlo engaged in additional conflicts throughout the eighteenth and nineteenth centuries, and as European merchants began to view the area as a potential source of large numbers of slaves, especially when the same were unavailable elsewhere.[1] Not all whom the Anlo captured in war or purchased on the market were sold for export, however. Family genealogies, Anlo oral traditions, and European documentary accounts concur that many of the enslaved individuals were also retained and integrated into Anlo families.[2] These same sources indicate as well that the majority of those retained were women and female children. In his study of the Danish role in the Atlantic slave trade, Sv. Green-Pedersen noted that between July 1777 and October 1789, the Danes purchased at Keta roughly twice as many men and boys as women and girls (Green-Pederson 1971: 193). And according to Anlo oral traditions and documentary sources from the late nineteenth and early twentieth centuries, this was not simply because there existed more male prisoners of war. Rather the Anlo opted to retain as slaves the females they had captured or purchased to serve as wives and workers (Schlegel 1858: 398).[3]

Incorporation into free Anlo families almost never removed from these enslaved women or their descendants the social stigma associated with such origins, however. In 1858, the German missionary Bernhard Schlegel reported that "a slave stands, I think, seven times lower in respect than a free man" (Schlegel 1858: 398). And in a diary written between 1879 and 1925 by a local Anlo man of slave descent, the author noted that he and his family—who were all fairly wealthy—were still referred to as "*Da awa li fe mamayoviwo*": grandchildren of a war-captive, despite the fact that his grandmother, who had been captured as a young woman in 1811, was married to and had children by her master/husband and was then later redeemed by her family before her own death in the mid-1800s.

The source of the lowly social status of both slaves and their descendants had to do, in part, with the fact that they or their ancestors had been personally and forcibly removed from their own communities, a situation that left them without kin, either maternal or paternal, from whom they could derive protection. Among the Anlo, for example, we know that both first- or subsequent-generation slaves could be sold at any time, based on the immediate financial needs of their masters. This was the case whether an individual was captured or purchased, whether she was single or married to another slave or to her master. Evidence in support of this observation comes from a number of German missionary accounts, two of which are quoted below. The first, recorded by Bernhard Schlegel, describes the situation for such wives in 1858. The second was written by D. Westermann in the early twentieth century.

[Among the Anlo, the enslaved] wife is so loosely connected with him. . . . [This kind of wife] lives independently and provides for herself and her girls. She cooks for her husband and looks after the bare necessities of his household. The man buys her with money, and if she becomes unfaithful, he sells her . . . and he buys another one from the proceeds. . . . The children of slaves were called "the ones that are born in-between." When you bought a slave and wife for him, their children would be "born in-between." The "born in-between" is like putting money into a business and it gets more. The master viewed him as a child, but he was more valuable to him than his own children, because when the master has large debts, which can happen occasionally, he can always pawn the "born-in-between" and that way get the money needed for the payment, or he can also sell him since he is the master's property. (Schlegel 1858: 399)

Slaves were reminded of their status as object in a number of ways. Slave owners who were also economically prominent within the community measured their wealth by the number of their slave dependents. The owner offered proof of this acquired wealth by stringing a cowry, representative of each slave (as opposed to each free dependent) in his or her possession, around the central pillar of a stool which was then carried by a member of the person's household before the master during ceremonial occasions (Greene, Field Note 53). Family elders also kept written and/or oral records of the origins of every family member. This record was then consulted when family elders had to select one of their members for an important office within the lineage, clan, or community. No slave descendant would be assigned to such an important office. Information about the slave origins of specific family members would also be revealed to the free children in the family who could then use this information to keep slave descendants in their place.

Slaves were also reminded of their low social status by the way in which their masters managed their marital affairs. During the late eighteenth and nineteenth centuries, free women were rarely if ever betrothed to stranger men, even financially prosperous ones. Anlo elders reserved unions with such men for the enslaved women in their families. They did so because of the perceived risks involved. As Anlo elder L. A. Banini noted, "If you tried to send your own child [i.e., your offspring from a marriage to a free woman] to the Europeans, your wife wouldn't like her [child] to go" since there existed a real possibility that a stranger about whom the family knew little would disappear with their daughter and never return. "So, the slave descendants were sent."[4] This same situation obtained with regard to those children chosen to be handed over to a lender as a pawn. As the German missionary D. Westermann noted of the system as it existed in the late nineteenth and early twentieth centuries, because a free child's maternal relatives would object to the possible loss of their niece or nephew if the father did not pay the debt for which the child served as collateral, it was the children of slave descent, who had no maternal relatives or parents to protect them, who were placed in pawn (Westermann 1935: 126, 284–285).[5]

The social stigma associated with slave origins that existed so overtly in the terminology, religious life, public performances, and marriage patterns among the Anlo-Ewe throughout the nineteenth century did not necessarily prevent enslaved women or their descendants from obtaining prominent positions within the economic hierarchy of Anlo society. Their ability to achieve such statuses had to do with the ways in which slave masters used enslaved women, and the abilities of these women and their descendants to take advantage of the situations in which they found themselves. If, for example, an enslaved woman had been taken by her master as a wife, and the master was deeply involved in trade activities and/or held important political positions, it was not unusual for one or more of the female children of such enslaved women to be offered as concubines to strangers who were resident in Anlo in order to reinforce the economic ties that existed between their father and their father's business partner. In a number of instances, these young women used their connections to their owner/father, and to the strangers to whom they were given, to take advantage of both the bonds of kinship and concubinage to obtain substantial wealth.[6] Before citing specific evidence to illustrate this phenomenon, however, it is necessary to review briefly the status of strangers in nineteenth-century Anlo in order to understand their own social position within this society.

RESIDENT STRANGERS IN PRECOLONIAL ANLO

Documentary sources and oral traditions indicate that the Anlo received throughout the late seventeenth, eighteenth, and nineteenth centuries, numerous groups of strangers who opted to remain as residents in the area. In 1679, for example, refugees from the Adangbe area west of Anlo crossed the Volta River and settled in a number of communities, including the town of Anloga. In 1702, when Akwamu conquered Anlo, they brought with them Ewe-speaking intermediaries to help them administer the area. Many of the latter remained in Anlo after the 1730 collapse of the Akwamu empire and formed a group known as the Agave. In 1742, when Anlo was again conquered, this time by the polity of Anexo to the east, individuals associated with this latter polity who often came to Anlo to trade also settled in the area, remaining even after the Anlo expelled the Anexo political administrators in 1750. In the early 1800s yet another wave of immigrants moved in and settled. Many were Afro-European businessmen who entered Anlo initially to escape British efforts to abolish the slave trade.[7]

By the mid- to late nineteenth century, all of these immigrants—whether resident in Anlo since the late seventeenth century or the early nineteenth century—were known as *bluawo*, resident strangers. Most had joined preexisting social groups (clans, *hlɔwo*, or lineages, *tɔ-fome*) in order to gain some of the benefits (protection and financial support) associated with membership in such groups. Others for the same reasons had formed their own clans or sub-clans according to their time of arrival, their geographical origins, and/or supposed kinship ties to one another. Thus, in the early twentieth century, Westermann noted that five clans had non-Anlo ethnic origins. These included the Amlade, Agave, Tsiame, Dzevi, and the Wifeme. All were defined as such based on the prevailing custom among the Anlo that any descendant of a non-Anlo male (or any descendant of an Anlo man and a non-Anlo woman who chose to affiliate with their mother's relatives) was defined ethnically as non-Anlo (Westermann 1935: 147–148).

The social status of strangers in nineteenth-century Anlo was not unlike that of strangers in other societies. They were often welcomed because of the possible economic benefits, new knowledge systems, and ritual expertise they brought to their host communities. Yet, these same individuals and groups were often viewed simultaneously with a degree of wariness. Their loyalty to the new homes could not be assumed; they might use their advantageous knowledge to disrupt the existing social order; they constituted not only a potential source of wealth, but also competition. Thus, the Anlo denied strangers throughout the late seventeenth, eighteenth, and nineteenth centuries the right to claim ownership of land and access to important political offices. Even the gods that were controlled by stranger groups were often characterized as untrustworthy and potentially dangerous (Westermann 1935: 146).

Those who were defined in such terms often attempted to counter such notions using a variety of means. Some—like the Amlade—offered their services as the custodians of particularly powerful gods to the political elite in Anlo, and then used this relationship to disseminate new traditions about themselves and their origins that identified them with the founding ancestors of the polity (Greene 1996: Chapter Two). Others—after failing to overcome the limitations imposed on them because of their foreign origins—opted to maintain connections to their home areas. The Agave clan, for example, reinforced its ties to the Agave area—a district located to the northwest of Anlo from which they claim their ancestors originated—by continuing to claim land there. The Tsiame insisted on continuing to perform the rituals associated with the worship of their gods, Tsali and Tesi, not in Anloga where other clans performed their rituals, but in the town of Tsiame, their ancestral home (Greene 1996: Chapter Four). Still others focused not on long-term social acceptance or maintenance of ties to their ancestral homes, but rather on immediate economic goals. They did so by establishing marital ties with prominent families within Anlo society. This strengthened their ability as ethnic outsiders to gain through their marriages the political clout needed to support their economic activities. But because such marriages often linked the stranger to prominent Anlo families through the enslaved women attached to these families, these ties also continued to mark the social status of the stranger as less than socially acceptable, even as all involved gained immediate economic benefits. More important for this study, however, is the fact that these unions often became the foundation for enslaved women, stranger men, and their descendants to challenge economically their low social status within Anlo society. This is most evident if one examines the histories of the many stranger and enslaved lineages and clans resident in Anlo during the late eighteenth and nineteenth centuries. For the sake of brevity, however, I discuss here only one lineage. I also use pseudonyms for all who are cited here in order to protect their identities.[8]

OF MARRIAGE AND OTHER MATTERS: ENSLAVED WOMEN AND STRANGER MEN IN PRECOLONIAL ANLO

1769 is the date when the Tetteh family first entered Anlo. In February of that year, a woman by the name of Madui of Ada was captured in war and retained as an enslaved wife by her captor, Lotsu of Anloga. She and a number of other women from Ada had been sent by their male relatives to an area twenty miles north of Ada to protect them from the Anlo. Unfortunately for Madui and her travel companions, the Anlo discovered their canoes before they arrived at their destination and captured them with the intent of retaining them or selling them into the Atlantic slave trade. Many were indeed sold, but Madui caught the eye of her captor, Lotsu, who decided to keep her as a wife. Immediately after the cessation of hostilities, Madui's relatives attempted to ransom her from the Anlos, but Lotsu refused the offer. Madui had already had a child by him, and had thus proven herself to be a serviceable member of his family. He was not prepared to give her up. Over the years, Madui had five more children with Lotsu, one of whom, a daughter named Ama, would later become a particularly important asset to her master/father. As a financially prosperous resident of Anloga (the capital of the Anlo polity), Lotsu had regular dealings with the various European and Afro-European traders who occupied the Danish fort in Keta. All of these traders were men; none were accompanied by their own women. This fact—and the power all slave masters had over the children of their slave wives—provided Lotsu with a ready means to enhance his economic relations with the only individuals in the area who had immediate access to the European goods in demand in Anlo and elsewhere in the region. Thus, when Ama came of age, Lotsu gave her as a concubine to one of the traders in the fort, Komla Datevi, who himself was the slave of a Danish officer, A. Pederson, posted for duty to Keta.

Datevi's own enslavement began in the early 1800s when his father handed him over to the Danes in Accra as collateral for a loan he had received from them to engage in trade. Because his father never repaid the loan, Datevi remained with his European masters in Accra, and there learned their language as well as the skills associated with blacksmithing. When Pederson was posted for duty to Keta fort during the first decade of the nineteenth century, he brought Datevi with him, presumably to serve as a linguistic intermediary (Datevi spoke Danish, Ga, and Ewe as well as Agotime), as a personal servant, and to help maintain the fort with his black-smithing skills.

Datevi did more than serve his master, however. He also took advantage of his-torical circumstances and his relationship with the Danes to achieve something for himself. During the first decade of the nineteenth century, Denmark was unable to ship goods to their African forts because of the Napoleonic wars in Europe. Those Danish officers and servants who had been posted to the outforts were often forced to sustain themselves as best they could by engaging in private trade. In such a situation, servants like Datevi, who were attached to these officers, found themselves in a partic-ularly advantageous position. Their masters were quite dependent on them to estab-lish and maintain those contacts with the local population that could sustain them during lean times. This, in turn, gave servants expanded opportunities to conduct a portion of their master's business for their own benefit (Nørregård 1966: 183, 184, 190, 195). By taking advantage of this situation, Datevi managed to obtain title to land next to the fort that had been given to the Danes by the local community. He also established himself in Anlo more generally as an individual not only closely asso-ciated with the Danes, but also as a stranger in his own right to whom others could bring their goods (ivory as well as slaves) for exchange.

By giving his slave daughter, Ama, to Datevi, Lotsu strengthened his relations with an important source of the few European trade goods available on the coast. By accepting Lotsu's daughter, Datevi gained access to the political, military, and reli-gious hierarchy of Anlo society that continually demanded European goods in ex-change for slaves and other locally generated commodities.

Existing sources provide very little information about Ama's perspective on the events that so deeply affected her life. What we do know, however, is that even though she continued to be viewed by her master/father and his relatives as property to be manipulated in ways that they could never employ with the children of free wives, Ama managed to transform her disadvantageous relationship within her father's fam-ily and the stigmatized position of being the concubine of her husband[9] into one that became beneficial to her own interests. She used her position as the "wife" of a wealthy stranger to obtain access to European trade goods and to begin trading on her own. After her husband's death (or departure?) in the late 1840s, she assumed owner-ship of his house and the land on which it was built. And by the time of her death in 1859, she had managed not only to establish herself as a woman of means in her own right by dominating the supplying of foodstuffs to the various Europeans who operat-ed in Keta as traders and later as missionaries, she had also purchased her own and her children's freedom and acquired the services of sixteen slaves (the majority of whom, by no coincidence, were women).[10] Ama then used her husband's connections to the Afro-European community that operated on the lower Gold Coast and upper Slave Coast, her own status as a wealthy woman, and her ties to her father's family in

Anloga to secure advantageous marital unions for her children and female slaves. She betrothed the daughter of one of her enslaved women, Mawudem, to a particularly prominent Afro-European trader from Accra by the name of Edgerton. She also supported the marriage that her son, John Tetteh (then fully independent), had arranged between himself and a woman by the name of Kafui, who was the daughter of the brother of the center wing chief of Anlo. Both of these unions reinforced and enhanced Ama's economic status as a major trader in the area, since these ties strengthened her ability to obtain the slaves and the European goods that were in constant demand by traders in Anlo. This in turn boosted her social status, since her position as a woman of means also meant that she could be of assistance to the Anlo when they were in need of financial support for their military efforts.

None of Ama's accomplishments totally erased, however, the stigma that others in Anlo continued to attach to her social origins. When her son arranged—with Ama's support—his own union with Kafui, for example, the marriage was not just between the son of a prominent female trader and the daughter of a politically powerful family. It was also a marriage between Tetteh, as a male stranger (defined as such according to the Anlo customary law because his father was a stranger), and Kafui, a woman who was not only the daughter of the brother of the Anlo center wing commander, but also the offspring of an enslaved woman. Ama and her son may have wished to establish ties to Kafui's family through a free member of the family, but social custom dictated to Kafui's family that this was the appropriate person that they should give in marriage to Tetteh because of his own origins. Even more significantly, Ama herself did not attempt to challenge this system. She only tried to distance herself from it when possible. Thus, when she betrothed her own slave's daughter, Mawudem, to Edgerton, she also operated according to the prevailing social norms of her time. As a woman who had redeemed herself and her children from slavery, Ama was not prepared to give one of her own daughters to a stranger to marry. Such unions were only appropriate for enslaved women. Only with the coming of British colonial rule did these boundaries, stigmatized identities, and social practices begin to change.

CHANGING GENDER RELATIONS IN TWENTIETH-CENTURY ANLO: FROM STIGMATIZED SLAVE TO ESTEEMED ANCESTRESS

In 1874, Britain extended colonial rule over Anlo, including it within the Gold Coast Colony. In that same year, it also passed Ordinance No. 2, which abolished slavery. Both events had a profound influence on every aspect of Anlo society. Of concern here is the effect these events had on the way in which the Anlo socially defined those individuals and groups that were the descendants of strangers and slaves. Did abolition create a widespread movement by slaves to return to their former homes or to new communities as Gerald McSheffrey (1983: 349–368) has argued was the case in Akyem Abuakwa? Or did most slaves opt to "remain close to their districts of adoption," as noted by Ray Dumett and Marion Johnson (1988: 71-115)? Information about the situation in the Anlo area is difficult to obtain given the existing sources, but there is evidence that many slaves did, indeed, opt for freedom by leaving their masters. Diary entries dated 7 March 1878 by Anlo resident Christian Jacobson, German missionary accounts, and the records of cases adjudicated by the District Commission of Keta between 1875 and 1888 contain numerous reports of slaves who fled their masters.[11] Several family histories that I recorded in 1988 also refer to specific female slaves who decided to return to their original homes (Greene, Field Note 60 and Field Note 70). More important for this study, these same sources also indicate that the departures and escapes prompted a vigorous reaction from Anlo family heads. Some masters relocated their slaves to more remote corners of Anlo where they would be outside the routine policing of the district by the British. Others, recognizing the possibility of even these relocated slaves attempting to escape, terrorized the individuals whom they suspected of having such interests by selling them to other masters or attacking them after sending them on an errand far from their residences.[12] The more long-term method that the Anlo adopted to deal with this situation involved neither of these, however. Instead, they modified the way in which slaves and slavery were discussed.

In European documentary sources and local court records, it is apparent that in the late nineteenth century and early twentieth century, it was acceptable for all within Anlo society to discuss publicly the slave origins of particular individuals. Fifty years later, however, that is, by the mid-twentieth century, such discussions were considered not only indelicate, but illegal according to customary law. Thus, when I inquired in the late 1970s and late 1980s about the extent to which people at that time used the slave origins of others to gain advantages, I was told in no uncertain terms that:

> If someone refers to your slave as a slave, they threaten the prosperity of the
> family who owns the slave and the clan of that family. It is a serious matter.
> No court will allow it. No elder will bring [a] case [that allows such informa-
> tion to be used]. If you don't know and you try it, you will be revealing the
> secrets of all the families in the town and they will form a gang and you will
> disappear immediately. They will kill you spiritually, instantly. It is not
> done. (Greene, Field Note 54)

Changes have occurred not only in the acceptability of discussing slave origins, but also in the opportunities available to those of slave descent. As Togbui Dzobi Adzinku, elder of the Bate clan, noted in 1988:

> In former days [that is, before the early twentieth century], slaves were not given either political or religious positions because they might run away and reveal secrets. But with the passing of time, they now can hold both. There is [only] one exception, the *awoamefia* stool. They investigate you properly so it would be very difficult for slave descendants to become the *awoamefia*. They investigate both your maternal and paternal side. (Greene, Field Note 65)

Similar changes have occurred in the way in which the Anlo manage the strangers who have been resident in their communities. During the late nineteenth century, the Anlo clearly defined the members of several clans as foreign *hlowo* whom one could distinguish from others in Anlo because their patrilineal ancestors did not emigrate from Notsie, the ancestral home of ethnic Anlos, as seen most clearly in their naming and funeral customs. While this social distinction did not prevent the Anlo from taking advantage of the knowledge and skills possessed by such individuals, suspicions about strangers did keep to a minimum the number of ethnic outsiders who were given leadership positions within the polity. This situation began to change in the twentieth century. Today, for example, the Anlo note that while members of the Dzevi clan have names that are identical with those found in the Ga and Adangbe areas of Ghana, they, nevertheless, define their origins as the town of Notsie. The fact that their clan names are still not ones associated with the Ewe or the Anlo is explained by the notion that the ancestors of the Dzevi simply lost their way on their westward journey from Notsie. Instead of settling on the coast with the Anlo ancestors, they crossed the Volta and lived among the Ga and Adangbe peoples where they adopted a number of Adangbe customs before they returned to their relatives in the Anlo area. The reasons for this recasting of family histories have been discussed elsewhere (Greene 1996: Chapter Five). Of significance here is the fact that this process has meant that the Anlo now deemphasize such differences as naming and funeral customs. Given priority instead is the newly generated notion that the vast majority of those resident in Anlo are full-fledged members of the society because their ancestors came from Notsie even if the latter took a detour before settling in the Anlo area.

How did these changes affect the position of those in Anlo who were descendants of enslaved mothers and stranger men? Evidence suggests that those in leadership positions, as well as those stigmatized as ethnic outsiders, took advantage of the noted changes to expand the criteria for leadership in Anlo. This is most obvious from the way in which the descendants of enslaved women and their stranger husbands managed to obtain and retain prominent political positions within the Anlo polity.

Perhaps the most well-known example of this involves Ama's descendants. During his lifetime, John Tetteh (Ama's son) followed his mother's example and established himself as an economic and political power in Anlo by associating himself with influential members of Anlo society as well as with the other stranger communities that operated in the region. In 1847, for example, when the Anlo military retaliated against the Danes who had murdered an Anlo citizen by blockading and besieging the fort at Keta, Tetteh secretly provided his European trade partners with corn and fowl in order to sustain them while they attempted to extricate themselves from their predicament. In 1865, Tetteh reinforced his ties with the political elite of Anlo by serving as translator for the Anlo army when they were negotiating with the British forces and the Adas immediately before the outbreak of the Attiteti or Funu War. At no time during the mid- or late nineteenth century, however, were the Anlo prepared to recognize Tetteh or his own sons as leaders who would exercise influence within the decision-making council of the Anlo *awoamefia*. This only began to change in the early twentieth century when the British began to administer the Anlo area as a colonial possession.

In 1909, the colonial administration sought to simplify its political relations with the different communities in Anlo by recognizing one person as the head chief of each town and village. One of the communities affected by this was the town of Drakofe, which had numerous chiefs (*fiawo*), none of whom were considered the political or religious head of the town. That position was held by Togbui Dra II, the descendant of Togbui Dra I, the founder of Drakofe. Recognizing, however, that the person who held this colonial government-recognized office on behalf of the town and the Anlo polity, the *awoamefia*, the leaders of the Anlo military, and Togbui Dra II opted to ignore the fact that Tetteh and his descendants were technically the descendants of strangers and slaves. They appointed A. F. Atsu, a descendant of John Tetteh, to assume the head chiefship of Drakofe on behalf of Dra II, because, in their words, ". . . of the services which the late Chief Tetteh Akoe [father of A. F. Atsu] had rendered the country, the good services which the present Chief A. F. Atsu has rendered to the town of Drakofe in all matters before His Majesty's colonial government and his being also a scholar, able to read and write. . ." Such decisions were not unique. Several other towns and villages in Anlo also chose to deal with the demands of British colonial rule by expanding the boundaries that had formerly governed the extent to which ethnically and socially distinct individuals could operate as insiders within the Anlo political system.[13] What this decision did not do, however, was prevent others from challenging the rights of these families to retain such positions. In 1902, the Tettehs faced a legal challenge as to their right to provide the head chief of Drakofe; in 1960, they faced another challenge. Accordingly, when I interviewed the descendants of John Tetteh in 1988, they expressed great reticence about discussing their paternal linkages, for it was this aspect of their ancestry—their stranger rather than their slave origins—that opponents could then use to strip them of their political power.

Even more important for this study is the fact that individuals and families who traced their descent to enslaved women and stranger men responded vigorously to the possibility that others would continue to hold their ethnic outsider origins against them by elevating to much greater importance the status of their enslaved grandmothers. Again, the most salient example comes from the Tetteh family. Faced with legal challenges that defined them as outsiders and therefore ineligible to hold the head chiefship position of Drakofe, Togbui Akoe IV and his advisors have begun to emphasize instead their descent from their enslaved foremother, Ama. They do not describe her as a slave. This would have been contrary to their own interests and would have disclosed information that was no longer permitted to be discussed in public. Rather they described Ama as the daughter of Lotsu, one of the most prominent families in nineteenth-century Anloga, the traditional political and religious capital of the Anlo polity. She, they emphasized, was the head of their lineage, having established their branch of the Lotsu family in Drakofe, and it was her residence in this town, her wealth, her connections to the Lotsu family (which obtained its own right to chieftancy through warfare, the most acceptable means for doing so) and the fact that Togbui Dra II, a direct descendant of the founder of Drakofe had sanctioned Akoe being head chief of the town, that legitimated their claim to the head chiefship position.

This same strategy has been pursued by a number of clans that trace their origins to a marriage between an enslaved woman and a stranger man. Late-nineteenth-century accounts about the Vakpome clan, for example, describe it as a social group founded by Amega Tsi, a male ancestor who entered Anlo from the Adangbe district. Like a number of other strangers, those who formed this Vakpome clan came from a particular region, in this case, the Ga and Adangbe districts to the west of Anlo. They established their *hlo*, in part, to obtain the kind of support they needed to operate independently as a distinct cultural and social group within Anlo. They were also encouraged to form themselves into such a group by the political authorities so that there would exist a body that could be held responsible for the actions of the individual strangers who lived in Anlo and were affiliated with that group. Throughout the late eighteenth and nineteenth centuries, the Anlo defined them as strangers because of their supposed descent from Amega Tsi. They then used this social identity to deny them access to important political offices within the polity. By the mid-twentieth century, the descendants of those who founded the clan began to take advantage of the changes in Anlo social values to alter their own history. They deemphasized completely their connection to Tsi, and gave priority instead to their new identity as the descendants of an Anlo woman by the name of Va. The latter is said to have lived with the Do clan's founding ancestor, not as a wife, daughter, or niece, but simply as a member of his household (i.e., as a slave). She was given in marriage to the stranger, Tsi, and it is she whom the Vakpome clan now define as the founding ancestor of the clan.[14]

By elevating women like Ama and Va to the status of lineage and clan head, respectively, the family elders of the lineages and clans that developed from the marriages of enslaved women and stranger men have redefined themselves so that they can cross the boundary that determines who is socially respectable within Anlo society. They have also contributed, wittingly or unwittingly, to major changes in Anlo gender relations. Prior to the late nineteenth century older women were rarely defined as house owners, household heads, or the founders of their own lineages or clans, but they played a vital role in the various production activities in which the Anlo were involved. This, in turn, gave them particular rights that insured their economic independence. Early travelers' accounts and oral traditions indicate, for example, that women took principal responsibility for weeding and then processing the grain crops (millet and sorghum and later corn) grown by their fathers and husbands. In recognition of their role (and in response to the fact that land was still relatively abundant), they—like their brothers—inherited land from their lineage elders which they could pass on to their own children. They also received land from their husbands on which to grow food for the household; and they inherited additional lands from their mothers on which they harvested the reeds and wickers they used for basketmaking. After the late nineteenth century, however, with the expansion of colonialism, commercial agriculture, and an increase in the population resident in Anlo, much changed. Family elders decreased the amount of agricultural land they allocated to their daughters. Husbands refused to allocate separate plots to their wives, and women lost to their brothers access to the lands they had previously been bequeathed by their mothers.[15]

How did women respond to these developments? Pushed out of land ownership, they embraced trading and a variety of other activities as a means to maintain the kind of economic independence that they had had when they possessed land on which to grow their own crops for sale. They also formed unions or cooperatives—organized on the basis of their gender and their occupation—to protect their particular economic interests within the commercial economy of the area. In 1975, for example, the women who sold shallots to wholesalers who then distributed this commodity to markets throughout Ghana successfully organized to protect their own interests as well as the interests of their wholesaler business partners by preventing Anlo men from circumventing their trading network. Four years later, in 1979, several hundred women who had organized themselves into groups to carry sand for the male shallot farmers who used this material to prepare their plots before the planting of the shallot crop, also successfully defended their interests when they went on strike to demand the same wages and benefits received by their male counterparts (Patten 1990: 187–195).

The success of these and other efforts not only have helped women maintain a degree of economic independence, they have also challenged nineteenth- and early twentieth-century conventions about the place of women within Anlo society. As noted, Anlo women rarely held the position of house owner or household head prior to the late nineteenth century. But as Sonia Patten and G. K. Nukunya have recently observed:

> . . . in the last two decades [i.e., since the 1960s] increasing numbers of women have been using their money to construct houses for themselves on building plots which they purchase. One consequence of this is that many wives both first and second, now live apart from their husbands [not in their father's or brother's house, but] in housing which they provide for themselves. (Patten 1990: 200)

> In 1962–63, [in] Woe . . . and Alakple. . . 44 percent of the households were headed by women. . . The high proportion of households headed by women shows not only the importance of women as homemakers but also the authority they can now wield in their own right. (Nukunya 1975: 169)

> In the past, it is said that women did not build their own houses: men would have been offended by such an openly competitive display of wealth and sought supernatural reprisals. Today, women fear such reprisals for other kinds of behavior, but not for the building of houses. (Patten 1990: 201)

Contributing significantly to this change in attitude toward the rights and roles of women in Anlo society have been those male elders who trace their origins to an enslaved ancestress and male stranger. When the latter began to recognize in the 1950s that their identities as outsiders limited their ability to retain the prestigious political positions they had obtained during the colonial period, they began to redefine themselves as the descendants not of their stranger male forefathers, but rather as the descendants of their esteemed female ancestresses. Their success in gaining acceptance of this redefinition—coupled with the response by Anlo women to their own economic marginalization—has meant that the norms that govern Anlo conceptions about the proper position of women and men in their society have changed enormously since the late nineteenth century. Contemporary Anlo elders may continue to disadvantage their daughters relative to their sons within the context of the landed inheritance system. And Anlo husbands may continue to refuse their wives land on which to grow crops of their own, but they can no longer deny the fact that women—like men—can be lineage and clan founders as well as house owners and household heads, positions formerly defined as male domains.

CONCLUSION

This chapter has illustrated the fact that Anlo contacts with other societies throughout the precolonial period generated a socially distinct group of individuals and families that had a profound influence on gender and ethnic relations within the polity. Throughout the nineteenth century, those defined by their descent from stranger men and enslaved women found themselves on the social margins of Anlo society because of their origins. They were denied access to leadership positions within their lineages and the polity. They were forced to operate within a value system that dictated that the only individuals whom they should marry were other outsiders or slaves. Despite this, many managed to distinguish themselves by obtaining substantial wealth and contributing to the welfare of the polity. This, in turn, provided their twentieth-century descendants with the opportunity to manipulate the changes generated by colonial rule for their own advantage. By the middle of the twentieth century, many who had previously been stigmatized because of their social origins had gained access to leadership positions within their lineages and the polity by focusing, in part, on their mother's connections to prominent families within the polity. This action, in turn, altered the we/they ethnic boundary that previously defined who could hold such offices. These same descendants also helped alter gender relations by elevating for the first time in living memory their foremothers to the status of lineage and clan heads. The fact that in both instances it was their foremothers rather than forefathers on whom these individuals and families focused their efforts also illustrates the role that enslaved women have played throughout the past two centuries. During the nineteenth century, enslaved women associated with prominent Anlo families became the vehicle through which ethnic outsiders were able to improve their relations with the wealthy and powerful within Anlo society. In the twentieth century, these same women (whose social origins were redefined) became for their descendants the means to reposition themselves within the Anlo social hierarchy. In playing such a role—as mediators between insiders and outsiders within Anlo and between Anlo and the larger world—enslaved women have been critical in connecting the local with the global in Anlo society.

NOTES

1. For more detailed discussion of the conflicts in which the Anlo were involved and the increasing European interest in the Anlo area, see Greene 1981. For information on the Danish slave trade, see Green-Pederson 1971:149–197 and Hernæs 1995.

2. Note that warfare and trade were not the only sources of slaves. The latter were also generated by a number of Anlo religious institutions and legal practices. See C. Spiess 1907:206; Greene, Field Note 56, 63, 100, 25 and 33. See also Greene 1996.

3. See also Greene, Field Note 70; Judicial Council Minute Book 1919; Egi of Srogboe -v- Awade Kportofe of Srogboe, 21 October 1919, 6; Special Collections: 14/2, 141, 146.

4. Greene, Field Note 63.

5. See Brooks 1976:27 and 1983:298, as well as Mouser 1983:321, for examples from other societies in which female slave descendants were the ones who became associated with male strangers. Data from Anlo about the gender of pawns is very limited. If what obtains elsewhere was also true in Anlo, women during the nineteenth century constituted at least half of the pawns in Anlo society. See, for example, Falola and Lovejoy 1994 and Austin 1994.

6.   Scholars writing about African slavery have established that this was a common pattern among slave-trading communities in West Africa, although none has pointed out the fact that marriages between stranger men and enslaved women were a cultural norm among many cultures in West Africa. See note 5.

7.   For a more detailed discussion of these various movements of strangers in Anlo, see Greene 1996.

8.   I have also omitted any references to the location of the information used here in order to protect the reputation of the families discussed.

9.   For evidence that such marriages were, indeed, stigmatized in the late nineteenth century, see G. Binetsch 1906:44–47.

10. The Danes who retained possession of the fort until 1850; the English who assumed control thereafter, and the North German missionaries who established themselves in Keta in 1853.

11. See for example Special Collections 14/2:211; "Ein Alter Heide" 1880:80–84; Administration Papers (ADM) 41/4/20: Criminal Record Book, Quittah, District Commissioner Court, Quittah: Regina -v- Dehsehoo and Agboko, 30 May 1882:75–76, 81; Private Dada -v- Afue, 9 April 1883:425; Complaint of Agbake of Tegbi, 28 April 1886:196; Corporal J. Wilson -v- Joan, 17 October 1888:124.

12. See, for example, "Ein Alter Heide", 1880. ADM 41/4/20: Criminal Record Book, Quittah, District Commissioner Court, Quittah: Regina -v- Dehsehoo and Agboko, 30 May 1882:75–76, 79–82. ADM 41/4/21: Criminal Record Book, Quittah:122, 137. Regina and Moshi -v- Chief Amagashie of Afrengba and Quittah, 28 July 1886:139–158.

13. See Anlo Traditional Council Minute Book, No.3, (14/4/60–23/7/87) 123 on the appointment of Acolatse as the head chief of Kedzi by the descendants of Abofrakuma; See Greene, Field Note 87, on the appointment of Chief James Ocloo to be head chief of Keta by Amegashie Afeku and the Anlo **awøamefia**, Amedor Kpegla. In both these cases, the individuals selected to hold the mentioned positions were not the descendants of stranger men and enslaved women, but they were chosen, in part, because of their long association with the Europeans with whom it was presumed they knew how to negotiate.

14. Amega Tsi is mentioned only when the person speaking is also prepared to emphasize that despite his Adangbe name, Tsi came originally from Notsie and acquired, and passed on to his descendants, an Adangbe name and other Adangbe cultural characteristics only because he remained in the latter area for a long time before joining his relatives in Anlo.

15. For more information on why these developments occurred, see Greene 1996: chapter six.

BIBLIOGRAPHY

Administration Papers (ADM). Ghana National Archives, Accra.

Alpers, Edward A. 1984a. "State, Merchant Capital and Gender Relations in Southern Mozambique to the End of the 19th Century: Some Tentative Hypotheses," *African Economic History* 13:23–55.

———. 1984b. "Ordinary Household Chores: Ritual and Power in a 19th Century Swahili Women's Spirit Possession Cult." *International Journal of African Historical Studies* 17(4):77–102.

Anlo Traditional Council Minute Book, Anlo Traditional Council Archives, Anloga, Ghana.

Austin, Gareth.1994. "Human Pawning in Asante, 1800–1950: Markets and Coercion, Gender and Cocoa." In *Pawnship in Africa: Debt Bondage in Historical Perspective.*

Toyin Falola and Paul E. Lovejoy, eds., 119–159. Boulder: Westview Press.

Binetsch, G. 1906. "Beantwortung mehrerer Fragen über unser Ewe-Volk und seine Anschauungen." *Zeitschrift für Ethnologie* 38:34–51.

Bosman, William. 1705. *A New and Accurate Description of the Guinea Coast*. London: J. Knapton.

Brooks, Jr. George E. 1976. "The Signares of Saint-Louis and Gorée: Women Entrepreneurs in Eighteenth Century Senegal." In *Women in Africa: Studies in Social and Economic Change*. Nancy J. Hafkin and Edna G. Bay, eds., 19–44. Stanford: Stanford University Press.

———. 1983."A Nhara of the Guinea-Bissau Region: Mãe Aurélia Correia." In *Women and Slavery in Africa*, Claire C. Robertson and Martin A. Klein. eds., 295–319. Madison: University of Wisconsin Press.

Dumett, Raymond and Marion Johnson. 1988. "Britain and the Suppression of Slavery in the Gold Coast Colony, Ashanti and the Northern Territories." In *The End of Slavery in Africa*. Suzanne Meirs and Richard Roberts, eds., 71–115. Madison: University of Wisconsin Press.

"Ein Alter Heide." 1888. *Monatsblatt der Norddeutschen Missionsgesellschaft* 5:80–84.

Eldredge, Elizabeth. 1991. "Women in Production: The Economic Role of Women in Nineteenth Century Lesotho." *Signs*, 16(4):707–731.

Falola, Toyin and Paul E. Lovejoy. 1994. "Pawnship in Historical Perspective." In *Pawnship in Africa: Debt Bondage in Historical Perspective*. Toyin Falola and Paul E.Lovejoy, eds., 1–26. Boulder: Westview Press.

Greene, Sandra E. 1996. *Gender, Ethnicity and Social Change on the Upper Slave Coast*. Portsmouth: Heinemann.

———. 1981. The Anlo-Ewe: Their Economy, Society and External Relations in the Eighteenth Century. Ph.D. Dissertation, Northwestern University.

———. Field Notes. On Deposit with the author:

    Field Note 25: Interview with Boko Seke Axovi, Anloga, 5 September 1978.

    Field Note 33: Interview with Boko Seke Axovi, Anloga, 3 October 1978.

    Field Note 53: Interview with Togbui Alex Afatsao Awadzi, Anloga, 16 December 1987.

    Field Note 54: Interview with Togbui Tse Gbeku, Anloga, 16 December, 1987.

    Field Note 55: Interview with Togbui Kosi Axovi, Anloga, 17 December 1987.

    Field Note 56: Interview with Mr. William Tiodo Anum Adzololo, Anloga, 16 December 1987.

    Field Note 60: Interview with Togbui Tete Za Agbemako, Anloga, 5 January 1988.

    Field Note: 63: Interview with Mr. L. A. Banini, Anloga, 5 January 1988.

    Field Note 65: Interview with Togbui Dzobi Adzinku, Anloga, 6 January 1988.

    Field Note 70: Interview with Mr. Kwami Kpodo, Woe, 12 January 1988.

    Field Note 87: Interview with Togbui James Ocloo IV, Keta, 3 February 1988.

    Field Note 100: Interview with Togbui Awusu, II, Atoko, 29 March 1988.

Green-Pederson, Sv. E. 1971. "The Scope and Structure of the Danish Negro Slave Trade." *Scandinavian Economic History Review* 19(2):149–197

Hernæs, Per O. 1995. *Slaves, Danes and African Coast Society*. Trondheim: University of

Trondheim, Trondheim Studies in History.

Guy, Jeff. 1990. "Gender Oppression in Southern Africa's Precapitalist Societies." In *Women and Gender in Southern Africa to 1945*. Cheryl Walker, ed., 33–47. London: James Curry.

Judicial Council Minute Book- 1919, Anlo Traditional Council Archives. Anloga, Ghana.

Law, Robin. 1982. "Jean Barbot as a Source for the Slave Coast of West Africa." *History in Africa* 9:155–173.

Mc Sheffrey, Gerald. 1983. "Slavery, indentured servitude, legitimate trade and the impact of abolition in the Gold Coast, 1874–1901." *Journal of African History* 24:349–368.

Mouser, Bruce L. 1983. "Women Slavers of Guinea-Conakry." In *Women and Slavery in Africa*. Claire C. Robertson and Martin A. Klein, eds., 320–339. Madison: University of Wisconsin Press.

Musisi, Nakanyike B. 1991. "Women, 'Elite Polygyny' and Buganda State Formation." *Signs* 16(4): 757–786.

Nørregård, Georg. 1966. *Danish Settlements in West Africa, 1658–1850*. Boston: Boston University Press.

Nukunya, G. K. 1975. "The Family and Social Change." In *Colonialism and Change: Essays presented to Lucy Mair*. Maxwell Owusu, ed., 163–177. The Hague: Mouton.

Patten, Sonia Gustavson. 1990. The Avuncular Family, Gender Asymmetry, and Patriline: The Anlo Ewe of Southeastern Ghana. Ph.D. dissertation, University of Minnesota.

Robertson, Claire C. and Martin A Klein, eds. 1983. *Women and Slavery in Africa*, Madison: University of Wisconsin Press.

Schlegel, Bernhard. 1858. "Beitrag zur Geschichte, Welt- und Religionsanchauung des Westafrikaners, namentlich des Eweer." *Monatsblatt der Norddeutschen Missionsgesellschaft*. 7/8 (7/93):397–400; (7/94):406–408.

Special Collections, National Archives of Ghana, Accra, Ghana: 14/2, 141, 146.

Spiess, C. 1907. "Ein Erinnerungsblatt an die Tage des Sklavenhandels in West Afrika." *Globus (Braunschweig)* 92:205–208.

Westermann, D. 1935. "Die Glidyi-Ewe." *Mitteilungen des Seminars für Orientalische Sprachen* XXXVIII:v–332.

DIASPORA AFRICAN REPATRIATION:
THE PLACE OF DIASPORA WOMEN IN THE PAN-AFRICAN NEXUS

OBIAGELE LAKE

There is a plethora of literature that focuses on nineteenth-century diaspora African repatriation to Africa (Shick 1980; Redkey 1969; Esedebe 1982), but very little on contemporary diaspora African repatriates. Even less has been written about diaspora African women in Africa and their roles in forging pan-African alliances. This chapter discusses the repatriation of diaspora African women to Ghana, West Africa, and the process of their integration into this society.

Diaspora Africans in Ghana do not constitute a monolithic group who claim a perfect memory of the past or "essential cultural continuity" (see Hall 1993). Instead these repatriates are assuming a number of identities that at times are experienced separately and at other times all at once. As Hall (1993:359) suggests:

> Modern people of all sorts and conditions, it seems have had, increasingly, as a condition of survival, to be members, simultaneously, of several, overlapping "imagined communities"; and the negotiations between and across these complex "borderlines" are characteristic of modernity itself.

Where diaspora Africans are included in transnational and diaspora discourse, the complexity and validity of their experiences in Africa and the diaspora are abbreviated and misrepresented (Van den Berghe 1976; Legum 1972: 108–110; Safran 1991: 89–90). Safran declares that "African 'Zionist' efforts have not been successful" and goes on to limit his discussion of repatriation to eighteenth-century migration to Liberia and Sierra Leone. He further asserts that "American [B]lacks no longer have a clearly defined cultural heritage to preserve." This is an interesting, if not ethnocentric, claim that repeats at least two historical approaches to diaspora African people. One is to presume the authority of people of European descent in outlining the parameters of diaspora African culture (see Basch, Glick Schiller, and Szanton Blanc 1994:268), and the other is to define our successes.

The emic perspective (both mine and that of my informants) is opposed to the suggestion that diaspora Africans are without a cultural heritage or homeland. For some contemporary repatriates, the goal was simply to leave their country of birth. In this regard, they have been successful. Others migrated to become part of a pan-African experience. For some repatriates this experience included being part of a newly independent African nation. For others it meant searching for roots or just living among other people of African descent. While many repatriates did not espouse a pan-African ideology before migrating to Ghana, some of these same repatriates came to value their emerging identities born of their experiences in Africa. Using excerpts from life histories, I illustrate the various expressions of this emergent process and focus on the psychosocial aspects of identity and how these dimensions articulate with political-economic pan-Africanism.

The movement of diaspora Africans from west to east[1] is significant from a number of perspectives, not the least of which is the inclusion of this population within the wider discourse on transnational populations (Basch, Glick Schiller, and Szanton Blanc 1994; Buijs 1993; Lake 1995; Sorenson 1992). The fact that diaspora African women are migrating from regions of greater to lesser economic opportunities is also significant and suggests a strong commitment to building new lives in the motherland. This entails developing networks and forming ideologies that encompass aspects of their national (places of birth) identities and those they have developed in their host societies. Repatriates from the Caribbean, South America, and the United States who have settled in Ghana offer a wide range of views that articulate with pan-African ideology and identity. In contemporary Ghana a large proportion of diaspora women are engaged in educational, medical, and legal professions. Others are housewives or have established private businesses. The reasons that initiated their move from the diaspora are intricately tied to issues of race and colonialism.

In the past decade there has been a proliferation of literature regarding homelands and diaspora communities (Scott 1991; Safran 1991; Hall 1993) that speaks of the "return" of diaspora people to a "homeland myth" (Safran 1991) and a search for an "authentic past . . . persisting in the present" (Scott 1991:268). While many diaspora communities around the world are described as constructing their identities within this framework, people of African descent are depicted as the most imaginative in claiming cultural continuities and an African cultural consciousness. What is never explicitly stated is that Africans in the diaspora have a past, as all people do, which guides and influences their present. Moreover, while the separation of Africans from Africa did weaken sociocultural ties, it did not totally erase cultural practices and beliefs. This is a significant preface to the following discussion regarding diaspora Africans in Ghana because, although this essay is not an account of continuities à la Herskovitz (1941), Price (1983), and others, my informants are descendants of African people, a fact that has racial, social, and cultural meaning in both Africa and the diaspora.

Although much of the literature concerning identity and transnational populations questions the effectiveness of race as a unifying principle (Basch, Glick Schiller and Szanton Blanc 1994; Davies 1994; Safran 1991), many diaspora Africans embrace race as the basis of cultural and political-economic solidarity. This is especially true for many diaspora repatriates in Ghana.

Diaspora African emigration to Africa is not a new phenomenon (Kilson 1976). People of African descent have been "returning" to the motherland since the eighteenth century (Esedebe 1982; Bittle and Geiss 1964; Miller 1975; Uya 1971). Most students of Africa are familiar with African Americans who were taken to Liberia by the American Colonization Society beginning in the first quarter of the nineteenth century (Shick 1980; Liebenow 1969).[2] In addition to thousands of African Americans who migrated to Liberia in the nineteenth century, a sizeable number migrated to Sierra Leone from Jamaica and Barbados (Walker 1976; Fyfe 1962; Skinner 1982) and to Nigeria from Brazil (Boadi-Siaw 1982). Women figured prominently among these migrants to West Africa as well as other parts of the continent, where they played significant roles in religious and educational institutions (Jacobs 1982).

My focus on contemporary repatriates is significant because racism continues to affect the life chances of diaspora Africans. In spite of the continuing struggle against racial hegemony in the United States and the rest of the African diaspora, many mainstream anthropologists are deemphasizing the idea of race as well as the dynamics of racism. While academics attempt to erase racism from the tapestry of American life, people of African descent continue to feel the impact of economic, political, and cultural oppression (Pinkney 1984; Edmondson 1979; Marable 1991). This predicament is not limited to African Americans, who constitute a minority in the United States, but also applies to people of African descent who constitute a majority in the Caribbean:

> It must be emphasized that [B]lack minorities (as in the United States) and [B]lack majorities (as in Africa and most of the Caribbean) were equally subject to patterns of racial deprivation and indignity. This historical phenomenon seems to reinforce the need for distinguishing race from ethnicity because in the former instance (unlike typical cases in the latter) the relevant considerations have in the past cut cross majority/minority distinctions. (Edmondson 1979: 420)

Williams (1989:410) reiterates these distinctions in her discussion of power differentials "between two categories of citizens," those whose ideologies are paradigmatic in institutions of control and "those identified with patterns not consistent with the institutionalized ones." Historically, it has been people of European descent who have maintained institutional control in the United States, Latin America, and the Caribbean. This political-economic hegemony has its counterpart in the culturalization of racism. In spite of these realities, academics and nonacademics alike have factored the United States and other parts of the western hemisphere out of the context of racial hegemony that emerged out of western European expansion. In fact, extraction of Africans for the purposes of enslavement and the colonization of Africa were part of the same process by which African peoples' economic and sociocultural systems were undermined. In order to legitimate the process of slavery and racism, people of European descent in the Americas created an elaborate system of stereotypes that degraded the African image, and at the same time psychologically separated diaspora Africans from their kin on the motherland.

Although many people of African descent have internalized these images to varying degrees and are reluctant to acknowledge or lend significance to their African ancestry, others have sought to reincorporate Africa as part of their historical and empirical experiences. This chapter runs counter to other works (Legum 1962: 108–110; Van den Berghe 1976; Safran 1991; Howe 1962, 1961; Isaacs 1961; Bond 1961) on diaspora Africans in Africa that tend to insist that "you can't go home again." What I offer is a more complex view that encompasses the vicissitudes of integrating into one's ancestral home. The joys and disappointments are part of an ongoing process.

DIASPORA AFRICAN REPATRIATES TO GHANA: PAN-AFRICAN PERSPECTIVES

From 1987 to 1989, I spent a total of fourteen months in Ghana, where I collected life histories from 81 of the approximately 120 diaspora Africans who have settled there. The thesis (Lake 1990) from these data suggests that diaspora Africans construct their identities along a broad spectrum of pan-African ideas. For the purposes of this paper, I have chosen to concentrate on women returnees, who constitute 70 percent of repatriates.

Some of the important questions relative to this population are: Why do more diaspora women migrate than men? What particular problems do women face in a largely patriarchal and polygynous society? How do these women's experiences inform debates regarding transnational identities? Before addressing these questions directly, it is useful to briefly define two conceptions of pan-Africanism that have been discussed at greater length in the sociohistorical literature (Legum 1962; Miller 1975; Harris 1982; Essien-Udom 1962).

Continental pan-Africanism is an idea which speaks to the political, economic, and military unification of African nations (Nkrumah 1963; Padmore 1956; Logan 1955). The idea of pan-Africanism was initiated by diaspora African leaders who organized pan-African conferences beginning in 1900. At the first conference, organized by Trinidadian Henry Sylvester Williams in London, England, diaspora and indigenous African leaders came together to discuss principles and strategies for liberation. This important international forum paved the way for several subsequent meetings, the latest of which took place in Uganda in 1993. Continental pan-Africanism became a unifying concept that advocated the creation of a United States of Africa.

What I call holistic pan-Africanism incorporates the notion of continental pan-Africanism and also advocates the return or repatriation of diaspora Africans to Africa. Throughout history, personalities such as Edward Wilmot Blyden (from St. Vincent, Virgin Islands), Henry McNeal Turner (from the United States), Marcus Garvey (from Jamaica), and Kwame Toure (originally from Trinidad) have insisted that the only way to achieve sociocultural integrity and political-economic autonomy lies in the unification of Africa and the repatriation of diaspora Africans to the motherland.

Kwame Toure (formerly Stokely Carmichael), the most recent proponent of holistic pan-Africanism, maintains that diaspora Africans

> . . . must now begin to call ourselves Africans. We have to have a land base. I think the best place for that is Africa and in Africa the best place is Ghana. Black people must begin to understand that there needs now to be a clear sharpening of our ideologies. Our ideology must be pan-Africanism. . . . We must fight for the unification of Africa. Unification of Africa means that you have one state. Everybody speaks the same language, one government, one army. (Carmichael 1969:40,41)

Toure, who formed the All African People's Revolutionary Party in 1968, follows a long line of pan-Africanists who propose that people of African descent will never experience equality in the diaspora. Toure also proposes that based on the enslavement and ethnocide of indigenous and diaspora Africans by a common European oppressor, diaspora and indigenous Africans are one people.

The purpose of my research in Ghana was to find the articulation, if any, between the pan-African notion of "one people" and the experiences of diaspora Africans in Ghana. I chose Ghana as my research site because, since its independence in 1957, it has been one of the countries most often chosen by diaspora Africans (Jenkins 1975:151; Dunbar 1968:39–109). Many diaspora Africans, reacting to segregation, discrimination, violence, and a lack of adequate wages or employment turned to independent Ghana for a chance to participate fully in an African state that espoused peace, egalitarianism, and a pan-African ideal (Legum 1962; Padmore 1956). Given the instability of the Ghanaian polity and the decline in economic growth beginning in the mid-1960s (Bretton 1966; Howell and Rajasooria 1972) many repatriates either returned to the diaspora or settled in other countries on the continent. Since that period there has nonetheless been a slow, but steady, migration to Ghana.

Some diaspora women came to Ghana because they were married to Ghanaian men. As their testimonies will show, this was not their only motivation. The fact that a number of women came to Africa before meeting their husbands is indicative of an early curiosity about Africa. Moreover, marrying a Ghanaian may be a statement in and of itself that speaks to a "choice" for Africa. In addition, the fact that women marry and must make cultural adjustments to this marriage as well as other kinds of compromises, does not mean that they do not hold other cultural and political ideas and philosophies at the same time. While a few diaspora Africans stated that they came to Ghana to search for their roots, most other repatriates cited other reasons. Some came to Ghana via other African countries, "just to tour the motherland." Others came as teachers and entrepreneurs.

As shown in Figure 1,[3] the diaspora population in Ghana consists predominantly of women. Informants explained this disparity by suggesting that women often come to Ghana with their husbands who have land and family. "[Diaspora African men] are already outsiders when they come."

The larger proportion of African Americans[4] to African Caribbeans (see Figure 2) is mainly due to the presence of a group who call themselves the Nation, and who are referred to by others as the Black Hebrews (Gerber 1977). They consider themselves to be Israelites and believe that Israel is part of northeast Africa. They have lived in Ghana since 1965 in an area known as Madina in the Accra region. The group mainly consists of African Americans, although there are several Ghanaians among them. Among repatriates as a whole, most are professionals who work in the fields of education, medicine, engineering, and law. Three are clergy. Most repatriates have settled in the capital city, Accra. Others are located in Kumasi and the Cape Coast.

Figure 1

PERCENTAGES BY AREA AND SEX

	Women	Men
African American	60	40
African Caribbean	88	12
African South American	71	29

Figure 2

DIASPORA AFRICAN POPULATION—1989
(Ghana, West Africa)

	AA	AC	ASA	Total	Total Percentage
Men	30	5	2	37	30.8
Women	42	35	6	83	69.2
Total	72	40	8	120	100

Even though the vast majority of women had thought about Africa long before their migration, their actual experiences varied in significant ways, as did their orientations regarding the concept of pan-Africanism. Some informants deemphasized their African ancestry and considered themselves "citizens-of-the-world." Others recognized their African identities, but also identified themselves in terms of their places of birth. A smaller percentage considered themselves Africans and felt that Africa was their "country."

One of the ways that I attempted to ascertain people's sense of connections to Africa was by asking "What made you come to Africa?" While informants' answers varied in particulars, the majority stated that they migrated to Africa because they were curious about Africa. Some were introduced to Africa through Crossroads Africa[5] while still others said that they wanted to be part of an independent African nation. Ghana seemed particularly suitable because the country's first president, Kwame Nkrumah, was the seminal indigenous African to promulgate continental pan-Africanism (Nkrumah 1963) and welcomed diaspora Africans into his country.

Most of the informants I spoke to came to Ghana in the 1960s or 1970s but a few families arrived in the late 1950s. Some belonged to nationalist or civil rights organizations in the United States; others were introduced to pan-African ideas through their parents' activities. For example, several informants from Jamaica and Trinidad had parents who were active in the Garvey movement. The geographical origins of African Americans may also influence their social integration into Ghanaian society since most of these informants were from the southern part of the United States where more African cultural and social practices may have been retained (Baber 1987; Osburn 1988; Stuckey 1987:306ff.; Levin 1977).

Some informants expressed their affinity with Africa by becoming Ghanaian citizens. Even though a number of the women came to Ghana with their husbands, they indicated that their views on pan-Africanism were formed before their arrival in Ghana. The following informant exemplifies this aspect.

> Asteri:[6] I think [pan-Africanism] is a sense of unity on the continent. I see it broader than Africa. I see it as a movement, as an ideal. To me it has a lot of connotations that are not just political. As a Black identity you should be concerned with other Africans.[7]

Other informants indicated that their membership in nationalist organizations in the diaspora facilitated their incorporation into Ghanaian society. Witness the following excerpt from a woman belonging to the Nation.

> Reyah: [Being a member of the Nation] gave me an awareness of what my purpose should be because before then I was, you know, I was kind of mixed up, to the point where I didn't have any direction . . . nothing to really steer

me in the right direction in regards to African people.It gave me an awareness of who I was and just about Black people in general.

Jeunef, an African American primary school teacher, had been a member of
Kwame Toure's All African People's Revolutionary Party before she met her husband.
Her ideas regarding transnational communities of African descended people are
well-defined.

> Jeunef: [The All African People's Revolutionary Party] was a very intense
> study group. We learned quite a bit, plus we were fortunate in that we had
> quite a few African students in our work-study group. They gave us realistic
> ideas of what the continent [Africa] would be like. . . .We learned quite a bit
> about Nkrumah. It was a blessing to get an in-depth view of material reality.
> You're not going to live in trees, yet you're not going to be in a situation like
> the United States. But in the long run, it's going to be a better life—which I
> agree it is.

> Lake: Better in what sense?

> Jeunef: Better in that the quality of living is better here. I have a better sense
> of who I am.

Jeunef and others who had some preparation for what to expect in Africa tended to be better adjusted to the vagaries of living in Africa than others. Informants who
had not adjusted well, that is, who expressed that they were not happy in Ghana, were
those who had not studied aspects of African history or culture, had not had indigenous African friends in the diaspora, and who thought that Ghana would not be
much different from their homes in the diaspora. One individual expected that Africa
was "going to be like Trinidad." Not finding this, she had little positive to say about
being in Africa. There were only two or three individuals who fell in this category.

One African American informant came to Ghana in 1988 looking for a job.
She had studied law at the Black Law School in Chicago, Illinois, and received her
J.D. from the Community College of Law in international diplomacy in 1980. Later
she had received her Ph.D. from the University of Wisconsin, where she wrote her
dissertation on international human rights.

> Ajetey: Based on my working relationship with the Black Law School and my
> commitment to African Americans and human rights, African Americans fall
> through the cracks with human rights because they don't place us on the agen-
> da on a regular basis. *Incidentally* they do, but they don't address it head on.

My decision to settle here was more of an ideological decision. But my trips to Africa made me more realistic about what I would encounter. It's nice to be totally free of racism.

Race figures prominently in other informants responses, especially among "Africanists." An informant whom I call Nguyen came to Ghana in 1967 and provided a purely racial explanation for her perspective on pan-Africanism and the role diaspora Africans have to play in that process.

> Nguyen: Pan-Africanism to me means a united Africa. Well, it's supposed to be the whole of Africa including North Africa, but I don't think those Arabs think of themselves as Black or Africans. They're only Africans when it's in their interest politically. So I think that we have to somehow limit that Pan-Africanism to sub-Saharan Africa. We should be able to communicate with the Northerners, but I don't think it's going to be integrated, united like the United States of America was envisioned. I don't think it's possible because the two cultures are too different, you know. And it's such a different race of people.

> Lake: Do you think that diaspora Africans have a role to play in the development of pan-Africanism in Africa?

> Nguyen: Yes, certainly. And we have the heroes who started long before even Nkrumah had the idea of pan-Africanism. That West Indian . . . Marcus Garvey, he had the idea. You know, I admire him. And there are others. Frantz Fanon, he's a Black. So indeed, we should bring in all our people. If they're in the Caribbean or wherever they're from. As long as they are Black they have a role to play in uniting Africa—I mean sub-Saharan Africa.

Nguyen's comments lie at the center of the pan-Africanist discourse in that they merge the concepts of continental and holistic pan-Africanism. Most indigenous Africans with whom I spoke also felt that there needed to be stronger relationships between diaspora and indigenous Africans and that coming to live in Africa was one way of reestablishing that link. These responses to diaspora African repatriation are at variance with the scholarly rhetoric, which tends to situate the experience and goals of diaspora and indigenous Africans as separate if not antithetical (Basch, Glick Schiller, and Szanton Blanc 1994:291; Fanon 1968:216). Informants place a great deal of emphasis on race and common origins as bases for proclaiming an African identity. These factors constitute two aspects of identity. The fact that informants' identities have been shaped by cultural, political, and economic factors as they existed during and after slavery constitutes the situational aspects of their identities.

Common racial and political backgrounds notwithstanding, most repatriates in Ghana felt that interaction between indigenous and diaspora Africans needed to be increased. The informant cited below speaks of a cultural knowledge that would enhance the self-confidence of potential repatriates and the benefits that Africa would accrue from the skills of diaspora Africans.

> Andoh: We [African Americans] still don't have the confidence that it takes to put us where we could be. No matter how much we talk about it and how much Black history they teach, there are certain things that have to come through experiences, through really getting something done—really seeing Blacks [Andoh is referring to indigenous Africans here] doing things and really being proud. Black Americans are still not proud of themselves. They can talk about it as much as they like, but deep down in their subconscious, it isn't there. And it will never be there until they come down and assist here in Africa—to make Africa what it could be—and until Africa really opens its doors and realizes that they have a lot to learn from what the Black Americans have done in America. Because they basically built the U.S., but nobody has really realized that.

Several informants said that they had gained a renewed sense of pride in seeing Africans in all spheres of society. An informant from the Nation echoes Andoh's view, but does so in more positive and reciprocal terms.

> Momree: I feel we should be striving for the unification of all Black people whether in the diaspora or out. And that Black people should become brothers and sisters and love one another and respect one another and to lean on each other for the different knowledges we have. Black people in the [United] States have a lot to offer the people here on the continent as far as technology is concerned. And I feel that the people here have a lot to offer us as far as our cultural background which we've lost. So I feel we can both benefit each other.

Other informants referred to the expertise and skills that diaspora Africans could bring to Africa. The encouragement of diaspora African repatriation on the part of African leaders historically has been targeted to skilled individuals (see Weisbord 1973:126–127, 132ff). More recently some African heads of state have proposed the diaspora African "right of return" and automatic citizenship in Africa (Abuja Declaration 1993).

While most informants understood the unifying concept of pan-Africanism, they felt that actualizing this theory would not be easy. The next informant emphasized that indigenous and diaspora Africans have different needs relative to pan-Africanism.

Falim: I feel that [diaspora Africans] need [pan-Africanism] more than Blacks within Africa. It's an identity, it's a search for identity that was stripped away in a lot of ways [but] it will have a hard time working.

The people themselves are not ready for the concept because they themselves are drenched in tribalism and sectionalism. And, you know, if you can't even get a village ten miles from another to agree, how are you going to get somebody from across the ocean who you have no knowledge of to agree with what you do and what you think? . . . Pan-Africanism is just a term to [indigenous Africans]. But to those of us outside of Africa, in America, Europe, the Caribbean, and even in South America, it's a strong push for pan-Africanism because we have a need that's met here in Africa.

IDENTITY FORMATION AND AFRICAN CULTURE

When asked more specifically about whether they think of themselves as Africans, informants offered a range of responses.

Even though the majority identified as African American or African Caribbean, they also expressed feelings of continuity with Africa. These feelings of extended kinship were experienced in many ways, including the recognition of Ghanaian names in their (diaspora) families, similar communication styles, and resemblances in physical features. These encounters are not separate from larger, macro political-economic issues; however, they have the effect of being mutually reinforcing. Some informants were hardly acquainted with larger notions of pan-Africanism, while others had clearly formed their ideas before coming to Ghana.

Repatriates from various parts of the Caribbean were no more or less African-identified than African Americans and most felt affinities to their places of birth as well as a recognition of their African roots. Among the African Caribbean population, most of the informants are from Jamaica—a place that absorbed African slaves and laborers into the late nineteenth century (Schuler 1980). Similarities have been widely reported between contemporary Jamaican and African cultures in religious ceremonies, family structure, and language (Mintz 1977; Allenye 1971; Abrahams and Szwed 1983). While many informants pointed to these similarities, they made it clear that the societies were not identical.

Nobari: I am African basically, but I still think Caribbean. I still think so. I tend to think I mustn't lose my identity. I feel that for marriage and for life. I feel that one should not try to submerge themselves into somebody else's culture or somebody else's life for that matter. So I think it works better for us. I'm Nobari, he's Thomas. I'm from the Caribbean and I still have some things that I grew up with that make me who I am. And he is the way he is.

And we meet each other halfway on some things. On other things, we are poles apart.

African food, for example—I choose the ones I like and I leave the ones I don't like. I think I've tried to introduce him to the Caribbean . . . like I say, we eat bananas boiled. At first he would resist that. He'd say, "Oh, no, we don't eat such things here." Until 1983 when we had famine in Ghana, near famine—then he was ready to eat anything.

Nobari, who has five children, has taught piano in her home for the past thirty-five years. She seems satisfied with her life in Ghana and attributes this to her not having "had any bad experiences."

Nobari: So that's something to say about Ghanaians. You know this is very much spoken about, the Ghanaian hospitality. How they receive strangers and that sort of thing. Also, of course, it depends on the person. If you make yourself proud and that sort of thing, they'll keep away. But if you're the normal sort of person and you smile at everybody, you get on all right, I think.

Another Caribbean from Trinidad, whom I call Egala, also felt this way.

Egala: You have to be in touch with customs if you want to get along. Where matters Ghanaian are concerned, my children have a Ghanaian instinct. Doing it any other way, you won't achieve anything . . . trying to change things willy-nilly. When I came here I didn't want to associate with West Indians to the detriment of maintaining close relationships with Ghanaians. Because I felt if you did, you would not be able to integrate into Ghanaian society, really. In addition, you would be trying to live like West Indians in Ghana. . . . My husband certainly wasn't going to tolerate my making a West Indian household. My mother-in-law taught me to prepare a lot of dishes.

Acquiring a taste for and preparing new foods, wearing African clothes, and adapting to styles of communication were only part of the adjustments diaspora Africans had to make. I suggest, along with a number of other scholars (Thompson 1983; Holloway 1990; Gay and Baber 1987; LaFrance and Mayo 1978), that these adjustments are facilitated because diaspora Africans are aware of a number of African cultural practices before coming to Ghana. As indicated earlier, the degree of success experienced by any particular informant was predicated on a number of issues, one of which was her pre-Ghanaian experiences. One informant who first came to Africa with Operation Crossroads had this to say:

Asteri: I was prepared to enjoy [Africa]. Whatever the discomforts were, it was part of the African experience. I have found that those students who have gotten along the best, and gotten the most out of it, were those who prepared themselves. They read about the country. They knew what they were coming to look for. They understood the political situation; they had spoken to people. And they seemed to have the best kind of experience here.

On an everyday level, diaspora African women as well as men have integrated well into Ghanaian society. Even though marriage constitutes the most fundamental link between Africa and the diaspora, diaspora and indigenous Africans come together in a number of other arenas, including religion, employment, and purely social areas.

Although most repatriates said that they had "integrated socially," most felt that they had not done so culturally. This is true for repatriates as a whole, but women are faced with a dual adjustment: They are both a foreigner and a woman, which in Africa entails playing roles and accepting or combating the status of second-class citizen. Diaspora women repatriates are expected to conform to the institution of polygyny, which, formally or informally, is alive and well in Ghana, as it is in the rest of Africa. Being part of a wider kinship network also means spending resources—time, money, and energy—caring for relatives who come and "visit" for extended periods of time. Some repatriates learn to live with this reality, but often feel compelled to make major adjustments to African family life. Marriage proved to be one of the most difficult. Although most women did not tolerate polygynous arrangements, some did. Some women bring values with them that are consonant with polygyny.

The Hebrew Israelites, unlike other repatriates, live as a community, and most of those who are married have married other African Americans (rather than Ghanians). The portion of an interview I had with one Hebrew informant reveals the many ways that women's subordination is manifested. When I asked her whether the Hebrew Israelites practiced polygyny, this was her response:

Merez: Well, we call it Divine Marriage. In polygyny we have plenty of minds, but in Divine Marriage there's one mind. And the husband is the head of the family. And all of his extensions, all of his wives, are one in the spirit with him. So this is the difference between polygyny and Divine Marriage. I find that in talking to women about the kingdom of God and in talking about our relationship with men in the community and talking about the order of the family and the order even as it was set forth by God in the beginning from creation, it was God first, then he created man. He created woman out of man. And then he gave them children, so the divine order of the family is God first, and then the man keeping his hand in God's hand, and then the women and children.

Although most women in Ghana did not subscribe to this hierarchical view, some did tolerate their husbands "marrying" other women and having children by them. The next excerpt comes from a Barbadian woman, Pouver, who has been married to a Ghanaian lawyer for almost thirty years. Her story is the most complex, and maybe the saddest, but other women have experienced their share of similar problems. Pouver had five children, three of whom had sickle cell anemia. One died as a young child, another died at twenty-eight years old—shortly before I met Pouver. In addition to these five children, Pouver raised nine other children that her husband had with other women.

> Pouver: That idea is the thing that jammed my brains and made me quite irrational sometimes because it didn't stay the [first] two [children], it increased in number until all together he had nine. . . . So I've raised all of his children. I've raised every one of them! I'm not afraid of [the other women] coming back, but I just do think about it and it makes me nauseated at times where it seemed like I've swallowed something and don't want it. And then suddenly it comes. It's like a dog lapping up what he doesn't want. . . . [My husband] is by nature a polygamous person.

In addition to problems in the marriage, challenges continue after the death of their husbands. When these women's husbands die, more often than not relatives lay claim to the wife's property. One woman who had observed this practice among her diaspora friends put it this way:

> Falim: At the funeral, of course, they will be courteous to [the widow]. And the friends will still say she's our friend and what have you. But the relatives are not going to feel like she's a relative. Now they will verbalize otherwise, but their actions will show, you see. We've had people when the husband dies, they've taken everything from the woman. Taken everything!

One informant whose husband had recently died attested to this practice.

> Alomar: You could have bought a home together, both wife and husband, bought cars together and other properties. But you find that after years pass by, if your husband dies and you're from another country, you could find it's not unusual that the extended family will come in. They come in quite nicely at the beginning, being quite helpful during funeral time. And they could be quite hostile too. And it's possible that they want to take most of your things away. They don't even ask, they demand it! . . . Really, if you marry an African and you stay together happily, in the end, you can be quite unhappy, so you have to prepare yourself for such things and plan your life according-

ly. Always have something for yourself separately away from your husband because once it's together, the family would like to get their hands on it. And that's not nice.

Ghanaian women, as well as other African women, go through similar changes with their in-laws (Cohen and Atieno Odhiambo 1992; Potash 1986) but, as diaspora repatriates informed me, the difference is that Ghanaian women have a family in Ghana to turn to for support in times of trouble. In spite of women's particular position in Ghana, diaspora women's problems in identifying with and assimilating into Ghanaian society have aspects that are not gender-specific. This is not surprising given the internal cultural conflicts that characterize all African nations (Ungar 1978). Although many Ghanaians with whom I spoke felt that "it is time for [diaspora Africans] to come home," many others pointed to cultural differences between diaspora Africans and Ghanaians. These differences were most frequently marked by referring to repatriates as *oburuni*. *Oburuni* is a Ga (one of approximately fifty-nine Ghanaian languages) word that means "white person." Although it is clear to Ghanaians that diaspora Africans are not phenotypically "white," the fact that they are from cultures outside Africa renders them foreign enough to be *oburuni*. The term *oburuni* is also used to describe Ghanaians who are lighter-skinned than normal, or who have wavy or straight hair; however, this does not lessen the blow for many repatriates who want to feel like they "are coming home." While this labeling is one aspect of Ghanaian life that makes distinctions between "we" and "they," diaspora African behaviors contributed to differences between these populations.

In all but a few cases, diaspora repatriates had not bothered to learn any of the Ghanaian languages and felt that this was one of the main reasons they were not culturally accepted. The fact that the vast majority of people in Ghana speak English, most of them fluently, acts as a deterrent to learning indigenous languages. One woman from Trinidad was exceptional in this regard.

> Garnes: When I came here at first, I had lived many years in Europe. I settled in Ghana and started to examine things more critically. Then I thought that to really get an understanding, you should know the language. And if I'm going to be living here, always, it would be silly to be living in a country and not be able to express yourself to the people, somehow, anyway. . . . I studied Twi. . . . When you hear them speak, it doesn't sound like anything . . . just like a bunch of noise. But I found it very interesting. The grammar is tremendous. I was astonished to find that they have such a great grammar behind their language.

Almost all informants mentioned language as a barrier to integrating culturally into Ghanaian society. Those who did learn an indigenous language were not necessarily more pan-Africanist, but they seemed more positive about their experiences with Ghanaians. Even though most Ghanaians speak English (I never encountered any Ghanaians in Accra and most of the other regions who did not), the unwillingness of repatriates to speak Ghanaian languages may be perceived as a lack of interest in Ghanaian culture. I suggest that if it is cultural acceptance that repatriates desire, then learning the native tongues is a place to begin. Not only would this be a statement indicative of a willingness to become part of Ghanaian culture, but it would facilitate a deeper understanding of Ghanaian cultures as well. As Fischer (1987: 198) asserts:

> Language itself contains sedimented layers of emotionally resonant metaphors, knowledge, and associations, which when paid attention to can be experienced as discoveries and revelations. Indeed, much of [the] contemporary philosophical mood . . . is to inquire into what is hidden in language . . . what is repressed, implicit, or mediated.

The other most frequently mentioned obstacle was the long-standing ethnic conflicts in many neocolonial African societies. The obstacles notwithstanding, all but three informants indicated that being in Ghana gave them a sense of freedom—freedom to reflect, spiritual freedom, and freedom from racism.

> Conway: I've always thought of myself as just being a Black female—a woman. But I'd say over the years I see where I really am African to a great extent. Since being here, I've seen all of my family, all of your family, and all the friends and everyone I've ever known—the whole range of shades and features. And they're all African. Being in Africa has made me feel more open in terms of knowing who I am.

> Jeunef: Yes, I'm a descendant of slaves and I am from Africa. So I have the advantage. I can take a little of everything. I can take a little of Yoruba [culture], I can take a little bit from the Gas, and just shape it into what I am. So I don't get offended *anymore* [by what people say], because I don't have a specific group.

> Momree: [Becoming a member of the Nation] gave me an awareness of what my purpose should be, because before then I was, you know, mixed up to the point where I didn't have any direction. It gave me an awareness of who I was and just about black people in general. . . . We're the Chosen People of God.

CONCLUSION

Most diaspora repatriates expressed a sense of relatedness to Africa—albeit not identical with the notion of "one people." While expressing an affinity to their places of birth, they also incorporated an African identity that speaks to cultural, psychological, and emotional orientations. Informants who were more willing to declare a pan-Africanist identity, one that spans both hemispheres, were those who had experiences in the diaspora that were consonant with a pan-Africanist ethos.

While informants were receptive to cultural and political pan-Africanism, they were realistic about the difficulties of actualizing these ideas. Continuing internal conflicts as well as European and European-American impact on the political economy of African nations constitute the most formidable obstacles.

While diaspora Africans have difficulties integrating into Ghanaian society, based in part on historical experiences and language differences, there are points of convergence. Just as European culture was thrust upon people of African descent in the diaspora, so it was in Africa as well (Lloyd 1966:108–109; Ferkiss 1966: 155–167). The intrusion of European norms, manifested in dress, religion, and other practices, is as common in Ghana as it is in other parts of Africa. Western imports such as TVs, VCRs, American television programming, and other cultural technologies are also integral to African culture. Although cultural imperialism has had deleterious effects for indigenous Africans, Western cultural norms provide another place of intersection between indigenous and diaspora Africans. These points of intersection are coupled with points of divergence, one of which is language.

Diaspora women repatriates' continued presence in Ghana, in the face of language and other cultural obstacles, is a statement about their commitment to finding their way in this new nation-state. Their difficulties in the domestic sphere are, nevertheless, important to emphasize because their lack of autonomy in the family is a reflection of their subordinate status vis-à-vis men in other spheres.

In this regard, diaspora women are not in a very different position than indigenous Ghanaian women. In Ghana, as in other African countries, the man is considered the head of the household. They also predominate in the higher echelons of polity and economy. Although laws give women *de jure* rights, the actualization of these rights is something else again. Differences in female and male opportunities are equally evident at the level of employment and of salary differentials. These disparities are a consequence of a bias in favor of educating males, especially at the tertiary level, while at the same time relegating females to domestic responsibilities (Frederikse 1992; Moumouni 1968).

Although, in general, opportunities for diaspora African women are greater than for their indigenous counterparts, they have been subject to sexist norms in the diaspora (hooks 1981; King 1988) that condition them for life in Africa. These women, like Ghanaian women, work outside the home and are still expected to carry the burden of being the primary homemaker as well. Moreover, although polygyny is illegal in the diaspora, women are accustomed to their husbands' involvement in informal liaisons with other women. Even though diaspora and indigenous women in Ghana face similar problems with their spouses and families, they have not joined together in efforts to bring about change. While the ideology of holistic pan-Africanism emphasizes egalitarianism, male hegemony over women and class divisions among women continue to characterize on-the-ground relationships. These political and economic divisions add to the complexity of cultural differences between indigenous and diaspora Africans.

Nevertheless, adjustment to Ghanaian cultural norms is not always an uphill battle. Women's stories that elaborated on difficulties with their husbands or in-laws were matched by those that praised the benefits of being part of an extended family. Mothers-in-law and sisters-in-law were frequently mentioned, particularly in terms of the supportive roles they played during childbirth. In addition to being incorporated into the Ghanaian family structure, diaspora Africans have integrated into all other arenas of Ghanian life, including the workplace and religious institutions. Relatives of these repatriates also come to visit for varying periods of time, which further extends the pan-African nexus and gives these visitors firsthand experience of the motherland that, in many ways, counters the rhetoric that tends to divide indigenous and diaspora people. While diaspora repatriates' stories may not be consistent with the notion of "one people," neither do they exemplify people who "cannot go home again." Instead, repatriates grapple with their multiple identities, which include, but are not limited to, being women, being Africans, being diaspora Africans, and others. This tension among racial, sexual, and national identities is a dynamic one; however, as Geertz suggests (1973:260), managing different affinities "[does] not consist simply of the expansion of one at the expense of the other." These multiple identities find their intersection within the ever-changing and complex pan-Africanist landscape.

NOTES

1. Diaspora Africans have migrated to most of the African nations. In addition to Ghana, other countries most often chosen as host societies include Togo, Kenya, Tanzania, Nigeria, and Zimbabwe (Washington 1989).

2. While much of the literature depicts African Americans as the oppressors of indigenous Africans in Liberia, African Americans and other diaspora Africans assumed a number of different positions in Liberian society. Moreover, the role of the United States and European control over the Liberia/Sierra Leone area has been underemphasized.

3. The data for the figures is based on my own surveys.

4. The term "African American" is used here to denote people of African descent from North America.

5. Crossroads Africa was formed in 1957 by James Herman Robinson, an African American who sought to give "American and Canadian students the experience of

living and working alongside Africans in the independent countries of Africa" (Shavit 1989:55).

6. All of the names used in this chapter are pseudonyms.

7. All of the excerpts presented in this chapter are in unedited form.

BIBLIOGRAPHY

Abrahams, Roger and John F. Szwed. 1983. *After Africa*. New Haven: Yale University Press.

Abuja Declaration. 1993. *A Declaration of the First Pan-African Conference on Reparations for African Enslavement, Colonization and Neo-Colonization*. Sponsored by the Organization of African Unity, Group of Eminent Persons and the Federal Republic of Nigeria.

Africa News. 1992. "The Changing Face of Africa." December 23–January 6: 8.

Alleyne, Mervyn. 1971. "The Linguistic Continuity of Africa in the Caribbean." In *Topics in Afro-American Studies*, Henry J. Richards, ed. Buffalo: Black Academy Press.

Anderson, Benedict. 1987. *Imagined Communities: Reflections on the Origin and Spread of Nationalisms*. London: Verso.

Basch, Linda, Nina Glick Schiller and Christina Szanton Blanc. 1994. *Nations Unbound: Transnational Projects, Postcolonial Predicaments, and Deterritorialized Nation-States*. Switzerland: Gordon and Breach.

Bittle, William and Gilbert Geiss. 1964. *The Longest Way Home: Chief Alfred C. Sam's Back-to-Africa Movement*. Detroit: Wayne State University Press.

Boadi-Siaw, S. Y. 1982. "Brazilian Returnees of West Africa." In *Global Dimensions of the African Diaspora*, Joseph Harris, ed. pp.291–308, Washington, DC: Howard University Press.

Bond, Horace Mann. 1961. "Howe and Isaacs in the Bush: The Ram in the Thicket." *Negro History Bulletin* 25(3): 67–70, 72.

Bretton, Henry L. 1966. *The Rise and Fall of Kwame Nkrumah: A Study of Personal Rule in Africa*. New York: F. A. Praeger.

Buijs, Gina. 1993. *Migrant Women: Crossing Boundaries and Changing Identities*. Providence, RI: Berg Publishers.

Carmichael, Stokely. 1969. "Pan-Africanism, Land and Power." *Black Scholar: Journal of Black Studies and Research* 1(1):36–43.

Cohen, David W. and E. S. Atieno Odhiambo. 1992. *Burying SM*. Portsmouth, NH: Heinemann.

Davies, Carole Boyce. 1994. *Black Women, Writing and Identity: Migrations of the Subject*. London: Routledge.

Dunbar, Ernest. 1968. *Black Expatriates*. New York: Dutton.

Edmondson, Locksley. 1979. "Black Roots and Identity: Comparative and International Perspectives." *International Journal* 34(3):408–429.

Esedebe, P. Olisanwuche. 1982. *Pan-Africanism: The Idea and Movement*. Washington, DC: Howard University Press.

Essien-Udom, E. U. 1962. *Black Nationalism: A Search for an Identity in America*. New York: Dell Publication Company.

Fanon, Frantz. 1968. *The Wretched of the Earth*. New York: Grove Press.

Ferkiss, Victor C. 1966. *Africa's Search for Identity*. New York: George Braziller.

Fischer, Michael M. 1986. "Ethnicity and the Post-Modern Arts of Memory." In *Writing Culture*, James Clifford and George Marcus, eds. pp.194–233, Berkeley: University of California Press.

Frederikse, J. 1992. *All Schools for All Children*. Oxford: Oxford University Press.

Fyfe, Christopher. 1962. *History of Sierra Leone*. London: Collier Books.

Garvey, Amy Jacques. 1971. *Philosophy and Opinions of Marcus Garvey*. New York: Atheneum.

Gay, Geneva and Willie Baber, eds. 1987. *Expressively Black: The Cultural Basis of Ethnic Identity*. New York: Praeger.

Geertz, Clifford. 1973. "The Integrative Revolution: Primordial Sentiments and Civil Policies in the New States." In *The Interpretation of Culture*. New York: Basic Books, Inc.

Gerber, Israel. 1977. *The Heritage Seekers: Black Jews in Search of Identity*. Middle Village, New York: Jonathan David Publishers, Inc.

Hall, Stuart. 1993. "Culture, Community, Nation." *Cultural Studies* 7(3): 349–363.

Harris, Joseph. 1982. *Global Dimensions of the African Diaspora*. Washington, DC: Howard University Press.

Herskovitz, Melville J. 1941. *The Myth of the Negro Past*. Boston: Beacon Press.

Holloway, Joseph E. 1990. *Africanisms in American Culture*. Bloomington: Indiana University Press.

hooks, bell. 1981. *Ain't I a Woman: Black Women and Feminism*. Boston: South End Press.

Howe, Russell. 1961. "Strangers in Africa." *The Reporter* 24(13):34-35.

———. 1962. "A Reply to Horace Mann Bond." *The Negro History Bulletin*. 25(5):102,104.

Howell, Thomas A. and Jeffrey P. Rajasooria. 1972. *Ghana and Nkrumah*. New York: Facts on File, Inc.

Irwin, Graham W. 1977. *Africans Abroad: A Documentary History of the Black Diaspora in Asia, Latin America, and the Caribbean During the Age of Slavery*. New York: Columbia University Press.

Isaacs, Harold. 1961. "Back to Africa." *The New Yorker*, May 13: 105–106.

Jacobs, Sylvia. 1982. *Black Americans and the Missionary Movement in Africa*. Westport, CT: Greenwood Press.

Jenkins, David. 1975. *Black Zion: The Return of Afro-Americans and West Indians to Africa*. London: Wildwood House, Ltd.

Kilson, Martin. 1976. *The African Diaspora*. Cambridge: Harvard University Press.

King, D. K. 1988. "Multiple Jeopardy, Multiple Consciousness: The Context of a Black Feminist Ideology." *Signs: Journal of Women in Culture and Society* 14(1): 42–72.

Lake, Obiagele. 1990. "A Taste of Life: Diaspora African Repatriation to Ghana." Ph.D. dissertation, Cornell University.

———. 1995. "Toward the Formulation of a Pan-African Identity: Diaspora African Repatriates in Ghana." *Anthropological Quarterly* 68(1):21–36.

LaFrance, Marrianne and Clara Mayo. 1978. "Gaze Direction in Interracial Dyadic Communication." *Ethnicity* 5(2):167–173.

Legum, Colin. 1962. *Pan-Africanism: A Short Political Guide*. London: Pall Mall Press.

Levin, Lawrence W. 1977. *Black Culture and Black Consciousness: Afro-American Folk Thought from Slavery to Freedom*. New York: Oxford University Press.

Liebenow, J. Gus. 1969, 1973. *Liberia: The Evolution of Privilege*. Ithaca, NY: Cornell University Press.

Lloyd, P. C. 1966. *New Elites in Tropical Africa*. Oxford: Oxford University Press.

Logan, Rayford. 1955. "Historical Aspects of Pan-Africanism: A Personal Chronicle." *African Forum* 1(1):90–104.

Marable, Manning. 1991. *Race, Reform and Rebellion: The Second Reconstruction in Black America, 1945–1990*. Jackson: University of Mississippi Press.

Martin, Tony. 1983. *The Pan-African Connection: From Slavery to Garvey and Beyond*. Cambridge, MA: Schenkman Publisher.

Miller, Floyd. J. 1975. *The Search for Black Nationalism: Black Emigration and Colonization, 1987–1863*. Urbana: University of Illinois Press.

Mintz, Sidney. 1977. *An Anthropological Approach to the Afro-American Past: A Caribbean Perspective*. Philadelphia: Institute for the Study of Human Issues.

Moumouni, A. 1968. *Education in Africa*. New York: F. A. Praeger.

Nkrumah, Kwame. 1963. *Africa Must Unite*. New York: International Press.

Osburn, Margaret. 1988. "Along the Side of the Road: Creating Sea Grass Baskets." *American Visions: The Magazine of Afro-American Culture* 3(2):16–21.

Padmore, George. 1956. *Pan-Africanism or Communism*. New York: Doubleday.

Pinkney, Alphonso. 1984. *The Myth of Black Progress*. London: Cambridge University Press.

Potash, Betty. 1986. *Widows in African Societies: Choices and Constraints*. Stanford, CA: Stanford University Press.

Price, Richard. 1983. *First Time: The Historical Vision of an Afro-American People*. Baltimore: Johns Hopkins University Press.

Redkey, Edwin S. 1969. *Black Exodus: Black Nationalist and Back to Africa Movements, 1890–1910*. New Haven, CT: Yale University Press.

Rushdie, Salman. 1991. *Imaginary Homelands: Essays and Criticism, 1981–1991*. London: Granta Books.

Safran, William. 1991. "Diasporas in Modern Societies: Myths of Homeland and Return." *Diaspora* 1(1):83–99.

Sarris, Alexander. 1991. *Ghana Under Structural Adjustment: The Impact on Agriculture and the Rural Poor*. New York: International Fund for Agricultural Development by New York University Press.

Schuler, Monica. 1980. *Alas, Alas Kongo: A Social History of Indentured African Immigration into Jamaica, 1841–1865*. Baltimore: John Hopkins University Press.

Scott, David. 1991. "That Event, This Memory: Notes on the Anthropology of African Diasporas in the New World." *Diaspora* 1(3):261–284.

Shavit, David. 1989. *The United States in Africa: A Historical Dictionary*. Westport, CT: Greenwood Press.

Shick, Tom. 1980. *Behold the Promised Land: A History of Afro-American Settler Society in Nineteenth Century Liberia*. Baltimore: Johns Hopkins University Press.

Skinner, Elliott P. 1982. "The Dialectic Between Diaspora and Homelands." In *Global Dimensions of the African Diaspora*, pp. 17–45, Joseph E. Harris, ed. Washington, DC: Howard University Press.

Sorenson, John. 1992. "Essence and Contingency in the Construction of Nationhood: Transformation of Identity in Ethiopia and its Diasporas." *Diaspora* 2(2):201–228.

Stuckey, Sterling. 1987. *Slave Culture: Nationalist Theory and the Foundation of Black America*. New York: Oxford University Press.

Thompson, Robert Farris. 1983. *Flash of the Spirit: African and Afro-American Art and Philosophy*. New York: Random House.

Touré, Kwame. n.d. "The Relevance of the People's Revolutionary Party to Africans World-Wide." Mimeograph No. 3. All African People's Revolutionary Party.

Ungar, Sanford. 1978. *The People and Politics of an Emerging Continent*. New York: Simon and Schuster.

Uya, Okon. 1971. *Black Brotherhood: Afro-Americans and Africa*. Lexington, MA: D. C. Heath.

Van den Berghe, Paul L. 1976. "Ethnic Pluralism in Industrial Societies." *Ethnicity* 3:242–255.

Walker, James W. St. G. 1976. *The Black Loyalists*. New York: Holmes and Meier Publishers, Inc.

Washington, Elsie B. 1989. "The Front Line—Ten Proud Years of Freedom." *Essence* 20(6): 97–110.

Weisbord, Robert. 1973. *Ebony Kinship*. Westport, CT: Greenwood Press.

Williams, Brackette. 1989. "A Class Act: Anthropology and the Race to Nation Across Ethnic Terrain." *Annual Review of Anthropology* 18:401–444.

POPULAR MUSIC, URBAN SOCIETY, AND CHANGING GENDER RELATIONS IN KINSHASA, ZAIRE (1950–1990)

CH. DIDIER GONDOLA

This chapter delves into the complexities of gender as a set of power relations by high-lighting a *terra incognita* that, until recently, researchers have tended to disregard. Barber (1991) points to a variety of sociocultural phenomena (e.g., painting, cooking, theater, humor, and popular culture more generally) that make it possible to address political issues without explicitly doing so. This was especially important during the colonial period. Martin (1991) has brought out new elements in the history of colonial Brazzaville by stressing how the struggle (between the colonial authorities and the African soccer players) to control the organization of soccer led to a political confrontation.

Music in colonial Africa also had political and social implications (Waterman 1988: 233). I have demonstrated (Gondola 1992) that in the case of Zaire, the former Belgian Congo, musical discourse was already demanding the total abolition of the colonial system, even before political leaders began the struggle for political reforms. Music is viewed here as a vehicle of political discourse and one of the responses against the colonial system. The colonial city, by virtue of its history as a milieu of fusion and diffusion and a breeding ground for new cultural patterns (Coquery-Vidrovitch 1993), enabled African actors to reshape and reinterpret different structures and relations, including gender. Before showing how music became a medium of gender negotiation, I will examine the extent to which the triptych gender, colonization, and urbanization functioned in Léopoldville (now Kinshasa), and how in its origins Congolese popular music appeared as an eminently male culture.[1]

GENDER, COLONIZATION, AND URBANIZATION

Although there were precolonial cities in West Africa, the dominant view about Central Africa equates urbanization with colonization (Lacroix 1967: 103). Since the pioneering research of Dresch on Congolese cities, nobody has really questioned the idea that "the city, creation of the white man, is populated by blacks" (Dresch 1948: 5).[2] Even though the city was an ally of colonization (Bairoch 1988: 508), it is incorrect to attribute to colonization the creation of cities *ex nihilo*. Central African cities were undoubtedly "tools" and "place[s] of colonization," but it is hardly true that colonization created them (Coquery-Vidrovitch 1991: 17, 35, 71). Bairoch views colonization as "an urbanizing factor in thinly urbanized regions and a deurbanizing factor in heavily urbanized regions" (1988: 506). To this, I add a violent deurbanization immediately followed by a reurbanization (Gondola 1994). In this latter case, colonizers used preexisting African patterns and frameworks to organize the land. In Léopoldville, this phenomenon occurred in a brutal way. Prior to building Léopoldville, the Belgian colonizers destroyed the important African settlements of Ndolo, Kintambo, Lemba, and Kimpoko, thus expelling their residents. A similar process has been analyzed in the case of the Spanish colonial establishment in Latin America, where cities such as Mexico City, Cuzco, Quito, and Arequipa were built over the ruins of native cities (Roberts 1978: 37).

Thus, if the colonial city was a "place of colonization," it should be stressed that it was therefore chiefly a place of exploitation. Léopoldville—situated on the banks of Malebo Pool, where the Congo River becomes unnavigable as its rapids melt into the Atlantic Ocean—was settled in 1881 and constituted an important industrial center. Until the Depression of the 1930s, the only population encouraged to migrate to the city consisted of young male workers whom the Belgian authorities labeled HAV (*hommes adultes valides*) and squeezed into poor housing far from the white residential areas.

If men were encouraged to settle in Léopoldville, women were dissuaded from moving there. In the rural areas, Congolese men wanted to keep women in the villages for economic reasons. Women comprised the majority of the labor force and were present and active in all the stages of the food crop production process. The Catholic authorities who organized missions all over the Belgian Congo were even more reluctant to let women migrate to Léopoldville. In fact, Léopoldville and most Congolese cities were stigmatized as negative, depraved, even evil milieux. In contrast, villages were viewed as safe havens, even the repository of the authentic and innocent Africa. In the urban milieu, the administrative authorities were also unwilling to promote female migration. From the colonial perspective, the African city (as well as the European city itself) was a male bastion from which women had to be excluded.[3]

In the Belgian Congo, as in Europe, the status of women was directly linked to their marital status. A married woman could not leave the village without the permission of her husband. In 1922, the legislature prohibited married women from being hired as servants unless they obtained written permission from their husbands. The official stance generally construed the migration of women to Léopoldville as a desire on the women's part to become prostitutes. Single women were then legally tagged with the awkward term *femmes indigènes adultes et valides vivant théoriquement seules* (indigenous able-bodied adult women officially living alone) and were taxed fifty francs annually (roughly the wage a domestic earned for ten days' work). In Stanleyville (now Kisangani) from 1939 to 1943, this tax was the second-highest source of revenue for the city (MacGaffey 1986: 174). Consequently, the number of women in the Congolese capital particularly remained low. In 1928, Léopoldville I, the biggest camp of workers, was populated with 21,500 men and only 5,000 women, among whom 358 were legally married, while the majority had been illegally introduced into the city. This demographic situation entailed a precarious urban life as depicted by the Reverend Father Van Wing in 1924: "I walked around the immense black city, where live, only God knows in which moral indiscipline, 20,000 negroes . . . it's a camp, it's not a village. There is little greenery, even fewer children . . . not many mothers, little joy. Of all the places that I went, I have only seen two children" (quoted in by Saint-Moulin 1976: 468).

Between 1924 and 1930, as economic activity expanded in the Belgian Congo (Bezy and Peemans 1981: 20), the African male population almost doubled in Léopoldville and, as in the Zambian copperbelt townships, "colonial authorities were [from then on] concerned with the problems [e.g., strikes and epidemics] that were beginning to arise from the rapid growth of substantial African populations in the towns, which were not designed to house and service them" (Hansen 1989: 116). The authorities faced a dilemma: either reinforce the camplike aspect of the black city (that is, stop women from migrating) or redesign African settlements. They opted for the latter and started, in 1933, to build standardized houses in remodeled African suburbs henceforth segregated from white residential areas by "ecological barriers" (i.e., greenery).

During World War II and thereafter, women were at last allowed to reside in Léopoldville. There were four principal reasons for this. First, women migrated to meet the needs of the white male urban dwellers. At the beginning of this century the distribution of Léopoldville's European population was strikingly unbalanced: only 600 women for 2,500 men in the late 1920s. The demographic imbalance seems even more pronounced since the majority of the white female population constituted the missionary staff in the religious missions. Up until the 1930s, contacts between European men and African women were heavily stigmatized. Simply to be on familiar terms with a black woman invited derogatory labels such as *petit blanc* (white trash). As industrial activity picked up momentum after the Great Depression, the number of white male settlers increased, and so did these interracial contacts. But even during the Depression, European men began to show less reluctance to accept black women as some white urban settlers experienced economic hardship. The rise in the number of abandoned biracial children, which almost doubled between 1932 (108 children) and 1934 (191 children), confirms this phenomenon.

The second reason women were legally permitted to move to the city was the official desire to eradicate prostitution and to stabilize African manpower by encouraging family life. Decline in employment for men during the Great Depression constituted the third reason. Between 1929 and 1937 many Europeans left Léopoldville and returned to Europe. Several European companies closed shop. Consequently, the majority of African workers became unemployed. They were detained by the colonial police and sent back to the villages: 6,000 were sent back in 1930 and 7,000 in 1932. Thus, the male population of Léopoldville decreased by one-half between 1930 and 1935, from 26,932 to 13,442, while the female population increased by 8 percent. By 1934, the female population was half of the male population.

The last reason was the women themselves. In Léopoldville, they succeeded in carrying out food crop production and small-scale trade which men were not willing to undertake during the Depression. After World War II, women gained status in the city. They were allowed to live in the city, but they still were fewer in number and, therefore, could choose partners from many suitors. Many women decided to have more than one male partner at a time while remaining single. These women were called *femmes libres* (free women) or *ndoumba* (courtesans). Some women also enjoyed better economic positions than many men because they had married Europeans and/or because they were entrepreneurs.

Once they entered the cities, however, women were neglected, even excluded from urban development and confined to activities such as small-scale trade, gardening and housekeeping. Whereas African men were labelled *évolués*, by which the white colonists acknowledged their efforts to evolve from "indigenous" to "civilized" status, women were labeled *musenzi*, a derogatory Lingala term meaning "uncivilized." As a result, young girls were encouraged to attend establishments where they could learn sewing, knitting, nursing, and housekeeping rather than attend regular schools. In 1953, more than 5,000 women and teenagers were enrolled in such activities in six establishments sponsored by the colonial municipality of Léopoldville and headed by 150 European female instructors. A year earlier, the Council of the Indigenous City of Léopoldville, a powerless organization entrusted to the Congolese elite, petitioned in vain for equal educational opportunities for women (Mission pédagogique Coulon-Dheyen-Renson 1954: 235).

Thus, Léopoldville represented a correlation between urbanization and women's emancipation. Pons (1969) in his remarkable study of colonial Stanleyville stresses the reverse. Stanleyville was one of the rare cities where the Belgians eventually closed their eyes to the settlement of women. As a result of the relative balance in the gender demography, and because the Belgians made life difficult for women who rejected marriage, the major issue was the absence of women's economic and social power. "Urban feminine roles inevitably came to be defined as more specifically sexual and domestic than the tribal roles to which most women had been reared in youth" (Pons 1969: 219). To some extent, it is true that in the colonial city, the more balanced the gender demography, the less gender relations favored women.

Denied access to education, with few employment opportunities, and preceded by men in occupations such as servant, most women had no other choice but prostitution if they wished to remain in the city. Through this activity they gained some wealth. Most female bar owners in Léopoldville were former prostitutes who had accumulated some money. A similar process is described by White in colonial Nairobi, where prostitution enabled women to accumulate wealth: "Women from societies in which they could not own property built houses and rented out the rooms at extremely profitable rates" (1990: 119). This shifting economic status is boldly stated by one of her informants: "I used to go with different men and make a lot of money, and then I became a strong woman. . ." (88). Indeed, as Little points out, Léopoldville was one of many cities that constituted "the only place where women can acquire property" (1973: 21).

Not only did women benefit economically by migrating to colonial Léopoldville, they also gained social status. Nowhere but in the colonial city could women attain social mobility and initiative. Unlike the men, who were relatively mobile while in the villages and managed to leave for short stays in the city, women through their involvement in agriculture were firmly bound to the land. Once in the city, men were coerced into wage labor and overwhelmed by heavy schedules. By contrast, women had more freedom. Thus, women were able to travel occasionally from the city to the countryside, to negotiate matrimonial unions and, through marriage and remarriage, to enjoy some upward social mobility. The development of Congolese popular music created new social and economic opportunities for women as they began to question gender relations. Women's initiative through the medium of popular music was even more significant considering that this music was a male cultural domain.

THE ORIGINS OF GENDERED MUSIC

The term "popular," which defines the music styles that began to spread in the Belgian Congo and in the French Congo in the early 1930s, refers to the fact that this music reached a great number of people of various ethnic origins. Some researchers prefer the term "modern music" to "popular music" and contrast it to "traditional music." I would rather use the term "popular music" since the opposition between "modernity" and "tradition" forms one more Eurocentric taken-for-granted construct. Within the field of African studies most people equate westernization with modernity and Africanity with tradition. However, Congolese popular music presents a different perspective on these notions. For example, during the 1950s, for every musician searching for something new, "traditional" instruments and dances were incorporated. This dual character of Congolese popular music was well put by the musician Serge Essous in his comments on folk music: ". . . it remains my main source of inspiration. I immerse myself in it *whenever I want to create something new*" [Essous 1970, my emphasis].

The popular music of Congo-Zaire originated in the twin landscapes of Brazzaville and Léopoldville, the two closest capital cities in the world (Gondola 1990). In its early stages it was nothing more than folk music introduced to the cities by the diverse residents of Léopoldville and Brazzaville. In the beginning the favorite instruments of popular musicians were therefore the drum and the *likembe* (a small keyboard played with the thumbs). As Léopoldville, which contributed more than Brazzaville to the emergence of this music, was mainly a workers' camp, the music became a male creation. After long hours of hard labor, the men would gather at dances in their neighborhoods and listen to the village drum. Special occasions such as marriages, wakes, or births also provided opportunities to perform music in a compound or on a street corner. The "nocturnal noise pollution," as it was called by colonial authorities, of these African workers prompted white settlers to distance them from the workplace.

Congolese music culture owed much to various musical currents that were also characterized by male initiative. The most important musical style that influenced Congolese popular music was highlife, introduced to Léopoldville by Nigerians, Ghanaians, Liberians, and Dahomeans. These West Africans were hired by two important companies (Huileries du Congo belge and SEDEC, owned by Unilever) to fill clerical positions. Highlife typified the imbalance of gender relations in West African colonial urban societies. It remained mostly an elite musical style radiating from the Fanti coast, a region exposed to European influence since the fifteenth century. Between the World Wars, highlife became the most popular form of music in Ghana and one of the first syncretic cultural manifestations of the Anglophone elite groups living in cities such as Accra, the Cape Coast, and Kumasi (Collins 1978: 33). Mann (1985:17–18, 27–29) has emphasized the social importance of these elite groups and stressed the gender gap. Fashion, for instance, was one of the elements that manifested this gap and fostered the invisibility of women and, by contrast, the visibility of men. Music was surely another element that played a significant role along with education and sports. But marriage remained one of the very few social institutions that afforded women any real prospects. Even then, however, women were used by men to promote male social strategy and status.

European music, which also greatly influenced Congolese popular music, manifested gender inequity as well. In French and Belgian societies between the wars, musical performances usually took place in male domains. Cabarets, bars, and cafés located in low-class neighborhoods were reputed to be, if not places of outright debauchery, at least places where a woman might feel uncomfortable. Heavy smoking, drinking, obscene and sexual jokes, and sexual talk were the favorite pastime for male customers. However, in Léopoldville, women, both as customers and as employees, frequented bars. Congolese musicians also learned French *guinguettes* and love songs of the 1930s and 1940s from resident European women (*femmes libres*), most of whom were the musicians' own mistresses.[4]

The maringa and rumba, brought to Léopoldville in the early 1930s, greatly affected Congolese musical creation. The rumba was introduced to the international public during the 1932 World's Fair in Chicago. In France, Tino Rossi from Corsica contributed to the spread of the rumba, most especially through his famous love song

"Marinella." Kru sailors from Liberia played an important role in transmitting these Latin American styles to the area from West Africa. Antoine Wendo, one of the most famous Congolese musicians, was a sailor traveling on the Congo River. Once, at the port of Matadi, he attended performances given by the Kru sailors and was strongly impressed by the rhythm and the instrumentation.

The colonial trilogy of the religious choirs, the scout songs, and the military parades were fundamental in the formation of Congolese music. These musical styles were also dominated by men. Several Congolese musicians began as Catholic choir members. Pascal Tabu was among those who attended only missionary schools. At the age of twelve, the young Pascal sang while at the Institut Saint-Pierre. In fact, since the 1920s in Léopoldville, religious songs were performed in secular realms. In 1925, a Belgian priest, Raphaël de la Kethulle, created the Fanfare Sainte-Cécile, a choir composed exclusively of male elementary-school students, which performed on July 21 (the Belgian national holiday), Christmas, and New Year's Eve. The Catholic Boy Scouts were founded in Léopoldville in 1928 by the Belgian Henri Dunant. Music was a major part of the educational, recreational, and camp activities. Serge Essous began his tremendous career as a saxo-clarinetist while a boy scout: "It was there that I learned how to play the reed-pipe and wood flute; I was even able to make some out of bamboo" (quoted in Gondola 1992: 467). Military parades, the last element of this trilogy, were a purely male cultural form. These influenced Congolese musical style, which had adopted their brass instruments. Antoine Kasongo, the founder of the band Martinique, grew up in the atmosphere of military parades at Boma, where his father participated. The name given to his band, formed in 1942, was not accidental. During World War II, French soldiers from Martinique arrived in Brazzaville, which was then capital of de Gaulle's France Libre. Kasongo was awed by the *biguines* of the French Antilles, characterized by their stirring rhythms. He began to cultivate the soldiers.

It is obvious that Congolese popular music began as a male preserve. This bias was reinforced by the nature of the early colonial city, which favored men over women. However, as soon as they were tolerated in the city, women managed to influence the musical culture. One main reason for this was that music, unlike other recreational activities, remained outside colonial tutelage. In the world of sports, the rules were European; in music, the initiative was totally in African hands. Congolese popular musicians sang in Lingala rather than in French, performed in informal places, violated the curfew, and conveyed critical discourse against the colonial system. Women were therefore able to intervene without incurring colonial wrath.

GENDER AND POPULAR MUSIC

Following all these influences, and because it was eminently a production of the colonial city, Congolese popular music was originally dominated by men. Today, the artists include a relatively equal number of men and women. Up until the 1950s, few women appeared on stage either as regular singers or as dancers. One notable female artist of the period was Eyenga Moseka. Though popular, she is not known as a singer but as the hostess of the female recreational associations for which she sometimes performed in bars. Only male musicians composed and interpreted songs.

Two generations of musicians contributed to the emergence of what Sylvain Bemba (1984) identifies as *la musique du Congo-Zaïre*. Antoine Wendo gave his name to the first set of musicians who are usually known as musicians of *tango ya ba Wendo,* "the era of the Wendos." They composed and performed as early as 1942 and reached the height of fame during the early 1950s, thanks to the creation, in Léopoldville, of recording studios by Greek refugees (Lederer 1983). The second generation is considered the golden age of Congolese music which began to spread beyond the Congo. The formation of the band African Jazz by Joseph Kabasele, in 1951, marked the beginning of this *siècle d'or* which ran its course in 1970 with the arrival of the Congolese musician Pascal Tabu (Rochereau) at *l'Olympia* theater in Paris.

How did this music, once characterized by male dominance, also become an arena in which women could pursue their own interests? Although women were not composing or performing, all musical creation, diffusion, and performance revolved around them. Woman was a powerful source of inspiration for the musicians. She was revered as in *Marie-Louise* (1949) sung by Wendo and in *Parafifi* (1951) by the band African Jazz, where she appeared as a goddess, inaccessible and perfect:

> *Félicité dit Fifi motema ya paradizo*

> [Felicity, alias Fifi, pure of heart]

> *Elongi na yo Fifi anzelu mobateli*

> [Your face is like a guardian angel's]

Conversely, she could be disparaged. Ngombe Baseko sang *Albertine mwasi ya bar,* "Albertine, The Night Club Woman," which portrayed woman as a "heavy beer drinker, [with] no cooking pots, or dishes, or bed. If you see her walking down the street, you would think that she is a respectable lady, but it's a nothing which sleeps around." Adulated or degraded, woman remained the central musical theme and captivated musicians.

The appearance of the *associations féminines d'élégance*, women's social clubs whose main purpose was mutual assistance, during World War II (M'Bokolo 1992: 544–545) also explains how women became influential through music. Though the war period favored the arrival of women in Léopoldville, they still constituted a smaller group than men. Rather than marry, most chose to remain single. This meant sexual freedom, multiple partners, and brief liaisons (Mambou Gnali 1967). Through a system of revolving credit they provided, the *associations d'élégance* helped women avoid economic dependence on men (Ntambue 1983). These clubs initially met in a member's compound, but later began patronizing the bars that flourished during the 1950s. Léopoldville, with a population of roughly 300,000, had some 400 bars. Based on his research in colonial Brazzaville, Balandier (1955: 146) suggests that, apart from recreation and mutual assistance, these clubs provided sex for sale. While surveying Poto Poto, the largest indigenous neighborhood of Brazzaville, in 1950, he identified eight clubs whose names—Violette, Elégance, La Rose, Dollar, Diamant, Lolita raised suspicions. Clubs such as Les Diamants, Rosette, La Lumière, and La Beauté flourished in Léopoldville during the same period (La Fontaine 1974).

The club La Reconnaissance illustrates the significant role acquired by women in the bars and through music. La Reconnaissance competed with two other clubs for the social mobilization of the free women of Dendale, one of the most heavily populated neighborhoods of Léopoldville. The club was created in August 1958. Mbuta Mingiédi, owner of the bar Chez Mingiédi, commissioned his friend, Victor Monguba, "to create a club of neighborhood young women and to gather them [in his bar] three times a week in order to attract male patrons" (Malingwendo 1958: 10). The club was organized in three days. Victor Monguba established a hierarchy with himself as the head, called tata mokônzi (president), at the club's second meeting. Miss Henriette Aziza was designated mama mokônzi, and Miss Suzanne Nganze became the secretary. The members, called bana ("children"; sing. mwana), numbered only twelve in the beginning. The statutes were as follows:

1) The meeting days are scheduled on Mondays and Tuesdays [Chez Mingiédi]. If a member comes late the penalty is ten francs; fifteen francs in case of absence.
2) The committee, including the *tata* and *mama mikônzi*, and the secretary, meets each Sunday morning.
3) The main advantages of membership:
   a) Upon marriage the member receives a set of dishes.
   b) In case of death of a family member (siblings or parents), the club provides the casket, sheets, and candles.
   c) Whenever a member is hospitalized, there will be daily visits from members, each person in turn, and meals will be cooked for the patient. In case a member's husband is hospitalized, each member gives twenty-five francs to the member.
   d) Because no member is now pregnant, the club will not consider benefits for newborn children.

During the club La Reconnaissance meetings at Chez Mingiédi, the owner offered members beer and grilled food. Because of this club the crowd at the bar kept growing. This growth led a *mwana* to comment: "We've already achieved great success: There are more clients on our meeting days than usual." Twice a month, the club purchased a whole piece of colorful wax-printed cloth with matching headscarf and sandals. All the *bana* wore this uniform at their gatherings. La Reconnaissance scheduled its formal opening for March 1959. The club was to organize a big party at Chez Mingiédi and to invite family, friends, and three other clubs from the neighborhood. This would have allowed La Reconnaissance to be "officially" recognized and to participate in dance, beauty, or fashion contests. Sources do not mention whether this big event actually took place. Because these women's social clubs were generally short-lived, it is not inconceivable that the club never had an official opening. However, its statutes and activities show that musical culture provided new opportunities for young single women, and that these women eagerly embraced them.

Two points may be made with respect to the significance of women's social clubs. First, the fashions adopted by these clubs suggest resistance to European values. Unlike African men, who rapidly borrowed the European suit, African women avoided wearing European dresses and skirts. Even today, European dress has not succeeded in displacing wax-printed cloth. Up until the 1950s, some women continued to walk barefoot while wearing a lavish wax print along with matching blouse. These wax prints all received names such as *King Georges, Messo ya putain* ("Eyes of a Bitch"), *Massa ya la mer* ("Seawater"), *Les six bougies* ("The Six Candles"), *Inzo ya Nzambi* ("The House of God"), and *Marie simba vélo* ("Marie Rides the Bike"). The "official" night out of the *bana* in a bar often coincided with the launching of a newly designed wax print, called *maï ya sika* ("new water") in Lingala. The popularity of this new wax print among the women of Léopoldville depended on the night's success. The majority of club members also refused to speak French, preferring Lingala instead, and rejected European cooking, which they found tasteless.

Second, most of the successful songs of the 1950s, beginning with Wendo's "Marie-Louise," were popularized by the women's clubs. Whenever they were particularly enthused by a song, the women would create a dance for it. Many musicians, following the example of Wendo, had their Egerias among the members of the clubs. Though many of these clubs were initiated to increase the number of male clients in the bars and to offer them sexual favors, women were able to turn these opportunities to their own advantage. And even though men played a role in the clubs, they did not have real power. The great majority of the clubs, as in the case of La Reconnaissance, had a *tata mokônzi* who officially represented it. However, this person was simply a figurehead. Aware of their low status, women knew that they would not be permitted to do anything without a man as the head. Some of these clubs hired a *tata mokônzi* to circumvent certain colonial prescriptions; a man, for example, was needed to open a savings account. Instead of just being used by men, women also used the privileges conferred on men in the colonial system to gain power and to attain higher social and economic standards.

That the women's social clubs contested colonial values and patterns was well understood by the colonial authorities. In 1954, the colonial administration urged the associations that had mutual interests to open savings accounts in an effort to control them. The authorities listed only eighty-nine registered associations in Léopoldville that year, but they were perfectly aware that many more were unregistered. In 1958, a decree regulating the mutual associations restricted the enrollment of married women in the women's social clubs. To become affiliated with a club, a married woman needed her husband's permission. A married woman who had joined a club while single could not continue her membership without her husband's consent.[5] This shows that the colonial authorities considered these associations places of corruption and depravity. The 1958 law also effectively institutionalized these clubs as single women's associations. Many married men who patronized the bars and even had affairs with *bana* were strongly opposed to their wives' involvement with any club. Married women could only venture out at their own risk. Hence colonial intervention helped turn the bar into a space for single women and married men.

Congolese musical culture was a vehicle that allowed women to question gender relations. At the same time, women subverted the rules of the colonial city. Polygamous practices forbidden under colonial law were overtly undertaken and encouraged through the women's social clubs. For the first time, men were not the only ones privileged to have multiple partners. Most of the *bana* also had more than one male mate at a time and were proud of being "shared," or of offering themselves to several men. They took advantage of this situation to enhance their social position and income and to provoke competition among their suitors. They forged a new image of the Congolese woman by challenging the one created by both African and European men. In the colonial image, the Congolese woman was a daytime creature confined to domestic activities under male subordination. Yet the *bana* did not conform to this and maintained a "corrupted" lifestyle instead. One anti-*bana* feminist commented condescendingly: "She generally lives with her mother or another relative, i.e., an aunt or a sister, who does the marketing, the cooking, and child rearing; in a word, keeps or runs the house. The *ndoumba* dresses up, runs all over town in search of the latest fashions and beauty products, places orders with the jeweller, tries on outfits at the dressmaker's, and gets her hair braided by friends as they chat, if she is not showing herself off in the bars" (Mambou Gnali 1967:1).

However, the challenge to colonially sanctioned patriarchy was never total. Most women were still under the tutelage of men. They could not leave the village for the city without the permission of a male benefactor. Women in the city were registered as dependents of men and received no identity cards of their own.

The complexity of gender relations in the colonial urban milieu resembles the intricacy of the interaction between African men and European colonizers. Though the entire Belgian colonial system held African men in subjugation, there were some domains where Africans had room to maneuver. Christian missions, for instance, remained one of the rare domains where the colonial policy of *indigenization* was applied. In other words, the missionary church was the only formal colonial institution where Africans could interact with Europeans in less hierarchical ways.

Interactions between men and women in the colonial context revealed the same complexity. In Léopoldville, women were seen as masters of the evening social game and men as sovereigns of daytime society. This observation shows the obsolescence of the dichotomy of domestic vs. public domains, commonly used by some authors. Daytime society remained a male arena while evening society, which can be considered as the public space, was dominated by women. In bars, married men who "wore the pants" in their household became subject to women's rules. Thus, women who were living in a daytime society in which they had no say lorded it over men in the bars at night.

"ATA NDELE . . ."

Women's influence through music also brought them in contact with nationalist politics since Congolese music of the 1950s was an important vehicle of social discourse and political awakening. In 1954, musician Adou Elenga composed and sang "Ata Ndele" following the death of one of his friends. When family and friends held a wake punctuated by women mourning and singing songs of farewell, Adou Elenga sang too. He communicated that his pain was so deep, no one other than the colonial system could be responsible for the death, adding:

Ata ndele mokili ekobaluka, ata ndele mondele akosukwama

[Sooner or later the world will change, sooner or later the whites will be kicked out.]

"Ata Ndele" was banned and Adou Elenga jailed for "disturbing the peace," a euphemism for political dissension. Apart from the syncretic religious movements, Congolese music was the only medium for expressing dissent. No political parties existed in Léopoldville at that time, and all the future Congolese politicians were not yet involved in politics. Even Patrice Lumumba, the first prime minister of independent Zaire, was still an obscure postal clerk in Stanleyville. Popular music stimulated the development of political consciousness and the first political meetings were held in bars. Between 1956 and 1959, Lumumba gave regular speeches in the bar Petit Pont ("Little Bridge") in Léopoldville. This link between music and political awakening in colonial Kinshasa has been widely acknowledged.

At the beginning of his play *Une saison au Congo,* the Martiniquan writer Aimé Césaire has a musician (*le joueur de sanza*) sing "Ata Ndele" in a bar (Césaire 1966:

13) as if the author wanted to show that political consciousness first manifested itself through music. He also has Lumumba in the bar Chez Cassian dancing with a beautiful Lulua girl (Hélène Bijou) to celebrate a major political and military victory (p. 67). In another bar, Césaire has Lumumba make a statement to the press and hold a conversation with a *mama makosi* (mother chief), the owner of the bar (p. 51). The role of *mama makosi [mokônzi]* in Césaire's play is very political. Not only does she provide Patrice Lumumba a political platform, but she also protects him when his life is threatened, and continues to support his views even after his death. While attending a speech by Mokutu (Mobutu) in 1966, a year after his coup, *mama makosi* bravely shouts *"Uhuru Lumumba!"* ("Independence with Lumumba!") amidst a pro-Mobutu mob (p. 115). In the throes of the Congolese crisis, in November 1960, Césaire sets the scene for one of Lumumba's last press conferences in a bar. While talking to the journalists, Lumumba is told by *mama makosi* that the soldiers (Mobutu's) have raided his house (p. 97).

For the first African political leaders, including Lumumba, the bar represented a safe haven. The fact that the bars survived despite the protests of Catholic missionaries shows that they symbolized a shield against colonial oppression for many Africans.

"OH! RIO-MA"

Given women's roles in Congolese music culture, male dominance has diminished even in daytime society. The song "Mario" by the band OK Jazz portrays an inversion of gender relations in Kinshasa. "Oh! rio-Ma" is how the Zairean musician Luambo Makiadi (alias Franco) starts the lengthy "Mario," with 1,251 lyrics which kept dancers on the floor for nearly fourteen minutes.

"Rio-Ma," the inverse of Mario, is undoubtedly a reference to what poor French suburban youngsters have labeled *verlan* (vers-l'en), that is, a switch of syllables in a word. The French language, with its hard and distinctive syllables, allows for a wide-ranging vocabulary and syntax in *verlan*. Translated into *verlan,* a sentence may even take on a double meaning as in *laisse tomber* ("let it be"), which becomes *laisse ber-tom. Laisse ber-tom* in the mouths of youngsters living in public housing becomes *laisse béton* which can be translated as "leave the concrete," this suburban universe of hopelessness and promiscuity. The use of *verlan* in the very first sentence of "Mario" may be intended to signal the theme of upside-down gender relations in the song.

The original version of "Mario" came out in early 1984 and remained on the best-seller list for almost two years. Listeners' enthusiasm for "Mario" seemed steadfast for two main reasons. "Mario" is mostly a disturbing and captivating love story between a middle-aged woman and her younger male mate, Mario. The song is alternatively sung by Madilu "System" and spoken by Franco in a very persuasive and accusatory tone. Franco's startlingly humorous vein when relating the woman's complaints against Mario has been mentioned by listeners as another reason for appreciating the song.

Since its inception, and especially after 1965, when Mobutism prohibited any political expression, Zairean popular music has explored the last artistic frontier: day-to-day life. Musicians have felt compelled to denounce all deviant or delinquent proclivities of city dwellers. They have also denounced the single woman who patronizes bars, in songs such as "Albertine mwasi ya bar" ("Albertine, The Nightclub Woman"). In "Mbongo ezali suka te" ("Money Is Not an End") and its recent remake "L'argent appelle l'argent" ("Money Calls Money"), they vilify the ambitious urban young people who worship the god Money. Zairean popular music went even further and, to my knowledge, remains one of the rare African cultural media to end the secrecy surrounding Acquired Immune Deficiency Syndrome (AIDS). Franco sang "SIDA" in 1989 to express the suffering of many Zaireans, and to awaken his audience to this deadly syndrome that would take him away a year later, as it did many other famous and less famous Zairean musicians. In the same vein, "Mario" relates a social phenomenon that has become much more visible since the 1980s, facilitated by the convergence of two other phenomena: the new economic power attained by middle-aged women traders and the upsurge in the number of unemployed male high-school, and even college, graduates.

"Mario" is a biting critique of these young men who play the gigolo to older well-to-do women. Mario, a young man trying to build his future, is attached to a fairly rich fifty-year-old woman. He is of a relatively poor, if educated, background. Upon obtaining his college degree, Mario did not look for work, but greedily sought comfort and "social security" in the arms of a woman he ended up calling Mère.[6] Mère, we eventually find out, is considered a *mama kulutu* (mother's eldest sister). She is also *mama mobokoli,* a term conferred on women who have finished raising children. Nothing is mentioned about Mère's marital status, so she could be widowed or divorced. The story does reveal that she has adult children who still live with her. Mère's ostentatious lifestyle includes jewels, a luxurious rented house, and a brand-new Mercedes-Benz. She has a business in the market and uses her compound as a club *(nganda)* where clients dance, eat, and drink anytime of the day or night.

Mario's identity is dual and rather ambiguous. He is presented as the man, with all the prejudice that surrounds a certain type of masculinity in Zairean urban culture. He is domineering, violent, and, above all, a notorious womanizer. His relationship with Mère begins to unravel mainly for this reason. And here again, this side of "Mario" also shows the grudges Zairean musicians hold against a certain type of woman. Like many Zairean women, Mario began bleaching his skin by using every product that his older mate applied.

Oh ! rio-Ma, yo moto ozalaki elongi mwindo,
Tala elongi ekomi kotela mikolo oyo po na ba produits ya mama kulutu

[Oh! rio-Ma, you whose face was dark
Now your face is shining because of "Auntie's" products]

Of the two, Mario is the more jealous, the more capricious, and the more desirous of luxury, readily spending money that he just borrowed from benevolent neighbors, proudly driving Mère's Mercedes-Benz, and going regularly to the dry cleaner's with his laundry.

Mario, mokolo mususu nawuti zando nakuti Mario asiliki
Nakanisi balambeli ye malamu te
Nga moko nakoti cuisine nalambeli Mario
Nati biloko na mesa, Mario aboyi kolya
Abengi nga à côté alobi: "te Mère oyebi pourquoi nasiliki?"
Ngai nalobi: "nayebi te"
Alobi: "chaîne oyo ya munene ebimi na kuruzu epayi ya Jacques Desmeres,
Soki nazwi yango te, Mère, okolanda nga, oyoki hein!"

[One day I came back from the market, I found Mario upset
I thought they hadn't cooked well for him
I, myself, prepared Mario's lunch
I set the table; Mario refused to eat
He took me aside and said: "No, Mère, do you know why I'm upset?"
I said: "I don't know"
He said: "There is a new line of cross necklaces at Jacques Desmeres,
If you don't buy it for me,
Mère, you won't see me again, do you hear!"]

Mère is here providing her younger mate with what Zairean men usually give their wives or mistresses. Once Mario got his degree, she took him into her nice rented house and offered him all the financial support he needed in return for his attention and sexual favors. Nonetheless, what Mère does for Mario exceeds what a Zairean woman expects her husband to do for her. Mère soon concludes that Mario is just exploiting her.

Mario, nasala lisusu nini po na yo?
Nasi nasalisi yo ndenge nionso
Ba famille na yo basala matanga kaka nga mutu nakipaka bango

Mama na yo azanga bilamba nga mutu nasombaka
Mario, ba niongo ya mike mike okendaka kodefaka
Bakoya koyokis'o soni ti na misu na nga, nga mutu nafutaka Mario
Bipayi mususu kutu bakoma kobengaka yo "gang"
Mario, naloba nini, basalisaka mobali ndenge nini?

[Mario, what else can I do for you?
I have done for you everything I could
Whenever your family mourns, I'm the one who takes care of them
Whenever your mother needs clothing, I buy it
Mario, all the small debts that you owe,
People have come to shame you even to my face, I have always paid
At some places they're even calling you "thug"
Mario, what can I say, how far should a woman go in helping a man?]

In fact, the casual relationship between Mario and Mère, along with the age gap, is shameful for both. Neither of them wants the relationship to be public. Mario's apprehension is related to his reputation as a casanova with younger women. Mère, on the other hand, realizes that her affair with Mario could ruin her business. Mère's patience eventually wears thin. She ends up kicking Mario out. And it is a shamefaced Mario, trying to maintain a low profile, who returns to his parents' house with nothing but memories of the good life spent with Mère. For Mario, this return not only throws him back to a more impoverished and harsher lifestyle but also to infancy; he resorts to sleeping in a fetal position on the old, worn-out mattress of his childhood days. The expression used by Franco to describe this situation, "*Okuti obe berceau na yo*" ("You have encountered your crib"), humorously points to Mario's dereliction, a sort of second birth beyond Mère's protective care. Once the umbilical cord is severed, he is pushed back into the cruel world of his parents, who are as incapable of taking care of him as they are of themselves.

The didactic relevance of Mario rests not only upon the fact that it speaks of a new, yet authentic, phenomenon, but that the phenomenon itself is analyzed and morally judged by the singer. According to Franco, the relationship between Mère and Mario has no future and should never have started. The derisive tone used by Franco signals that Mario is a scandal.[7] In the latest version of the song, Franco criticizes Mario even more harshly:

Mario, papa, ebele ya basi oyo batondi Kisasa omoni nanu bango te?
Oyokisa nzoto na yo soni, yo moto ozwa ba diplômes ebele

[Mario, Daddy, Kinshasa is full of women, haven't you noticed them?
You shame your body, you with many degrees]

The gigolo Franco depicts in "Mario" appears to be a result of the new sociability and gender struggle launched through music culture. Mario's behavior and attitudes make us wonder if he is really a "man": He initiates quarrels and uses his fingernails in fights. And he is eventually the one asked to leave. All this was once associated with women. Ultimately, Mario represents the new African man, who, due to the economic crisis and the emergence of the *basi ya kilo,* is no longer predominant and supreme.

CONCLUSION

Women in the African city have gained social as well as economic power. They now participate in several sectors of the economy as entrepreneurs, trading with other African countries as well as with Europe. In Kisangani, the third-largest Zairean city, women are "achieving renown for their success in business. . . . [In 1980, 28 percent of big business owners] were women, specializing in long-distance retail and semi-wholesale trade, exporting and importing goods to and from Kinshasa or to the interior by boat, plane, and truck" (MacGaffey 1986:166). Some of them go to Europe several times a year; to Brussels and Amsterdam for wax prints, to Bologna and other Italian cities for shoes direct from the factory (p. 172). Claudine Vidal (1991) has written about a "battle of the sexes" in Abidjan, Côte d'Ivoire. Most of the female residents of Abidjan gain income through independent activities. They also work in factories and are paid regular salaries. Their financial autonomy and purchasing power leads to tension in the home. Vidal's analysis also deals with passions and representations. Gender then becomes a site of conflict between the ideal image each sex has of the other and lived reality. In Abidjan, the majority of men agree that their "ideal woman" should be a good homemaker, able to maintain the household budget and sustain harmony (Vidal 1991). The ideal woman should not work outside the home but rely on her husband for money. However, reality is different. The husbands, employed or unemployed, depend on their wives to make ends meet. Such economic conflict is only one dimension of gender struggle and negotiation.

Hansen (1989: 5) puts it well when she states: "Gender roles are not given; they are made. Their construction depends on a complex interweaving of cultural factors and social practices with economic forces and questions of power." In most African cities gender relations evolved in favor of women due to economic transformations. The phenomenon of *nana Benz* originating in West Africa is now common in major African cities.[8] In Kinshasa, women's autonomy is partly a consequence of the musical sociability of the 1950s and 1960s, which allowed women to reshape existing power relationships. For Congolese women, music, at first glance, seemed recreational. Further analysis shows that it served as a terrain of gender struggle and provided opportunities for social and economic advancement. In the colonial city, women were identified with "tradition" and therefore considered uncivilized. They accepted their status and rejected the "modernity" of European civilization. They chose African music, a cultural form treated with condescension by the colonizers, to question the European definition of the city itself. Since it was beyond colonial control, it enabled women to elaborate a model of gender relations which still operates in Kinshasa. Located at the crossroads of various cultural patterns and effectively functioning as "the factory of the new Africa" (Balandier 1955: vii), the colonial city proved to be a crucible where new interrelationships and identities were forged.

NOTES

My thanks to Maria Grosz-Ngaté and Omari H. Kokole for their editorial help and suggestions.

1. I have chosen to use the name Léopoldville when referring to the city before 1967. At that date the colonial designation Léopoldville was replaced by Kinshasa, which had been a village that the colonizers dismantled in order to build Léopoldville.

2. This and all subsequent translations are my own.

3. In Europe, women were granted the opportunity to live in the cities without being conceded citizenship. In most European countries women's legal rights were connected with their legal status as wives. In France, women gained the right to vote in 1944. This right was obtained in Belgium four years later, in 1948, for the same reason: women worked in the war industries and contributed to victory to the same extent as men who were in combat.

4. Musicians from Léopoldville used to cross the river to Brazzaville to meet the women. Unlike the Belgians of Léopoldville, French authorities of Brazzaville tolerated overt contacts between whites and blacks. Beginning in 1946, Africans in Brazzaville were allowed to frequent European bars, and vice versa, whereas in Léopoldville all recreational establishments, including hotels and restaurants, remained strictly segregated.

5. *Bulletin officiel du Congo belge*, 15 juillet 1958, p. 1169.

6. Lingala speakers use this French word for older women while in the same familiar tone *tantine* (aunty) designates younger women.

7. The word *Mario* is now commonly used in Lingala for "gigolo."

8. The *nana Benz* (*Benz* for Mercedes-Benz) are well known for their wealth and their luxurious lifestyle built through the international commerce of Dutch wax prints, bought in the Netherlands and sold in West African cities, especially Lomé, Togo. In Kinshasa, these women are called *basi ya poids* or *basi ya kilo* (heavy women), which refers not only to their financial wealth but also their physical weight.

BIBLIOGRAPHY

Bairoch, Paul. 1988. *Cities and Economic Development: From the Dawn of History to the Present*. Chicago: University of Chicago Press.

Balandier, Georges. [1955] 1985. *Sociologie des Brazzavilles noires*. Paris: Fondation Nationale des Sciences Politiques.

Barber, Karin. 1991. "Popular Arts in Africa," *African Studies Review*, 30(3):1–78.

Bemba, Sylvain. 1984. *Cinquante ans de musique du Congo-Zaïre, 1920–1970*. Paris and Dakar: Présence africaine.

Bezy, F. and J. P. Peemans. 1981. *Accumulation et sous-développement au Zaïre, 1960–1980*. Louvain-la-Neuve: Presses universitaires de Louvain.

Césaire, Aimé. [1966] 1973. *Une saison au Congo*. Paris: Seuil.

Collins, J. 1978. "Sixty Years of West African Popular Music." *West Africa*: 16 October: 2041–2044.

Coquery-Vidrovitch, Catherine. 1991. "The Process of Urbanization in Africa (From the Origins to the Beginning of Independence." *African Studies Review* 34(1):1–98.

———. 1993. "La ville coloniale: 'lieu de colonisation' et métissage culturel." *Afrique contemporaine*, 168:11–22.

Dresch, Jean. 1948. "Villes congolaises." *Revue de géographie humaine et d'ethnologie*, 3: 1–24.

Essous, Serge. 1970. "Le folklore, ma principale source d'inspiration . . ." *Fraternité-Matin*, (Abidjan), 17 December.

Gondola, Ch. Didier. 1990. "Kinshasa et Brazzaville: Bréve histoire d'un mariage séculaire." *Zaïre-Afrique*, 249–250:493–500.

———. 1992. "*Ata ndele* . . . et l'indépendance vint. Musique, jeunes et contestation politique dans les capitales congolaises." In Les Jeunes en Afrique: La politique et la ville, vol. 2, pp. 463–487, C. Coquery-Vidrovitch & Alii eds. Paris: l'Harmattan.

———. 1994. "Ville en Afrique ou ville d'Afrique? Quelques remarques sur le fait urbain dans le "pool" congolais précolonial." In "Echanges Franco-Allemands sur l'Afrique," (special issue), *Bayreuth African Studies*.

Hansen, Karen Tranberg. 1989. *Distant Companions: Servants and Employers in Zambia, 1900–1985*. Ithaca, NY: Cornell University Press.

Lacroix, Jean-Louis. 1967. *Industrialisation au Congo: La transformation des structures économiques*. Paris: Mouton.

LaFontaine, Jean. 1974. "The free Women of Kinshasa: Prostitution in a city in Zaïre." In *Choice and Chance: Essays in Honour of Lucy Mair*. pp. 89–113, J. Davis, ed. London: Athlone.

Little, Kenneth. 1973. *African Women in Towns: An Aspect of Africa's Social Revolution*. Cambridge: Cambridge University Press.

Lederer, André. 1983. "L'odyssée des réfugiés grecs au Congo pendant la 2e Guerre Mondiale." ARSOM *Bulletin des séances* 27(3):315–330.

MacGaffey, Janet. 1986. "Women and Class Formation in a Dependent Economy: Kisangani Entrepreneurs." In *Women and Class in Africa*, pp. 161–177, Claire Robertson and Iris Berger, eds. New York: Africana Publishing Co.

Malingwendo, D. 1958. "Une nouvelle association de jeunes filles: 'La Reconnaissance.'" *Actualités africaines*, 10 octobre.

Mambou Gnali, Aimée. 1967. "La femme africaine, un cas: la Ndumba congolaise." *Etumba*, 28 septembre (a), 1–4; 16 novembre (b), 1–3.

Mann, Kristin. 1985. *Marrying Well: Marriage, Status and Social Change among the Educated Elite in Colonial Lagos*. London: Cambridge University Press.

Martin, Phyllis. 1991. "Colonialism, Youth and Football in French Equatorial Africa." *The International Journal of the History of Sport* 1(8):56–71.

M'Bokolo, Elikia. 1992. *Afrique noire: Histoire et civilisations*, Paris: Hatier-Aupelf.

Mission pédagogique Coulon-Dheyn-Renson. 1954. *La réforme de l'enseignement au Congo belge (rapport présenté au ministre)*.

Ntambue Katshay Tshilunga. 1983. "Le 'likelemba' et le 'muziki' à Kinshasa: nature et prob-lémes socio-juridiques en droit privé zaïrois." *Zaïre-Afrique* 177:431–440.

Ortner, Sherry. 1974. "Is Female to Male as Nature to Culture?" In *Women, Culture, and Society*, pp. 67–88, M. Rosaldo and L. Lamphere, eds. Stanford: Stanford University Press.

Pons, Valdo. 1969. *Stanleyville: An African Urban Community under Belgian Administration*. London: Oxford University Press.

Roberts, Bryan. [1978] 1979. *Cities of Peasants: The Political Economy of Urbanization in the Third World*. Beverly Hills, CA: Sage Publications.

Saint-Moulin, Léon de. 1976. "Contribution à l'histoire de Kinshasa (I)." *Zaïre-Afrique* 108: 461–473.

Vidal, Claudine. 1991. *Sociologie des passions (Côte-d'Ivoire, Rwanda)*, Paris: Karthala.

Waterman, Christopher Alan. 1988. "Asiko, Sakara and Palmwine: Popular Music and Social Identity in Inter-War Lagos, Nigeria." *Urban Anthropology*, 17(2–3): 229–258.

White, Luise. 1990. *The Comforts of Home: Prostitution in Colonial Nairobi*. Chicago: University of Chicago Press.

"TO DETERMINE THE SCALE OF WANTS OF THE COMMUNITY": GENDER AND AFRICAN CONSUMPTION

Barbara A. Moss

Consumption is a complex phenomenon, both an enrichment by acquisition and often an impoverishment created by dependency (Brewer and Porter 1993:4). For Africans in colonial Rhodesia, the shift from subsistence to consumer-oriented economy reveals transformations in material culture as well as in social relations. While colonialism forced Africans to consume foreign items, their own desire for many of these items softened the burden of economic dependency. Ironically, it was on the backs of African women that most authorities, African and European, placed the blame, or rested the responsibilities, for changing African consumption patterns.

The imposition of colonial rule marginalized African women, emphasizing political discourse between European and African men. However, they were pivotal to the transfer of culture. Women as symbols, workers, and nurturers were essential to colonialism (Enloe 1990). Both colonial officials and missionaries tacitly viewed women as socializing agents whose influence within the household could shift Africans into consumer dependency. The creation of the "housewife" as an agent of consumption was an important strategy (Mies 1986). Women were both the targets of campaigns to marginalize them and unsuspecting allies in the battle against African tradition.

All Europeans practiced cultural imperialism to some extent, but it was at the very core of the church's "civilising" mission. For this reason, we shall focus on missionary influence, using Methodist data collected in the eastern portion of the colony, where the majority of European missions and settlements were established. After military victory, even the most passive Europeans aroused fear. Lawrence Vambe (1972:218), born on a mission station, was brought up with the belief that any *murungu* (European) was likely to use violence against Africans. Africans were wary of the invaders; their preferences, as well as orders, held authority. Wrapping themselves in the security of their own material culture, Europeans set the norms for Africans both consciously and unconsciously. As colonial administrators and employers they established rules for subordinates, creating standards of dress and consumption. As new neighbors, settlers introduced their values and rituals. From the vantage point of conquest, Europeans touted their material culture as superior, beneficial, and necessary.

However, the consumer items that transformed African society were embraced as a result of African desires as well as European influence. Some individuals in pre-colonial society were receptive to changes which allowed them to circumvent the authority of chiefs, elders, spirit mediums, and the obligations of communal living (Ranger 1986:28). Youth desiring more autonomy, and women seeking alternatives to custom, formed the nucleus of potential colonial allies. When colonial strategy and African objectives coalesced, cultural transformations accelerated.

Investigating African women as traders and consumers of imported goods from the 1890s to the 1940s reveals cultural ramifications which affected Africans economically, socially, and politically.

AFRICAN CONSUMPTION AND EUROPEAN OBJECTIVES

Cecil J. Rhodes and the British South Africa Company (BSAC) created the colony of Rhodesia for the sole purpose of extracting the country's mineral wealth.[1] The British government gave the Company the authority to administer the colony "in such ways and manners as it shall consider necessary."[2] Women were initially overlooked in early policies geared toward providing land and laborers. However, African consumption of European goods was a necessary corollary of wage labor; this brought African women into the colonial scheme. Officials assumed that women would provide the impetus for purchasing consumer goods which would, in turn, nudge African men into wage labor.

As Appleby (1993:172) emphasized, consumption is a form of self-expression, allowing individuals to become masters of their own dollars and shillings, if not their destinies. For most this mastery is fleeting, threatened by responsibilities; however, the illusion is powerful and appealing. When free to choose, individuals buy items to take possession of a small, concrete part of the style and standard of life to which they aspire (McCracken 1988:111). Purchasing goods is a means of investing in a new lifestyle, accumulating "cultural capital" that pays off as later generations become part of the changing society.[3] These assumptions were true for Africans in colonial Rhodesia.

Despite military defeat in 1897, Africans believed their society still belonged to them. This conviction was facilitated by the fact that they remained in possession of most of the land, even though it was claimed by Europeans. The new commodities that came with colonialism were also perceived as part of *their* changing world. However, wage labor was not a part of their world and Africans resisted making it so. Consumer goods were not tied to wages; Africans chose commodities that often exposed their aspirations as well as their needs, revealing new standards of womanhood and manhood. Africans sought commodities to improve their lives and reinforce their claim to their changing society. They incorporated items by choice when they could, and by necessity when forced.

Under colonialism, any aspect of African freedom of choice bordered on rebellion. As in European societies a century earlier, new consumption patterns provided fresh avenues for rebellion, "not the grand stuff of revolutions, but splendidly innovative in the minor skirmishes of everyday insubordination" (Appleby 1993:172). Challenging the colonial perception of themselves as "uncivilized," Africans selected from a diverse array of clothing as well as foodstuffs and household items. Most of the time, new commodities were not forms of resistance; every cup of tea or imported strip of cloth was not a call to revolt. Africans, like everyone else, derived a sense of satisfaction and improved self-esteem from new acquisitions. These items also transmitted social messages, which signaled African involvement in colonial society. However, possession of certain European goods took on political significance when Africans used them to challenge European hegemony. However, women's freedom of choice was constrained by "customary" laws, domestic responsibilities, and diminishing income-generating opportunities.

"CUSTOMARY" LAW, CHRISTIANITY, AND GENDER

The colonial regime used law as a major tool for attaining its economic objectives. The BSAC designed legislation to establish a climate in which it could prosper. Interfering as little as possible in the everyday running of society resulted in "customary" law based on European understanding of traditional law as related by African men (May 1979:13).

"Traditional," or precolonial, law was local and ad hoc, taking into account individual needs and specific circumstances. As such it was extremely flexible and not amenable to standardization. It was thus inevitable that "customary" law would deeply transform African society at the expense of women.

Women benefited least from the establishment of "customary" law; special circumstances involving family obligations, bridewealth, and women's productive role were ignored. The exaggerated powers of chiefs to decide "criminal" cases completely overlooked diviners, spirit mediums, and n'angas—the influential preserve of women. The new law became the common ground upon which European and African men met. Customary law replaced the control that African men felt they were losing over African women (Chanock 1982:63).

The British Wesleyan Methodist Missionary Society (WMMS), like other denominations, entered Rhodesia as an integral part of the colonial system. In 1891 the WMMS received an extensive concession of land from the BSAC. In 1897 the American Methodist Episcopal church likewise accepted the grant of the abandoned town of Old Umtali from the BSAC. As the self-appointed conscience of the new colony, missionaries occasionally called into question legislation that overtly discriminated against Africans. Nevertheless, they fervently believed in Anglo-Saxon superiority and the need to Christianize Africans. Synonymous with Western culture,

Christianity was more than a religion, it was a way of life. The patriarchal focus of Christian denominations also exacerbated women's status.

However, it was not only the adoption of a male perspective that led colonial officials to ignore certain areas in which African women had been active. They also denigrated women's productive role. Unaccustomed to viewing the physical labor that African women performed, European traveler accounts bemoaned their "slave status." Some missionaries saw Christianity as their only hope. Missionary John White was representative in his condescending assessment:

> I was much impressed with the backwardness of the native women. They do not, like the men, have occasion to go much from home and know nothing of the privileges and benefits of our Christian civilization. Some of their heathen customs fraught with abominable cruelty and demoralization to their own sex they seem to cling to even more tenaciously than the men. Nothing can really set them free but the Grace of our Lord Jesus Christ.[4]

Coupled with the need to justify their own colonial existence to their parent church, missionaries used African women as an excuse to promote the spread of Christianity. Missionaries like John R. Gates linked their civilizing mission directly to African women:

> To furnish a place and the instruments for God to make a WOMAN out of this down-trodden, helpless sex, is to be engaged in one of the biggest tasks that either the Church or the Nation has to do. . . . It is a conviction in my heart as deep as the center of its core that to save Africa we must save the African WOMAN, yea, if we are to lift Africa a foot out of the mire of paganism toward the Eternal Christ, we must lift the African woman a little higher.[5]

But behind this self-proclaimed noble effort was the realization that African women were the linchpin to African self-sufficiency. Europeans generally believed that African women provided the means by which African men avoided wage labor. Many young men, returning from migrant labor in the Transvaal, retired from employment after using their wages for *lobola* (bridewealth). Native commissioner Peter Neilsen referred to this transaction as converting the money into "real value" (a wife). This practice was deplored as detrimental to civilization itself:

> There remains a not inconsiderable number of able-bodied men who form a class of their own in that they contrive to live without ever doing any work for an employer . . . they manage to procure a first wife with whom to procreate, as they hope, female children to be sold as such and thus provide money for the payment of tax . . . whereas the getting of goods or wealth,

through labor must necessarily result in . . . civilization, the acquisition of women, the Natives' wealth, not through labor but through the unearned increment furnished by female children, must necessarily lead through continued inactivity to stagnation which is the antithesis of civilization.[6]

Although crudely stated, Neilsen recognized that women were essential to African self-sufficiency. Subsequent prohibitions of arranged marriages were rooted in economic as well as cultural objections. While missionaries condemned it, the colonial government passed legislation to prohibit the marriage of girls under the age of twelve. Precolonial customs concerning women had to be changed before women could adopt new societal roles. Women were considered essential to "set the standard of civilisation and . . . determine the scale of wants of the community as a whole."[7] Although more subtle in tone, the missionary view coincided with this agenda. Missionaries sought to transform African women into "true helpmeets," literate, skilled in sewing and housework while dependent upon their husband's wages. These women, it was hoped, would help create a new consumer-oriented society.[8]

Both church and state united in placing African women soundly under the guardianship of African men. Codified customary law overlooked women's rights and delegated their possessions to their husbands. As interpreted by colonial courts, "property acquired during a marriage becomes the husband's property whether acquired by him or his wife" (Ncube 1987:10). Tradition acknowledged women's economic rights over their *mavoko* and *umai* property; formal recognition was unnecessary.[9] But formality was the order of the day under colonialism: Record keeping relegated property to a male preserve, which placed women's property in jeopardy. Officials listed cattle dipping and tax receipts in the husband's name and filed them at the district administrator's office, where few women ventured (Mpofu 1983:19). Property inherited by the wife's family was diverted to the husband's family in divorce cases and after the wife's death. Women also lost their land-use rights when land was allocated to the male head of the family by the chief, subchief, or headman (Kazembe 1987:382). Politically women lost significant leverage. Given the European bias for male leadership, officials removed women from future leadership positions in colonial society with the stroke of a pen. Public recognition of diviners, spirit mediums, and *n'angas* diminished. The relatively powerless and nonproductive role assigned to women effectively left them outside of decision making in the consumption of commodities. Yet colonial authorities assumed that they would be able to determine the level of commodity consumption for the African community.

DISCRETIONARY TRADE AND CONSUMPTION, 1889–1910

Between 1889 and 1910 changes in African society were unhurried and moderate. Europeans co-opted tradition by commandeering the channels of power and delegating their authority through them. Traditional rulers requisitioned taxes or labor in the name of the colonial officials. Thus the shift to wage employment and a consumer-oriented economy often bore a familiar face, which may have muted the edge of cultural differences. Women were neither sought as laborers nor forced by necessity into employment, yet they were active in trade and consumption.

During the first decade of colonialism, consumer goods failed to entice Africans into wage employment and had little impact on African societies. Commodities were basic, offering few discernible benefits. Since Africans were self-sufficient, able to sell their produce or cattle, participation in wage labor was "discretionary" rather than "necessary" (Arrighi 1970:206). When they chose to participate, Africans were also very selective about consumer goods.

Gearing up for an expanding market, Africans produced surplus grain for sale at the colonial out-stations and along the main trade artery. The grain trade was a thriving business at Fort Victoria, with grain traded for blankets, cloth, hoes, beads, and salt. Itinerant traders passing through the villages exchanged goods for guinea fowl, milk, pumpkins, sweet potatoes, and eggs (Hyatt 1914:67, 75). As the primary agriculturists, women were heavily involved in the trade. Beads and calico were the prevailing currency in the 1890s, with beads of specific sizes and colors and empty metal cartridge cases in demand (Wood 1974:176). But these were hardly essential to the indigenous economy. Africans were discriminating in their choice of consumer items, as two visiting British nurses witnessed:

> Each family had something to sell, pumpkins, white beans, or eggs. They were very particular about the colour and size of the beads they accepted. Fashion is as autocratic in a native kraal as in the big village by the Thames. Blue and white beads had been the rage six months before; now no one could possibly wear anything but red ones. They were very particular too about the limbo they liked. Far from delighting in gaudy and grotesque patterns, they only approved of plain colours—dark blue or crimson. They preferred white to anything. (Blennerhassett and Sleeman 1893:245–246)

Africans began to slowly augment indigenous items with foreign goods. However, imported fabric, blankets, enamel basins, and cups were still rare in African homes, rather than the norm. They nevertheless reflected slight transformations in society. By increasing agricultural surplus to accommodate the anticipated itinerant trader, women gradually altered their labor and expectations. Nonetheless, their societies functioned basically the same as they had previously.

As cultures rubbed against each other, exchanges took place. Colonial officials recognized the power of culture contact to achieve what some called "civilisation by mingling" (Schreuder 1976:297). Proximity to European settlements increased the flow of European goods into African households. As legislation removed Africans from their land, European settlements slowly displaced Shona villages, though in reality both settlements existed side by side. European settlers sprawled onto African land, forcing Africans to work on European-claimed farms or to found new settlements. By 1902 Africans had been deprived of three-quarters of the land in the colony; however, in actuality they still had possession, remaining as squatters and laborers. Custody reinforced their hold on the land, although Europeans controlled much of their movements. Many were also hesitant to leave and risk retribution from the *mudzimu* for abandoning their ancestral graves.[10] Thus, entire villages were incorporated into European farms, with Africans assimilated slowly into wage labor. Women, as well as men, provided labor on the farms, especially during harvest.

Urban and industrial areas provided a conducive environment for the flow of goods. There, surrounded by the trappings of a foreign culture, Africans more readily used new material goods as part of their daily lives. Laborers, especially migrant workers, bought clothing, utensils, blankets, soap, and even foodstuffs. Exigency determined the new "wants" as much as desire. The workplace necessitated material goods; Europeans required Africans in their employ to dress in appropriate Western clothing. As Mukerji (1983:15) suggests, materialism was becoming a semiautonomous force, integral to the colonial setting. Driven by cultural contact and, in some instances, high-pressure sales techniques, Africans in the mines and in the urban areas became steady consumers. According to Burke (1993:137–138), storekeepers coerced Africans into accepting goods instead of cash for produce, ignoring them until they chose goods. Some, lulled into a sense of false acceptance by friendly resident mine vendors, "opened their wallets in a spending spree" (Vambe 1972:220). But the work environment was principally a male realm. Women, who were sought as laborers only during harvest, lagged behind men as consumers.

European settlements afforded African women the opportunity to participate actively in the consumer market. Africans living within walking distances of European areas hawked poultry, eggs, vegetables, and fruit from door to door. As Schmidt (1992:56) points out, it was usually the women and young girls who peddled the produce. Vendors engaged in a lucrative trade in milk and vegetables. European consumers appear to have been at the mercy of some African suppliers during the early years. As one native commissioner's wife recalled, "One local wife sold milk in whisky bottles and when one day I complained that it had arrived full of broken glass, she refused to supply us any more" (Masterson 1977:398). The cash or material goods bartered in return had not become a necessity for this vendor to the extent that she felt compelled to cater to her clientele. Women were intricately involved in groundnut cultivation as well. At the end of the reaping season they sold the nuts in enamel basins, paraffin tins, and baskets. This exchange reveals that women were consumers of manufactured items, like enamel basins and paraffin tins.

However, for these vendors, foreign commodities were still incidental to their lives, functioning alongside woven baskets. At this early stage the goods had become a part of their lives without significantly changing them.

As European settlers increased, the market for surplus meat and produce expanded. In 1903 trade between the European and African populations was estimated at £350,000 (Arrighi 1970:201). Trade represented approximately three times the value of wages (£100,000–£150,000) that Africans earned during the same year (Palmer 1977:229). This income not only paid taxes, but was converted into cloth, foodstuffs, and other commodities.

Women's participation in this early trade did not go unnoticed. As in many other cultures, men criticized their involvement (Breen 1993:257). Perhaps because women's assertive role did not conform to colonial expectations, Europeans were quick to condemn them. They blamed African women for a lack of male laborers, claiming that women's increased revenue was used to pay taxes, thereby rendering wage labor unnecessary. In 1902 only an estimated 13 percent of able-bodied Shona men worked at least three months for wages (Palmer 1977:229). Reportedly, women refused to allow their sons to work for whites for fear of death or injury. Women sold their own cattle or persuaded their husbands to sell cattle to pay the tax of an adult son.[11] If we believe colonial observers, women were still very influential despite decreasing political power. Whether women were exerting undue pressure on potential male laborers or not, they were players in the new exchange of goods and services. And as such they had the potential for effecting change.

Although a male arena, mining brought women as well as men closer to European culture. Hoping to garner sufficient laborers, mine owners offered rations for wives and children. This policy was instituted to justify reduced wages and encourage longer wage contracts, but it also brought more Africans into a consumer-oriented economy. As women joined their husbands on the mines, their households lost rights to village land (Schmidt 1992:54). This migration, therefore, reflected a commitment to a new lifestyle that loosened familial and cultural ties. Cut off from their villages, Africans began to utilize manufactured goods. While women obtained some food as rations, many women started small vegetable gardens. Not content with mere subsistence, they also cultivated additional acres by intensifying their labor on land adjacent to the mines. Officials estimated that women could earn more money in a month selling their produce than their husbands did in three months working at the mines.[12]

Brewing beer for profit, instead of ritual, became a lucrative outlet for women. Some village women reportedly went to the mines at their husbands' insistence to sell beer. Others went on their own initiative, selling beer or maize sprouts to make beer.[13] District commissioners estimated that women earned twice as much during a single weekend as their husbands did in a month working in the mines.[14] This *mavoko* income, generated by women's own labor, was traditionally theirs to dispose of as they wished. It could be converted into cloth, utensils, foodstuffs, corn crushers, school fees, or even sewing machines. The status of these hardworking women was ambiguous due to customary law that formally placed the proceeds in their husbands' hands. However, contemporary observations indicate that some of these women were able to use their earnings to improve their material conditions (Schmidt 1992; Vambe 1972). Thus some women on the mines were becoming consumers almost as rapidly as men. However, it was on mission stations that women, more so than men, were drawn into deeper cultural transformations.

THE "CIVILISING" MISSION

Christianity in colonial African societies was more than a religion; it was a whole way of life. Conversion became a physical transformation, replete with clothing, housing, mannerisms, and speech. Seemingly, missionaries found it easier to measure conversion by external rather than inner transformations (Comaroff and Comarroff 1991; Beidelman 1982).

In the Methodist churches, conversion plans aimed at adults met with little success. After two years of intensive proselytizing, missionaries and African evangelists turned their attention to young children, taking runaway, motherless, and abandoned children into their homes. Fervently believing in European cultural superiority, missionaries thought that children would make the best converts, not having become fully entrenched in their own culture. As one missionary explained, "It is in their plastic days that the lessons of our holy religion can best sink into their minds and their actions before ingrained prejudices and vicious habits have acquired a permanent hold" (Sykes 1902). Missionaries hoped that these children would become evangelists and teachers. With no other cultural or familial ties, these converts did indeed become some of the strongest adherents to Christianity and European culture.

African evangelists, teachers, and their wives were essential to the success of the new strategy for conversion, with each family adopting up to five orphans. Missionaries theorized that as friends and relatives gathered, these groups would develop into Christian communities, acting as "beacons of light" to attract others. Government appropriation of land and creation of African reserves aided missionary success. By 1901, mission stations were reportedly overflowing with marginal people, especially childless widows and elderly women looking for refuge.[15]

Christian villages were established to make the converts proud of their faith, instead of ashamed, as some early converts were in non-Christian communities (Zvobgo 1986:53). Predominately composed of elderly women, prepubescent girls, abandoned infants, war refugees, and other relatively powerless people in African societies, the villages became dependent upon the missionaries in their new environment. Often ridiculed as "bleached" Africans by the surrounding community, these individuals had to be devout Christians in order to practice their new faith. They became European in everything except color, living according to the "Christian [meaning European] code of Godliness, orderliness and morality" (Kapenzi 1979:20). Prospective converts were reminded that minimal Christian living standards in housing and dress signaled the internal transformations assumed to be taking place (Comaroff and Comaroff 1992:54). Since they had to shed their African heritage, assimilating a Victorian lifestyle, they often clung to the new teachings with their material appendages for security in the new surroundings. Mission residents assimilated more readily than all others, leading Africans in the use of European manufactured goods.

As missionaries spread the gospel, they also distributed their material culture, passing out blankets, mirrors, plates, and sugar. Children were enticed to mission schools with lumps of sugar.[16] Some traders, like Hyatt (1914:242–243), viewed the missionary competition with contempt:

> They live comfortable, almost luxurious, lives . . . only in missionary camps will you find numbers of native women—they are well-paid from Home, and consequently, when they enter into competition, as they always do, with the ordinary trader, they have a most unfair advantage, especially as, in very many cases, the trading goods are sent free by the Faithful at Home. . . . Some become fanatics . . . others, saddened, weary, true Servants of their Master, recognize the essential hollowness of it all . . . the gross commercialism . . . but many, the majority . . . join in the scramble for the shekels.

At the core of mission communities was the mission school. For the first year or two, missionaries provided clothing and paid prospective pupils, initially all male, to attend school. Then around 1904, coincidentally when African girls began to attend voluntarily, wages ceased, but boys continued to be furnished with free clothes.[17] Missionaries routinely took mission students into the surrounding villages to show off their reading skills and their "modern" clothing. Mission children also requested to go preaching in crowds, stating: "When we stand up to sing they will see that we look different from them and our faces are different and they will say: 'We want to be like that'" (Ranger 1987:40). The image of neatly dressed children in European clothing was not only a testimony to missionary success, it also implied inclusion into the rulers' society. These children spoke, or sang, in the rulers' language, they dressed in the same type of clothing, and they had learned the secrets of "making the paper talk." The inference was that they had indeed joined an exclusive club, privy to the new secrets and material goods that it offered. To the surrounding villagers it appeared as if a conversion of some sort had taken place. Although some missionaries worried that the wrong message was being sent, by 1906 students became less hesitant to attend schools and requests for schools increased.

Women were central to the physical and cultural transformation at the missions. The vast majority of residents at the missions were women. From the day a girl arrived at the mission, she became part of the transformation of clothing and culture. If she had any acquaintances in the school, they immediately loaned her their clothes, taught her their songs, and pulled her into their social circle (Springer 1909: 145–147). In short order she was making her own clothes and possibly those of nearby villagers. Sewing was the point where missionary objective and African desire met. Missionaries taught sewing in response to newly introduced cultural sensibilities about nakedness. Associating nakedness with sexuality, they were instilling these sensibilities in Africans. African women sought sewing lessons as a means of addressing changing societal norms on acceptance, respectability, and power.

When Rev. Erwin H. Richards brought a few blankets and some fabric to the mission, he observed a near fascination among women:

> None knew how to cut or sew a garment. So impromptu sewing classes were arranged at the new stations. No one wanted to take time to cook or eat. While the heathen women crowded round not asking for clothing or gifts but begging the privilege of holding that little sharp, shining thing which had no name but could fasten pieces of cloth together.[18]

Pieces of cloth sewn together in European fashion had by this time become accepted and desired apparel for African women in the villages as well. Many women were not satisfied with simply sewing in the classes, but brought cloth to be cut out for them to sew in their own homes, while others asked for patterns to cut and sew their garments at home.[19] The union of Christianity and European fashion produced a solid marriage. In South Africa, the desire to be "dressed" or "clothed" was synonymous with seeking Christian instruction or baptism (Gaitskell 1990:255). African womanhood was measured by a foreign standard, with European women providing the model.

Sewing became a major part of the curriculum. Missionaries provided instruction for women from the villages as well as for resident students. Missionary Ellen Bjorklund recalled that:

> in the afternoon from two to three hours were spent in teaching industrial work such as sewing, basket making, tape weaving, laundry work, etc. . . . . my boarding girls make all of their own clothes and some for the kraal people, thus providing a little more money for cloth. Two afternoons each week a few kraal women came in to be taught sewing.[20]

For several hours each day, African girls learned a new way of conceptualizing themselves and their domestic responsibilities. Tied to instructions on sewing, ironing, and laundering were moral imperatives concerning cleanliness and filth, morality and sin.

As an integral part of the mission program, sewing developed into a thriving industry on some stations. Missionary Edith Bell recorded that in 1908, she and eleven African girls turned out 153 skirts, 125 blouses, 126 dresses, 226 shirts, 76 head wraps, 758 body wraps, and 317 sundry articles of clothing.[21] They sold and bartered some of the garments for mission supplies. As Africans clothed themselves in European garb, they embodied changing tastes and aspirations.

Clothing was the most visible indication that European fashion and ideas had made an impact on African tastes. By 1907 ready-made clothing was becoming popular for men and women living near missions and European settlements. Women fancied not only colorful blouses but shoes and stockings as well. These garments did not completely replace indigenous items but rather augmented them.

On the mission stations, women not only led the cultural crusade, they were transformed by it. The good Christian woman was also a good consumer. Mothers' meetings, organized by missionaries' wives, were extremely popular among African women, whose identity was associated with motherhood. The meetings dispensed information about child care, while providing escape from physical labor. But these social settings also introduced consumer goods and associated cultural values. As Mrs. Carson recorded:

> Monday evenings I have a mothers' meeting. I think the women enjoy it, perhaps because of the cup of tea or coffee. I have them bring their own cups and they see to it that they bring pretty big ones. After we have had the Scripture read, explained and discussed, coffee and cake or bread are handed around, and as it is our afternoon tea, tongues are loosened, and then I speak to them about keeping their homes, their persons and their children clean. We discuss children's ailments and simple remedies.[22]

Women who participated needed an enamel cup and were expected to dress in appropriate clothing. The novelty of the foods, the setting, and the company heightened the impact of the cultural message. The fact that European women, respected as models of womanhood, shared food and conversation with them transmitted a sense of acceptance and respectability to African women. This ritual of tea and sugar, legitimated by the sanctity of religion, introduced African women to a practice which had by the nineteenth century become a mainstay of British culture. Although exclusively an elite practice in the eighteenth century, it had been appropriated by the commoners. Colonial settlers, by establishing tea breaks identified with the elite, enhanced their respectability (MacClancy 1992; Austen and Smith 1990). Africans, especially women, may have also sought validation of their worth as confusing signals on propriety were exchanged in colonial society. Africans were well aware of European prejudice, which relegated them to "uncivilized" status. Living on settler farms, near mines, and at mission stations, out of reach of local rulers and family members, Africans were often re-creating themselves according to new standards. They clung to the new commodities which marked transitions in their lives while seeking direction from their peers.

In motherhood African women combined new standards with old status symbols. Weekly mothercraft classes, held for the African evangelists' wives, taught them hygiene, sewing, and knitting. Missionaries awarded prizes to the best baby and mother in baby shows. They encouraged mothers to make complete layettes and fathers to make cradles. This practice emphasized not only the birth of a new child, but the birth of a new lifestyle. Tradition had warned that the baby would die if parents provided anything before its birth, but public legitimation of new customs helped to dampen such concerns.[23] By teaching pride and setting new standards for motherhood, missionaries attempted to reshape African womanhood and, with it, African society.

Despite the cloak of culture, mission education and Christianity remained firmly under their colonial mantle. Concerned that African converts might become unfit for their proper place in colonial society, district chairman Frank Noble, among others, cautioned against Africans becoming over-Europeanized.[24] Missionaries kept the specter of equality at bay by substituting indigenous products as much as possible, creating a Western veneer over African reality. Wearing handmade aprons of coarse brown material, embroidered with dyed wools, African women learned to make boiled puddings, scones, and soup using mealie meal, their staple. Although the menu was British, the ingredients were African.[25] African women's involvement in colonial society was meant to be limited.

However, African men were not so constrained by mixed messages, minute resources, or, in many cases, family obligations. While purchasing blankets, work clothes, and food, they also purchased items for leisure activities, such as playing cards, candles, cigarettes, and bicycles. These goods reflected a shift in lifestyle as laborers spent more time in the urban and work environments than in the villages. Cotton cloth dominated women's choices, which were constrained by domestic responsibilities. The majority of young single women were not employed and thus minimally influenced consumption patterns.

Missions fostered social and cultural change by emphasizing the Protestant work ethic of industry, wage labor, and Western education, creating a generation with new values and customs. All parents residing on, or ploughing on, the mission farm had to send their children to school for at least two hours per day. No work was allowed in the fields on Sundays.[26] Missionaries noted a greater variety of crops and vegetables grown both for consumption and sale. Wealth and prestige were becoming increasingly associated with the trappings of colonial society.

As African converts migrated from the mission stations they spread Christianity and the material culture with which it was linked. Establishing villages, they laid the foundation for religious and educational institutions in their areas. When James Zinyengere, a local preacher, left Epworth accompanied by the usual retinue of friends and relations, they founded a new village and erected a tiny church about four miles away. His wife became leader of the church's women's organization and his daughter Dinah, educated to Standard IV (the equivalent of tenth grade in the U.S.), became the teacher in the village school.[27] Families like this one set the standards by which women and men would begin to measure themselves. No longer ridiculed, their experience and education propelled them to leadership positions in a changing society. Elders competed with teachers and evangelists for their children's loyalty and obedience. As youths moved to missions and urban areas, generational conflict arose over family obligations. Individualism, nurtured by a growing emphasis on material goods, tore at family ties and tradition.

CONSTRAINTS AND CONSUMPTION, 1910–1949

After 1910 colonial culture embedded itself more deeply in African lives. Casual consumer items were increasingly visible in households, marking cultural changes in the villages. Whereas precolonial houses had low doors which required individuals to enter on their knees, by 1910 houses with taller doors were commonplace.[28] Since individuals had not increased in height, one can only attribute the new doors to changes in taste. The Western plough was slowly taking the place of the hoe. African men readily purchased wagons and carts, while women invested in corn crushers.

Indigenous industries of basket weaving, woodcarving, net and mat making, pottery, and ironwork faced stiff competition from imports. By 1911, imported material had virtually driven fabric woven from bark fiber out of the market. Cotton fabric not only aided British textile mills but appealed to African women as well. Women had spent hours chewing bark to make it sufficiently pliable for weaving and thus welcomed the convenience of ready-made fabric. Mission education also sanctioned the change.

As consumers, Africans contributed a significant amount to the colony's economy. For the 1910 fiscal year Africans supplied over one-third the revenue, £206,051, by direct taxation and an additional £27,661 in customs duties.[29] Many imported items, including beads and cotton manufactures, were purchased solely by Africans. Foodstuffs predominated, with newly acquired tastes added to old wants. Syrup was becoming commonplace which, added to tea, heralded a new ritual in African circles among wage laborers and mission residents. As in other cultures, sweetened teas rose in popularity among working classes due to their carbohydrate boost and harmony with breads, or in this case, grains (Mintz 1985:149).

Changing tastes often withstood economic pressure. With wages at a virtual standstill, and a 100 percent increase in the cost of goods in 1917, the demand for many goods remained steady. New items appeared on Africans' wish lists as their aspirations rose. That same year, African women in Matabeleland bought fifty-five sewing machines, for a total of £400.[30]

After World War I, substantial increases in commodity prices placed many articles beyond the means of most Africans. The price of clothing and blankets skyrocketed: blankets 145 percent, suits 136 percent, shirts 150 percent, vests 175 percent, enamelware and utensils 237 percent, fabric 212 percent, women's clothing 150 percent, agricultural implements 150 percent, foodstuffs 115 percent.[31] Farm laborers were particularly handicapped. Observers witnessed many wearing grain bags for want of better apparel. Having developed a taste for European clothing and without ready access to precolonial supplies, they were left adrift in the sea of fashion. In several districts new preferences gave way to necessity as women and girls reverted to wearing bark blankets and skins. High prices also temporarily spurred a dormant indigenous industry. Reportedly "quite good hats" were made from palm leaves, locally made pipes replaced the imported articles, and skins were used in the place of blankets.[32] But by the 1920s Africans were on an irreversible path to wage bondage and consumerism, as drought and related famine made food purchases a necessity.

Women's employment dramatically increased in 1925 due to food shortages that forced those remaining in the villages to buy food.[33] At that time, wage opportunities for women were limited to agricultural work on white-owned farms or in domestic service.[34] As they entered the tobacco and cotton industries, their access to cash allowed them to register some preferences for new consumer items, although most of their meager purchasing power was ploughed back into food consumption. By 1927 store keepers reported an increasing demand by African women for European clothing, including "under-linen." The woman dressed entirely in traditional garb was becoming the exception.[35] Changing tastes were reflected in the absence of indigenous articles of decoration. By 1928, women had abandoned precolonial adornment like the thick brass wire leg and arm bangles, and *indoros*, a popular white ring of ornamental shell. Women replaced shawls with blouses made to order from material selected over the trader's counter.[36]

Retailers conducted a lucrative business, converting imported fabric into dresses. One local trader employed twelve tailors to meet his customers' demands. A 1929 native commissioner report revealed changing tastes on a large scale:

> All these "dresses"—and there is not a girl within the length and breadth of
> the Colony who does not wear one if obtainable—are made to a stock pattern of hideous design and grotesque proportions, at every trading station or

store. . . . No doubt such apparel, however ill-made, dirty or ragged, may be regarded by many as an advance, since it is believed to show a growing sense of modesty compared with the wearers of the more scant but picturesque attire of former days.[37]

Fashion commentary aside, the changes in style also reflected women's increasing participation in a European-dominated society which many men resented. As women ventured from patriarchal authority, they were roundly condemned. According to colonial officials, women's "desire to indulge in clothes and other finery" was undermining the whole social fabric of African society.[38] The Methodist church blamed women's "inordinate love for dress" for a reported rise in immorality sweeping the country. It recommended that teachers' wives set an example of simplicity in dress to girls who were reportedly "selling themselves for finery."[39] However, with few opportunities and low wages, they were selling themselves very cheaply.

Before the Depression, wage employment was based on individual choice for many; afterward it was a necessity for most, linked to taxes, school fees, and diminishing land resources. The 1931 Land Apportionment Act forced an estimated fifty thousand Africans into the already overcrowded reserves by 1941. The reserves were fast becoming a women's preserve, with a two-to-one ratio of women to men.[40] During World War II the forced labor system (*chibaro*) conscripted African men to produce food. With less manpower, women were forced into unpaid road work, thereby decreasing their time for agriculture.[41]

Responding to economic conditions, women's wage employment rose dramatically during the 1940s, from 3,769 in 1941 to 13,524 in 1946. The largest increase occurred in the tobacco industry.[42] Most tobacco growers used their employees' wives in the grading shed and in the fields.[43] In the 1930s and 1940s, some women on farms had their terms of employment set by their fathers and husbands (Phimister 1988:206). Presumably the income went to them as well. Women's "wants" were silenced by patriarchy and women's responsibilities.

A disastrous drought in 1947 drove thousands in search of food. Missionaries reported a constant stream of people, predominately women, on the roads in search of a scant ration of meal:

We meet people on the road who have walked in from . . . 16 miles away or similar distances to buy two shillings worth of mealie meal at the store in Plumtree because they have already finished their own grain. That is all they are allowed at a time and when it is finished they must come in again. I have never seen so many women on the roads.[44]

With the removal of price controls in 1949, many areas became food-purchasing rather than food-producing areas.[45] These trends were irreversible as imported foods became a part of everyday life which tied Africans to wage labor.

CULTURAL BAGGAGE

Foreign consumption brought with it cultural baggage, which predominately African women carried. Some burdens were relatively light, like tea, which evolved into a necessity for Christians since beer was prohibited. Other baggage was more weighty, bringing unfamiliar and unwanted burdens such as postponed marriages, domestic strife, and additional domestic expense.

Christian African women were taught to redefine themselves, not as farmers, but as dependent housewives. Activities that diverged from "homemaking" were severely criticized, with women missionaries recommending that "we preach to them Paul's injunction 'Let the wives be subject to their husbands.'"[46] Missionaries believed that wives spent too much time in their gardens, neglecting their houses and children. Rev. Holman Brown at Epworth complained that "it must not be laid upon the women so much to be the food-producers. The man (husband) in living Christian circles is the breadwinner and the woman (wife) is the homemaker."[47] This strategy was not only contrary to tradition, it was not viable. While conceding that higher wages were necessary, missionaries recommended that men give their wives more money for food. Some mission residents were plagued by poverty, as many struggled to feed their families.[48]

Christian mothers found it difficult to comply with the new order and their domestic responsibilities. Children had to be sent to school properly clothed, posing difficulties for women without income. Sewing thus attained a high priority.

Agricultural production proved to be a challenge for women, who remained the principal food suppliers. Teaching children lessons in Christianity took time away from farming. Lessons in domestic science and vegetable gardening were frequently difficult to put into practice. Women reported that their husbands often refused to purchase the accessories necessary for vegetable gardening, forcing them to revert to precolonial methods of agriculture which they had learned from their mothers. In addition, men's absence due to wage labor exacerbated the problem of pillaging baboons, since men generally made nets and organized hunts.[49] It was difficult for women to pursue their "wants" given the needs of their families.

Marital problems were aggravated by scarce job possibilities, high aspirations, and gendered opportunities. Many Africans, especially Christians, experienced money problems due to increased demand for material possessions.[50] Customary law granted men greater authority, while women's traditional autonomy exacerbated their new needs. This left men with little domestic responsibility. Even when some men earned wages of £1 to £5 per month, they spent it on luxuries, like fashionable clothes and bicycles.[51] According to one contemporary, the bicycle was more a status symbol than a means of transportation (Sithole 1970:80). In actuality, wants were gendered. Necessities, such as food and basic clothing, fell to women to provide.

Aspirations rose higher than wages. Economic necessity may have pushed men into the work force, but they sought entry at the highest levels. Mission-trained Africans had lofty middle-class job aspirations, envisaging themselves as post office messengers, drivers, clerks, foremen, waiters, cooks, and policemen, roles which provided of the some prestige of European society. However, the demand for this type of labor was extremely limited. Nevertheless, even when relegated to lower-level jobs, Africans' ambition and personal perceptions soared above reality in private social functions. Vambe (1972:243) related how on Sundays

> they put on their best clothes, and they could have held their own in any fashionable society anywhere . . . most of these people, particularly the men, were dressed flawlessly, according to the latest fashions. They put on well-cut suits as well as such things as spats, coloured waist-coats, watches with gold or silver chains, gold rings and white gloves, while others wore tweed jacket and knickerbockers and carried walking-sticks and indeed, in some cases wore pince-nez. These were things they had seen worn by Europeans and had set out to save hard for and acquire, despite their small incomes.

There was no second-class status exhibited here, but the money spent for these luxuries deprived families of much needed income.

Mission education, while preparing Africans to read and write, also created disdain for precolonial pursuits in their villages. Some Christian men were true to the adage "They sow not neither do they reap." In 1923 the Mrewa native commissioner reported periodic complaints from women whose "educated" husbands refused to help in their gardens or supply money for food and clothing.[52] Some men set their own standards by refusing to participate in "demeaning tasks" such as carrying water for dip tanks (Davis and Dopcke 1987: 77–78). These new standards added to women's workload.

Women responded to these burdens in a variety of ways. Some ignored missionary edicts and continued to work in the fields to provide surplus for sale. Others produced beer for profit, even selling it on church property.[53] And several rejected the life of a struggling homemaker altogether. Teachers at Fairfield Girls' School complained that "a large number of the girls . . . refuse to become the wives of our pastor-teachers, as the boys working in the towns earn more money and are therefore able to provide them with more things."[54]

Similar conflicts occurred in other societies where foreign cultural, politico-economic constraints restricted women's opportunities. In Liberia, "settler" women were deemed "civilized," and restricted from public marketing. Concentrating on marriage, housekeeping, and training children publicly, they used kin and friendship networks to participate in nonpublic marketing (Moran 1990:7–8). In Lagos, elite Christian women also ignored Victorian ideals, becoming involved in trading to supplement meager incomes (Mann 1983:44).

In Rhodesia, Christian African women reshaped the Methodist women's prayer union, Ruwadzano/Manyano, to generate income and share labor (Moss 1992). Rejecting the dependent image that Christian missionaries and colonial authorities concocted, they created a self-help organization. Through survival strategies, prayers, and shared experiences they provided practical and psychological relief in their midweek meetings. By contributing labor and pooling their resources, earned through their domestic skills, they helped themselves and women in the community. The African women who led Ruwadzano did so by virtue of their educational expertise and legitimacy based on age and spirituality.

Nonetheless, African elites identified with Europeans. Having assimilated their lifestyle, they felt that they, too, should be exempt from discriminatory legislation, such as the poll tax. At a 1933 "Native" Board meeting in Chipinga, Mubuso Tabete proposed that those with a fair standard of education, who lived in a "civilized" manner, be exempt from the tax. He observed very little difference in lifestyle between Africans in Chipinga district and Europeans. They all wore the same sort of clothing; lived in square houses with windows, divided into rooms, furnished more or less in the same way; and they all had about the same amount of education, that was to say, they could all read and write and reckon with numbers sufficiently well for ordinary purposes.[55] Challenging European hegemony, the assemblage saw no rationale for discriminatory taxes. However, race, not class, determined status in Rhodesian society.

Once African men were securely tied to wage labor, women's "wants" were ignored, although their needs surfaced in men's demands for better wages. Missions may have cultivated foreign tastes, but employers disregarded them, assuming that laborers only needed money for taxes and maize meal. However, even the lowest-paid laborer had needs that went beyond mealie meal. In 1944 Aaron Koanza explained:

> We don't only need mealie meal and meat but other things too which are home and life necessities. . . . Africans are becoming more and more used to European food and customs. There are things such as education, dipping fees, supporting parents and families . . . the cost of living has risen a great deal recently, and we still have to meet the expenses of food such as mealie meal, meat, vegetables, sugar, bread, milk, tea, kitchen utensils, blankets, rent in the Location, medical expenses and entertainment.[56]

Life's necessities had expanded, yet businesses were built upon the assumption that male workers had no familial obligations. As African families became more dependent upon wages, this fiction created even more conflict.

Consumerism and wage employment deeply affected family structure. Wage employment led men into migrant labor, with unmarried men postponing marriage and final *lobola* payments. Reportedly, women were expensive to maintain, demanding clothes for themselves and their children.[57] Rhodesian migrants commoditized *lobola* by offering the only wealth they possessed, cash.[58] The amount of *lobola* slowly increased as the cost of living rose.

Migrant labor itself might not have disrupted the rural household to the extent that it did, had not the household become dependent upon wages. In fact, May (1983:34) argues that women's positions might have been strengthened by men's absence if they could freely produce for the market. But cash dependency bred male dependency and placed the woman-headed household in a precarious position.

As women in the villages struggled to maintain their families, they increasingly turned to the new skills offered at the missions and through the women's organization. Using religion, their traditional resource, to cope with colonial obstacles, some African women were able to address some of their wants in a changing society.

CONCLUSION

The shift into a wage and consumer-oriented economy was a complex process with cultural ramifications based on gendered options. Women's choices acted as a barometer of family involvement in the consumption of foreign goods. The occasional pot or piece of fabric gave way to routine food purchases, reflecting deep transformations in African society that eroded customs, challenged beliefs, and altered tastes. What made many of choices offered to Africans exploitative was the diminishing area of control in which those choices were made. Taxation and discriminatory legislation forced African men into wage labor, while African women were pulled into the economy by newly developed consumption. As Africans became wage-dependent, consumer prices rose while income opportunities decreased. Land expropriation pushed the majority of Africans, predominantly women, into overcrowded reserves, making them even more dependent upon men in migrant labor.

As the colonial system became deeply entrenched, it transformed all facets of African society, fragmenting the religious, social, and economic spheres. Community life was altered and family structure modified on missions and in villages. Wealth and prestige became increasingly associated with colonial commodities and European education. Social obligations reflected new cultural baggage as marriages were postponed to allow for final, commoditized payments. Women bore the brunt of these changes more heavily than anyone else.

African women were central to the transfer of culture during colonialism. Changes in their lives charted transformations of African society. Before the European invasion it was said that a woman could support a small family with her hoe and the use of a milk cow. Grain had not become commercialized by sale and barter to traders. However, by 1949, the lifestyle of most Africans had changed significantly. A cow no longer represented wealth, since even that cow had to be dipped, and dipping fees necessitated money. Children in many localities were expected to attend school, clad in European clothing. European utensils and implements, including ploughs, had become near essentials.[59] This made African women more dependent upon African men as the main breadwinners. African women were indeed balancing the load of new consumption patterns, although they were unable to determine its direction.

NOTES

1. In 1886 the country was known as Southern Zambesia; in 1895 the name was changed to Rhodesia in honor of Cecil J. Rhodes. The BSAC continued to rule the colony until 1924.

2. *Charter of Incorporation of the British South Africa Company*, October 29, 1889.

3. Peggy Bartlett, Second Southern Conference of Women's History, University of North Carolina at Chapel Hill, June 7, 1991.

4. Rev. J. White to Mrs. Bradford, April 30, 1918, MMS Box 1052.

5. John R. Gates, District Supt., Umtali, East Central Africa Mission Conference. *Minutes of the East Central Africa Mission Conference of the Methodist Episcopal Church*, 1911.

6. Peter Neilsen, N. C. Chipinga, *Annual Reports, District Native Commissioners*, January 23, 1929. S235/506, NAZ.

7. The Southern Rhodesia Cost of Living Committee, *The Rhodesia Herald*, 4/8/21, 16.

8. Report of Helen E. Springer, East Central Africa Mission Conference. *Minutes of the East Central Africa Mission Conference of the Methodist Episcopal Church*, 1905. See also Meintjes 1990.

9. *Mavoko* property was that which women earned by virtue of their own labor. *Umai* property was that which was given to them after childbirth or after the birth of a grandchild.

10. *Mudzimu* are ancestral spirits who communicate with the living. They are believed to influence the actions of the living, providing guidance and delivering retribution in the form of sickness, drought, famine, and even death. Misfortune was not arbitrary; it was caused by a displeased spirit. Thus, ancestor veneration was essential to African belief.

11. *Report of the Native Affairs Committee of Enquiry*, 1910–1911.

12 *Reports of the Inspectors of Native Compounds for the Year Ended 31st March, 1893*.

13. *Report of the Native Affairs Committee of Enquiry*, 1910–1911.

14. *Hartley District Annual Reports*, 1926, S235/504, NAZ.

15   East Central Africa Mission Conference, *Minutes of the East Central Africa Mission Conference of the Methodist Episcopal Church,* 1901.

16.   Dunmore T. Maboreke, "A History of Nyadire Mission, 1921 to 1970." B.A. honours dissertation paper, History Department, University of Zimbabwe, 1981, p. 1.

17.   Rev. Jonah Tariwa Citombo, transcribed Interview 9/5/79, AOH/61, National Archives of Zimbabwe.

18.   *East Central Africa Mission Conference. Minutes of the East Central Africa Mission Conference of the Methodist Episcopal Church,* March 13, 1907.

19.   *Rhodesia Mission Conference, Official Journal. Minutes of the Rhodesia Mission Conference of the Methodist Episcopal Church,* 1916.

20.   *Minutes of the East Central Africa Mission Conference of the Methodist Episcopal Church,* 1913.

21.   *Minutes of the East Central Africa Mission Conference, Sixth Session,* 1909.

22.   Mrs. L. Carson, East Central Africa Mission Conference. *Minutes of the East Central Africa Mission Conference of the Methodist Episcopal Church,* 1911.

23.   Margaret Dry to Miss Bradford, March 26, 1929, MMS Box 1258; Elizabeth A. Noble to Miss Bradford, November 26, 1929, MMS Box 1052. Similar public displays of domesticity were practiced in the Belgian Congo. See Hunt 1990.

24.   Frank Noble to Miss Walton 1936, MMS Box 1049.

25.   Elizabeth A. Noble to Miss Bradford, November 26, 1929, MMS Box 1052. The fear of over-Europeanization was prevalent in other areas. Belgians also advised the use of local items to encourage thrift (Hunt 1990).

26.   "Rules," Chimanza Circuit, 1911–1912, MH.H.

27.   Muriel Pratten, "More Jottings From Mashonaland," May 7, 1932, MMS Box 1052.

28.   Tegwani Circuit Report 1909, Jan. 10, 1910, MMS Box 346.

29.   *Report of the Native Affairs Committee of Enquiry,* 1910–11.

30.   Secretary, Dept. of Customs and Excise, *Report of the Chief Native Commissioner for the Year 1917.*

31.   The Southern Rhodesia Cost of Living Committee, *The Rhodesia Herald,* 4/8/21, 16.

32.   *Report of the Chief Native Commissioner for the Year 1920.*

33.   *District Annual Reports of All Native Commissioners & ANC Year Ending 31 December 1925,* S235/503, NAZ.

34.   Reports from most districts indicate few women working in wage labor and not desiring to do so, although there were exceptions in Melsetter, Umtali, Bulawayo, Bubi, Mtetengwe, and Nyamandhlovu districts. *Native Commissioners District Annual Reports, Year Ending 31 Dec. 1923,* S235/501.

35.   *Shabani District Annual Reports,* 1927, S235/505, NAZ.

36.   *Darwin District, Native Commissioner's Annual Report,* 1928, S235/506, NAZ.

37.   *Native Commissioner, Marandellas District Annual Report,* 1929, S235/507, NAZ.

38.   *Marandellas District Annual Report,* 1929, S235/507, NAZ.

39.   Report of Woman's Conference, Rhodesia Mission Conference, *Official Journal, Minutes of the Rhodesia Mission Conference of the Methodist Episcopal Church,* 1916.

40.   *Report on the Census Population of Southern Rhodesia Held on 7th May 1946.*

41. Private Secretary, Premier's Office to Chief Native Commissioner, 9/16/39, S235/430. NAZ.

42. *Report on the Census.*

43. *Report of the Secretary for Native Affairs, Chief Native Commissioners, and Director of Native Development, for the Year 1948.*

44. Dora Warwick, Tegwani Circular Letter, May 4, 1947, MMS Box 1298.

45. Dora Warwick, Tegwani Circular Letter, November 1949, MMS Box 1298.

46. Mrs. H. I. James, Secretary, Report of Woman's Conference, Rhodesia Mission Conference, *Official Journal, Minutes of the Rhodesia Mission Conference of the Methodist Episcopal Church*, 1916, 71–72.

47. Rev. Holman Brown, *Minutes of Leaders' Meeting at Epworth*, 10/28/31, MH.H. See also Meintjes 1990 and Moran 1990 for similar problems which Christian women faced.

48. *Minutes of the Leaders' Meeting at Epworth*, 10/28/31, MH.H.

49. N.C. Inyanga, *Annual Reports, District Native Commissioners*, 1928, S235/506, 6–7.

50. Native Commissioner, Mrewa District, *Annual Reports of the District Native Commissioners*, 1924, S235/502.

51. D.M. Pratten and C.W. Phillips, *Annual Report*, 1938, MMS Box 1033.

52. Report of the Native Commissioner, Mrewa, for the year ending 31 December 1923, S235/501, NAZ.

53. Herbert Baker, Annual Report of the Selukwe Circuit, December 1905, MMS Box 345.

54. Rhodesia Mission Conference, *Official Journal, Minutes of the Rhodesia Mission Conference of the Methodist Episcopal Church*, 1917, 24–25.

55. Native Board Meeting, Chipinga, 7/3/33, S1542/N2, NAZ.

56. Aaron D. Koanza, Chairman of the African Welfare Association, Que Que, Evidence 1944.

57. *Native Commissioner, Umtali District Annual Report, 1929*, S235/507, NAZ.

58. Native Commissioner, the Range to Chief Native Commissioner, 4/20/32, S138/47, NAZ.

59. Chief Native Commissioner Memorandum, 1/27/30, S138/55, NAZ.

BIBLIOGRAPHY

Appleby, Joyce. 1993. "Consumption in Early Modern Social Thought." In *Consumption and the World of Goods*, pp. 162–173, John Brewer and Roy Porter, eds. London: Routledge.

Arrighi, G. 1970. "Labour Supplies in Historical Perspective: A Study of the Proletarianization of the African Peasantry in Rhodesia." *Journal of Development Studies* 6(3):197–234.

Austen, Ralph A. and Woodruff D. Smith. 1990. "Private Tooth Decay as Public Economic Virtue: The Slave-Sugar Triangle, Consumerism, and European Industrialization." *Social Science History* 14(1):94–115.

Beidelman, E. T. 1982. *Colonial Evangelism: A Socio-Historical Study of an East African Mission at the Grassroots.* Bloomington: Indiana University Press.

Blennerhassett, Rose and Lucy Sleeman. 1893. *Adventures in Mashonaland by Two Hospital Nurses*. London: Macmillan and Co.

Breen, T. H. 1993. "The Meaning of Things: Interpreting the Consumer Economy in the Eighteenth Century." In *Consumption and the World of Goods*, pp.249–260, John Brewer and Roy Porter, eds. London: Routledge.

Brewer, John and Roy Porter, eds. 1993. *Consumption and the World of Goods*. London: Routledge.

Burke, Timothy J. 1993. "Lifebuoy Men, Lux Women: Commodification, Consumption and Cleanliness in Colonial Zimbabwe." Ph.D. dissertation, The Johns Hopkins University.

Chanock, Martin. 1982. "Making Customary Law: Men, Women, and Courts in Colonial Northern Rhodesia." In *African Women and the Law: Historical Perspectives*, pp.53–67, Margaret J. Hay and Marcia Wright, eds. Boston: Boston University Press.

Comaroff, Jean and John Comaroff. 1991. *Of Revelation and Revolution: Christianity, Colonialism, and Consciousness in South Africa*, vol. 1. Chicago: University of Chicago Press.

———. 1992. "Home-Made Hegemony: Modernity, Domesticity, and Colonialism in South Africa." In *African Encounters With Domesticity*, pp. 37–74, Karen T. Hansen, ed. New Jersey: Rutgers University Press.

Davis, Benjamin and Wolfgang Dopcke. 1987. "Survival and Accumulation in Gutu: Class Formation and the Rise of the State in Colonial Zimbabwe, 1900–1939." *Journal of Southern African Studies* 14(1):64–98.

Enloe, Cynthia. 1990. *Bananas, Beaches and Bases: Making Feminist Sense of International Politics*. Berkeley: University of California Press.

Gaitskell, Deborah. 1990. "Devout Domesticity? A Century of African Women's Christianity in South Africa." In *Women and Gender in Southern Africa to 1945*, pp. 251–272, Cherryl Walker, ed. London: James Currey.

Hunt, Nancy Rose. 1990. "Domesticity and Colonialism in Belgian Africa: Usumbura's *Foyer Social*, 1946–1960." *Signs* 15(3):447–474.

Hyatt, Stanley P. 1914. *The Old Transport Road*. London: Andrew Melrose, Ltd.

Kapenzi, Geoffrey Z. 1979. *The Clash of Cultures: Christian Missionaries and the Shona of Rhodesia*. Washington, DC: University Press of America.

Kazembe, Joyce L. 1987. "The Women Issue." In *Zimbabwe: The Political Economy of Transition, 1980–1986*, pp.377–404, Ibbo Mandaza, ed. Harare: Jongwe Press.

MacClancy, Jeremy. 1992. *Consuming Culture: Why You Eat What You Eat*. New York: Henry Holt and Co.

Mann, Kristin. 1983. "The Dangers of Dependence: Christian Marriage Among Elite Women in Lagos Colony, 1880–1915." *Journal of African History* 24:37–56.

Masterson, G.M. 1977. "Memories of a Native Commissioner's Wife." *NADA* XI(4):397–406.

May, Joan. 1979. *African Women in Urban Employment*. Harare: Mambo Press.

———. 1983. *Zimbabwean Women in Customary and Colonial Law*. Gweru: Mambo Press.

McCracken, Grant. 1988. *Culture and Consumption: New Approaches to the Symbolic Character of Consumer Goods and Activities*. Bloomington: Indiana University Press.

Meintjes, Sheila. 1990. "Family and Gender in the Christian Community at Edendale, Natal, in Colonial Times." In *Women and Gender in Southern Africa to 1945*, pp. 125–145, Cherryl Walker, ed. London: James Currey.

Mies, Maria. 1986. *Patriarchy and Accumulation on a World Scale: Women in the International Division of Labour*. London: Zed Books Ltd.

Mintz, Sidney W. 1985. *Sweetness and Power: The Place of Sugar in Modern History*. New York: Viking Penguin, Inc.

Moran, Mary H. 1990. *Civilized Women: Gender and Prestige in Southeastern Liberia*. Ithaca, NY: Cornell University Press.

Moss, Barbara A. 1992. "'Holding Body and Soul Together': Women, Autonomy and Christianity in Colonial Zimbabwe." Ph.D. dissertation, Indiana University.

Mpofu, Joshua M. M. 1983. *Some Observable Sources of Women's Subordination in Zimbabwe*. Harare, Zimbabwe: Centre for Applied Social Sciences.

Mukerji, Chandra. 1983. *From Graven Images: Patterns of Modern Materialism*. New York: Columbia University Press.

Ncube, Welshman. 1987. "Underprivilege and Inequality: The Matrimonial Property Rights of Women in Zimbabwe." In *Women and Law in Southern Africa*, pp.3–34, Alice Armstrong and Welshman Ncube, eds. Harare: Zimbabwe Publishing House.

Palmer, Robin. 1977. "The Agricultural History of Rhodesia." In *The Roots of Rural Poverty*, pp. 221–253, Robin Palmer and Neil Parsons, eds. Berkeley: University of California Press.

Phimister, Ian. 1988. *An Economic and Social History of Zimbabwe, 1890–1948*. London: Longman.

Ranger, Terence O. 1986. "Protestant Mission in Africa: The Dialectic of Conversion in the American Methodist Episcopal Church in Eastern Zimbabwe, 1900–1950." Paper presented at the Religion in Sub-Saharan Africa Conference, Brigham Young University, October 22–25.

———. 1987. "Religion, Development and African Christian Identity." In *Religion, Development and African Identity*, pp. 29–57, Kristen Holst Peterson, ed. Uppsala: Scandinavian Institute of African Studies.

Schmidt, Elizabeth. 1992. *Peasants, Traders, and Wives: Shona Women in the History of Zimbabwe, 1870–1939*. Portsmouth, NH: Heinemann.

Schreuder, D. M. 1976. "The Cultural Factor in Victorian Imperialism: A Case-Study of the British 'Civilising Mission.'" *The Journal of Imperial and Commonwealth History* IV(3):283–317.

Sithole, Ndabaningi. 1970. *Obed Mutezo: The Mudzimu Christian Nationalist*. London: Oxford University Press.

Springer, H. 1909. *Snapshot from Sunny Africa*. New York: Katanga Press.

Sykes, R. 1902. "A Visit to Our Mission Station at Empandeni." *Zambesi Missionary Record* 11(15):225–240.

Vambe, Lawrence. 1972. *An Ill-Fated People*. Pittsburgh: University of Pittsburgh Press.

Van Onselen, Charles. 1976. *Chibaro: African Mine Labour in Southern Rhodesia, 1900–1933*. London: Pluto Press.

Wood, Joseph Garbett. 1974 [1893]. *Through Matabeleland: The Record of Ten Months' Trip in an Ox-Waggon through Mashonaland and Matabeleland*. Reprint. Bulawayo Books of Rhodesia.

Zvobgo, C. J. 1986. "Aspects of Interaction Between Christianity and African Culture in Colonial Zimbabwe, 1893–1934." *Zambezia* XII:53–57.

EMBODYING THE CONTRADICTIONS OF MODERNITY:
GENDER AND SPIRIT POSSESSION AMONG MAASAI IN TANZANIA

Dorothy Hodgson

Gender relations, in Africa as elsewhere, have never been merely a self-contained matter of "local" ideas or "local" practices. Throughout history and across space, "local" gender relations and ideologies have been constituted in interaction with translocal material, social, and cultural processes; both men and women take advantage of the opportunities and constraints provided by these translocal flows to either reinforce or renegotiate not only their relationships, but their dominant concepts of masculinity and femininity as well. These "local" responses and resistances have, in turn, informed the translocal flows, producing what Watts calls "a working and reworking of modernity . . . Globality and locality are inextricably linked, but through complex mediations and reconfigurations of 'traditional' society; the nonlocal processes driving capital mobility are always experienced, constituted and mediated locally" (1992: 6).

In this paper, I examine *orpeko,* or spirit possession, among Maasai in Tanzania as one site where Maasai men and women negotiate the profound gendered contradictions generated by the complex, interconnected processes of capitalism, missionization, and "development" that, among others, comprise "modernity." In its celebration of the individual, progress, civilization, and rationality (cf. Hall 1992), "modernity" has been a profoundly gendered process. The penetration of capitalist relations of production, for example, not only restructures economic and political relations of power between men and women, but their social and cultural relations as well: the oppositional categories of modern/traditional imposed by modernity both valorize and stigmatize certain masculinities and femininities. The symptoms and spread of *orpeko,* I argue, marked the penetration, impact, and reshaping of modernity with all its contradictions: the increasing disenfranchisement of Maasai women from their historical rights over certain economic resources, their political marginalization, their exclusion from the expanding opportunities for education and income generation, and their marginalization from a sense of Maasai identity.[1] But *orpeko* has simultaneously been a "counter-hegemonic process" (cf. Boddy 1989: 5), as it has not only critiqued the intrusion of "modernity" and the consolidation and reinforcement of patriarchal authority in the lives of Maasai women, but strengthened relationships *among* women, and partially enabled the creation of an alternative female community beyond the gaze and control of Maasai men. In other words, spirit possession is one site where the translocal ideas and practices of "modernity" and patriarchy intersect with "local" gender relations, at once constraining as well as initiating opportunities for their reconfiguration.

To explain *orpeko* in terms of gendered mediations of modernity, I will first briefly review the history of its emergence among Maasai, then use three studies of the phenomenon among Maasai in Tanzania to offer one reading of the cultural meanings and political ramifications of *orpeko*'s symptoms, diagnosis, and treatment. The three studies were undertaken at approximately ten-year intervals: a set of twenty case studies based on interviews by David Peterson in 1971 when outbreaks of *orpeko* were sweeping through southern Maasailand;[2] a 1984 study of *orpeko* by Arvi Hurskainen, commissioned by the Catholic and Lutheran churches as a means to settle their disputes over the diagnosis and cure of *orpeko*; and finally, my own data collected during field research from 1991 through 1993 in three Maasai communities in northern Maasailand, including 150 transcribed narrative interviews from men and women of all ages.[3]

OUTSIDE IN: "MODERN" SICKNESS

Most studies of spirit possession examine cases of long-established cults with complex rituals and procedures for identifying, appeasing, and negotiating with rich pantheons of spirits, but rarely casting them out permanently. Further, many of these spirit possession cults operate in societies with a significant Muslim influence and presence. The distinctions of the Maasai case in Tanzania are therefore intriguing: First, Maasai have no long-term tradition of spirit possession; instead, spirit possession, or *orpeko,* is a recent phenomenon. Second, although *orpeko* emerged through Maasai interaction with Muslim-influenced spirit possession practitioners and cults, it spread in tandem with increased missionary activity by the Lutheran and Catholic churches. Third, most Maasai now interpret *orpeko* as possession by "the devil" (*setan*), rather than by a range of individual, unique spirits. Finally, rather than seek ways to accommodate the spirit in a long-term relationship or through institutionalized spirit cults, most Maasai seek a permanent "cure" for the "sick" and "inoculation" for the "healthy" through Christian baptism. Despite these many distinctions, however, there are similarities: As in most cases in Africa, the preponderance of possessed Maasai are women, generally younger, married women.[4]

To understand the distinct, gendered manifestations of Maasai spirit possession, we must look beyond the "local" frames of reference, the "local" ideas and practices. *Orpeko* is vividly perceived by Maasai men and women themselves as an outside, nonlocal force that has entered and disrupted their lives. The "otherness" of *orpeko* is immediately evident both linguistically and spatially. First, the word *orpeko* is not indigenous to the Maa language, but an adaptation of the Swahili word *upepo* (spirit, wind). Secondly, *orpeko* spread from the outside in—the first cases occurred in the south, near the borders with non-Maasai peoples, then slowly spread northward, into the heart of Maasailand.[5]

Maasai stories about *orpeko*, as well as the case histories, emphasize its foreign origins: *Orpeko* emerged from Maasai contacts with non-Maasai peoples, both African and Euro-American. Maasai say that the first cases of *orpeko* were brought by Maasai who had dispersed to "Swahili" lands after the devastation of livestock and people in the late 1800s wrought by rinderpest, bovine pleuro-pneumonia, and smallpox, as well as the resulting famine and intersectional wars.[6] Although *orpeko* seemed to have faded for years after a spate of outbreaks in the 1930s, it reappeared dramatically in the mid-1950s and spread rapidly throughout southern Maasailand (Hurskainen 1989: 141–142). By 1971, when Peterson made his study, hundreds of Maasai women were reportedly possessed by *orpeko*. Most women he interviewed claimed that their first symptoms occurred from two to fifteen years earlier. The renewed outbreaks coincided not only with the incursion of non-Maasai, Muslim-influenced *waganga* (healers) who specialized in identifying and treating *orpeko* cases, but also with the rapidly expanding evangelization activities of the Catholic and Lutheran churches (Hurskainen 1985: 9–11).[7] Slowly the outbreaks spread north, with occasional cases being recorded in Monduli district in the mid-1970s, and significant numbers in my three research communities by the early 1980s (Hurskainen: 1985, 11).

The earliest recorded case of spirit possession is that of Nanoto (DP/3), an elderly woman who told Peterson that she was first possessed between 1900 and 1910, when she was in her late twenties. Her story, as summarized by Peterson, is as follows: Although she was born in northern Maasailand, she was living at the coast near Pangani during this period. The elders took her to a non-Maasai healer for treatment when their normal methods for treating her symptoms, a fever and rapid, strong pulse, failed. He diagnosed her problem as spirit possession, prepared a brew of medicinal herbs for her to drink, and charged twenty-one cows for the treatment. For three months following the treatment, she was far worse—she had no appetite, rarely slept, and refused to talk to anyone. Just when her family thought she was going to die, she recovered, was better for a while, then suffered a relapse of the same symptoms. In 1930 a Lutheran evangelist and another man visited her *enkang'* ("homestead," cf. Swahili *boma*), telling people to gather around and hear God's word. "She heard this, came, listened and became very, very happy—'like the white cloud on top of a mountain.'" After the evangelist left, she ate and slept well for four days, then began to hear voices directing her to go to church. She convinced her father to let her go, partly by reminding him of all the cattle he had lost trying to heal her. She walked to the mission, attended devotions that evening, then stayed on in the area to attend baptismal instruction classes. "After hearing the First Commandment on her first day of baptismal instruction, she began to shake and wail and then the demon left her for good. She then finished instruction and was baptized."

The details of Nanoto's account provide a template through which to examine the symptoms, diagnosis, and treatment in both early and contemporary cases. As in Nanoto's case, *orpeko* most commonly afflicts women of childbearing age, although a few cases of possessed men have been reported and recorded.[8] A range of symptoms can be diagnosed as *orpeko*, including headaches, pains in the head; fevers; pains and burning sensations in the womb and/or stomach; backaches; swelling in the neck, breasts, and often belly; general listlessness and apathy; lack of appetite; and insomnia. Later symptoms often include wailing, shaking, thrashing fits, choking sensations, and nightmares (cf. Hurskainen 1989: 143). The most prominent symptoms seem to cluster geographically, so that, for example, women in Naberera complained of fever, while most from Kisongo spoke of terrible burning sensations in their stomach/womb. In the communities in Monduli that I studied, the acute symptoms of *orpeko* are fits characterized by body rigidity, vigorous shaking, and a low, growling moan. Its ongoing symptoms include a general malaise, negligence of household duties, rudeness, and terrifying nightmares. Many of these symptoms, of course, can be attributed to other diseases and maladies—it is the "naming" as *orpeko*, usually by other women, that makes the difference.[9]

These symptoms, I believe, signify and embody the contradictions modernity has produced in the lives of Maasai women. Elsewhere, I have shown how colonial and post-colonial interventions contributed to the economic, political, and cultural disenfranchisement of Maasai women (Hodgson 1995). Influenced by their gendered ideas as well as popular imagery of "the Maasai," British administrators recognized only Maasai men as the "true" pastoralists, native authorities, taxpayers, decision makers, property owners, and political actors. As such, most interventions were directed at men, who used the opportunity to consolidate their control over livestock, land, and money. For example, both the British and later Tanzanian governments have tried to encourage, bribe, coerce, or force Maasai men (as the livestock "owners") to perceive their cattle as commodities and sell them in the interests of "overstocking," "better" animal husbandry, and the "benefits" of a cash rather than barter economy. As a result, livestock (especially cattle) has shifted from a resource with multiple, intertwined layers of rights between men and women to an individually male-"owned" commodity. Similarly, as the "sellers" and "buyers" of livestock, and the "taxpayers," men have come to control most primary sources of income.[10] Women's increasing disenfranchisement from their former economic rights has been accompanied by their political marginalization: Men have used their role as the chosen intermediaries with first the British and now the Tanzanian government to increase their control over "domestic" disputes and affairs (see, e.g., Hodgson 1996). At the same time that Maasai women have been gradually losing both prestige and power, their workloads have been increasing. Many have been compelled to cultivate to subsidize household consumption as livestock resources have dwindled, and most walk farther in search of fuelwood and water now that sedentarization has depleted nearby resources (Hodgson 1995). Finally, women's movements outside the boundaries of their households and communities have been curtailed; their former travels as traders to local markets and neighboring agricultural villages, as well as visits to mothers and brothers, have been hindered by both the monetization of the subsistence food economy and the constant demands for their individual labor in their fields and those of their husbands. Days spent working, relaxing, or traveling together with other women have been replaced by the incessant pace of lonely labor. In conversations I had throughout Maasai areas, Maasai women complained bitterly about their loss of rights, heavy workloads, and mistreatment by their husbands. Most women were resentful and despondent; few of them saw any way to improve their situation.

The project of modernity has therefore produced contradictions in the lives of Maasai women. Monetization, commoditization, and "development" have produced separate male-dominated domains of "the economic" and "the political," among others (as opposed to the female domain of "the domestic"). Meanwhile, the gendered modernist ideologies of "individualism" (i.e., individual male control of property), "rationality" (male "thinking" over female "feeling"), and "progress" (in terms of increased productivity for profit) have empowered Maasai men to consolidate their control in these realms through such categories as "taxpayers," "heads of households," and "livestock owners" (Hodgson 1995). These processes have converged to displace Maasai women from their rights and roles and heighten their sense of despair and isolation. Furthermore, the oppositional categories of modern/traditional that are central to modernity's meaning have been mapped onto Maasai gender relations: Maasai men have been valorized as the cultural ideal, promoted as the symbol of "tradition," an image of "being Maasai" that has been increasingly reified in the images of the warrior, pastoralist, patriarch. The result of this rigid gender coding of Maasai ethnicity has been to further marginalize women, in this case from their sense of being Maasai.[11]

The one obvious alternative open to women—to embrace "modernity" in opposition to men and ethnic identity—is neither an easy or attractive option. Not only do women lack the economic or political means for such a direct challenge to the consolidation of patriarchal authority, but they are unclear as to whom or what they would be opposing. Maasai women do have a ritual means of organizing to rebuke individual affronts by men or women to certain cultural rules which involves cursing, physical attacks, and the destruction of property.[12] But the gradual, overlapping processes and practices of "modernity" which have empowered Maasai men provide no *specific* violation to be condemned or individual to be punished. Women cannot launch a ritual attack of words and beatings on all men. Instead, silenced from either verbal or violent forms of protest, women have initiated a powerful moral critique of modernity and its gendered effects on their lives in the language of the body. Through spirit possession, women voice their complaints about their economic, political, and social disenfranchisement, at once internalizing their despair and expressing their predicament.

Other Africanist scholars have recently discussed spirit possession in terms of embodiment. Janice Boddy describes *zar* spirit possession in Sudan as "embodying power relations" (1989: 8), while Michael Lambek discusses spirit possession in Mayotte as "embodied knowledge" (1993: 305). Most recently, Paul Stoller, in an evocative article about Hauka spirit possession in Niger entitled "Embodying Colonial Knowledge" (1994), argues that by considering spirit possession "sensuously as an embodied practice, we are likely to sense it as a phenomenological arena in which cultural memory is fashioned and refashioned to produce and reproduce power" (1994: 637). Furthermore, Stoller urges that we go beyond just considering "body-as-text"; "embodiment is not primarily textual; rather, the sentient body is culturally consumed by a world filled with forces, smells, textures, sights, sounds and tastes, all of which trigger cultural memories" (1994: 636). In discussing the relationship of modernity and embodiment, I adopt Stoller's suggestions, but I pursue them in terms of a third relationship which he, oddly enough, ignores—that of gender. Although Stoller acknowledges that the preponderance of possessed among Hauka adepts are women, he fails to discuss embodiment as a gendered process: It is not just any body, but a *female* body, that is possessed.[13]

Considered broadly, *orpeko* is a metaphor for women's outrage at the gendered changes produced by modernity. *Orpeko*'s association with devastation and disease is stressed in contemporary discussions, where it is obliquely referred to as *emuoyian*, or "sickness," but a sickness that comes from the outside and afflicts only women. Like modernity, *orpeko* has ambiguous origins, multiple manifestations, and devastating gendered effects. One cluster of *orpeko* symptoms, for example, condenses the multiple, indistinct sources of the sickness of "modernity" into a vague category, "the other"—that is, outsiders, non-Maasai, the external, imposed processes, practices, and people over which women exert little control. For example, possession fits are often triggered by "foreign" sounds, such as radios and drumming; and when possessed, some women speak in "strange" languages in which they are not fluent, most often Swahili or Arabic. As Pastor Stanley Benson reports:

> One case in which I was present exhibited a manifestation of being another person than what she actually was. This lady knew no Swahili, yet when we Christians were seeking God's help by prayer and hymn singing, she started to speak Swahili. It came from her but in a voice that was not like hers in timbre or pitch. In order to check if she knew Swahili at a later time I asked

her questions which would require her to use the same words she spoke in the trance. She could not nor did she understand what I was talking about in Swahili. (Benson 1980: 55)

But the terror of women over the changes in their lives is most evident in the nightmares they described to Peterson, nightmares filled with signs of the invasion of "the other." Many women spoke of a sense that "darkness" or "a black cloud" was descending on them, suffocating and even strangling them:

> She would wake up at night with a start as "darkness" would come and try to strangle her. Being very frightened, she would cover herself quickly before the "darkness" could cover her and then she would scream. After this she was unable to sleep for the rest of the night. She also began to feel something very heavy in her chest. (DP/1)

Sometimes the choking sensation came from within themselves, rising from their stomach to their chest and throat:

> The first occurrence of trouble was in 1969 when this girl became quite sick with a fever. A few days later she saw "darkness," felt that she was being strangled and ran out of the *boma*. She was caught by her family and they decided that she was crazy. From then on she would shake everyday—first on one side, then the other and then her whole body would shake. She always had a burning sensation in her stomach and felt something very hot moving upwards to strangle her. She felt like a dying woman at this time, and she almost did die. (DP/5)

Most women complained that their symptoms were always worse during the night, in the darkness. In a few cases, "the other" was symbolized by whiteness: a few women dreamt that something or someone white was either coming towards them or beckoning them—a white light or moth, a white man, or a half white/half Maasai man. Perhaps these images signified the white settlers and administrators infiltrating their lives and lands, or the white cassocks of pastors and priests.[14]

If these symptoms, as I have argued, identify the source of women's increasing despair—their unhappy encounter with the political economy of "modernity"—another cluster of symptoms marks the dimension in their lives where they feel most threatened, and therefore most anxious: their roles as mothers. Being a mother, especially the mother of sons, is still fundamental to attaining not only respect and prestige as a woman, but ensuring one's maintenance and subsistence in old age. Although important, their roles as wives, daughters, and sisters are less prestigious and critical in comparison. Pregnancy, or anxiety about pregnancy, is therefore central to most occurrences: Not only is possession prevalent among infertile women, but pregnancy can trigger possession, and possession is in turn said to cause miscarriages (cf. Boddy 1989, especially Chapter Five). One of the most common symptoms could be read as an embodied expression of women's anxieties about pregnancy, motherhood, reproduction: Many women report a burning, painful womb or stomach, occasionally with a hard lump in it. Here the notion of spirit possession as a gendered embodiment of the contradictions of modernity is quite clear: Women fear the effects of the changes in their lives on both their biological and social reproduction.

Finally, as Pastor Benson has argued, another cluster of symptoms can be read as expressions of the isolation women feel: Possessed women run away from their families and communities, or enter into "a coma-like trance where no communication is possible" (Benson 1980: 54). Similarly, Peterson described how women still suffering from possession would often cover their heads, faces, and eyes when talking to him, as if to hide and distance themselves (1971). Possessed women's withdrawal from contact—whether physical, verbal, or emotional—with family members signified their economic, political, and social isolation, their enforced physical and symbolic enclosure within the domestic domain.

Read together, these symptoms narrate a story about some vague, powerful, malevolent "other" that threatens not only the well-being but the bodies of women. The precise origins of this "sickness" are unclear; all that is known is that it is "foreign" and has come from "outside." Its effects, however, are dramatic: women are marginalized, isolated, even suffocated by its presence. The triggers and symptoms of *orpeko* embody the ambivalent position of Maasai women in relation to the contradictions in their lives generated by "modernity."

INSIDE OUT: "MODERN" HEALING

Paradoxically, while *orpeko* thus marks the structural crisis of individual women, it has also enabled their "healing" in two ways. First, *orpeko* has strengthened relationships among Maasai women: When a woman becomes possessed, it is usually other women who help her. Since *orpeko* cases have become more prevalent, it is mainly other women, often Christian women, who diagnose or "name" a woman's symptoms as *orpeko*. The ability to "name" *orpeko* is simultaneously an assertion of power, the recognition of a common condition, and the first step toward healing. Sometimes they beat *debes* (metal containers—also a foreign import) to confirm their diagnosis, and invoke, then appease, the spirit, causing the woman to dance and sing until exhausted or the spirit has subsided. Non-Maasai healers can also temporarily placate the spirits through *ngomas*, or dances with drumming, but most *ngomas* these days, as in the past, are usually performed for afflicted women by other Maasai women.[15] Also, when a possessed woman has acute attacks of fits and thrashing, other women gather around her and physically hold and comfort her until the fit has passed. Finally, it is generally Christian women who encourage the afflicted woman to go to church, or if a church is not nearby, instruct her themselves in the teachings of Christianity.[16] (Occasionally, however, a woman's brother or husband who has seen *orpeko* cases elsewhere will insist that she go to church to be healed.)

Orpeko, in other words, has enabled women to establish multidimensional, textured relationships among themselves. Through physical touch, emotional bonds of empathy and sympathy, and the sharing of knowledge and experience, women have addressed the isolation, despair, and loneliness produced by modernity. Although women might not be able to describe the source of *orpeko* beyond vague attributions to some foreign, outside "other," they can name the symptoms as *orpeko* and, through the naming, begin to work together toward healing.

Orpeko has also enabled women's healing by facilitating the creation of an alternative female community within the Christian church: The most popular and prevalent means to heal *orpeko* has been to attend baptismal instruction, become baptized, and participate regularly in the Christian church (see Hodgson n.d.). The pattern in Peterson's earlier cases was for men to take possessed women to non-Maasai healers, to *oloiboni/iloibonok* (Maasai healers and ritual experts), and/or to doctors in government hospitals and dispensaries, all of whom failed to cure the women. Their impotence in the face of *orpeko* could be read as a sharp gendered rebuke and protest of both the increasing powers of "traditional" patriarchal authorities and the male medical institutions of modernity. If *orpeko*, as I have argued, is a gendered critique of the consolidation of patriarchal control achieved through "modernity," then certainly the cure would not be found in further empowering these patriarchs. And so possessed women, like Nanoto, would eventually be taken, usually by other women, to church, where they would find permanent healing.

Such was the case with another woman interviewed by Peterson, who first described her early symptoms, which began after a miscarriage. On the advice of the elders, she took a trip to a traditional healer, who beat drums for her. She danced and thrashed on the ground so hard, however, that she miscarried again:

> After this second loss of a child, she returned home sick, very weak and with the same symptoms as before. They fed her cow and goat fat in their efforts to give her strength. When they saw that she wasn't getting any better, the elders decided to send her to another traditional doctor. She, however, refused to go because she had heard from Masai Christian women at Ngojoha who had been cured that Christianity was the only true cure. The elders consented so she went to church in about 1966. She was taught by a Masai evangelist . . . and then baptized on the 24th of September, 1967.

> As soon as she began baptismal instruction, she started improving as far as the shaking, the burning sensations in the groin and the headaches.

All of these symptoms left her before baptism. She still had occasional problems mentally, i.e. confused thinking, amnesia. These mental lapses continued until baptism.

The day before baptism when she first heard she was to be baptized, all the original symptoms returned in full—yelling, dancing, shaking, burning sensations. They continued until the moment when she was baptized (first application of water). Afterwards she became normal and has been so since that time. When she was baptized, she said she felt a heavy feeling pass over her and then afterwards she felt very relaxed. (DP/8)

All of Peterson's, Hurskainen's, and my accounts emphasized this point: that only the Christian churches can *permanently* heal *orpeko*.

So what is the appeal of Christian churches to Maasai women? As I have discussed elsewhere (Hodgson 1995, n.d.b), despite the persistent efforts of Lutheran and Catholic missionaries to convert Maasai men, the vast majority of converts have been women. The appeal of the church is partly due to women's greater religiosity: Maasai women perceive themselves and are perceived by Maasai men as far more religious and closer to God (*Engai*) than Maasai men. As women themselves say, the church enhances their already substantial spiritual life by providing a place to sing and pray to God. But the church also overcomes women's isolation by providing a forum for gathering as a group. Unlike ceremonies and celebrations which provide only infrequent opportunities to gather, the church enables women to gather together on a frequent, regular basis. In addition to the class or service, women meet beforehand to chat in small, circulating groups, and often remain long afterward to talk. Finally, the church is also described by some as a place where one can learn new things and gain wisdom (*eng'eno*). Women go to church so that they can "get that wisdom (*eng'eno*) which is taught to people" (SUR/440) (see Hodgson n.d.b).

As many feminist scholars (among others) have argued, the Christian churches are themselves modernist and patriarchal institutions. Unlike the government, development agencies, and other "modern" institutions, however, the churches are less implicated in the consolidation of male Maasai power since Maasai men have generally rejected Christianity as "not-Maasai," as not in accordance with their rigid sense of "traditional" masculinity (see Hodgson n.d.a, 1995). There is no consensus between Catholic and Lutheran missionaries as to whether *orpeko* is a hysteric response to women's declining status or a manifestation of "the devil" (see Hurskainen 1985). This dispute notwithstanding, the association between *orpeko* and Christianity is now quite direct: Most contemporary Maasai have adopted the missionaries' naming, interpret *orpeko* as possession by "the devil" (*setan*), and believe that Christian baptism, whether in the Catholic or Protestant churches, is the only way to exorcise the devil and achieve permanent healing.[17] As one elder man explained:

There is a sickness (*emuoyian*) which has spread into this area recently which was not here before, this thing called *setan*, this *orpeko*. It hasn't entered men, but women. But when you take a woman to the *oloiboni* he says "she is cursed." And if you take her to another, "she is cursed." *Basi*, . . . this wisdom of Christians showed that a thing called the church (*ekanisa*) could heal this sickness. When we put women in there they were healed, really it helped them. *Shie*, why else would so many have joined? Also, it is said that a healthy person who is baptized cannot be possessed. (SUR/134)

His narrative was reiterated by another elder man:

Another thing which often admits women [into church] is *setan*, they have entered church because of *setan*. I mean, many have gotten *orpeko*, and they say that church is the only cure, since they have seen many others who became ill with *orpeko*, went to church and were cured. Others decided to go to church so that they wouldn't get *orpeko*. (SUR/892)

One woman, when asked if she attended church services, answered quite bluntly: "I have not gone to church; I don't have satan (*maata setan*)" (SUR/48) (see discussion below about involuntariness).

Despite the appeal of the Christian churches, most women have to receive some man's permission—most often her father or husband—to attend baptismal instruction and church services. Several women interviewed by Peterson, like Nasirian below, spoke of the difficulty obtaining permission from reluctant men:

Upon returning home [after visiting several healers whose treatments failed] a Christian woman told her [that] if she would accept her instruction about Christianity, she would be healed. Her husband became very angry and refused. Her grandmother said, "If you play around with Christianity, you will become like an Mswahili." However, when her husband saw that she was getting no better, he consented and she began instruction from this woman . . . [after eight days of instruction from this woman she was cured] . . . Now that she was alright again, her husband and others in the *boma* tried to keep her from having anything to do with the church. She did manage to sneak off to church occasionally but suffered a lot of grief because of this. Finally her husband allowed her to go because she began having the same trouble again and another wife and a daughter also became possessed (they also went to church). (DP/12)

As in the above case, other women told Peterson how their husbands were very reluctant about their continuing involvement in the church:

Although the rest of the *boma* inhabitants think her cure quite amazing, she has suffered a lot of grief because of her husband who is a type of local medicine man. He doesn't like at all the fact that she is a Christian. He thinks it is an excuse for moving towards civilization and Swahili ways. (DP/9)

The only baptized man interviewed by Peterson suffered continual harassment: "He is really bothered by other Maasai men. They come and ask him, 'Are you the one who sits among women and children? You aren't worthy to be a Maasai!'" (DP/13). Many Maasai men whom I interviewed spoke disparagingly about the church, dismissing it as the mere "nonsense" of women, a waste of time.

Orpeko has helped women overcome men's resistance to their participation in church. Listen to one woman's story, as paraphrased by Peterson in 1971:

There are eighteen women in her *boma* who are Christians, and when they heard that she had a demon they gathered and sang for her. Three of these women who had been demon-possessed are in her immediate family. (In this *boma* demon possession became such a common thing that husbands of women once possessed but now Christians, gave their wives permission to have their children baptized. Up to this time, permission for baptism was given only to those who were possessed.) (DP/2)

Orpeko continues to overcome the reluctance of Maasai men to allow their wives to become involved in the church. As one young married woman told me:

Men just don't want it [baptism]. There are men, for instance, like mine, who insult the church and say "*Shie*, child, where are you going? Church? And what do you intend to find there? Have you changed? Have you become an *emeeki* [derogatory term for "female non-Maasai"]? If you go, you'll leave a bad omen here."

But they all have to put you in that house of God *(ena aji Engai)* on the day when satan comes inside you. If you are unable to cook his *uji* and he is stricken by hunger, then he says, "*Shie*, yesterday I slept without eating, perhaps my wife is crazy with *orpeko*, let me take her to church."

And he doesn't know what else to do to cure her. I mean, he left her for a long time until the day when he missed his food because saetan prevented her from cooking. Then and only then did he take her [to church]. But when he takes her, she will embarrass him there since she might jump about and tear off her clothes. But he left her [at home] without taking her so that she could pray to God when her spirit was still good *(supat oltau)*; he left her until she got blemishes on her spirit *(oldoai oltau)*, then and only then did he take her. (SUR/1416)

Several women spoke of how they became sick and their husbands had to "put" them *(etipika)* in church. Even men spoke of "putting" a sick wife in church to cure her of *orpeko*: "I put [*atipika*] one wife in that house [the church], I took her to be baptized . . . I mean she had *orpeko*, that was the reason I put her in . . . everything else I did failed" (SUR/196). Disputing notions of individual choice, one man claimed that women did not want to go to church, but were forced to go by *orpeko*:

> If you examine the women from here who are there, you'll see that what makes so many go is the sickness called *orpeko* which had infected them. If there is a young Maasai woman who does not want to go to church, she is taken anyway by this craziness. It is the place to wipe out this curse, the church is the only place. So, as I see it, it is not that the women badly want [to go to church], but that they are afraid of this sickness. The sickness has not yet spread much among men, or else many of them would also enter the church. (SUR/1051)

This theme of involuntariness—that *orpeko* is forcing women to do things, like join the church, that they would not otherwise choose—is repeatedly expressed in numerous early and contemporary accounts. First, other people (usually women) usually diagnose or "name" the symptoms as *orpeko*. Second, possessed women often refuse to go to church, despite insistent pleas by family and friends. Most are forced to go to church, often physically dragged to church for the first time, only to run away or have violent possession fits in the doorway. Finally, just before baptism or the application of water, a woman's symptoms may occasionally return violently, as if making a final statement of her unwillingness and lack of intention (see, e.g., DP/8, above).

The very ambiguousness and ambivalence of *orpeko* in terms of questions of women's agency and intentionality is crucial to its ability to resolve, in some measure, women's dilemma (cf. Boddy 1989: 5). Even if men are reluctant to allow their wives or daughters to join the Christian churches, they can hardly argue with the demands of the devil. By displacing responsibility for going to church from the women to either the devil *(setan)* or decisions by men, women get what they want—to go to church—without *directly* threatening the authority of men. Husbands either allow their wives a weekly respite from their heavy workloads to attend church or suffer the social and economic consequences should a woman become possessed and quit working altogether. Once *orpeko* spreads through an area, it is often enough for women just to invoke its possibility to receive permission to join the church. Although some "never-possessed" women choose not to join the church, those who are interested need only remind their reluctant husbands about the possibility of *orpeko*. Ever-fearful about malevolent forces threatening the well-being of their children, many women (such as the ones discussed above by Peterson) also receive permission to baptize both their sons and daughters as a precaution. Unlike the earlier cases where baffled men took their wives, mothers, and sisters to *iloibonok*, healers, and medical doctors to seek a cure, the cure is now universally recognized and acknowledged. The extended endeavors sparked by earlier *orpeko* episodes, such as those described by the women interviewed by Peterson, are now condensed into a familiar, almost stereotypical pattern: Once a woman's affliction is named as *orpeko*, she bypasses the *iloibonok* and doctors and goes directly to church and its community of women for healing.

CONCLUSION

Given the above studies and accounts, how then can we understand the distinct manifestations of Maasai spirit possession? Why has *orpeko* affected women and not men? In her study of spirit possession among factory women in Malaysia, Aihwa Ong explores how women use the vocabulary of spirit possession to indirectly attack male control and capitalist discipline, without directly challenging male authority. Ong describes the profound contradictions generated by capitalist relations of production in the lives of young Malay village women employed as industrial labor, especially "the rigidity of the work routine, continual male supervision, and devaluation of their labor in the factory" (1987: 7). Beginning in the 1970s, large numbers of women in different factories would simultaneously be seized by spirits, disrupting production for days at a time. Spirit possession episodes for these women, according to Ong, "are to be deciphered not so much as a noncapitalist critique of abstract exchange values . . . but as a protest against the loss of autonomy/humanity in work" (1987: 8). As a response to being treated like "things" and the intensified external male control of their work routine, these continuing incidents have called attention to women's situation and produced some minor improvements in their working condition. But they have not fundamentally challenged male authority or factory discipline.

Similarly, I have argued that the symptoms of the "sickness" spreading through Maasai women have embodied and expressed Maasai women's anxieties about their increasingly isolated, precarious position in "modern" Tanzania (cf. Alpers 1984). *Orpeko* has emerged and spread alongside a particular historical, political-economic conjuncture between the increasing pressures and alienation produced by the intensifying economic, political, and social disenfranchisement of women, and the alternative possibilities for female community and solidarity provided by the Christian missions. As the parallels between my study and Ong's suggest, although the particular contradictions produced by capitalist relations of production and, more broadly, "modernity" vary according to the historical moment, forms of capitalism, and "local" contexts, the contradictions seem to be always gendered. But why have Maasai women, like Malay factory women, expressed their frustrations in the embodied narratives of spirit possession? The parallels of spirit possession with the vast literature on "hysteria" are equally intriguing: Is spirit possession perhaps just a culturally appropriate expression of female "hysteria"? Are such embodied expressions the only means of expressing power left to otherwise powerless women (cf. Micale 1995)?

Although discussing the relationship between gender, embodiment and capitalism in yet another context (Baltimore in the 1980s), Emily Martin offers a possible answer to the question of why embodiment may be a particularly female response to capitalism. After analyzing women's embodiment of the distinctions that dominate postindustrial capitalist society (such as "home vs. work, sex vs. money, love vs. contract, nature vs. culture, women vs. men" (1987: 197)), she argues that "because of the nature of their bodies, women far more than men cannot help but confound these distinctions every day. For the majority of women, menstruation, pregnancy, and menopause cannot any longer be kept at home. Women interpenetrate what were never really separate realms. They literally *embody* the opposition, or contradiction, between the worlds" (Martin 1987: 197, emphasis added).

Orpeko has, however, been more than an embodied expression of capitalist and modernist contradictions; it has also enabled Maasai women to resolve their structural crisis by strengthening their relationships among themselves and facilitating the formation of alternative female communities under the auspices of the Christian churches. But such a resolution is itself partial and contradictory. Spirit possession and the Christian churches may provide alternative forums for women to congregate and interact, but they do not directly address the underlying causes of women's predicament—their displacement from economic control and political power by Maasai men. By providing an outlet for women's dissatisfaction that does not directly challenge male authority, *orpeko* may serve merely to reinforce the existing gendered relations of power (cf. Ong 1987: 210). Furthermore, despite their failure to convert many Maasai men, Christian churches are themselves profoundly patriarchal institutions, with their general exclusion of women from leadership positions, and conservative teachings about "proper" gender roles. Yet for Maasai women in Tanzania, these same churches offer a space beyond the control of Maasai men for them to come together and be "healed." And these same communities of "church" women may even, in the future, become the platforms for the collective female action necessary to restructure gendered relations of power.

Whatever their future, Maasai women have had the spirit to critique the malevolent forces shaping their lives and transcend their isolation and anxieties. In the Maasai case, like the Hauka case, spirit possession has the power "to evoke the past, manipulate the present and provoke the future" (Stoller 1994: 642). Rather than the last resort of the powerless, embodiment is all the more powerful as a form of protest because of its fierce meaningfulness and resonance, its multidimensionality and undeniability. *Orpeko* therefore provides a crucial site for examining how such transnational cultural flows as Christianity, "modernity," and patriarchy intersect with Maasai gendered relations of power, at once constraining as well as initiating opportunities for their reconfiguration.

NOTES

Sections of this paper appear in Chapter IX of my dissertation, "*The Politics of Gender, Ethnicity and "Development": Images, Interventions and the Reconfiguration of Maasai Identities, 1916–1993.*" A version of the paper was also presented at the 1994 annual meeting of the American Anthropological Association in Atlanta on a panel I co-organized and co-chaired with Sheryl McCurdy entitled "The Spirit Calls But the Responses Differ: Gender and Spirit Possession in Tanzania." Research for the dissertation, carried out from 1991 to 1993, was supported by a Fulbright-Hays Doctoral Dissertation Abroad Award; an International Doctoral Research Fellowship funded by the Joint Committee on African Studies of the Social Science Research Council and the American Council of Learned Societies with funds provided by the Rockefeller Foundation; a National Science Foundation Doctoral Dissertation Improvement Grant (BNS #9114350); and an Andrew W. Mellon Candidacy Fellowship from the University of Michigan (summer and fall, 1991). Dissertation write-up was supported by an Andrew W. Mellon Dissertation Fellowship (1993–94) and a Rackham Fellowship (1994–95), both from the University of Michigan. I am indebted to the Tanzanian Commission for Science and Technology for permission to carry out the research, and to Professor C. K. Omari and the Department of Sociology at the University of Dar es Salaam for research affiliation. Special thanks are also due to Neil Smith and the Center for the Critical Analysis of Contemporary Culture at Rutgers University for providing me with an Associate Fellowship (1994–95), and, more important, a warm, vibrant intellectual community in which to work, write, and laugh. Finally, I am grateful to Maria Grosz-Ngaté, Cindi Katz, Michael Lambek, Sheryl McCurdy, and Rick Schroeder for their insightful critiques and comments on earlier drafts of the paper.

1. Other scholars have also examined spirit possession as a response to certain historical transformations that resulted in a decline in women's economic power or social prestige (see, for example, Harris 1957; Alpers 1984; and Vail and White 1991).

2. I am very grateful to David Peterson for sending me a copy of his unpublished paper and allowing me to use the valuable case studies described within it. In his paper (1971), Peterson included summaries of his interviews with nineteen women and one man who had been possessed. Each case study is between one and four pages long and provides the name, father's name, clan, birthplace, present residence, date of interview, and approximate age of the interviewee. Each study explored when the person first thought she or he was possessed, the initial and later symptoms, how possession was diagnosed and treated, and their involvement with the church, among other details. References to Peterson's case studies are abbreviated as DP/Informant #.

3. From August to October 1992, a disproportionate stratified sample of five adults in each gender-age category, in each of three research communities, were interviewed using an interview guide that explored topics such as marriage, economic rights and relations, religion, education, and perspectives on development. One hundred fifty interviews were taped, transcribed, and sections translated into Swahili. All quotations are my translation, based on the original Maa interview transcript, and my assistant Morani Poyoni's Swahili translations. References to survey materials are abbreviated as SUR/Informant #.

4. Many scholars of spirit possession have supported I. M. Lewis' argument in *Ecstatic Religion* (1971) that possession is a mechanism used by women and other "oppressed" members of society to cope with difficult circumstances in their lives. But studies by Janice Boddy (1989) and Michael Lambek (1981, 1993), among others, have shown the value of exploring spirit possession in terms of its relationship to the cultural meanings, social relations, and historical context of the wider society.

5. The colonial border between Tanzania and Kenya cut through the center of areas historically occupied by Maasai, so there is no "northern" border between Maasai and non-Maasai in Tanzania.

6. See Hodgson 1995, especially Chapters II and III, for a detailed discussion of the "disasters," the resulting scattering of Maa-speaking peoples, and their eventual reconsolidation by British administrators beginning in 1919 onto the Maasai Reserve. Waller (1988) also provides a valuable description of the crisis, although his material focuses on Maasai living in Kenya.

7. According to Shorter (1970), the *migawo* spirit possession cult and Christianity appeared at the same time in southern Ukimbu, but were seen by Kimbu people as incompatible, and "[t]he picture which the Kimbu have of the *migawo* differs radically from the traditional Christian concept of the Devil" (1970:124).

8. Out of the three communities, only one man was afflicted. He underwent instruction for baptism, was baptized and cured, and quit going to church. Male symptoms are reported to be different: During an acute attack, the man sits silently like a deaf and dumb person. Peterson discovered only two cases of possesssed men out of hundreds of women (1971), and only two of the eighty-three case studies of orpeko collected by Hurskainen were men (1985:24). Other factors, including clan membership, number of children, economic status of household, and relationships with co wives and husband, were not found to be significant indicators of which women became ill (Hurskainen 1985:24–26).

9. Koritschoner discusses another kind of relation between naming and the symptoms: "The number of sheitani is almost countless, but it seems that the different names are merely the names for the different symptoms" (1936:211).

10. Although women do have a few sources of income, including selling milk, alcohol, or tobacco, or, for a very few, providing midwifery or circumcision services, none of these provide a substantial income (Hodgson 1995, especially Chapter VII).

11. As were certain Maasai men who went to school, became Christians, participated in state political structures, or otherwise failed to conform to this reified and essentialized notion of Maasai masculinity—they were called *ormeek*, a derogatory term for non-Maasai and other Africans who adopted the attributes of modernity. See Hodgson n.d.a for a detailed exploration of the formation of these mutually exclusive masculinities, as well as contemporary shifts in their attributes and valuation as more and more Maasai men necessarily embrace education and political involvement in the nation-state.

12. According to Spencer (1988:205) these ritual attacks *(olkishiroto)* occur primarily if a woman has a series of stillbirths or miscarriages, both signs that the woman engaged in prohibited intercourse during the tabooed pregnancy period. Furious, neighboring women descend at sunrise on the guilty woman's home, beating her with sticks, cutting her brow, destroying her house, beating her husband unless he can convince them of his innocence, and beating then eventually slaughtering one of the husband's prized oxen. Similarly, during women's fertility gatherings *(oloiroishi)*, women may attack men who prevent their wives from participating in the ritual or beat them during this time (Spencer 1988:201).

13. Lambek (1993) also discusses embodiment as a seemingly gender-neutral phenomenon, although mainly women are possessed in Mayotte. In contrast, gender is central to Boddy's analysis of *zar* spirit possession, but she frames her discussion of embodiment in terms of a "body-as-text" analysis, which, as Stoller warns, mutes its sensory richness (1989).

14.   Koritschoner reports that women possessed by the Ruhani *sheitani* dreamt about white turbans, figures of a white color (not Europeans) that alternately approached and receded (1936:211). All of the spirits in Ujiji in western Tanzania are also white, but not European (Sheryl McCurdy, personal communication). Janzen argues that "across the ngoma region, whiteness defines the special transitional status of the sufferer-novice in the course towards health" (Janzen 1992:101).

15.   The incidence of *ngomas* is decreasing as attendance at church increases.

16.   Small churches and communities of Christians are now scattered throughout Maasai areas, although usually only one denomination is present in an area. Possessed women will therefore attend the closest church, regardless of denomination. Some pastors and priests are more understanding than others about *orpeko*, but even baptism by an unsympathetic priest will "cure" possession.

17.   Since Peterson presents only his English summary of his interviews, it is difficult to know whether the women spoke of *orpeko* as Satan, the devil, or demons. He infers that most perceived *orpeko* in terms of demon possession, which explains the success of the church in exorcising the demons.

BIBLIOGRAPHY

Alpers, Edward. 1984. "'Ordinary Household Chores': Ritual and Power in a 19th-Century Swahili Women's Spirit Possession Cult." *International Journal of African Historical Studies* 17(4):677–702.

Benson, Rev. Stanley. 1980. "The Conquering Sacrament: Baptism and Demon Possession Among the Maasai of Tanzania." *Africa Theological Journal* 9:52–61.

Boddy, Janice. 1989. *Wombs and Alien Spirits: Women, Men and the Zar Cult in Northern Sudan*. Madison: University of Wisconsin Press.

Comaroff, Jean and John Comaroff. 1993. "Introduction." *Modernity and Its Malcontents: Ritual and Power in Postcolonial Africa*, Jean Comaroff and John Comaroff, eds. Chicago: University of Chicago Press.

Comaroff, Jean and John Comaroff, eds. 1993. *Modernity and Its Malcontents: Ritual and Power in Postcolonial Africa*. Chicago: University of Chicago Press.

Gomm, Roger. 1979. "Bargaining from Weakness: Spirit Possession on the South Kenya Coast." In *Women and Society: An Anthropological Reader*, ed. by Sharon Tiffany, Montreal: Eden Press.

Hall, Stuart. 1992. "The West and the Rest: Discourse and Power." In *Formations of Modernity*, Stuart Hall and Bram Gieben, eds. Cambridge, UK: Polity Press.

Harris, Grace. 1957. "Possession 'Hysteria' in a Kenya Tribe." *American Anthropologist* 59(6):1046–1066.

Hodgson, Dorothy. n.d.a. "'Once Intrepid Warriors': 'Development,' Modernity and the Modulation of Maasai Masculinities." Unpublished paper.

———. n.d.b. "Engendered Encounters: Men of the Church and the 'Church of Women' in Maasailand, Tanzania, 1950–1993." Unpublished paper.

———. 1995. "The Politics of Gender, Ethnicity, and 'Development': Images, Interventions, and the Reconfiguration of Maasai Identities, 1916-1993." Ph.D. dissertation, Department of Anthropology, University of Michigan.

———. 1996. "Patriarchal Authority and the Case of the Disobedient Daughter: Marriage, Maasai and the Tanzanian State." *Canadian Journal of African Studies* 30(1). In press.

Hurskainen, Arvi. 1985. "Tatizo la Kushikwa na Pepo Umasaini Tanzania" (The Problem of Spirit Possession in Maasailand, Tanzania). Helsinki. Privately circulated paper, commissioned by the Catholic and Lutheran churches, Tanzania.

————. 1989. "The Epidemiological Aspect of Spirit Possession among the Maasai of Tanzania." In *Culture, Experience and Pluralism: Essays on African Ideas of Illness and Healing*, Anita Jacobson-Widding and David Westerlund, eds. Uppsala: Almqvist and Wiksell International.

Janzen, John. 1992. *Ngoma: Discourses of Healing in Central and Southern Africa*. Berkeley: University of California Press.

Koritschoner, Hans. 1936. "Ngoma ya Sheitani: An East African Native Treatment for Psychical Disorder." *Journal of the Royal Anthropological Institute* 66:209–219.

Lambek, Michael. 1981. *Human Spirits: A Cultural Account of Trance in Mayotte*. New York: Cambridge University Press.

————. 1993. *Knowledge and Practice in Mayotte: Local Discourses of Islam, Sorcery, and Spirit Possession*. Toronto: Univerity of Toronto Press.

Lewis, I. M. 1971. *Ecstatic Religion: An Anthropological Study of Spirit Possession and Shamanism*. Middlesex: Pelican.

Martin, Emily. 1987. *The Woman in the Body: A Cultural Analysis of Reproduction*. Boston: Beacon Press.

Micale, Mark S. 1995. *Approaching Hysteria: Disease and Its Interpretations*. Princeton: Princeton University Press.

Ong, Aihwa. 1987. *Spirits of Resistance and Capitalist Discipline: Factory Women in Malaysia*. Albany: SUNY Press.

Peterson, David. 1971. "Demon Possession Among the Maasai." Unpublished paper.

Shorter, Aylward. 1970. "The *Migawo*: Peripheral Spirit Possession and Christian Prejudice." *Anthropos* 65(1/2):100–126.

Spencer, Paul. 1988. *The Maasai of Matapato: A Study of Ritual of Rebellion*. Bloomington: Indiana University Press.

Stoller, Paul. 1994. "Embodying Colonial Memories." *American Anthropologist* 96(3): 634–648.

Vail, Leroy and Landeg White. 1991. "The Possession of the Dispossessed: Song as History Among Tumbuka Women." In *Power and the Praise Poem: Southern African Voices in History*. Charlottesville: University Press of Virginia.

Waller, Richard. 1988. "Emutai: Crisis and Response in Maasailand, 1883-1902." In *The Ecology of Survival: Case Studies from Northeast African History*, Douglas Johnson and David Anderson, eds. Boulder, CO: Westview.

Watts, Michael. 1992. "Capitalisms, Crises, and Culture I: Notes Toward a Totality of Fragments." In *Reworking Modernity: Capitalisms and Symbolic Discontent*, by Allan Pred and Michael Watts. New Brunswick, NJ: Rutgers University Press.

Wilson, Peter. 1967. "Status Ambiguity and Spirit Possession." *Man* (n.s.) 2(3):366–378.

ISLAM, TRANSNATIONAL CULTURE, AND MODERNITY IN RURAL SUDAN

Victoria Bernal

Global cultural flows are usually presumed to originate in the West. Islamic culture, on the other hand, is often seen as static and monolithic (Said 1979). Islamic cultural flows, thus, have been rendered invisible within the world system. While the so-called Islamic revival has commanded much attention, this has centered on political groups and the state. Less recognized is the cultural component of global Islamic trends and the changes taking place among ordinary Muslims in ritual practice, expressions of identity, and consumption patterns. Muslim societies, in particular, are often simplistically seen as resisting "Westernization." It has been assumed, moreover, that to be modern is to be secular. Islam has been cast as the authentic and indigenous, while foreign often is equated with Western. This has led many observers to misunderstand the contemporary Islamic "revival" as a rejection of modernity and the West.

This chapter explores the rise of Islamic fundamentalism in a Sudanese village (Wad al Abbas) where the course of change runs counter to established assumptions.[1] Foreign influences in Wad al Abbas are as likely to be Islamic as they are Western, and Islamic culture blurs the distinction between foreign and indigenous, because it is both. Western and Islamic cultures, moreover, are closely intertwined in villagers' experience, rather than appearing as irreconcilable opposites. Furthermore, for the villagers of Wad al Abbas, the fundamentalist forms of Islam that predominate in the global Islamic revival are not traditional; they represent a cosmopolitan, modern Muslim identity (Bernal 1994). Local rituals and religious practices are seen as deviating from orthodox Islam, which in the 1980s was largely represented by Saudi Arabia (McDonnell 1990). Thus, modernity enters in the guise of (Islamic) tradition, and foreign ways claim an authenticity denied local practices. New understandings of Islam and new styles of Islamic dress are appealing to villagers in part because they are associated with sources of power and prestige abroad, rather than rooted in local social formations.

Through practices of sex segregation and female seclusion, gender is a central organizing principle of social life in Wad al Abbas. Gender plays a significant role in the intersection of local and global cultures in Wad al Abbas, where women are cast as custodians of local tradition and men represent modernity. The behavior and appearance of women have assumed particular significance for villagers in the process of reevaluating their way of life.

This essay explores the complex processes shaping the ways villagers reproduce and transform gender, culture, and identity in a global context.[2] The first section, "Labor Migration and Transnational Culture," explores the significance of villagers' relations with Saudi Arabia. The next section, "'Westernization' and Islam," explores the ways in which Western and Islamic cultures are fused in the global culture reaching Wad al Abbas and in local practices. "Ambivalence, Modernity, and Gender" turns to the contradictory character of villagers' integration into global circuits and explores the ways in which women come to represent local identity and tradition, and become the symbolic focus of fundamentalist reform. The final section, "Forging Modern Identities and Folkloric Traditions," considers the ways in which culture becomes style in the expression of individual identity, and folklore replaces tradition as a symbol of communal identity.

The global Islamic revival is, among other things, a movement from local particularized Islams to Islam as a world religion. Certain forms of religious practice, identified as truly Islamic because they have roots in the holy texts, are gaining ascendency over other, localized Islamic traditions. This clearly is a modernist project if we accept, for example, Rabinow's definition of modernist as "the attempt to efface history and cultural specificity through universal formal operations which are ultimately their own referent" (1992:249). Thus, in one sense globalization *is* contributing to cultural homogenization, as has so often been predicted, but for some people this homogenization does not mean Westernization but rather becoming more like their fellow Muslims elsewhere. As Hefner (1987:75) points out, the concern of world religions with

> formal education, the written word, abstract ethical codes, universal prophets, and holy lands for all of humankind serves to elevate their appeal above more restricted terrains. They provide the discourse for the elaboration of a secondary moral and ideological identity beyond that given in the immediacy of local groupings.

The villagers of Wad al Abbas have always identified themselves as Muslims. Their community was founded by a Sufi holy man for whom it is named. But, in the 1980s, local practices such as the veneration of holy men and their tombs increasingly came into question. A growing number of villagers began to argue, in keeping with fundamentalist ideas, that worship of holy individuals or sites contradicts the monotheism so central to Islam. Thus, the network of local allegiances and regional loyalties, the veritable religious landscape of Sudan, was being transformed as religion was mapped along a much more international axis. At the national level, Sudanese politics shifted from the decentralized system of parties connected with Sufi orders that participated in various ways in the apparatus of the state (Al-Karsani 1993) to the formation of a centralized Islamic state under the influence of the fundamentalist

National Islamic Front. At both the local and national levels the move toward a more scripturalist Islam is a movement away from local parochial identities toward perceived conformity with a more universal set of beliefs and practices. Fundamentalist Islam appeals to the villagers of Wad al Abbas as a solution of sorts to the challenges posed by their growing social integration into the world system.

LABOR MIGRATION AND TRANSNATIONAL CULTURE

The villagers of Wad al Abbas have long been linked to the world economy—as producers of cotton since the 1950s and as consumers of imported goods (Bernal 1991). But international labor migration and improvements in transport and communications over the past two decades have altered profoundly the character of villagers' participation in the world system. Information about chances of employment in Saudi Arabia, Abu Dhabi, Iraq, Yemen, and other locales circulates continually in the village, as does news from relatives and fellow villagers working or studying abroad. From the mid-1970s through the 1980s the incorporation of Wad al Abbas into the world system was mediated to a great extent by Saudi Arabia.[3] The national economic and identity crises of Sudan and the labor migration of villagers to urban Sudan and Saudi Arabia were catalysts of change, stimulating the rise of "fundamentalist" Islam in the village.

The most significant source of global Islamic culture reaching Wad al Abbas during the 1980s was Saudi Arabia. As guardian of the holy cities to which Muslims the world over make pilgrimages, Saudi Arabia has long wielded worldwide influence over Islamic practice. The wealth of the 1970s oil boom, however, gave Saudi Arabia and other Middle Eastern states and individuals the economic means to support various Islamic endeavors and organizations around the world (Hijab 1988; Sanad and Tessler 1990; von der Mehden 1993). It also brought Muslims from many lands to Saudi Arabia as migrant workers. Saudi Arabia exerted influence on Sudan at the national level, pressuring then-president Numeiri to institute *shari'a* law in 1983, for example, and funding fundamentalist opposition groups such as the Muslim Brotherhood (Riad 1990; Voll 1986; Warburg 1991). At the same time, Saudi Arabia drew ordinary Sudanese from all walks of life to its shores as labor migrants. While in past generations some villagers from Wad al Abbas had made the Hajj, in the early 1980s every villager knew someone from Wad al Abbas working in Saudi Arabia.

There was a steady traffic between the village and *"al Mumlika"* (the kingdom), as some local cognoscenti liked to refer to it. Moreover, as one villager explained, "Before, people went to Saudiya just for the Hajj. They didn't see anything else. But now they go everywhere." Even in the 1980s it was common practice for villagers making the Hajj to travel as a group and to bring with them most of the supplies they expected to use on the pilgrimage—dried meat, clarified butter, spices, and various ingredients for meals and drinks. Labor migrants, who usually stay for a year or two and are generally employed in urban areas, experience life in Saudi Arabia much more fully than pilgrims, shopping in the markets, riding public transportation, interacting with Saudi employers and the public. While the majority of Wad al Abbas households own land and continue to do some farming, none of the villagers employed in Saudi Arabia worked in agriculture. They performed such jobs as truck drivers, electricians, factory workers, and shopkeeping. Migration abroad drew villagers into international culture as never before. In the 1980s the movement of people, ideas, and things between the village and Saudi Arabia touched the lives of all villagers whether they traveled themselves or not.

Villagers encounter new things and ideas from other parts of Sudan, of course, most particularly in the capital city, Khartoum. However, the primacy of Saudi Arabia was evident in a number of ways. A ten-year-old girl remarked in surprise, "I thought Khartoum was in Saudi Arabia," a telling statement revealing how national boundaries are blurred by the flows of people and culture, and indicating at once both the relative remoteness of Khartoum and the proximity of Saudi Arabia. An older woman said her relative went to "some place near Saudiya—what's it called?— London," her statement reflecting a Saudi-centered geography in which divisions between East and West are not significant. Indeed, from villagers' standpoints such divisions may pale beside the glaring differences in wealth that separate Sudan from the Gulf States and the West.

Migrants brought home clothes, shampoo, tape decks, TVs, VCRs, and even refrigerators (years before the village was electrified). Through migrants' purchases abroad, new products and things unavailable in Sudan circulate in the village. Local consumer culture is shaped in part by what men bring back, but having seen what neighbors have, women also make specific requests. One adult married woman recounted with pride how she had continually repeated her demand that her brother bring her a watch, until he finally did. In the village, a woman has little practical use for a watch—since time is not reckoned by minutes or even hours, but by markers such as dawn, lunchtime, evening prayer, and the like. Yet by the early 1980s watches had become a fixed part of the groom's "traditional" gifts to the bride. These gifts, called *shebka*, include a gold wedding band, a watch, and sometimes other gold jewelry as well.

The watch, like the jewelry, is an ornament and a luxury consumer good symbolizing affluence and well-being. But the watch is also a symbol of modernity, harking to the rhythms of urban life and formal employment. That the watch is a symbol of a certain world order rather than a true timepiece is illustrated by an exchange I had with a young man. Noticing he sported a watch, I asked the time. He indicated his watch and replied offhandedly, "Oh, it doesn't work." It was clear from his manner that this was of little consequence. The image of this man dressing in the morning and strapping on his stopped watch in some way encapsulates the dynamic of northern Sudan in the 1980s, where development was deadlocked and people could do little to satisfy their aspirations but embrace icons of progress. Women's desire for watches is one testament to their participation in the mystique of modernity even if they have little opportunity to experience urban life or travel outside the village.

Since women do not have direct access to employment abroad or in most cases much cash income from any source, they are reduced to satisfying their demands for consumer goods through male relatives whom they can pressure for things. Women are in that sense the quintessential consumers; men experience them as a drain on their resources. While in the West, the image of women eating men's leftovers signifies an extreme form of subordination, one local man expressed the image of women as voracious consumers jokingly, saying, "They eat their own food and ours, too!" (He was referring to the fact that at big feasts, women eat leftover delicacies from the men's trays when they are sent back to the kitchen.) The image of woman as consumer is not particularly new in Wad al Abbas, but it takes on new meanings when production, the generation of wealth, and the sources of consumer goods are so removed from the village.

Migrants bring back not just consumer goods, but also new understandings of what it means to be Sudanese, to be Arab, and to be Muslim. Travel abroad is transformative. One way this is symbolized in Wad al Abbas is through dress; people returning from abroad often dress differently, at least in the initial period upon their return. One migrant, for example, sported a tailored Western-style suit jacket over his *jellabiya* when he got back from Saudi Arabia. An older woman who had traveled to Saudi Arabia to visit her migrant sons and also made the *umra* pilgrimage[4] received the guests who came to welcome her home attired in a long shocking-pink nightgown, a brightly patterned *towb* (the head-to-toe cloth wrap worn by adult women), Dr. Scholl's sandals, and a lime-green string of prayer beads around her wrist. Her choices were a striking departure from the simple, austere clothing such as beige or black *towbs* usually worn by senior Wad al Abbas women.

Travel abroad is a special category of experience and labor migrants who go abroad are referred to by the special term *mukhteribiin* (singular, *mukhterib*), unlike men who work outside the village within Sudan. *Mukhterib*, furthermore, is a social status and an occupational category in its own right—the actual work that the person does abroad is secondary. Children and even wives might describe their father or husband as a *mukhterib* without knowing exactly what work he does. In contrast, labor migrants from Wad al Abbas who work elsewhere in Sudan are described simply in terms of their occupation or by their occupation and place of work, such as "he is a trader in Renk." The gendered nature of *mukhterib* status is captured in the fact that I never heard anyone utter the hypothetical feminine form of *mukhterib*—*mukhteriba*. Through the 1980s Wad al Abbas men were highly mobile, while women remained basically immobile.

Since salaries are much higher abroad, *mukhteribs* are associated with wealth and luxury consumption. A returning *mukhterib* is greeted like a king. The celebration of a *mukhterib*'s return begins with an impromptu parade from his disembarkation point in the village as news spreads and people begin to flock over. Ideally a sheep is slaughtered before the migrant's foot crosses the threshold of his home. A *karama* (a feast with an animal sacrifice) is performed if at all possible to give thanks for the safe return. Through the ritual of *karama* the occasion is invested with religious as well as social meaning. The whole village is alerted to an important event as men shoot off rifles and women ululate, attracting even more people. Migrants usually spend a week or more at home greeting guests and making the rounds to offer condolences to those families that lost loved ones during the migrant's absence. Migrants spend much time recounting their experiences.

In the early 1980s it was established practice for migrants to bring back suitcases loaded with gifts to distribute among relatives, neighbors, and anyone who came by to welcome them back home. Through the accounts of *mukhteribs* and the wealth and goods they brought back, Saudi Arabia captivated the imaginations of villagers. *Mukhteribs* arrived in the village with savings amassed from their wages, consumer goods purchased abroad, and a new sense of the world and their place in it. New sources of wealth, consumption patterns, and new understandings of what it means to be a Muslim were intertwined.

One way that villagers (migrants and others) articulated the changes in their lives was through pronouncements about Islam and what was and was not truly Islamic. Thus, after describing in detail the pattern of funeral and mourning practices (*bika*) in Wad al Abbas, a villager ended his account with the caveat "but in Islam and *shari'a* there is no *bika*." Village wedding practices, funeral rituals, and reverence for holy men were particularly held up as examples of local deviation from true Islam. When I began fieldwork in the early 1980s most villagers I spoke with understood being Muslim to mean being like, and living like, them. For example, before new notions of "Islamic" dress came to the village, a woman described the *towb* to me as "from God." By the time I returned to the village in 1988, the locus of moral authority had shifted. Islam clearly had its center outside the community; local culture and behavior were now being measured against new standards derived from external sources.

"WESTERNIZATION" AND ISLAM

Globalization means that villagers live their daily lives in a larger world. It is a world in which during the 1980s some villagers were watching *Dallas* on battery-operated TVs and some local young women began to wear new forms of "Islamic" attire fashioned after that worn by women in Saudi Arabia and the Gulf states. Yet the Islamic revival in Wad al Abbas is misunderstood if seen simply as a rejection of all things Western or as a contest between East and West. In fact, contemporary Islam and perhaps its revivalist forms in particular are inextricably intertwined with Western institutions, technology, and consumer goods. The leader of Sudan's National Islamic Front (NIF), Dr. Hasan al-Turabi, is the product of a Western education. Indeed, it has been suggested that Islamists are simply applying Western intellectual tools to Islam (Simone 1994). Moreover, Simone (1994), referring to the Sudanese case, warns that Islamic movements may become the West in Islamic garb. Rather than resisting the influence of Western culture, the villagers of Wad al Abbas have embraced it through the medium of a modernizing Islam.

Islam and "Westernization" often are presumed to be opposed; the case of Wad al Abbas reveals a much more interesting relationship. The complexity of Wad al Abbas—and Sudan's positions in global circuits—is illustrated, among other things, by the fact that the *towbs* regarded as the finest by Sudanese (Risala brand) are manufactured in England. Villagers are well aware of this fact, often referring to these *towbs* as "Risalat London," the *towb's* provenance adding to its cachet. Photographs brought back by *mukhteribs* show that some of them wear Western dress in Saudi Arabia. Wedding exchanges in the 1980s often included Nivea creme, Prophecy perfume, and Wella shampoo along with the cloth, flour, coffee, and incense given by the groom to the bride's household.[5]

The influence of Western culture reaches into villagers' lives through varied and diffuse means. Western media and Western institutions such as development schemes, public schools, and other bureaucracies communicate (by their very form as well as their content) a particular vision of society (Foucault 1979; Mitchell 1988). The pervasive influence of Western culture within Sudan is recognized by the current NIF-dominated regime in its attempt to "Islamize" knowledge and revamp university curricula, for example. Only three villagers that I knew of in the 1980s had traveled to the West, however, and only one had returned to Sudan by then. In contrast, there was a steady traffic between Wad al Abbas and the Arab world, but most particularly Saudi Arabia.[6] Travel is especially significant because, despite advances in media and communications technology, new ideas, new styles, and information were largely transmitted to Wad al Abbas by individuals from the community.

Media remained a small fragment of communication. Wad al Abbas was not electrified until 1988, and televisions were rare. A few villagers owned TVs operated by car batteries and shared viewing with relatives and neighbors. Among the villagers with access to television, Egyptian soap operas were popular. These shows embody a blend of cultures since the Egyptian characters are usually Westernized elites. Their allure is reflected in the fact that one village couple named a daughter after a soap opera character. Print media were virtually absent from Wad al Abbas, where literacy was not widespread. Cassettes were used to circulate some things, including music, sermons, and personal correspondence from *mukhteribs* to their families.

Radio was the most important medium and most Wad al Abbas households owned one. Radio programs were highly varied in form and content; among them were some that explicitly sought to teach about Islam. But even in more subtle ways radio was changing the character of religious life in the village. For example, during Ramadan some families listened to Radio Omdurman for the signal to break their daily fast, while others listened to the village muezzin. The radio formed part of the holiday ritual for many villagers who tuned in and heard chants of "*la allah ila allah*" and "*allahu akhbar*." On the Mawlid[7] some villagers listened intently to radio programs that taught about the Prophet. Women, in particular, usually cited radio as a source of their knowledge about Islam, because most adult women had received little *khalwa* (or public education).

Transnational culture as experienced by the villagers of Wad al Abbas is a fusion of Western and Islamic. Various Western goods and practices go hand in hand with imports of Islamic ideas and fashions. Many Western products enter the village via Saudi Arabia and some Islamic goods, such as Risala *towbs,* are imported from the West. Saudi Arabia is not a big producer of goods, but itself relies on imports from the world market, many of them Western products.[8] Thus, Western consumer goods commonly enter Sudan via Saudi Arabia, blurring the distinction between things Western and those Islamic. Villagers, moreover, perceive Saudi adherence to "orthodox" practice, their wealth, and the abundance of goods and modern conveniences in Saudi Arabia as interconnected. Modernity and Islamic orthodoxy are seen not as contradictory (as they may appear in the West, where it is assumed that to be modern is to be Western and secular) but as two facets of the same thing. At the national level, Islamic fundamentalist identity is "synonymous with wealth and economic success" (Al-Karsani 1993:152). For many villagers, Saudi Arabia was, therefore, a vision of the future. As one man expressed it, "Before there was no money, now there is some, soon it [Sudan] will be like Saudiya."

In villagers' minds the luxury consumption enjoyed by the Saudis is associated with a more literate, urban understanding of Islam, just as village poverty and local practice are intertwined. The words of one villager, who remarked that "before, people [in Wad al Abbas] were so poor and ignorant, now they understand Islam better," reflect this constellation of related things. Economic development and technological advance also are associated with Islam. Meetings concerning such issues as the village water pumps are held at a village *zawia*.[9] One of the prime movers in local efforts to establish running water and, later, electricity is also a leading figure in the local shift toward fundamentalist Islam. Villagers refer to this young man (who, in the early 1980s, was studying for a master's degree at the Islamic University in Omdurman) as the Mawlana, in recognition of his knowledge of Islam. Perhaps because of his piety, people of the region trusted him with the large sums of money collected for electrification, reportedly totalling £S500,000 in the late 1980s.

Western bureaucratic forms derived from colonial and post-colonial administrative practices are ubiquitous in Wad al Abbas. There is a board (*lijna*) for this and a board for that, including one to reform local wedding practices. Every ceremonial celebration, be it a wedding or a circumcision, has someone with a notebook, usually a schoolboy sitting at a table, who records the cash donation given by each guest.[10] Thus, ritual is bureaucratized, harnessing the power of literacy—a skill with both religious and material value. And bureaucracy is ritualized; through the ritual of formal record keeping, villagers can appropriate for themselves and demystify the powers of officialdom.

Asha, a village *shaykha* (*zar* possession cult leader), models her seances on the bureaucratic pattern of Western medicine, refering to the meetings as *keshif,* the term used for medical appointments. She keeps her incense and various things in a small box resembling a toolkit and similar to that used by the government-trained midwives and other health practioners. While entranced, Asha not only speaks Arabic, but *rhutan* (dialect) that is supposed to be *Habeshi* (Ethiopian), although it is actually a modified Arabic, and therefore not entirely unintelligible to the participants. Among Asha's paraphernalia is the colonial tarbush. The example of the *zar* (Boddy 1989) is instructive because it confounds any notion that local culture ever was unadulterated or produced autonomously by the community. The practices introduced in the name of true Islam in the 1980s build upon earlier syncretisms.

Wedding celebrations are another vibrant local tradition that is anything but static. Marriage contracts are formalized by men at the village mosque, but marriages are completed through a series of rituals, sacrifices, and feasts that lasts for seven days or more. Wad al Abbas brides decorated with henna dance barefoot to the lively beat of the *diluka* (Sudanese drum) and the singing of unmarried girls.[11] Among the wedding songs popular in the early 1980s was one about a Toyota pickup truck and another about gasoline in which Shell and Mobil were mentioned by name.[12]

Western-style white wedding dresses are worn by some brides for part of the festivities. As surprising as the revelation that traditions are invented (Hobsbawm 1983) is the realization that tradition is constantly reinvented. The invention of tradition is not an act but an ongoing process. Like the *zar* seance and the wedding, which blend various elements of African, Islamic, and Western culture, village ceremonial life draws its power and vitality from diverse sources. Islam plays a special role in this process, helping to fuse the indigenous and the exogenous.

Despite the fluid, syncretic properties of culture, the process of transformation in Wad al Abbas is nonetheless fraught with tensions. For example, in the early 1980s some young men got the idea of taking their brides to a hotel for a honeymoon, as some urban Sudanese were doing. As one of these men pointed out, a honeymoon would completely violate the tradition of secluding the bride; usually even the groom doesn't see his bride except at night for at least the first forty days of marriage. This particular groom was forbidden a hotel honeymoon by his father and uncles, who said, "We don't want one of our family to be the first one in the village to do this." The elder men's fear of standing out as a target for criticism sheds light on the role of Islam as an agent of change. Deviations from local practice that can be justified in terms of more closely obeying Islam clearly leave one less vulnerable to reproach.

Transnational fundamentalist forms of Islam thus provide a moral basis to argue against local tradition and practice. The indeterminacy of orthodoxy, moreover, allows a certain flexibility. In this way change can be represented as *tradition* rather than as innovation.

AMBIVALENCE, MODERNITY, AND GENDER

One thing communicated to the Sudanese in Saudi Arabia where their place—as immigrant workers, as blacks, and as Muslims from a poor country—is not an exalted one, is a vision of hierarchy. There is a great contrast, moreover, between the life that Wad al Abbas villagers actually live in Saudi Arabia, often sharing quarters with other workers and saving as much of their pay as possible, and the life of leisure and prosperity that villagers perceive the Saudis to enjoy and to which they aspire. Tensions are inherent in the process whereby villagers' vision of progress is one that devalues local identities and practices. In the global hierarchy perceived by the villagers of Wad al Abbas, it is better to be Arab than African, scripturalist understandings of Islam are superior to local ritual understandings, and the knowledge associated with worldly sophistication and formal education is more respected than local knowledge. Given the differences in women's and men's lives, this hierarchy is clearly gendered.

Through the 1980s villagers were actively articulating the distinctions between provincial and cosmopolitan, traditional and modern. In important respects women came to symbolize tradition, while men stood for modernity. The signs, symbols, and commodities associated with the Islamic revival were key components of local constructions of the modern.[13] Even trivial practices assumed importance as statements of conformity with either a more international Islamic sensibility or a provincial one. For example, some villagers made a point that it was *haram* (forbidden) to wear a watch (or anything) on the left hand. A woman explaining this to me added in support of this view, "The university students all wear their watches on the right hand," again linking "correct" Islamic behavior with education, sophistication, and elite status.

In Saudi Arabia migrants experience harsh exploitation and capitalist relations of employment unmediated by social ties. *Mukhteribs* generally do not dwell on the denigration they experience in the Gulf, perhaps because it would detract from the local view of the migrant as a success—a returning hero with booty from abroad. However, no migrant I spoke with had been invited into a Saudi home, something they were well aware of, given the open hospitality for which Sudanese are rightly renowned. Saudis treat the Sudanese as stigmatized outsiders, sometimes denigrating them as *abid* (slave) because of their dark skin. One villager actually filed a court case against a Saudi who insulted him by addressing him as *ya abid* ("hey, slave"). Another villager returned home earlier than expected, explaining, "The Saudis don't like people from outside. I will only go back there if I make the Hajj, otherwise not." Among a group of women talking about Saudi Arabia, one said, laughing at these uncomfortable thoughts:

> They won't give their daughters to a Sudanese. They don't want us. Like the
> Fellata [Sudanese of Nigerian descent who are regarded as inferior]. They
> call us *"abid al arab"* [slaves of the Arabs].

"You are a Saudi," said a *mukhterib,* congratulating the host of a huge circumcision celebration for his sons, meaning "you are wealthy" (from the cash donations offered by all of the guests). He went on to explain to a group of guests, "She [indicating me] comes from the *biggest* government in the world—you come from the smallest." This was in fact not the usual context of my social relations in Wad al Abbas at all, but his sojourn abroad had given him a different perspective on things. Another *mukhterib,* musing on his experiences abroad, asserted to me, "We Sudanese are *better* than the Arabs, because we are a blend of African and Arab." His statement suggests one way of resolving the ambivalence about African and Arab identity that many Sudanese seem to feel.[14]

More typically, villagers strive to claim a broader Arab Muslim identity. One means of expressing this is through adopting what they see as more orthodox Islamic practices or, at the least, paying lip service to "orthodoxy" by criticizing local practices as not properly Islamic. While few people were altering their behavior profoundly, many used disparaging statements about various local practices to assert "I know better." This ethos of estrangement from local custom added another dimension to village life—the vague presence of a global context in which things at Wad al Abbas were not as they ought to be. Given that women are particularly identified with the local, it is no surprise that women's behavior became a central focus of fundamentalist critique.

While men's lives were being transformed by the necessity of working outside the village and even outside of Sudan, the standards for women's comportment and dress became the focus of concern in a way that men's were not. A new construction of masculinity and male superiority was being forged and the differences in men's and women's life experiences were invested with meaning in terms of a natural order of difference between men and women. Comaroff and Comaroff (1993:xxviii) argue that capitalist ideologies of modernity "grouped counterimages under feminized signs—rural, preindustrial, ritualistic, primitive."

This is one way of understanding what is happening at Wad al Abbas when women are cast as provincial and ignorant, while men are seen as advanced and knowledgeable (Bedri 1987). I overheard one man complaining to another, for example, about the dangers of television, saying, "Women hear someone crying on television and mistake it for a *bika* [funeral] and get everyone up in arms." Women, thus, represent the unsophisticated and irrational. And a man can express his own disapproval of television through an argument about its effects on women and (through women) on the community. It is significant, moreover, that this man referred to crying because the local practice of ritual crying by women at funerals was deemed un-Islamic according to the newfound wisdom.

Wad al Abbas weddings also reflect the representation of man as modern and woman as traditional. For example, younger educated grooms wear Western dress rather than the *jellabiya* normally worn by men when in the village. Brides, on the other hand, always appear at least part of the time in Sudanese wedding regalia. Wedding portraits taken in Sennar studios capture this dichotomy; the Western-dressed man stands beside the bride bedecked with a headdress of braids and fake gold coins, a nose ring attached by a chain to her earring, henna up her arms and ankles, as if the man and woman had come from two different cultures.

One way new understandings of Islam are expressed is through the medium of feminine modesty. Villagers' reevaluation of local wedding practices, for example, focused on the ritual dance performed by the bride without a *towb* and before a mixed audience. Moghadam (1994) argues that "identity lies in the private sphere" and women therefore are key symbols in the Islamic resurgence because women represent the private domain. However, the distinction between private and public is itself a historical construction, and one that takes on particular significance in capitalist culture. At Wad al Abbas new Islamic ideals may have helped give meaning to the changing nature of domestic and communal life as villagers increasingly participated in the global economy in ways that drew them away from their households and community.

During the 1980s villagers constructed new forms of private space, and female seclusion increased as villagers adopted new forms of architecture and dress. Up until the early 1980s few village houses were enclosed by courtyard walls. Compounds were demarcated by low mud walls or thornbrush fences, if at all. By the late 1980s, villagers who had the means were building high brick or cement walls around their homes, separating domestic and public space definitively. Less fortunate villagers strove to achieve similar effects through such means as adding burlap screens on top of their mud walls.

The fluidity of the division between public and domestic in the early 1980s was reflected in the fact that women wore their *towbs* all the time, adjusting them in different ways depending on who was present or whether women were at home or in the public thoroughfare. In contrast, by the late 1980s it was common for women to take off their *towbs* completely once they were inside the *hosh* (courtyard). A woman of the family with whom I lived even instructed me to remove my *terha*[15] when I kept it on inside the *hosh* as I always had done before. Some women also began to wear ankle-length robes underneath their *towbs*, rather than the short, sleeveless smocks (*showal*) that had been standard in the early 1980s. Such "Islamic" dress was considered a mark of sophistication.

If fundamentalist forms of Islam represent sophistication and progress, local Islam is regarded as ignorant tradition. Its inferiority is symbolized through its association with women (Ibrahim 1989). Thus, a man dismisses the significance of local *fakis* (holy men) as *"kalam al niswaan"* ("women's talk" or "women's affair"), even though many village men as well as women continue to venerate *shaykhs*, participate in Sufi orders, and make pilgrimages to local shrines.

Women do, however, have less access to knowledge about the world beyond the village and "orthodox" Islam. Despite much talk in the village about other places and Saudi Arabia in particular, few women have seen much of Sudan, let alone been abroad. One woman, for example, does not know Khartoum and so remembers her son's work locale as "Burri" when he works in Bahri. Once, when I referred to the river in Khartoum, an elderly woman exclaimed, "Do they have a river there, too?" unaware that the Blue Nile that flows past the village merges with the White Nile at Khartoum to form the River Nile.

Standing with the women in the open space where villagers had gathered to celebrate *Aeed al Duhiya*, we were too far away to hear the words of the Khalifa and the Mawlana who were the speakers. At the Mawlid celebration where men were reading from the Qur'an to a large audience gathered outside the mosque, I asked a woman why no women were reading. "Do we know how to read?" she replied, "All we know is *surat al salah* [the verses of prayers]." Added another woman, "I don't know the words to the prayers, I only know how to perform the movements."

Women's experiences are rooted in the local. Nonetheless, local self-definitions and gender constructions are contingent on a global context and shaped by transnational cultural flows. From their vantage point in the village women are able, moreover, to perceive various hierarchies that extend beyond it. For example, one day some Nuba[16] girls were teasing a couple of village girls, saying things in a Nuba language the villagers did not understand. The village girls replied in turn with insults in schoolgirl English, adding in Arabic (the shared language) a further assertion of superiority: "*We* speak English, *you* speak dialect."

Despite their different positioning relative to sources of scriptural knowledge and "orthodox" practice abroad, women are active participants in the diffusion of new Islamic ideas entering the village. Women discuss and exchange information, such as that "sheikh so-and-so" said that dyeing your hair was *haram*, that it was said on the radio that women should not hold jobs, or that a newly fundamentalist village man said all pictures are *haram* and forced his family to dispose of their television set. New ideas like these circulated through the village like rumors. In discussing local practices that were being brought into question, women often used vague language such as "they say it is *haram*," this formulation reflecting the speaker's lack of direct knowledge of scriptural Islam. Such formulations also give a sense of the disembodied form in which cultural critique transpired in Wad al Abbas; rather than being definitively associated with particular proponents, the new fundamentalism was a pervasive ethos. Thus, a woman explained to me, "We used to go to the river for every [ceremonial] occasion, but now people are dropping it." Another said "When my father died I put dirt on my head and wailed, but now I learned that that is *haram* and when you die on the last day you will be interrogated." Another woman told me, "In the past [when a widow had completed her mourning seclusion] she would shave her pubic hair and cut her nails and bury them in the dust of his [her husband's] grave." All the women present laughed at this, and one exclaimed, "Isn't that bad! We don't do that anymore."

But women do not simply accept all new ideas or comply with them equally. For example, while in one discussion women seemed to be taking seriously the idea that hair dye might be unacceptable, they casually dismissed the idea that women should not be employed, saying, "We can't go by that." Telling about how girls, but not boys, are restricted in the high-school dormitories in Sennar (the closest high school to Wad al Abbas), a girl commented bitterly, "Only girls are forbidden everything." A young woman and her audience laughed disdainfully as she recounted how the Mawlana rode all the way from Sennar (an hour away) with his eyes shut because there were women present in the vehicle. An eighty-year-old woman, referring to the subdued funerals becoming more common as a result of the new fundamentalist sensibility, commented critically, "People have given up mourning the dead."

Since the younger generation of women have opportunities for formal education and literacy, the cultural gap between them and their male peers is smaller. The first two Wad al Abbas women ever to finish high school graduated in 1981. Over the course of the 1980s growing numbers of women gained experience outside the village, pursuing education, accompanying migrant husbands, and one even working abroad (as a teacher) along with her husband. One of the few women to travel to Saudi Arabia with her husband now talks to me as a fellow sophisticate, asking questions about where America is located. She has a new sense of the world and of our places in this larger system. She is one of the younger women who have adopted a new style of dress, wearing an ankle-length *ibaya* (long flowing dress).

Along with new Islamic sensibilities have come other new parameters of conduct for women in the expanding social field. One of the first female high-school graduates from Wad al Abbas got a job teaching school in the village. She said:

> People thought that a girl going to school or working in an office with men—there would be *aeb* [shame], that she would not know how to keep her honor [*sharafha*]. But now they saw that girls have studied and worked and nothing bad has come of it. So they're all letting their daughters study. In fact, many are paying to have their daughters in evening school now so they can get their degrees.

Another young woman told me:

> Before it was considered *aeb* [shameful] for a woman to travel. But people
> opened their minds and got educated a little and saw that it's OK and now
> so many go. . . . People in the past didn't let a girl work. Women weren't ed-
> ucated and she may bring *ayr* [dishonor] to her family and they're afraid of
> that. But now girls are educated and know how to behave.

While in the early 1980s women sent children to make purchases in the village
shops, by 1988 women made such purchases themselves. "We used to scold women
for that and say *aeb,* but not anymore," said one woman, linking this change in attitude to education and "understanding."

Young women are also consulted more often now as part of the marriage pro-
posal process. When I asked an older woman about this change, she said her recently
engaged son had talked to the girl "before he even talked to his own father."
She explained:

> Before, the boy and girl weren't educated. The girl would *tekhjil* [be shy].[17]
> It's better now. Before, you didn't know whether the girl wanted or not. If
> she was unhappy or if she was pleased, she was married all the same. Now if
> she wants, OK, if she doesn't want, she refuses right away. It's better.

By the late 1980s education was accepted as a positive thing for both boys and
girls by many villagers. Marriage nonetheless remained a priority in parents' concerns
for daughters. While parents generally wished to delay a son's marriage until the
young man had worked for a while and contributed economically to the family, a
good marriage was of such paramount importance where daughters were concerned
that girls were withdrawn from school to be secluded once engaged. There were signs
of change in the 1980s, however, as some grooms encouraged their prospective in-
laws to keep girls in school, in some cases even paying for school expenses. Young
men's greater opportunities, relative to older men, for labor migration, and particularly for work abroad, was giving them greater say in the matter of marriage because
grooms were assuming greater responsibility for their own wedding expenses and for
establishing the new conjugal unit.[18] The shift of generational power from older to
younger men is reflected in changing notions of what is desirable in a bride—young
grooms want a bride who is consenting to the marriage, and they are also more likely
to want a bride with some education.[19]

Thus, even as women become the symbolic focus of fundamentalist reform
and of local tradition, women are gaining greater control over their marital destiny,
obtaining education, and, in a few cases, even garnering their own incomes through
formal employment. Increasing Islamic "orthodoxy" and expanding horizons

for women are not so much opposing processes as two facets of the larger transformation of the village resulting from capitalist expansion and incorporation into global cultural circuits.

FORGING MODERN IDENTITIES AND FOLKLORIC TRADITIONS

A significant element in the process of transformation in Wad al Abbas is the objectification of culture and the ability of individuals to "play" with cultural forms and craft a more individualized identity and style. The intensified contact with powerful others such as the Saudis who do not share their culture allows villagers to see their culture through strangers' eyes. They thus experience a kind of alienation that allows them to be critical and self-consciously aware of their own culture (and alternatives to it). Migrants also become estranged from village culture after years away. The focus of fundamentalist critique on particular practices held up as bad examples both reflects and further intensifies this process, by isolating specific practices from the larger cultural context.

This process opens up space in which individuals can "play" with culture to create a personal style, inventing individual solutions to the questions of identity raised by global encounters. Culture is objectified and made manipulable as different imported and indigenous elements are combined in novel formations by various individuals. Thus, for example, appearance and presentation of self took on new meaning as the range of choices expanded.

Women's dress and hairstyles are an important area of such individual creativity. Islamic dress (*hijab*) does not so much replace the *towb* in Wad al Abbas as offer additional choices. Whereas in the early 1980s all women past a certain age wore *sirwal* (baggy shorts) or *showals* (short sleeveless dresses) under their *towbs*, in the late 1980s some women began to wear different outfits—usually *jellabiyas* or *ibayas*. Moreover, at the same time as self-consciously Islamic dress was being adopted by some women, for the first time I saw women walking around the village with curlers in their hair. In the early 1980s there was one basic hairstyle consisting of tiny braids worn by all adult women. In the late eighties I observed increasing heterogeneity as individuals made different choices. Nor is it that Western and Islamic styles are opposing choices—one sees curlers combined with the new Islamic attire as well as with the *towb*.

Rituals such as weddings and funerals are a conglomeration of symbolic public statements about identity, gender, and social relations. It should be no surprise then that they are central foci in the process of change in Wad al Abbas. Like hairstyles and dress, which are open to individual creative possibilities, rituals are areas of broader cultural creativity in which villagers can refashion their image of themselves. As they do so, symbols shift in meaning and traditions are recast. Subtle changes in wedding rituals illustrate this process. Among the regalia sometimes worn by local brides are *hijab* (Islamic amulets). At one wedding a woman pointed out to me that the amulets worn by the bride around each upper arm were not "real *hijab*" but "just for decoration." (*Hijab* were regarded as unacceptable from the fundamentalist perspective.) Thus, objects that once had real ritual significance may come to be valued merely as folkloric color—as *symbols* of tradition, rather than as true expressions of it. The fake thus stands for a certain kind of authenticity.

Similarly, villagers told me that in the past there was a part of the wedding called *jirtig* where the bride and groom spat milk at each other and on the guests. Villagers said this was replaced by spraying (commercial) perfume around. As one older woman put it, "They gave up milk and switched to perfume, because all the people laughed and the bride's clothes got dirty." However, at an urban wedding on the outskirts of Khartoum I was able to observe a milk-spraying *jirtig* ceremony. This *jirtig*, like the fake *hijab*, is decontextualized tradition enacted as a symbol of itself, no longer invested with deep ritual meaning. Such "traditions" can be performed as nostalgic folklore without tainting the family's reputation with the mark of backwardness. Local culture, thus, is reified at a certain level of abstraction that was not possible when it was simply the taken-for-granted way of being and doing. It is the decontextualized, ossified tradition created by modernity that therefore stands as a representation of tradition.[20] In this form tradition has been rendered powerless and therefore can be reintroduced to invoke local identity and community at a symbolic level now that communal ways no longer govern existence as they once did.

The rise of Islamic fundamentalism can be seen as part of the decline of the local community as the center of moral and social power. The fundamentalist perspective on Islam is part of the process whereby the role of the individual in making cultural choices is heightened and made visible. Fundamentalist Islam offers a more individual religious identity and means of expression than the kin-based structure of local Sufi brotherhoods (Umar 1993). The new Islam emphasizes self-discipline; to be Muslim is an achieved rather than an ascribed status. You as an individual make the *choice* to be a true Muslim; it is not simply a fact of your birth into a kin-group or community. While women have been constituted as symbols in the process of societal transformation, women also have shown their ability to manipulate symbols—casting aside at times their role as custodians of tradition, and using the symbol of Islamic dress to claim space in the emerging order of modern Sudan (Bernal 1994; Hale n.d.).

CONCLUSION

Many have suggested that Islam offers a stable identity in a rapidly changing society (Moghadam 1994:9). However, it may be the opposite that makes Islamic fundamentalism appealing—the pace of institutional change is so slow compared with the ability of individuals to change their ideology or mode of dress. A new Islamic identity is important to the villagers of Wad al Abbas, in part, because Sudan's political economy has proven so unresponsive to their aspirations. Fundamentalist Islam appears to hold out the possibility that change can come simply by willing it (Simone 1994).[21] It does not represent stability, but rather a process of transformation over which the individual exercises some control.

At Wad al Abbas and around the world women have assumed particular symbolic importance in the Islamic revival (Antoun and Heglund 1987; Mernissi 1991; Kandiyoti 1991). Gender relations operate as a marker in identity politics, and control over women may symbolize the reproduction of the community (Yuval-Davis 1994; Helie-Lucas 1994). Yet contemporary communities are not reproducing their current form so much as transforming themselves under changing conditions (Ong 1987; Appadurai 1990). This process gives rise both to new mechanisms for controlling women and new opportunities for women to renegotiate their positions in gender relations. Islamic ideologies serve as catalysts of change and as a means of inhibiting women, in particular, from fully exploring all the possibilities opening up in an expanding social universe. At Wad al Abbas regarding women as more backward and less Muslim than men also may be a way of representing in local terms the inequalities that villagers (and male migrants in particular) experience between themselves and others in the global system. Local inequalities thus are reconfigured as they are integrated into a global hierarchical schema.

The case of Wad al Abbas sheds light on the way local constructions of gender and modernity are contingent on global processes. The analysis presented suggests that Islam, which is both local and universal, provides a ready medium for crafting solutions to the contradictions between the local and global contexts that people increasingly must inhabit simultaneously. This casts the worldwide Islamic revival in a new light and helps explain why this movement has appealed to so many Muslims in the postmodern age.

NOTES

I am grateful to the National Science Foundation, the Social Science Research Council, and the American Council of Learned Societies for funding my fieldwork in Sudan. I thank the Women's Studies and Religion Program at Harvard, where I was a Rockefeller fellow, for providing such a stimulating environment in which to develop my ideas.

1. I use the (sometimes maligned) term "fundamentalism," rather than "Islamism," because fundamentalism is broader in meaning (e.g., some scholars use Islamism to refer to demands for an Islamic state), and because fundamentalism implicitly invites comparison to other religions rather than implying something unique about Islam.

2. All references are to the 1980s, when fieldwork was conducted, unless otherwise indicated. I spent 1980–82 in Wad al Abbas and returned there for a short stay in 1988.

3. This has obviously changed since Sudan's support for Iraq in the Gulf War.

4. The *umra* is like the Hajj but can be made at any time of year.

5. Villagers, moreover, are aware of brand names, distinguishing between name-brand goods and similar items or knockoffs by referring to the former as *al asli* ("the original").

6. The passports villagers were able to obtain in the 1980s were explicitly marked "valid for Arab countries."

7. Holiday celebrating the birth of the Prophet.

8. This fact is not lost on villagers. One man remarked that he had more respect for Egypt since it had its own factories while Saudi Arabia simply purchased things.

9. A place of prayer associated with a particular Sufi brotherhood.

10. The practice of giving money (*khut al grush*) was coming to be regarded as un-Islamic. Perhaps a handful of villagers, including the *Mawlana*, were known not to participate on religious grounds.

11. At most weddings the drum is more likely to be an empty plastic gallon container than a real *diluka*.

12. These were topics of popular interest since Toyota pickups were a hallmark of bourgeois status (elites had Mercedes cars), and the country was periodically racked by fuel shortages and skyrocketing prices.

13. This differs from the urban circles in Khartoum where a group opposed to the NIF called themselves "modern forces."

14. There is, moreover, tension between African and Arab identity within Sudan—not simply a division between an African southern Sudan and an Arab northern one, but an ambivalence that permeates northern Sudanese society. Local culture in Wad al Abbas is dynamically syncretic of African, Arab, and Western ideas and practices.

15. The *towb* requires some skill to wear, so early on I adopted the *terha* (cloth covering head and upper torso) that young girls wear as modest attire in the village.

16. There is a Nuba settlement adjacent to the village that supplies agricultural labor and illicit alcohol.

17. This refers to a formal ritual shyness/avoidance required by local etiquette.

18. I do not say "household" here because it was established practice for the newly married couple to reside with the bride's family for the first few years of marriage.

19. Nonetheless, since men generally do not want a wife's education to exceed their own, the issue had to do with the groom's educational background as well as his economic standing. *Mukhteribs* tend to have more schooling than the average villager, however.

20. Perhaps these examples prefigure the fate of many distinctive local Sudanese practices, if they are to survive at all.

21. This may shed light on the appeal of *shari'a* law, which in Sudan has become the key symbol of the Islamic revival at the national level (Warburg 1991). *Shari'a* is so powerful precisely because it is a symbol and not fixed to specific historical conditions (Simone 1994).

BIBLIOGRAPHY

Al-Karsani, Awad Al-Sid. 1993. "Beyond Sufism: the Case of Millenial Islam in the Sudan." In **Muslim Identity and Social Change in Sub-Saharan Africa**, pp. 135–153; Louis Brenner, ed. Bloomington: Indiana University Press.

Antoun, Richard and Mary Heglund, eds. 1987. **Religious Resurgence**. Syracuse: Syracuse University Press.

Appadurai, Arjun. 1990. "Disjuncture and Difference in the Global Cultural Economy." **Public Culture** (2)2:1–24.

Bedri, Balghis Yousif. 1987. "Food and Deferential Roles in the Feteihab Household." In *The Sudanese Woman*, pp. 67–91, Susan Kenyon, ed. Khartoum: Khartoum University Press.

Bernal, Victoria. 1991. *Cultivating Workers*. New York: Columbia University Press.

———. 1994. "Gender, Culture, and Capitalism: Women and the Remaking of Islamic 'Tradition' in a Sudanese Village." *Comparative Studies in Society and History* 36(1): 36–67.

Boddy, Janice. 1989. *Wombs and Alien Spirits*. Madison: University of Wisconsin Press.

Comaroff, Jean and John Comaroff. 1993. "Introduction." In *Modernity and Its Discontents*, pp. xi–xxxvii, Jean Comaroff and John Comaroff, eds. Chicago: University of Chicago Press.

Foucault, Michel. 1979. *Discipline and Punish*. New York: Vintage Books.

Hale, Sondra. n.d. "Gender and Politics in Sudan: Islamism, the Party, and the State." Manuscript.

Hefner, Robert. 1987. "The Political Economy of Islamic Conversion in Modern East Java." In *Islam and the Political Economy of Meaning*, pp. 53–78, William Roff, ed. London: Croom Helm.

Helie-Lucas, Marie-Aimée. 1994. "The Preferential Symbol for Islamic Identity: Women in Muslim Personal Laws." In *Identity Politics and Women*, pp. 391–407, Valentine Moghadam, ed. Boulder, CO: Westview Press.

Hijab, Nadia. 1988. *Womanpower: The Arab Debate on Women at Work*. New York: Cambridge University Press.

Hobsbawm, Eric. 1989. "Introduction: Inventing Traditions." In *The Invention of Tradition*, pp. 1–14, Eric Hobsbawm and Terence Ranger, eds. Cambridge: Cambridge University Press.

Ibrahim, Abdullahi A. 1989. "Popular Islam: The Religion of the Barbarous Throng." *Northeast African Studies* 11(2):21–40.

Kandiyoti, Deniz, ed. 1991. *Women, Islam and the State*. Philadelphia: Temple University Press.

McDonnell, Mary B. 1990. "Patterns of Muslim Pilgrimage from Malaysia, 1885–1985." In *Muslim Travellers: Pilgrimage, Migration, and the Religious Imagination*, pp. 111–130, Dale Eickelman and James Piscatori, eds. Berkeley: University of California Press.

Mernissi, Fatima. 1991. *The Veil and the Male Elite*. Reading, MA: Addison-Wesley.

Mitchell, Timothy. 1988. *Colonising Egypt*. Cambridge: Cambridge University Press.

Moghadam, Valentine. 1994. "Introduction: Women and Identity Politics in Theoretical and Comparative Perspective." In *Identity Politics and Women*, pp. 2–26. Valentine Moghadam, ed. Boulder, CO: Westview Press.

Ong, Aihwa. 1987. *Spirits of Resistance and Capitalist Discipline: Factory Women in Malaysia*. Albany: SUNY Press.

Rabinow, Paul. 1992. "A Modern Tour in Brazil." In *Modernity and Identity*, pp. 248–264, S. Lash and J. Friedman, eds. Oxford: Blackwell.

Riad, Ibrahim. 1990. "Factors Contributing to the Political Ascendency of the Muslim Brethren in Sudan." *Arab Studies Quarterly* 12(3–4):33–53.

Said, Edward. 1979. *Orientalism*. New York: Pantheon Books.

Sanad, Jamal and Mark Tessler. 1990. "Women and Religion in a Modern Islamic Society: The Case of Kuwait." In *Religious Resurgence and Politics in the Contemporary World*, pp. 195–218, Emile Sahliyeh, ed. Albany: SUNY Press.

Simone, T.A.M. 1994. *In Whose Image? Political Islam and Urban Practices in Sudan*. Chicago: University of Chicago Press.

Umar, Muhammad S. 1993. "Changing Islamic Identity in Nigeria from the 1960s to the 1980s: From Sufism to Anti-Sufism." In *Muslim Identity and Social Change in Sub-Saharan Africa*, pp. 154–178, Louis Brenner, ed. Bloomington: Indiana University Press.

Voll, John. 1986. "Revivalism and Social Transformation in Islamic History." *Muslim World* 76(3–4):168–180.

Von der Mehden, Fred. 1993. *Two Worlds of Islam: Interaction Between Southeast Asia and the Middle East*. Gainesville: University Press of Florida.

Warburg, Gabriel. 1991. "The *Shari'a* in Sudan: Implementation and Repercussions." In *Sudan: State and Society in Crisis*, pp. 90–107, John Voll, ed. Bloomington: Indiana University Press.

Yuval-Davis, Nira. 1994. "Identity Politics and Women's Ethnicity." In *Identity Politics and Women*, pp. 408–424, Valentine Moghadam, ed. Boulder, CO: Westview Press.

DYING GODS AND QUEEN MOTHERS:
THE INTERNATIONAL POLITICS OF SOCIAL
REPRODUCTION IN AFRICA AND EUROPE

GILLIAN FEELEY-HARNIK

> Who does not know that magnificent island, the queen of the Indian
> Ocean: the fertility of her soil, the variety of her products, her metallurgical
> riches, her vast and excellent ports, finally her admirable geographical loca-
> tion, two steps from the African continent, not far from the great Asian
> peninsula, between the two routes to India, China, and the western Ocean,
> between the Cape of Good Hope and the isthmus of the Suez? (Guillain
> 1845:148)

In the mid-nineteenth century, "the queen of the Indian Ocean" needed no introduction to an international audience. The land, resources, and seaways of
Madagascar attracted the interest of many countries, especially France and Great
Britain. By 1817, Malagasy monarchs had already begun sending diplomats to foreign capitals in Africa and Europe asking for help in fending off territorial claims. By
the 1860s, embassies had become standard practice in their foreign relations. France
(in 1862), Great Britain (in 1862), and the United States (in 1875) established consulates in Madagascar, while (in 1864) Malagasy established their own consulates in
London, Paris, Marseille, and Mauritius, already a British colony (Mutibwa
1974:111, 377, 379, 380). While Queen Victoria became the longest-reigning
monarch of Great Britain and Ireland (1837–1901), and Empress of India (from
1876), her rule was contested, and her monarchy transformed into a constitutional
form of government. This was a period of radical political change in France and
America as well. During Guillain's explorations of "the queen of the Indian Ocean"
for King Louis-Philippe's [First] Empire, and the international struggles that ensued,
Malagasy also debated and fought over hierarchy, shifting their loyalties from male to
female rulers in the two largest of the island's several rival polyarchies: the Sakalava of
the west coast and the Merina of the central highlands. Finally the French (now in
their Third Republic) won out, invading the island in 1895 and turning it into a protectorate, then a colony in 1896.[1]

Powerfully feminizing representations of Africa in Europe seem to have coincided with shifts in African polities from male to female rulers in the course of other
early struggles of Africans against European encroachment. The famed "Queen
Njinga" of Ndongo and Matamba, who dominated international politics and slave-

trading among the Mbundu, Portuguese, and Dutch in Angola for forty years (1624–1663), was followed by several generations of queens in the century after her death (Thornton 1991:40). The "Rain Queens" who succeeded male rulers among the Lovedu in the early 1800s acquired similar renown in Europe, especially after the publication of Rider Haggard's *She* in 1886. Joseph J. Walters's *Guanya Pau: The Story of an African Princess* was published in the United States five years later, in 1891, when the Liberian writer was a student at Oberlin College in Ohio. He set his Vey [Vai] heroine in Liberia, but depicted his Princess—the epitome of all African women "pure and good . . . blessed wives and noble mothers"—with an engraving of the Christian "Queen Ranavalona III, of Madagascar" (Walters 1994:ii, xxvi).[2] Ranavalona III, the last of the Malagasy queens who had ruled Imerina since 1828, was still so powerful after the invasion of 1895 that the first colonial governor exiled her to Algeria, where she maintained an international Algerian-Parisian court until her death in 1917. When her remains were repatriated in 1938, as part of an effort to gain *le loyalisme absolu* of the Malagasy people on the eve of World War II, a crowd of some 200,000 followers thronged the *chapelle ardente* installed in the train station of the capital of Antananarivo (Decary 1951:276). The French government of Madagascar was then negotiating with Poland to provide "asylum" for Jews, who would solve their persistent labor problems (Olivier 1938). The negotiations ended in May 1942, when the British invaded Madagascar to prevent the advancing Japanese armies from taking the western Indian Ocean, especially the Suez Canal.[3]

Grosz-Ngaté and Kokole urge us to attend to "the gendered nature of cultural flows across social and national boundaries or the ways in which such flows intersect with local gender constructs and relations."[4] In this chapter, I will discuss the flow and force of gendered representations of hierarchy and autonomy in international politics during the nineteenth century, at the intersection of events involving the transformation of European monarchies into states and African monarchies into European colonies. Drawing on case studies of Malagasy, British, and French relations in Madagascar, I explore the following question: How do gendered representations of political hierarchy inform and express the social-historical processes by which polities are reproduced, co-opted, and transformed?[5]

I take my inspiration from feminist ethnography on the ways that relations of sexuality and procreation are used to model large-scale processes of growth and change, which are realized in turn through political-economic interventions in the most intimate human relationships (Yanagisako and Collier 1987). My hypothesis is that the ideological power of generative political structures derives from the links that participants make between their phenomenological and political-economic dimensions, for example, in relating "person" to "office" in indigenous theories of European monarchies and republics. Historical data suggest that the Malagasy, French, and British involved in international relations in nineteenth-century Madagascar held competing ideologies of these generative processes. I am interested in how they interacted through their rival policies and practices to reproduce social hierarchies embodied in gendered forms. How—in considering the views of others—did they come to adopt newly gendered strategies for handling their "foreign relations" or co-opting the relations of others? Recognizing that "kinship" and "contract" are mutually constitutive relations, not sequential stages, how are we to understand the historical engendering of European states and African colonies out of international royal relations?

First I will argue that the European social theories used to analyze African political systems are part of the "cultural flows" we are trying to understand. Male-centered models of hierarchy and change appear to mask more complex assumptions about social reproduction that, if better known, might provide wider common ground from which to explore the dynamics of international relations between Africans and Europeans from a comparative and historical perspective. I explore these issues in a case study of how the Sakalava of Madagascar sought to transform the gendered structure of their political relations in struggles among themselves and with the Merina, French, and British during the nineteenth century. I conclude by discussing how research on Malagasy and African polyarchies might help us rethink the gendered dimensions of political-economic growth and change.

EUROPEAN POLITICAL THEOLOGY IN COMPARATIVE PERSPECTIVE: DYING GODS AND VIRGIN QUEENS

Frazer's *The Golden Bough* (1890) and Kantorowicz's *The King's Two Bodies* (1957) have had the most profound influence on anthropological and historical models for understanding the social reproduction of African monarchies (Feeley-Harnik 1985). Yet they must be understood as indigenous theories of human and social reproduction comparable to the African ideas and practices to which they have been applied. Here, I can only outline some of the cultural preoccupations that seem to have been involved in the flow of ideas and practices among European polities, especially those related to gender and the creation of states and colonies. Hayden's (1987:44–61) analysis of the internationalism of the British monarchy up to World War I, when anti-German sentiment contributed to its "anglicization," suggests a more general puzzle about cultural flows that warrants further study. The transformation of European monarchies into nations was inseparable from colonial expansion into Asia and Africa, as well as Europe; yet nationalism entailed a growing cultural localism in domestic politics.

Frazer did his research for *The Golden Bough* in the years following the Golden Jubilee (1887), celebrating the fiftieth year of Queen Victoria's reign. The possible relationship of Frazer's "Dying God" to the "Widow Queen," as Victoria was called after decades of publicly mourning the death of Prince Albert in 1861, has yet to be explored. Frazer's first edition was published in 1899, two years after the Diamond Jubilee (1897) celebrating the sixtieth year of Victoria's reign. Later editions appeared in the years following other major imperial displays, including Victoria's funeral (1901), the coronation of Edward VII (1902), his funeral (1910), the coronation of George V (1911), and his Delhi Durbar (1912). Frazer placed the Dying God in the "sacred grove and sanctuary of Diana" (Frazer 1899:1). Yet Diana's grove was always overshadowed by the broken bough of the "King of the Wood," whose death so powerfully evoked the crucifixion and resurrection of Jesus Christ, albeit in ever more shadowy form (Feeley-Harnik 1985:273–275).[6]

Frazer's paradoxical vision of the absolute king, absolutely at the mercy of the people who would kill him as his powers waned, peculiarly anticipated what European scholars found when they applied his model to African polities in the first decades of the twentieth century. With increasing evidence that ritual regicide was not common in Africa or anywhere, their focus shifted from the death of African rulers to what they saw as the structural weaknesses of African monarchies compared to the colonial bureaucracies into which former royals were being incorporated (*ibid.*:276).[7]

Some francophone Africanists, notably Luc de Heusch (1958), developed Oedipal themes perhaps implicit in Frazer's work.[8] Anglophone scholars taking a staunchly Weberian approach to succession, focusing on person and office, became interested in Kantorowicz's study of English political theology, *The King's Two Bodies* (1957). Fortes, for example, credits Frazer with inspiring him to expand his comparative perspective in (1959:1–3), but he recommends Kantorowicz (1957) in his work on "ritual and office," especially Kantorowicz's explanation of the English notion that "the king never dies" (1962:88). Kantorowicz concentrated on kingship in Tudor and Stuart England, mainly in the reign of Elizabeth I (1558–1603), when the doctrine of "the King's two Bodies," emergent since the twelfth century, was made law to decide a dispute over land against the Crown. Kantorowicz explained the legal fiction of "the King's two Bodies" as the jurists' way of reconciling the contradictions between person and office in English kingship. Like Frazer's "Dying God," the concept of "twin-born majesty" (as it was also called) derived from Christian theology (ibid.:19, 506). Conceptions of the "mystical body of the Church" (*corpus Ecclesiae mysticum*), extended to define the "mystical body of the State" (*corpus Respublicae mysticum*), and the corresponding conceptions of Jesus Christ and the king himself as a *persona mixta* or *gemina persona*, provided ways of merging, yet also distinguishing the king's "Body natural" and "Body politic," thus assuring continuity in government because "the king (in his corporate form) never dies" (Kantorowicz 1957:193–232).

Like Fortes, most followers of Kantorowicz have focused on the death and succession of kings. British colonists introduced English political theology into India, where some Hindu and Muslim rulers adapted it for their own uses (Mayer 1985:211). So Mayer explains his study of succession in the Hindu Princely States before 1947 as an analysis of "the king's two thrones." The dynastic throne (*rājgaddī*) is named for the cotton mattress *(gaddi)* and bolsters, collectively *gaddi,* considered to be its main parts. Mayer emphasizes that "the status of the king [as hallowed "child of the *gaddi*" or as hallowing the *gaddi*] may be the subject of conflicting theories, which may indeed be held concurrently" (ibid.). His own evidence suggests that Indian participants also held different theories about the gender dynamics of succession. Through invocation, the cotton *gaddi* were filled not with priests, but with goddesses: the Great Goddesses and sometimes also the guardian deity of the state, identifying the *gaddi* with the state in female terms (ibid.:208–209, 217). Some respondents compared *gaddi*-king to relations between mother and son, others to relations between wife and husband (ibid.:209), but Mayer does not pursue the female dimensions of the Hindu rulers who appear in their human forms to be male.

VIRGIN QUEENS AND QUEEN MOTHERS

Kantorowicz himself might have questioned the genders of "the King's two Bodies," precisely because the long-standing doctrine became law just as Elizabeth I was crowned queen of England. Elizabeth I (1558–1603) and her immediate predecessor, Mary Tudor (1553–1558), were the first queens regnant of England since the Norman Conquest in the eleventh century.[9] Yates (1975) challenged the singular focus on male figures in English models of political regeneration by arguing that the "cult" of Elizabeth I drew on the power of outlawed Catholic devotions to the Virgin Mary. Axton's study *The Queen's Two Bodies* (1974) explores the broader social context of the cult. She shows how the dramas of Shakespeare and other playwrights provided places where officially forbidden topics could be openly debated: her Protestant faith, "the fate of a land governed by a virgin queen" (ibid.:17), the legitimacy and purity of rival bloodlines and "foreign" births. Yet neither Yates nor Axton goes into the blood, semen, or soil that so powerfully animate rival conceptions of social regeneration in Elizabethan drama, poetry, and painting.

One of Kantorowicz's most interesting discussions concerns "the blood of kings," which became important with the shift to male primogeniture in deciding royal succession during the thirteenth century. Curiously, the shift occurred "not by any special act or decree, but *de facto,*" both in France in 1270 and in England two years later (ibid.:330). Besides obviating troublesome interregna, male primogeniture made the king's legitimacy

> dynastical, independent of approval or consecration on the part of the Church and independent also of election by the people. . . . The Holy Spirit, which in former days was manifested by the voting of the electors while his gifts were conferred by the anointment, now was seated in the royal blood itself, as it were, *natura et gratia,* by nature and by grace—indeed, "by nature"

as well; for the royal blood now appeared as a somewhat mysterious fluid (ibid.: 330, 331).

The concept of "the blood of kings" or *"le sang royal"* was eventually used to support the idea of the preeminence of a "royal race" in England and in France. Kantorowicz emphasizes that it is not clear which of several possible models of human procreation the medieval theorists might have had in mind; Aristotle's theory of a "male seed" co-existed with different Stoic and Hermetic doctrines. Kantorowicz himself is baffled by this "peculiar kind of scientific mysticism—irrational and material at the same time." He acknowledges that the "the royal birth itself manifested the Prince's election to kingship, his election by God and divine providence." But he does not discuss the particulars of royal blood or birth, and returns almost immediately to the ways in which the new approach to succession contributed to "the sempiternity of the Crown" (ibid.:333–336).

Kantorowicz's own account makes it clear that the doctrine of primogeniture never completely replaced the doctrines of ordination or election in either England or France. They have coexisted as competing theories and practices of social regeneration right up to the present in England (see Mayer 1985:213, 217–218) and possibly elsewhere. Yet the dynamics of their interaction, especially their gender dynamics, are far from clear. Jochens (1987) shows how the combination of primogeniture, monogamy, and unified rule in thirteenth-century Norway led to a new "politics of reproduction" confined to marriage, rather than the broader field of concubinage, where women had formerly sought to advance themselves and their kin through the sons they had with kings. Jochens (1987:328) states that "the influence of biblical or Aristotelian patriarchy and biology" led to the widespread European emphasis on male primogeniture, but does not explore the ways they may have been expressed in blood or birth.

Hackett (1995) insists that the "Virgin Queen" Elizabeth I neither represented, intended, nor accomplished a revolution in "the same basic misogyny" dominant in her lifetime and in later scholarly reassessments of her reign (1995:235–241). Like Warner on the Virgin Mary, Hackett argues that Elizabeth I was regarded as "an 'exceptional woman' whose marvelous gifts stand out in contrast to the general fallibility or even depravity of her sex" (ibid.:238–239). Elizabeth herself used "the King's two Bodies" to overcome objections to her femaleness by explaining how, as "Gods Creature," she could be "but one Bodye naturallye Considered though by his permission a Bodye Politique to Governe" (ibid.:40).[10]

In contrast to Yates's argument that Elizabeth I assumed the attributes of the Virgin Mary for Protestant iconoclasts, Hackett shows how Elizabeth I (like the Virgin Mary) took on the attributes of a much wider range of historic and mythical female figures, variously interpreted. Thus, her unmarried state could be a sign of purity to her supporters, a mask of sexual depravity to her detractors (ibid.:130–132).

The Virgin Queen was above all "the bride of the nation" and a nursing mother. The metaphor of marriage, which Kantorowicz (1957:203) found "all but nonexistent" in medieval England, "reached its fullest expression in England with Elizabeth" (Hackett 1995:56). In this imagery, the nation was regendered as masculine without replacing the usual representations of the church (*Ecclesia*) and the state (*Respublica*) as feminine, with which Elizabeth became more closely identified than any of her male predecessors (ibid.:60).

The image of Elizabeth as a nursing mother drew on Marian iconography, but also on "a key biblical text for the Protestant reformers, Isaiah 49.23 . . . 'And Kings shalbe thy nourcing fathers, and Quenes shalbe thy nources' (ibid.:4, 27–28, 50–51, 200–201). As this image became commonplace toward the end of her reign, Elizabeth's promotion of Protestantism was represented as an act of giving birth (ibid.:136, 138). Hackett is the first to examine systematically how Elizabethan debates about representation informed their interpretations of the polybodied queen and the power of her "image" and "presence." These debates originated in the controversies over the blood and body of Christ in the Eucharist and the unity of the Trinity, yet even Hackett does not discuss the relationship of Elizabeth's milk to "royal blood."

The current Elizabeth (the Second) creates her two bodies out of contrasts between state spectacles and factory visits (Hayden 1989:10–13). Yet one of Hayden's most valuable arguments has to do with mutually constitutive relations between family and state. The singularly encompassing queen of England "never appears alone in public. . . . Her most constant companions are the members of the Royal Family" (ibid.:35). Hayden shows how these domestic relations contributed to the anglicization of the Germanic House of Hanover in the early twentieth century (ibid.:44–61), and also its apparent transformation into a middle-class family. The role of changing displays of family life in creating a "constitutional" monarchy, subordinate to Parliament yet the hidden mainstay of an aristocratic class system, is yet another topic for further research. English royal births were still state spectacles in the nineteenth century. Queen Victoria's birth was witnessed by a crowd of notables (ibid.:140), yet her forty years of mourning for Prince Albert prevailed even over the imperial displays of her last fourteen years. Since the death of the "Widow Queen," English royal births and christenings have become virtually invisible. In contrast to Cannadine (1983), who stresses the emptiness of imperial ritual, Hayden (ibid.:140–142, 164–166) sees the private christenings, and the equally veiled but continuing governmental work of the queen, as the very wellsprings of privilege linking royals and aristocrats in contemporary Great Britain. Here again, we encounter a complex mixture of superficially familiar models of feminization as subordination (Hackett's "same basic misogyny") with quite the opposite. The assumption of a female form may have contributed to Parliament's apparent domestication of English monarchy, while renewing the vigor of class distinctions with which it remains associated.

I will close this brief comparative perspective on the gendered dimensions of European political theology by turning to France, the other main contender in Madagascar during the nineteenth century. England and France shared the shift to primogeniture around 1270 C.E. and consequent emphasis on "royal blood." Kantorowicz's student Giesey (1960) argued that English political theology and practice contributed to the development of embalming, effigies, and processionals in French Renaissance funerals designed to ensure the sempiternity of the French Crown. Walzer (1974) draws on "the King's two Bodies" to argue that the trial of Louis XVI and his subsequent execution as citizen Louis Capet, modeled on the earlier trial and execution of Charles I in England in 1649, was ritually required to destroy kingship in France in 1793. Yet the French (and Spanish) were unique in adopting the sixth-century C.E. law of the Salien Franks, originally excluding women from inheriting land, but extended to exclude women from succeeding to the throne. The distinctive *loi salique* against female rulers did not prevent the rise of powerful *reine-mères* as regents before, during, and after the reign of Elizabeth I, nor the emergence of a distinctively French "Family-State compact" that Hanley (1989) describes as "engendering the state" in the sixteenth and early seventeenth century, that is, contributing to the growth and centralization of the French monarchy through the emergence of a professional bureaucratic elite operating at every level of government (Mettam 1989). Hanley shows how family-state governance arose from mutual interests:

> The king and royal government, through the sale of offices, obtained the financial capital and professional service necessary to support a centralized polity and facilitate state building; and the legists (bourgeois or newly ennobled), through the purchase, exercise, and bequests of offices, obtained the prerogatives necessary to construct critical family networks and augment family fortunes (Hanley, 1989:7).

In the early 1500s, the legists discovered that the *loi salique* was a medieval forgery (Hanley 1994:107–109). From the 1520s into the 1650s, faced with Elizabeth I and other European queens, as well as their own powerful female regents, legists and *parlementaires* drew on family law to create a new theory justifying the exclusion of women from the throne: a "marital regime government," based on a king-kingdom conjugal pair, and a "seminal [refined out of blood] theory of authority," following Aristotle's theory of generation, according to which men gave birth to subsequent generations of men (see ibid.:117, n. 29). By the early 1600s, interconnected familial-state male authority, ever strengthened by the French system of transmitting government offices through sale, dowry, and inheritance, was expressed in two linked maxims. In the words of a contemporary legist: "The first maxim of our French [inheritance] law [is] *The dead [person] seizes the living [one].* . . . That is *The king never dies*" (cited in ibid.:115). Female rule became not only illegal, but unnatural. *The king never dies* had its unspoken corollary: "'The queen dies,' spells the imminent death of the state" (ibid.:120). From the 1650s, as women began taking cases to courts, claiming that marriage was a kind of slavery ruled by despots, French rulers reverted to earlier conceptions of the king as spiritual father rather than as legally defined husband of the people (ibid.:122-123), but still drew on blood-seminal theory, now entrenched in natural law.

We would benefit from more research following Hayden and Hanley in breaking down kinship-to-contract theory from within, and thus the evolutionism still inherent in the analysis of international relations among European and African polities. A study of how family-state relations were reformed in the struggles between French royalists and republicans during the nineteenth century, which coincided with the struggles between Madagascar and France, remains to be done. Hanley (ibid.:125–126) argues that royalists and republicans had a common commitment to perpetuating male rule. The new postrevolutionary constitution of 1791 went even further than the old *loi salique* in declaring that all regents must be male. The Code Napoléon (1804) did away with male primogeniture by preserving equal inheritance rights for children, but established stricter laws upholding male authority in the family right into the 1980s.

QUEEN MOTHERS AND ROYAL SISTERS

Given the gendered models of social reproduction still pervasive in British and French political theory, the dearth of data on women in African polyarchies is not surprising. The earliest studies by scholars like Roscoe (1911) on "queen mothers" and "royal sisters" in Buganda, and Rattray (1923) on Asante "queen mothers," still resist assimilation into "the King's two Bodies" and "*le roi ne meurt jamais*." Lebeuf (1963) documented the diversity of these forms. Sacks (1977) provided the first social-historical account of their relations by taking a Marxist approach to the politics of women's multiple and changing roles as sisters, wives, mothers, and daughters. Her argument, still set in a kinship-to-contract framework, is twofold: (1) women as sisters were politically powerful in "nonclass societies" of producer-owners; (2) the transformation of sisters into wives was critical to the creation of states based on the systematic dismantling of rival kin-based polities. We will return to these points shortly.

Bloch's (1986, 1987) analyses of Merina royal ritual in nineteenth-century Madagascar is superficially similar to Sacks's approach in positing an association between women and "biological birth." But in contrast to Sacks, who rejects the association as reductionist and focuses instead on the political implications of women's work, Bloch affirms that Merina (and people everywhere) make this association and ignores the subject of women's work, even the labor they once put into making the hand-woven shrouds that were the focal point of Merina secondary burials in the nineteenth century. Bloch interprets Merina circumcision ritual and the annual "bath" of the living ruler as being, like the secondary burials of Merina commoners today, male forms of social reproduction, designed to overcome the mortality of biological birth associated with women. Perhaps for this reason, Bloch discounts the historical dynamics of these events, including their relationship to international affairs. He analyzes the Merina royal bath in generic rather than historical terms, persistently referring to the central royal figure as "he" or "the king" (1986: *passim*). The terms are relevant to Hastie's account of Radama I's bath in 1817, but inapplicable to most of his five successors from 1828 to the French invasion of 1895, who were all women. The only exception was Radama II, strangled with a silk cloth in 1863 after less than two years in office.

Other studies confirm Sacks's emphasis on the cultural and historical evidence of women's political significance in Africa and Madagascar (Barnes 1991, Cohen 1977, Feeley-Harnik 1991, Ben-Amos 1983). They show that the social formation of a polity conceived as a perpetual corporation does not necessarily entail the elevation of a male model of social reproduction over a female model identified with the errors and infirmities of ordinary mortals, regardless of the possible relevance of such a model to European monarchies. The women so commonly called "queen mothers" were structurally significant, but they were not just figureheads; they were political actors in their own right.[11] In some historical circumstances involving struggles with Europeans, female political leaders seem to have come to the fore. In these instances, as in the European cases of female rulers, it is possible to get a better sense of the dynamics of social reproduction involving the two and many bodies from which singular rulers are made, and especially the importance of the gendered *unions* involved in their procreation, not only son-mother and husband-wife unions, superficially familiar from the gender politics of European royal history, but also sister-brother unions.

Krige and Krige's (1943) study *The Realm of a Rain-Queen* provides such an example. The Kriges begin their study with the "Fame of Mujaji," stating: "Among their neighbours and among tribes as far away as the Zulu, they [the Lovedu] have a great reputation. The fame of their queen, Mujaji, is spoken of even by white men as if it were the fame of the monarch of a mighty empire" (ibid.:1). Especially her "very light" color evoked speculations about her birth, and possible native or foreign affiliations, by people as different as Rider Haggard (She-Who-Must-Be-Obeyed, 1886, inspired in part by Mujaji II, who died in 1894) and Field-Marshal and Premier J. C. Smuts, J. D. Krige's uncle, who provided the foreword to *The Realm of a Rain-Queen*, then Mujaji III.

The differing conceptions of women held by the Lovedu and the Boers who subjugated them in 1894 clearly affected their later interpretations of the conquest and possibly the events themselves. The Boer government acquitted the Lovedus of complicity in the rebellion that led to the "defeat and wholesale transportation of several tribes in the lowveld" (ibid.:3). The Kriges attribute their acquittal to the missionary Rev. F. Reuter, who intervened on behalf of Mujaji II. Yet they also cite the view of Lovedu who attributed Mujaji II's acquittal to her own cunning in deceiving the Boer general, Joubert. Despite her seeming visibility to Europeans, her "very light[ness]," the Lovedu claimed that even after subjugation in 1894, Joubert was shown not the true Mujaji II, but someone who impersonated her (ibid.).

With rare exceptions (Beidelman 1966), most scholars of African kings treat these figures as if they were unitary individuals.[12] The literature on female rulers shows more awareness of their polybodied qualities. These encompass gender distinctions and other socially recognized differences, such as condition of life (living, dead, ancestral), relatedness (slave, free, royal), or locality (native, stranger). As in the European cases, these qualities might appear merged in any single manifestation of royalty, for example in the androgynous qualities of a living ruler. But the African data suggest that (1) these apparently unitary composite creatures are better understood as historically situational faces of more complex beings, having and showing other faces, facets, bodies, and dimensions, in other contexts; and (2) as the dynamic outcome of powerful unions among these different facets.[13] Here in particular, African polyarchies seem to show striking differences from European forms in their emphasis on what Weiner (1992:15–16, 67–68, 151–152) calls "sibling intimacy" in Polynesian polyarchies.

European models of political reproduction appear to emphasize queen mothers and sons, secondarily wives and daughters. Sisters are hardly mentioned. Queen mothers and *reine mères* also dominate in the African case studies of the colonial period. Yet when the African cases are read more closely, these "mothers" are so often "sisters" that Luc de Heusch (1958) has to invoke "substitution" to make his evolutionary Oedipal argument about mother-son incest as the *point de rupture* catapulting "kin-based societies" into bureaucratic states: *La demi-soeur est un personnage substitutif* (ibid.:135, emphasis in original) for the mother; the sister-brother union in whatever form is to be understood as an incestuous sacred marriage between mother and son.[14]

The comparative perspective from Melanesian ethnography suggests that we should not disregard these intimations of alternative theories of political reproduction by assimilating sisters to mothers. In showing that human procreation is not essentially "biological," feminist scholars have removed the main support from the kinship-to-contract reasoning that still pervades most theories of political-economic change. The social construction of birth is not isolated from politics in some "domestic" realm. The very conception of a separate, lesser, more natural or "biological" female domestic realm is itself an ideological construction, inextricable from historically particular political-economic processes (Yanagisako and Collier 1987). Furthermore, as we have already glimpsed from the European cases, people may hold more than one theory of family-procreation concurrently. Melanesian ethnographers have been most attentive to the varieties of social unions involved, notably the importance of brother-sister unions existing along father-son, mother-son, and husband-wife unions. According to Weiner's argument:

> When a woman marries, the full range of her reproductive powers is far too essential to be lost to her brother and the other members of her natal group. Whereas in most cases, a woman's biological procreative role is established within her marriage, thereby sexually upholding the sibling sexual relations taboo, her other productive and reproductive roles—those usually omitted in kinship theory—remain clearly tied to the relationship between herself and her brother. Even when the sibling taboo is rigorously upheld, the desire for and possibilities of sibling intimacy are present, giving women as sisters a unique kind of power. (1992:72)

Whereas Sacks (1979) anchors the political importance of sisters in the work they contribute to egalitarian, kin-based groups, Weiner (1992) sees the importance of brother-sister unions in "keeping-while-giving." Where Sacks (ibid.:10–64) analyzes the ethnocentricities in European models of production, Weiner (ibid.: 23–65) overturns conventional theories of exchange. In focusing my critique on theories of social reproduction, I will take a still more thoroughly historical and comparative perspective, including not only the social-cultural circumstances of the emergence of particular ideas and practices among Europeans and Africans discussed so far, but also the ways they have played out in international relations among them. My hypothesis is that Africans in dangerous encounters with Europeans used many offensive strategies based on their evaluations of their own and Europeans' assumptions about social reproduction. In addition to diplomacy and military combat, for example, they could show a female form of leadership they knew the British and French would dismiss as a figurehead. This form protected the generative force of their polyarchies in their own terms, and allowed them to keep trying to "keep-while-apparently-giving," especially to keep the land to which their sovereignty was increasingly linked during the nineteenth century. The Kriges' passing comments on the Lovedu interpretation of the seeming encounter between Mujaji II and Joubert suggests the existence of such a strategy (see also Rattray's (1923:84, 295) citations of Asante views). The purpose of the Malagasy case is to explore the dynamics of reproductive models of polyarchies in the context of international relations among the Malagasy, French, and British during the nineteenth century.

SPOUSES AND SIBLINGS: COMPETING MODELS OF REPRODUCTION IN MALAGASY MONARCHIES

Hierarchical forms of political organization began developing in Madagascar in the sixteenth century, eventually giving rise to five or six multicentered networks of dynastic relations: the Sakalava, which expanded north along the west coast; the Betsimisaraka, which expanded north and south along the east coast; and the Merina of the mid-highlands, which eventually incorporated the Betsileo and Tanala sovereignties to the south. My data on the Sakalava polities are based on ethnographic research in the Analalava region of northwest Madagascar and further research in Madagascar and France at intervals from 1971 through 1989. Residents of the Analalava region come from all over Madagascar and from abroad, but the area is commonly acknowledged to be Sakalava "ancestral land," the former domain of Sakalava rulers and their diverse followers. Sakalava royalty still command respect in postcolonial Madagascar, not only among "children of the land," but also "strangers" who—for decades—have adopted "Sakalava" practices as a way of integrating themselves into local networks of accesss to land and labor (Deschamps 1959, Feeley-Harnik 1991, Sharp 1993).

Throughout Madagascar, such terms as *razana, mpitondra, ampanjaka, andevo, mpanaraka*—ancestor, leaders, ruler, slave, follower—are not usually marked according to gender. When they are, concordant suffixes—"male" and "female" (*-lahy, -vavy*)—are used. More often, these states of being (or rather states of relations, for they are all implicitly relational) are embodied in more generic images of heads and feet, above and below, ahead and behind, laying out spatially and in other ways the changing structures of their historical relations.

In contemporary northwestern Madagascar, men are accorded certain priorities in relation to ancestors, but these are offset by priorities given to women (Feeley-Harnik 1991:155–364). According to Sakalava oral histories since the turn of the century, the earliest Sakalava rulers were men. But both Malagasy and European sources suggest that the succession practices of Sakalava and Merina changed radically during the early nineteenth century. Beginning among the Sakalava around 1778, and among the Merina in 1828, the position of living ruler shifted from men to women. The changing roles of men and women in the reproduction of singular rulers and their infinite numbers of followers, the vitality of ancestors and the deadness of corpses, are most clearly revealed in oral and written narratives about past generations called *tantara*.

The *tantara* show first that living rulers, recalled in all their uniqueness, were and are not the only or most important expressions of royalty. Sakalava royalty are polyform. Living rulers are the most clearly visible of their multiple presences, but living rulers, male or female, exist together with other dimensions of royalty embodied in diverse and historically changing forms, which may become more dominant depending on the circumstances. Among Sakalava, these forms included the relics of royal corpses known collectively as "grandparents" (*dady*) whose "bath" at the capitals of living royalty inaugurated the new lunar year; their entombed corpses, known as "difficult things" (*raha sarotra*), are hidden in separate cemeteries. Royalty appear in the bodies of commoners and slaves (*saha*, "channels"), through whom they can speak and act on a wide range of contemporary concerns. Royal ancestors are also manifest in words and stories of royal books and proclamations. In nineteenth-century Imerina, the range of royal presences included their "substitutes" (*solo*) in the form of clothes and beaded bags of earth from their tombs, their entombed corpses, and—at least toward the end of the nineteenth century—commoners serving as their mediums, which some Merina now claim is a borrowed "Sakalava custom."

Yet all these forms of sovereignty compounded of flesh, earth, cloth, and stone—living, ancestral, female, male, native, stranger, slave, free, and noble—were "one person" (*olo araiky*), albeit a "difficult thing," in contrast to the innumerable "thousands" of "simple people" (*olo tsotra*), interchangeable replicas of one another, who followed them. Further, these "one persons," rooted in the places of living and ancestral royalty among their generic "people," formed the generative source, literally the "royal genitals" (*doany*, the all-inclusive term for a living ruler's capital) of still larger, literally corporate bodies, realized in periodic gatherings of followers into these places. The formation of these bodies was and is marked at such events (especially funerals) by the places rulers assumed "at the head" of the crowd; their followers "at the feet," even as formerly the lowest of slaves were "at the anus" (*amporia*).

Social and historical data show that the power invoked and sustained in creating these different bodies of royalty is not unidirectional (see Feeley-Harnik 1991). The creative acts involved in every one of their "appearances" implicitly raise questions about the direction of government (*fanjakana*, "making sustain/endure"), who is governing whom. In contemporary spirit possession, for example, a royal ancestor is commonly said to "come down on the head" of a medium, and possession is clearly a burden for the one thus subjected to royalty. Yet the identification of a royal ancestor with a living commoner begins to turn around when adept spirit/mediums, who are the descendants of commoners or former slaves, deliver the royal spirit from the body of the afflicted person, and eventually bring about its departure in processes closely resembling childbirth and burial rites (Feeley-Harnik 1989). Once an ordinary living human being and a royal ancestor have become joined to one another "like a married couple," the now not-so-"simple person" may exercise considerable power of her or his own, as a political actor and/or curer. Thus, the distribution of power between "difficult things" and "simple people" in particular circumstances is best seen relationally, on the basis of specific questions concerning the workers and work involved in creating new forms. These "services" on the polyform body of royalty are precisely the places where relations of power and subordination are reworked in particular historical circumstances.

The phenomenology of contemporary Sakalava spirit mediumship shows that childbirth and death are not the only ways of modeling and transforming political relations. The seizure involved in "coming down on the head" of a medium is likely to be but a faint echo of the force of the mastery involved in enslavement, another form of social reproduction, which is still—in the carefully circumscribed recollections of elderly people—contrasted with the formation of relations through childbirth. Yet these are not completely distinct domains, as indicated in the persistence of "sword-battle" imagery in women's descriptions of childbirth from the turn of the century to the present (Feeley-Harnik 1995). The Sakalava oral histories set down in abbreviated form in the first two decades of colonial rule (a form suggesting that they may have been responding to the biblical histories of a generation of English and French missionaries) focus almost exclusively on the process of birth. The emergence of a living ruler out of the death of his or her predecessor is seen not as "conquest," "succession," "substitution," "replacement," or "descent," but as "birthing": "*X niteraka Y, Y niteraka Z* . . ."

"Standing up a child" (*mitsangana zanaka*) is now, and presumably was, no less difficult and delicate a social process than the process of "making a person stand up [in a particular social capacity]" (*mampitsangana olo*), through which it is achieved. "Standing up a child" begins in ancestors' blessing in response to earlier giving, followed by further gifts from both prospective parents and other exchanges until a "thing" in the woman's belly, exceedingly difficult in that it is completely unknown and mostly unknowable, finally emerges as a "red child" and later a person.

The process of "birthing" (*miteraka*) is not inherently gendered. Both women and men "bear children" (*miteraka zanaka*) together. The mutual growth of ancestors and their descendants is achieved through their union, celebrated in the sexual imagery of burial rites and spirit possession ceremonies, as well as in marriages, or the famed *lapa be* of nineteenth-century Imerina. In northwestern Madagascar, these new beings are born out of unions between "pairs" of "friends," who are—at least currently in the daily life of people in the northwest—the sought-after completion of unique individuals in spouses, who are compared and contrasted with siblings.

Brothers and sisters born of the same mother are "friends of one belly" (*namana kibo araiky*), a union as intimate in its own ways as the union of spouses who are "friends of one house" (*namana trano araiky*). Children born of a properly housed union are "children of men" (or "brothers' children") *and* "children of women" (or "sisters' children"), because they are cognatically connected to ancestries on both their father's and their mother's "sides," in contrast to an "outside child," reduced to one. In contemporary Madagascar, being only a "sister's child" is the condition of greatest vulnerability. Yet siblings of one belly may be situationally distinguished by these terms when they live with one or the other parent, or around their father's or mother's kin. Brothers as "children of men" may also be distinguished from sisters as "children of women" by relating them to their progeny (male and female), who will have different rights depending on where they live.

For most people who currently identify their "ancestral homeland" with Sakalava domains in western and northern Madagascar (and others in northern and northeastern Madagascar), spouses are very like siblings, but emphatically not siblings. A person is expected to go "searching" for the stranger who will become his or her spouse. Endogamous marriages are considered incestuous, with deadly consequences. Yet brothers and sisters so often foster each other's children that most people grow up as the children of both spouses and siblings. For most people in central and southern Madagascar, including people who identify themselves as Merina, in-marriage is considered the most fruitful, preferably marriages between the children, grandchildren, or great-grandchildren of a brother-sister pair. Beyond certain prohibited unions (including unions between full or half siblings), the closer the marriage partners are to the ancestral brother-sister pair, the better the union is considered to be. Yet "all these marriages, as indeed all marriages between cognates, are in various degrees [considered to be] incestuous" (Bloch 1971:53).

Such differences and ambiguities of opinion are still highly controversial in contemporary Madagascar, used to characterize or condemn whole peoples and regions not simply as "children of men" or "children of women," but as the outcome of legitimate or incestuous, fruitful or deadly unions (see Feeley-Harnik 1991: 84–88, 172–176). In short, Malagasy, like British and French, recognize several theories of social reproduction ranging from enslavement to controversially different models of procreation. The marked regional differences among people, notably the oppositions that "Sakalava" and "Merina" emphasize as distinguishing themselves from the other, suggest the need for a relational analysis that could include their international relations with the British and French bent on reorienting Malagasy forms of social reproduction to their own purposes. I will focus primarily on Sakalava relations with the French during the nineteenth century, with a brief comment about Merina relations at the end.

DEBATING THE LIFE AND DEATH OF SOVEREIGNTY: SAKALAVA-FRENCH RELATIONS IN THE NINETEENTH CENTURY

The relations between "children of men" and "children of women," now characterizing political and domestic relations in the northwest, changed shape in the course of the Sakalava royal histories. These histories date from the early nineteenth century, collected by Guillain (1845) among others, and from the early twentieth century, preserved by Sakalava royalty and their officials in *tantara* written down around 1925. Their common purpose is to trace Sakalava royal ancestors from their "first coming" in the late sixteenth century to the reign of a current ruler, which began in 1925 in the Analalava domain and is still continuing (Feeley-Harnik 1991:65–113).

The histories begin with tensions among "children of men," older and younger brothers whose "fights among kin" led to the departure of the younger brother and his formation of a new Sakalava domain further north. As they move from this early period of expansion into the period now recalled as one of constant flight, beginning in the early 1800s, the narratives shift from relations between brothers to relations between brothers and sisters: first an intense, possibly incestuous, union, followed by what is bitterly remembered by some as a worse violation, a brother's betrayal of his sister to the Merina. Finally, the focus is on the children of sisters, who predominate among the contemporary living Sakalava rulers.

Ravahiny ("Stranger"), who reigned in the Mahajanga area of the northwest coast from around 1778 to 1808, the first female to succeed a long line of men, is represented in Sakalava histories as the turning point. She is followed in the royal genealogies by the brother-sister pair of Andriantsoly and Agnitsaka, who are followed in turn by a succession of female rulers, including Agnitsaka's sister and sister's children (Tahosy, Oantity, Tsiomeko), as these rulers fled northward up the west coast, trying to escape from Merina soldiers. Finally, following a treaty with the French for protection against the Merina, eventually leading to the conquest of the island, the women's reigns are followed by a reestablishment of the dichotomy between brothers' and sisters' children, embodied in the descendants of Andriantsoly, who served the French in Nosy Be, and the descendants of his sister Oantity, who refused to serve them by fleeing south, where they remained independent until the French invasion and conquest in 1895.

Struggles for political sovereignty were inseparable from conflicts over land, first against the Merina, then with the French against the Merina, then during the Franco-Malagasy War of 1883–85, with the Merina, British, and Americans against the French (see Mutibwa 1974: 196, 259). *Capitaine de corvette* Guillain, who wrote down the Sakalava oral histories he heard in the 1840s, expressed his own arguments about political power and succession in gendered terms. He gathered his *Documents sur l'histoire, la géographie, et le commerce de la partie occidentale de Madagascar* in 1842–43. He saw them as providing the framework in which French economic interests and, eventually, Franco-Malagasy relations of economic cooperation in the French colony of Madagascar were to be understood. He completed his "historical sketch" with the *acte de prise de possession* of 5 May 1841, in which the French government claimed the Malagasy island of Nosy Be and adjacent mainland (1845:144). Guillain justified the French act of possession historically by arguing that Sakalava and Merina efforts to conquer Madgascar constituted prototypes of what the French would take further. Their efforts revealed indigenous impulses to expansion and colonization, but beyond a certain point, they were fatally affected by impulses to decline.

According to Guillain, the vital strength of Sakalava and Merina royalty was epitomized in their male rulers, especially the Merina king Radama (deceased 1828), who sought to civilize the country along European lines. The impulses to decline were revealed in the shift to female rulers beginning with Ravahiny's reign (ca. 1778–1808) among the Sakalava and Ranavalona's reign (from 1828) among the Merina. Guillain says explicitly:

The principle of *l'autorité absolue du souverain* is the fundamental basis of order and power in barbaric societies . . . by this alone prepar[ing] for the superiority of the Sakalava over their neighbors. But the monarchic constitution, cornerstone of the edifice of their grandeur . . . [was] profoundly modified by the admission of women to the throne, a truly lethal attack on the first law with chiefs as unruly as the Sakalava chiefs . . . There [in "their sovereign authority"] lay their vitality; when they stopped in this path of progress to fall asleep in the shade of acquired glory, political death began. (ibid.:145)[15]

For Guillain, the Merina monarchy, led by Andrianampoinimerina and his son Radama, took up the task of political unification and economic growth when the Sakalava, weakened by internal struggles, were fatally struck down by the admission of women to the throne. But the hope of a Merina empire

is dead with Radama, and the reign of Ranavalona [his sister, wife, and successor] is a proof that, beyond a certain point, these Malagasy peoples can do nothing on their own, not even set the bounds of their own country. To expect henceforth something to come from mere contact with our civilization would be to hope for a resurrection from the union of a living person with a corpse. (ibid.: 145–146).

Guillain argued that to leave the Malagasy in the hands of their female rulers was "to condemn them to die. . . . [They need] the direction of the elders of the human family" (ibid.:147). He concludes his summary with the words reproduced at the start of this chapter, extolling "the prize of such a possession," now wholly feminine and earthly in form.

Given the lack of ample data concerning Sakalava polities during the seventeenth and eighteenth centuries, when men are alleged to have ruled, it is difficult to assess the extent to which colonial observers have read more contemporary concerns back into the past. Other historical factors might have been significant in Sakalava controversies over brother-sister unions, the relative strengths of children of men and children of women as "masters of ancestors," and related matters. Yet historical data concerning the decades since the 1840s suggest that Malagasy participants also began to see their own tensions about gender and power from the perspectives of the French attempting to take their land and undermine their sovereignty.

Some backers of Andriantsoly (and Maka—a rival "child of men" now commemorated as the progenitor of another branch of Sakalava royalty) may have welcomed French views supporting the priority of children of men over children of women in the formation of ancestries. But there were clearly others in those decades who—even while they expressed their muffled alarm over sibling incest—nonetheless reevaluated the strength of sisters as the living face of power, and conversely the weakness of brothers who abandoned their closest "friends" and followers. Thus, while Guillain (ibid.:145) saw Ravahiny's reign as a peak after which "the power of the Sakalava . . . did no more than decrease," Sakalava followers commemorated her in the praise name Ndramamelooarivo, "Noble Who Gave Birth to Thousands," by which she lives on in the *tantara* and in contemporary mediums. They legitimated the priority of children of women as represented by Agnitsaka, Tahosy, Oantity, Tsiomeko, and their descendants in the Analalava region, governed by the female ruler who now holds the "long iron [knife]" (*vy lava*) emblematic of her legitimacy. What the French saw as ending in weakness, the Malagasy supporters of these women saw as being reborn in a new form.[16]

The likelihood that Sakalava were embroiled in controversies about the relative value of spousal and sibling unions in regenerating hierarchical forms of government that the French were trying to destroy and replace with their own is supported by historical data concerning the Merina with whom Sakalava followers were closely involved at this time. Three points are most relevant to the argument of this essay. With the exception of Berg (1995), who recognizes the administrative acumen of Ranavalona I in particular, most observers of Merina monarchy since the early nineteenth century have interpreted the sequence of queens as figureheads masking the real power of the prime ministers who were their successive husbands.[17] French observers writing in the late eighteenth and early nineteenth centuries (prior to 1817) argue that the Malagasy themselves preferred male heirs (Delivré 1974:235). Yet Malagasy documents from the Merina royal archives emphasize the role of a group called "brothers and sisters" in deciding succession, and a clear emphasis on brother-sister endogamous unions and heirs of such unions. Like the Sakalava debates in the early nineteenth century, the contemporaneous debates in Imerina (Delivré ibid.:235–283) seem to have focused especially on the relative power of "children of sisters" (*zanak'anabaviny*) in these unions and as heirs to the position of living ruler (see Feeley-Harnik 1991:506, n. 66).

Secondly, the statements that Merina queens made in their proclamations (*kabary*) to the people of Antananarivo, including foreign residents, suggest that they were well aware of French and English views of female rulers as figureheads, inferior to their male predecessors, subordinate to parliamentary officials like the prime minister, or simply weak in themselves, and in some instances explicitly countered such views.[18] Widespread Malagasy awareness of the ambiguously double, even multiple, significance of the Merina queens as emblems of power to Malagasy and European observers is suggested by their names as living rulers: Ranavalona, the common name of three of the four queens: "Beautifully Wrapped One," especially something wrapped well to protect and preserve it for use on a future occasion; and Rasoherina: "Chrysalis," especially the "child of the silkworm" (*zana-dandy*), wrapped in the cocoon of silk fibers used in making the finest royal cloth.

Finally, the Merina version of the Sakalava annual ritual of bathing the ancestors, called in Imerina *ny fandroana* ("the bath"), should be reconsidered as one of the major ways in which Ranavalona I proclaimed Merina conceptions about the generative power of "children of women" as living rulers to other Merina and Malagasy, and the power of "female rulers" to Europeans, using this form as a deliberate alternative to Christian baptism. Radama I, Ranavalona's brother/husband and predecessor, had told a British traveler, Sir Henry Keating, in 1825 that he considered circumcision "our ceremony of baptism, which is no doubt different from the European custom" (cited in Bloch 1986:127). In my view, Ranavalona I developed the royal bath of the living ruler (herself) not only as a commentary on the royal circumcision ritual, but also as a way of incorporating and countering Christian rituals of baptism identified with British and French challenges to Malagasy sovereignty.

Here in the Malagasy polities of the nineteenth century, as in European monarchies, there is a strong emphasis on the individual character of living and ancestral rulers, indeed the singularity of royalty by comparison to infinite numbers of "simple people" who are their clone-like followers, "everyone a thousand" (*sambarivo*), to use the Sakalava idiom. Yet here—perhaps because of their less familiar qualities—it is more obvious that a singular focus on these figures obscures the very relations from which their all-encompassing singularity is socially and historically created. In the Malagasy as in other African cases, there is a strong emphasis on the engendering of political-economic growth and transformation that should encourage us still further to reanalyze European monarchies from a broader comparative perspective. In the African and European cases, it is also evident that births may derive from different kinds of unions, perhaps involving alternative theories of conception. Following Kantorowicz, Aristotelian theories of procreation existed alongside those of the Stoics and Hermetics, perhaps persisting into the nineteenth century. Most European scholars have focused on relations between spouses, fathers, mothers, and sons. Yet Shell (1988) documents some recognition of the power of brother-sister unions during the reign of Elizabeth I that might prove to be more widespread and enduring. In Madagascar, the relationship of nineteenth-century debates to contemporary controversies about sexual and marital propriety and political leadership still needs to be clarified. Yet even the little evidence we now have indicates that such debates are highly sensitive to the historical circumstances in which people find themselves.

In making my argument, I am building on the earlier work of James (1978) on the "matrifocus" in African politics, Sacks (1979) on the significance of sister-brother links, and Barnes (1991) on female leaders in Africa as political agents, together with Weiner's (1992) insights on the political-economic dimensions of "sibling intimacy" in the Pacific. I suggest that Malagasy rulers in Sakalava domains and in Imerina adopted policies of countering British and French efforts in Madagascar that drew simultaneously on modes of force and also subtle organizational strategies. Malagasy queens were indeed actors in their own rights, but attuned to their significance as emblems of power and authority among Malagasy as well as those of others. They were *sisters*—emphatically marking a shift from "children of brothers" to "children of sisters" as living rulers (the fruit of sister-brother unions)—concerned with "keeping" Malagasy political-economic autonomy, increasingly identified with control over land. They deliberately enacted gender roles that would appear to mirror the dismissive assumptions of Europeans, but simultaneously defeat them, especially in the "showings" (*fisehoana*) of Sakalava and Merina sovereignty like the royal bath. Where the French thought they had achieved the subordination of the island, reduced to feminine forms, I have argued that Sakalava and Merina followers saw the female forms of the living dimensions of polybodied beings, inextricable from ancestral and other powerful qualities, protecting and regenerating new forms of autonomy.

CONCLUSION: RETHINKING THE "CULTURAL FLOWS" OF POLITICAL REPRODUCTION AND CHANGE

Nineteenth-century observers of Malagasy, French, and British relations provide ample evidence of "cultural flows" coming from all sides. French officials and merchants evaluated the possibility of Indian Ocean possessions with clear presumptions about gender and power, in which the degenerate, even "lethal" female form of Malagasy monarchies provided them with one of their main ideological justifications for their revivifying interventions. Likewise historical evidence from Malagasy sources indicates that Malagasy participants were aware of French and British presumptions and developed political countercultures designed to protect Malagasy ideologies and practices beginning well before the colonial period.

I have situated my brief analysis of Malagasy-French relations in the framework of comparable flows and counterflows on a larger political and ideological scale. The cultural presumptions evident in nineteenth-century French and British practice have their contemporary analogues in the cultural flows of influential theories of social analysis, the very development of which is inextricable not only from the history of European political forms, but also European-African relations. Indeed, European representations of African monarchies as exotic females (or as bloodthirsty males) must have served not only to legitimate the subordination of African polities, but to facilitate the transition from monarchy to constitutional monarchy or republic in Europe, while preserving the class systems with which they were articulated.

Here I have argued that we would benefit from the intellectual counterflow inherent in placing Melanesian, European, and African theories of the gender dynamics of social reproduction in a broader comparative perspective, drawing not only on theories of regicide, queen mothers, and the politics of marriage, but also the procreational imagery of African and Melanesian polyarchies, including "sibling intimacy." Such a common framework might allow us to ask still more substantive questions about the diversity evident even in the handful of cases cited in this chapter.

In concluding, I want to indicate how such a comparative framework might help to dismantle kinship-to-contract reasoning still further by breaching the monarchy-republic barrier by which it is constituted. At least for Malagasy-French relations, one of the most fruitful places to break down kinship-to-contract evolutionism, to show that procreational imagery is not simply metaphorical, but constitutive of "family-state" relations not only in monarchies, but in republics and their colonies, is to focus precisely on the bureaucratic forms that persist across the monarchy-republic divide, in fact confounding the person-office, spiritual-rational, kinship-contract, domestic-political antinomies still associated with this dichotomy.

In Europe, French family-state politics were distinctive not only for their persistant focus on the *loi salique*, which continued to be debated throughout the nineteenth century (Hanley 1994:125–126), but also for their pronatalist emphasis, intensified by widespread concern over the high death toll of French soldiers in the Franco-Prussian war of 1870. Just how pronatalist and other procreational policies figure into the repeated engendering of republican states out of monarchies during the nineteenth century in France remains to be explored. When these policies were adopted in the new legislation that colonial governor Gallieni used to form the French colony of Madagascar in 1897, they were clearly directed at creating a body of laborers considered essential to making the new polity grow and develop.

The link made between "social" and "biological" health and consequent "medicalization" of social issues that Nye (1982) has argued was a distinctive feature of French approaches to social crisis from 1885 to World War I, in politics and in social theory, may have contributed to the prominence of medical solutions in the formation of a strong French colony in Madagascar. Nye argues that "the alarming state of the French population . . . was regarded by nearly all observers as the 'master-pathology'" (ibid.: 106). Although Gallieni advocated a range of new laws for increasing the Malagasy population, public-health legislation was central (Feeley-Harnik 1995). Within months of his arrival, Gallieni founded a medical school, completed in 1897 (Wright 1991:261–262). The first "native hospital" and Institut Pasteur were finished shortly afterward, in 1898 and 1902 (ibid.:263). The first hospital building was "far and away the largest structure on the island," to which were added many more, creating a huge health district in the capital, and eventually what Wright calls "sanitary statism" (ibid.:263). The failure of these medical bureaucratic interventions into Malagasy procreation, evident already in the 1920s, was one factor in the development of alternative strategies for growth exemplified in the negotiations with the Polish, Japanese, and eventually Nazi governments to settle potentially millions of European Jews in Madagascar, mentioned at the beginning of this chapter.

Perhaps because public-health measures were made so critical to Madagascar's growth as a colony, they were also one of the earliest and most important sources of rebellion against French rule in the highlands where these measures were first imposed. The medical school at Befelatanana was the center of the first major anti-French nationalist organization, the VVS, founded in 1913. The same then-medical students were leaders again in the Malagasy revolt against French rule in 1947. One of them, Joseph Ravoahangy, was named the first Président de la Santé publique et de la Population in Madagascar's First Republic after independence in 1960 (Rajemisa Raolison 1966: 305–306, 311–313, 380). These natalist issues persist in international debates surrounding population growth and conservation in contemporary Madagascar.

NOTES

An earlier draft of this paper was presented in the seminar on "Women and Power in Africa" at Indiana University, February 1992. I am grateful to the participants of the seminar and its organizers, Paula Ben-Amos Girshick and Beverly J. Stoeltje, for their helpful comments. I thank Maria Grosz-Ngaté and Omari H. Kokole, editors of this volume, as well as T. O. Beidelman, Gerald Berg, Alan Harnik, Vanessa Harnik, and Frederick Klaits for their valuable comments on later drafts, and Sarah Hanley and Sylvia Schafer for their discussions of particular points.

1. The completion of the Suez Canal in 1869 disrupted the tenuous standoff between the British and French that Malagasy had sought to maintain. The British lost interest in protecting their seaway around the Cape of Good Hope and turned their attention to the headwaters of the Nile and to India. The Malagasy fought a "war" with the French over land rights in 1883–85, during which they made a failed appeal to the United States for support "on the grounds that the Americans had won their independence by having successfully fended off a 'foreign invasion' of their country" (Mutibwa 1974:267). In 1890, Great Britain recognized a French protectorate over Madagascar in exchange for France's recognition of earlier British claims. The French justified the invasion of 1895 on the grounds that they were defending their protectorate. Territorial and political sovereignty were the key issues in Malagasy international relations during the nineteenth century.

2. Walters was not unique in linking Madagascar, Liberia, and the United States. Vermonter John W. Phelps, a general in the Union Army, and active in the antislavery movement, published a history of Madagascar in 1883, shortly after the arrival of the Malagasy embassy seeking help against French land claims. Phelps's history of Madagascar was written to serve "the true interests of Africa, and . . . the best manner of serving these interests through our Liberian colony, which lies on the opposite side of the African continent from Madagascar" (1883:3). He too saw the Christian "Queen of Madagascar" as proof of the country's civilization (ibid.:92–93).

3. During the 1920s and 1930s, the Polish, Japanese, and French governments all explored the possibility of solving problems of "surplus population" and high unemployment by sending their poorest citizens to Madagascar. The German plan that Hitler adopted for sending the Jews of Europe to Madagascar was first proposed in 1931 and by the late 1930s involved Jewish leaders in Warsaw, Tel Aviv, Stockholm, and New York (Hevesi 1941:381, 389).

4. As stated in the description of the book project.

5. This paper, based mainly on verbal records preserved in Malagasy, French, and British written and oral historical accounts of royalty, barely skims the surface of the complex iconography of African and European international relations during this period.

A full study would have to take into account the wide array of gendered images found in official portraits and photographs, popular literature, postcards, cloth wrappers, tailored clothing, and commercial advertisements, made for domestic and foreign markets in Madagascar, Africa, Europe, the United States, and Asia.

6. In Frazer's letter of November 1889 to George Macmillan, asking if he would publish *The Golden Bough*, Frazer noted that "the resemblance of many of the savage customs and ideas to the fundamental doctrines of Christianity is striking. But I make no reference to this parallelism, leaving my readers to draw their own conclusions, one way or the other" (cited in Ackerman 1987:95). The second edition of 1900 (vol. 3:86–96) did include a short discussion of Christ's crucifixion, moved to the footnotes of the third edition of 1913–15 (vol. 6:412–423), which Frazer dropped from the abridged edition of 1922.

    In his letter to Macmillan, Frazer explained that the priest of Nemi had to die because "his slaughter was regarded as the death of the god" (ibid.). It turns out almost immediately that the goddess Diana "did not reign alone in her grove at Nemi" (1889:4), but together with two young gods, including Hippolytus, "chaste and fair . . . who spurned the love of women," thus bringing on a torrent of problems from women who loved and hated him, as a result of which he ends up as the "dying god" in Diana's grove. Frazer added a large section on corn maidens, inspired by the legends of Demeter and her daughter Persephone, mother-daughter unions that he saw as analogous to the father-son pairs of gods. He often referred to the gods' mothers and sisters whom they married. Yet the corn maidens soon give way to corn people, then corn animals, snatched from roadsides for sacrifices. Noting that Persephone's death and rebirth is what makes these corn figures relevant, Frazer returns to his main theme: the "dying god" that remained the centerpiece of the book through all four editions, including the abridged.

7. Meanwhile, contemporary British and French historians were overemphasizing *la monarchie absolue* embodied in such European rulers as Louis XIV (Mettam 1989:13–44).

8. Luc de Heusch (1958:7, 132) named *la pensée novatrice* of Lévi-Strauss as the most important source of his *Essai . . . on incest* in Africa. Like most of his contemporaries, he dismissed Frazer as an evolutionist. Paul (1982:305) suggests that Frazer was exploring Oedipal themes.

9. Matilda, daughter of Henry I, contested the rule of the grandson of William the Conqueror, Stephen of Blois (1135–54). Matilda claimed to be "Queen of the English" in 1141–47, but could not get herself crowned (Hackett 1995:246, n. 30).

10. Hackett herself pays closer attention than previous scholars to how the doctrine apparently celebrating "the union of diverse qualities in the sole person of the Queen" could also be used to "acknowledge, and even accentuate, division," thus serving as a covert form of criticism (ibid.:165–166).

11. Barnes (1991:1–2) emphasizes that in certain historical circumstances, female rulers not only "embodied and idealized the roles of supporter and protector but also politicized them," as in the polity of Lagos in 1816–1853, where maternal homesteads were common places of refuge for embattled rulers. Stoeltje's (1991) work on Asante politics shows that female officials could provide refuge for dissidents that their male counterparts had condemned to death (see also Lebeuf 1963). Indeed, as Ben-Amos (1983) shows for Benin, "queen mothers" could kill the very kings to whom they give birth.

12. Beidelman's pioneering (1966) study of the Swazi *Incwala* shows how the singularly plural king of the king-queen mother pair at the head of the Swazi dual monarchy is constituted and animated with power through the confounding of qualities ordinarily separated in persons and things. The queen mother is the focus of Swazi rain ritual (Kuper 1935), but the *Incwala* and rain ceremony have yet to be analyzed together.

13. As in the European cases, we need more research on the ideas and practices in-
     volved in creating such beings, including their "presence" and "image." Thus,
     Cohen's (1977) analysis of the gendered structure of government in the Pabir king-
     dom of Biu in precolonial northern Nigeria shows how the Maigira, "a senior daugh-
     ter of a previous monarch" (ibid.:18), was seen as giving birth to kingship during the
     interregnum between one male ruler and the next. Cohen emphasizes the utility of
     thus appeasing a lineage segment losing access to the king's position (ibid.:24), with-
     out exploring the gender dynamics implied in Pabir metaphors of birth or their ex-
     periential roots in everyday life. James (1978), though she too sees birth in biological
     terms, argues on the basis of Asante and Uduk ethnography and history that
     Africanists need to take into account the "indigenous view of the moral primacy of
     biological motherhood in the definition of social relations" (ibid.: 150). Schnepel's
     (1991) reanalysis of regicide among the Shilluk of the southern Sudan is organized
     around Shilluk conceptions of *wei* ("a spiritual life-giving force or vitality", ibid.:48),
     but restricted in focus to the *reth* ("king"). Similarly, Ifeka's (1992) study of the pow-
     ers of 'Nso "queen mothers," and Warnier's (1993) study of 'Nso "kings as contain-
     ers," emphasize the widespread importance of *sëm*, "transmissible life essence"
     (Warnier ibid.:306) for people in the Cameroon Grasslands historically and in current
     business and politics. Warnier emphasizes that *sëm* is "a genderless substance . .
     shared by both genders," carried by bodily substances like semen and breast milk; in-
     deed the mother's *sëm* is considered the more desirable (ibid.:307). Ideally, their in-
     sights should be combined in an analysis of the multifaceted dimensions of 'Nso
     leaders.

14. Documenting the pervasiveness of the "queen mother" approach to women's roles
     in African political hierarchies, and exploring why Belgian, French, British, German,
     and other European social theorists should have insisted on this category in the face
     of contrary evidence, would take us far beyond the page limits of this paper. Suffice
     it to say that queen mothers are clearly significant in several cases, e.g., Swazi dual
     monarchy. Yet the vernacular term may be better translated as "female ruler," not
     "queen mother" (as in the Pabir case, Cohen 1977:18), or it may be a generic term
     like *kabaka,* applied to the "king," "queen mother," and "queen sister" (who is the
     lubuga wife of the "king") in Buganda (Roscoe 1911:236, 84). Scholars need to be
     more specific about the kinship relations involved, as when Rattray (1923:82, n. 1)
     notes that the Asante queen mother is "not necessarily the chief's mother, often his
     sister," though he goes no further. We would also benefit from more specificity
     about the unions involved. For example, in the Pabir case (see Cohen ibid.:18–20),
     the figures isolated as "queen mother" and "head of women in capital" seem to be
     part of sister-brother pairs in adjacent, parent-child generations, and may be better
     understood in those terms. In Buganda, the pair of midwives who occupy such an
     important place at the royal capital are "the King's Mother's sisters" (Roscoe 1911:50).

15. Like Sakalava, Guillain and other French observers saw Ravahiny ("the Stranger") as
     the turning point in Sakalava history. Like the Sakalava, the French observers also de-
     bated about the incest, endogamy, or exogamy involved in the succession of "the
     Stranger" and her heirs, but the main French concern was for the "physical purity" of
     Sakalava "royal blood" (Feeley-Harnik 1991:79–84; see Hanley 1994:120 on the "alien"
     or "foreign" status of French women in the French blood-seminal theory).

16. As I have argued elsewhere (1991:93–113), Sakalava strategies concerning gender
     were inextricable from strategies involving even more radical confrontations with
     the dead. The diminishing autonomy of living rulers, harried and eventually con-
     quered by outsiders, seems to have led Sakalava followers to shift their attention
     from the living rulers to ancestors, embodied in forms they could protect even
     when cornered. Royal relics, the paramount symbols of legitimacy and the objects of
     the most important services honoring royalty in the south, were small, portable, and
     prone to theft. The current paired relationship between the capital of the living ruler
     (*doany*) and the royal cemetery (*mahabo*) for the burial of predecessors' corpses
     seems to have originated in new ways of birthing ancestors out of corpses in forms
     that would be harder to steal, probably after the Merina had indeed seized the relics
     constituting the "root" of the Sakalava domains in the northwest. Spirit mediumship,

whereby male royal ancestors live again in the bodies of female mediums, is another important dimension of Sakalava political action that has persisted through the colonial period into the present.

These Sakalava strategies could be seen as a kind of protective, yet regenerative "containment" (see Warnier 1993). In contrast to what Rowlands (1993) argues for Benin, and what many historians have argued about the conquest of Madagascar in 1895, I do not see evidence of nihilism or ceremonial involution in Malagasy politics, but continuing efforts before, during, and long after 1895 to thwart French goals. Many contemporary observers in late-nineteenth-century Madagascar thought that the Malagasy had been betrayed by those who purported to be their friends, and this is Mutibwa's (1974:374–376) conclusion based on an extensive reanalysis of their foreign relations.

17. Berg (1995:74) attributes the "received view of Ranavalona . . . [as] an atavist throwback to a dark age of superstition and brutality, in contrast to Radama's 'progressive' and 'modern' reign," as originating in the views of evangelical Christian missionaries from Great Britain. Ranavalona I questioned the universalism of their views and eventually removed them from Imerina. With some exceptions, most studies of Ranavalona and her successors focus on royal ritual, emphasizing what they see as empty or deceiving (see Berg ibid.:89, n. 3).

18. See, for example, Ranavalona I's sharp reply ("If it is because I am a woman . . .") in 1829 to Captain Gourbeyre's aggressiveness in negotiations leading to war with the French in 1829 (from a French observer's report, cited in Berg 1995:86) and the similar statements ("that because I am a woman . . .") in the *kabary* she made to Malagasy and Europeans at her coronation in 1829, when she was visibly pregnant (quoted in a British Colonial Office report and in London Missionary Society correspondence, cited in Berg ibid.). See also Ranavalona II's *kabary* ("God made me a woman, still . . .") of 7 June 1883, calling for Malagasy to defend their "ancestral land" against French claims (in the Franco-Malagasy war of 1883–85), translated by Rev. Richardson (cited in Mutibwa 1974:253 and Brown 1979:227, who compares Ranavalona II to Elizabeth I in this context); Rasoherina's proclamation published in the government-owned *Gazety Malagasy* of 6 June 1884, exhorting Malagasy to defend "the land of our ancestors" by "ris[ing] to the strength of manhood", reported in letters to the British Foreign Office and the London Missionary Society (cited in Mutibwa 1974:270–271, 299); and Ranavalona III's *kabary* of 25 September 1895 during the French invasion of Madagascar ("I am but a woman, but . . ."), reported by a contemporary English war correspondent (cited in Brown ibid.:248, 269, 298).

Berg's research on the documents written in Malagasy in the Merina royal archives suggests that the proclamations of Merina queens for their subjects made different claims about their gender in malagasy idioms. Thus, Ranavalona I stated in her *kabary* of 1831: "*Tsy vavy aho fa lahy. Fa izaho ny fanovan' ny roambin' ny folo manjaka*" ["Not female I but male, for I am the changeling of the twelve-who-rule [the royal ancestors]" (Merina Royal Archives, cited in Berg 1995:86; Malagasy phrase by personal communication, January 1992), drawing on the singular pluralism of Merina royalty.

BIBLIOGRAPHY

Ackerman, R. 1987. *J. G. Frazer: His Life and Work*. Cambridge: Cambridge University Press.

Axton, M. 1977. *The Queen's Two Bodies: Drama and the Elizabethan Succession*. London: Royal Historical Society.

Barnes, S. T. 1991. "Gender and the Politics of Support and Protection in Pre-colonial West Africa." Paper delivered at a conference on "Queens, Queen Mothers, Priestesses and Power: Case Studies in African Gender," April 8–11, New York University. Manuscript.

Beidelman, T. O. 1966. "Swazi Royal Ritual." *Africa* 36:373–405.

Ben-Amos, P. 1983. "In Honor of Queen Mothers." In *The Art of Power, the Power of Art*, pp. 79–83, P. Ben Amos and A. Rubin, eds. Monograph Series no. 19. Los Angeles: University of California at Los Angeles, Museum of Cultural History.

Berg, G. M. 1995. "Writing Ideology: Ranavalona, the Ancestral Bureaucrat." *History in Africa* 22:73–92.

Bloch, M. 1971. *Placing the Dead: Tombs, Ancestral Villages, and Kinship Organization in Madagascar*. London: Seminar.

———. 1986. *From Blessing to Violence: History and Ideology in the Circumcision Ritual of the Merina of Madagascar*. Cambridge University Press.

———. 1987. "The Ritual of the Royal Bath in Madagascar: The Dissolution of Death, Birth and Fertility into Authority." In *Rituals of Royalty: Power and Ceremonial in Traditional Societies*, pp. 271–297, D. Cannadine and S. Price, eds. Cambridge University Press.

Brown, M. 1979. *Madagascar Rediscovered: A History From Early Times to the Present*. Hamden, CT: Archon.

Cohen, R. 1977. "Oedipus Rex and Regina: The Queen Mother in Africa." *Africa* 47:14–30.

Delivré, A. 1974. *L'Histoire des rois d'Imerina: Interprétation d'une tradition orale*. Paris: Klincksieck.

Deschamps, H. 1959. *Les migrations intérieures à Madagascar*. Paris: Berger-Levrault.

Feeley-Harnik, G. 1985. "Issues in Divine Kingship." *Annual Review of Anthropology* 14:273–313.

———. 1989. "Cloth and the Creation of Ancestors in Madagascar." In *Cloth and Human Experience*, pp. 73–116, A. B. Weiner and J. Schneider, eds. Washington, DC: Smithsonian Institution Press.

———. 1991. *A Green Estate: Restoring Independence in Madagascar*. Washington, DC: Smithsonian Institution Press.

———. 1995. "Plants and People, Children or Wealth?: Shifting Grounds of `Choice' in Madagascar." *PoLAR: Political and Legal Anthropology Review* 18:1–21.

Fortes, M. 1959. *Oedipus and Job in West African Religion.* Cambridge University Press.

———. 1962. "Ritual and Office." In *Essays on the Ritual of Social Relations*, pp. 83–88, M. Gluckman, ed. Manchester: Manchester University Press.

Frazer, J. G. 1890. *The Golden Bough: A Study in Magic and Religion*. 2 vols. London: Macmillan.

Guillain, C. 1845. *Documents sur l'histoire, la géographie, et le commerce de la partie occidentale de Madagascar*. Paris: Imprimerie Royale.

Hackett, H. 1995. *Virgin Mother, Maiden Queen: Elizabeth I and the Cult of the Virgin Mary*. London: Macmillan.

Hanley, S. 1989. "Engendering the State: Family Formation and State Building in Early Modern France." *French Historical Studies* 16:4–27.

———. 1994. "The Monarchic State in Early Modern France: Marital Regime Government and Male Right." In *Politics, Ideology, and the Law in Early Modern Europe*, pp. 107–126, Adrianna E. Bakos, ed. Rochester, NY: University of Rochester Press.

Hayden, I. 1987. *Symbol and Privilege: The Ritual Context of British Royalty*. Tucson: University of Arizona Press.

de Heusch, L. 1958. *Essais sur le symbolisme de l'inceste royal en Afrique*. Brussels: Université Libre de Bruxelles.

Hevesi, E. 1941. "Hitler's Plan for Madagascar." *Contemporary Jewish Record* 4:381–394.

Ifeka, C. 1992. "The Mystical and Political Power of Queen Mothers, Kings and Commoners in Nso', Cameroon." In *Persons and Powers of Women in Diverse Cultures: Essays in Commemoration of Audrey I. Richards, Phyllis Kaberry and Barbara E. Ward*, pp. 135–157, Shirley Ardener, ed. New York: Berg.

James, W. 1978. "Matrifocus on African Women." In *Defining Females: The Nature of Women in Society*, pp. 140–162, Shirley Ardener, ed. New York: J. Wiley.

Jochens, J. M. 1987. "The Politics of Reproduction: Medieval Norwegian Kingship." *American Historical Review* 92:327–349.

Kantorowicz, E. H. 1957. *The King's Two Bodies: A Study in Medieval Political Theology.* Princeton University Press.

Krige, E. G. and J. D. Krige. 1943. *The Realm of a Rain-Queen: A Study of the Pattern of Lovedu Society.* Oxford University Press.

Kuper, H. 1935. "The Swazi Rain Ceremony." *Bantu Studies* 9:35–50.

Lebeuf, A. D. 1963. "The Role of Women in the Political Organization of African Societies." In *Women of Tropical Africa*, pp. 93–119, D. Paulme, ed. Berkeley: University of California Press.

Mayer, A. 1985. "The King's Two Thrones." *Man* (n.s.) 20:201–227.

Merrick, J. 1988. "Royal Bees: The Gender Politics of the Beehive in Early Modern Europe." In *Studies in Eighteenth-Century Culture*, vol. 18, pp. 7–37, J. Yolton and L. E. Brown, eds. East Lansing, MI: Colleagues Press (for the American Society for 18th-Century Studies).

Mettam, R. 1989. *Power and Faction in Louis XIV's France*. Oxford: Blackwell.

Mutibwa, P. M. 1974. *The Malagasy and the Europeans: Madagascar's Foreign Relations, 1861–1895*. Ibadan History Series. New York: Humanities Press.

Nye, R. A. 1982. "Heredity, Pathology and Psychoneurosis in Durkheim's Early Work." *Knowledge and Society: Studies in the Sociology of Culture Past and Present* 4:103–142.

Olivier, M. 1938. "Madagascar—terre d'asile." *L'Illustration* (Paris): 199 [February 19]: 197–199.

Phelps, J. W. 1883. *The Island of Madagascar. A Sketch, Descriptive and Historical.* New York: John B. Alden.

Rajemisa Raolison, R. 1966. *Dictionnaire historique et géographique de Madagascar.* Fianarantsoa: Librarie Ambozontany.

Rattray, R. S. 1923. *Ashanti.* London: Oxford University Press.

Roscoe, J. 1911. *The Baganda: An Account of Their Native Customs and Beliefs.* London: Macmillan.

Rowlands, M. 1993. "The Good and Bad Death: Ritual Killing and Historical Transformation in a West African Kingdom." *Paideuma* 39:291–301.

Sacks, K. 1979. *Sisters and Wives: The Past and Future of Sexual Equality.* Westport, CT: Greenwood.

Schnepel, B. 1991. "Continuity Despite and Through Death: Regicide and Royal Shrines Among the Shilluk of Southern Sudan." *Africa* 61:40–70.

Sharp, L. A. 1993. *The Possessed and the Dispossessed: Spirits, Identity, and Power in a Madagascar Migrant Town.* Berkeley: University of California Press.

Shell, M. 1988. *"Measure for Measure": Incest and the Ideal of Universal Siblinghood.* Stanford: Stanford University Press.

Stoeltje, B. J. 1991. "Asante Queenmothers: A Study in Female Authority." Paper delivered at a conference on "Queens, Queen Mothers, Priestesses and Power: Case Studies in African Gender," April 8–11, New York University. Manuscript.

Thornton, J. K. 1991. "Legitimacy and Political Power: Queen Njinga, 1624–1663." *Journal of African History* 32:25–40.

Walters, J. J. 1994 [1891]. *Guanya Pau: A Story of an African Princess.* Lincoln: University of Nebraska Press.

Walzer, M., ed. 1974. *Regicide and Revolution: Speeches at the Trial of Louis XVI.* London: Cambridge University Press.

Warnier, J. P. 1993. "The King as a Container in the Cameroon Grassfields." *Paideuma* 39:303–319.

Weiner, A. B. 1992. *Inalienable Possessions: The Paradox of Keeping-While-Giving.* Berkeley: University of California Press.

Wright, G. 1991. *The Politics of Design in French Colonial Urbanism.* University of Chicago Press.

Yanagisako, S. J. and C. F. Collier. 1987. "Toward a Unified Analysis of Gender and Kinship." In *Gender and Kinship: Essays Toward a Unified Analysis*, pp. 14–50, J. F. Collier and S. J. Yanagisako, eds. Stanford: Stanford University Press.

Yates, F. A. 1975. *Astraea: The Imperial Theme in the Sixteenth Century.* London: Routledge and Kegan Paul.

FOREIGN TONGUES AND DOMESTIC BODIES:
GENDERED CULTURAL REGIONS AND REGIONALIZED SACRED FLOWS

JUDY ROSENTHAL

The *Voduwo* are slave spirits. Hundreds of years ago peoples of the north—
Hausa, Mossi, Tchamba and Kabye—passed through Eweland. Some of
them suffered hardships and had to sell their children to our ancestors.
These children did everything for us. They worked their whole lives and
made their masters rich. When they grew old and died, the objects we had
taken from them upon their arrival—cloths, bracelets, fetishes, sandals—
these things became the Vodu, and the slave spirits came and settled in them
and became our gods. If we do not serve them, generation after generation,
we become ill and die. It is beautiful when the Vodu comes to possess you. It
is good. (Gorovodu priestess)

Gorovodu spirits are *amefeflewo* [bought people]. They made our law. If we
don't obey the law we become ill, and only Gorovodu can heal us. When we
play *brekete* drums and sing their songs, and dance, then they come out.
They want to dance too. When they come to possess us it is because they
need our arms and legs to dance. And that is why people crave to watch
Gorovodu ceremonies—when the gods come to us it is very beautiful.
Women receive Gorovodu into their bodies more often than men do. They
love the spirits more. Men are afraid because the gods are fierce. Our women
are stronger than our men. (Gorovodu priest)

In this essay I explore Ewe and Guin-Mina conceptualizations of gender, slavery, and the foreign "north" as they operate within Gorovodu and Mama Tchamba
Vodu and Tro (spirit, divinity) orders in southern Ghana, Togo, and Benin.[1] I hope to
give readers a lingering interest in practices of Gorovodu and Mama Tchamba spirit
possession and memories of Ewe slave possession, in their gendered and "(dis)en-
slaved" traveling to and fro, across various borders, literal and symbolic. Permutations
of binary oppositions, especially female/male, south/north, and master/ slave, are
central to these religious orders and to the ethnographic materials that follow. They
constitute an implicit cultural critique of Western concepts of gender, place, and

caste. While spirit possession in this case definitely includes what Janice Boddy calls "historical consciousness" (1994:417), it is also an event and a state that exists for itself, for the ecstasy and pleasure of both gods and spirit hosts.

I have employed the forum of the present volume to ask more questions than it is possible to answer in a single paper, for they loom too large to ignore, although convincing answers are not yet in print; nor are they more than tentative in my own interpretive efforts.

It is difficult to establish exactly when Gorovodu and Mama Tchamba orders began, given that spirit possession itself and the worship of *trowo* had apparently always been crucial to the lives of the Adja-Tado emigrants toward the coast (via the city of Notse), who began to call themselves "Ewe" by the seventeenth century.[2] This was also true of surrounding peoples, including Asante, Fante, Ga, Fon, Guin, and Mina. Documents from the early sixteenth century[3] mention "fetishes" and ceremonies that are undoubtedly the precursors of modern Vodu religion, of which there are numerous specific orders. However, archival research indicates that the divinities of one of these orders, the present Gorovodu pantheon, sprang up one by one under diverse names all along the coast, in various ethnic communities, during the colonial period, around the turn of the twentieth century.[4] Probably only since the 1940s has the pantheon as it stands today come together as a "family" of some six to twelve protective spirits; and not every community has the very same collection.

These spirits "do the same work" as numerous related gods, including deities before them who are somehow still a part of the more recent avatars. Different *trowo* have always protected worshipers from illness, envy (*n'bia*), and violence; they have insured fertility of women and fields, abundance of game and fish, healing of physical and spiritual sickness, availability of jobs, just arbitration of disputes, and blessings of respect, joy and community. The Vodu orders central to this paper also perform these tasks. But the "work" (*edowowo*) that is specific to Gorovodu and Mama Tchamba, and missing in older Vodu orders indigenous to Ewe regions, includes a celebration of exchange between north and south, foreigners and family, slaves of yesteryear and descendants of their masters, all permuted with categories of maleness and femaleness.

Gorovodu ("kola nut Vodu") is a coming-together of a wide array of witch finding spirits and other deities "from the north" that were worshiped during the colonial period. Asante and Fon related orders were called by the name of the father god, Kunde, as well as by the name of his wife, Ablewa (or Abrewa).[5] Ewe eventually grouped Kunde and Ablewa with Sunia Compo (Senya Bupo, Senyon Kipo, etc.), Sacra, Banguele, and Nana Wango, which at one time were separate orders, also present among Fante and other Akan groups. Another name for Gorovodu is "Brekete," which is actually the name of the drumming rhythm necessary to produce trance.

This particular collection of spirits, said by some priests to be spirits of slaves, rather quickly changed focus from witch finding (although that remains one of their tasks) to performing the usual protective and healing work demanded of most deities, and, above all, to a symbolic (implicit) restatement of exchange relationships between north and south. Asante Abrewa worship did focus mainly on witch finding, according to the missionary Debrunner (1961); it may have included some of the misogynous abuses known in Tigare or Atinga.[6] It is possible that such excesses also occurred in Ewe Ablewa and Kunde cults at the turn of the century. In any case, the "fetishes" that now compose the Gorovodu order were accused of all sorts of evil by the Christian clergy, as well as by numerous British and German colonial administrators.[7] Fiawoo (1971) insists, however, that Gorovodu was never mainly a witch-finding cult, but was rather an *atike* or "medicine" (literally, "tree root") society, focused on healing.

Mama Tchamba, also "northern" and marked by consumption of kola nuts, is an order consecrated specifically to the honoring of northern slaves who married into Ewe patrilines and are therefore ancestors of their worshipers.[8] Most in-marrying slaves were women. There is, to my knowledge, nothing in print about Mama Tchamba. Etienne Ahiako (ORSTOM Lomé) believes this specific order began only a few decades ago, about the same time that the Gorovodu pantheon was gathered together out of various witch-finding cults.

Gorovodu and Mama Tchamba religious communities say that their *trowo* come from the north, the savannah regions, or from Muslim countries. They celebrate cultures of the "north" and welcome "stranger gods," including the spirits of slaves, into their midst, even the midst of their individual minds and bodies, in trance. This hosting of the foreigner deities is conceived of as a wifely act. The Vodu orders themselves are sometimes categorized as female, although many worshipers, notably most priests (who may be called "*vodu* mothers"), are men. They maintain a practice and a discourse of admitting the husbandly north into the wifely south, of eating and marrying the north, of ritually "becoming" the savannah spirits, thereby canceling north/south and husband/wife dichotomies for the period of trance. This practice takes on a certain political irony in Togo at the present time, as numerous members of the ruling party accuse southerners of tribal hostility against the peoples of the north.

SPIRIT POSSESSION AS MIMESIS OF NORTHERN SLAVES

The ambiguity in the title of this section—"Mimesis of Northern Slaves"—is the same as the ambiguity of identity in Gorovodu and Mama Tchamba spirit possession today in southern Benin, Togo, and Ghana. The question in both cases concerns who exactly is performing the mimesis, the "northern" slaves or someone else, namely, the Ewe and Guin-Mina (also Ga, Fanti, and Asante, etc.) "southerners" who are being possessed. In terms of Western common sense there can be no doubt; the southern spirit hosts, most often women, are there in body and in person, whereas the northerners are only evoked during trance, only mimed or acted out. But Ewe and Mina[9] spirit hosts say that they are not performing; they are being performed. They themselves are not dancing; they are being danced. To be sure, they have desired this host position; they have made known to the spirits of the north that their southern bodies and minds are hospitable to being taken over by northern beings during Vodu celebrations. Just as their forebears provided homes and succor for slaves of the north, and often married them, they in turn, generations later, give of their own person in an ideal wifely fashion to provide ritual homes—dancing bodies—for northern spirits. Home is also a locus of speaking organs for a glossolalia full of southern and northern sounds, rapturously intermingled. The act of giving oneself to the spirits is spoken of through metaphors of sexual intercourse. Although it is said that "the vodu has seized her" (*vodu foe*), which in itself does not give the spirit host an active role, it is also said that "she has seized the *vodu*" (*efo vodu*). Possession is fraught with mutuality in spite of protestations that spirit hosts are swept up against their own will or intentions (as slaves were swept up and taken away against their will). I believe this denial of mutuality to be a ritual device to enhance historical mutuality, or the symmetry of reciprocal possession over time.

These husbandly northern spirits still accessible to human desire in the south are also desirous; they are impatient to eat and drink and dance. They long to perform in a state of grace, seductive and beautiful, sometimes raucous and brilliantly hilarious. They want *brekete*, the drumming rhythms of the north, to be played. They want to see and feel the material trappings of northern culture, such as the little Hausa drum (*adodo*), which speaks to them, and the metal kettles full of water that are brought out to cool their spirit hosts in trance. They want the tunics (*batakali*) and boubous and leather purses of the Sahel to be worn, displayed, and admired. They want the red fez to be on the heads of the priests and on their own heads (momentarily the same as the heads of the spirit hosts). They want the Ewe priests and priestesses to wear the *oheneba* sandals of the Asante royalty.

When Gorovodu and Mama Tchamba spirit hosts first enter into trance they often have the bulging eyes, shaking limbs, and monstrous expressions typical of spirit possession in Africa; they are said to look "wild" (*ada*), like ferocious animals and hunters. But as they give in to mimesis and "become" the northern spirits they may become elegant and beautiful, dancing in a state of unmistakable grace, the very personification of art and refinement. Similar aesthetic conventions of movement during trance may be observed throughout the coastal area, among Fanti, Ewe, Guin-Mina, and Fon. Possessed "wives" are guided into the Vodu houses by *senterua*, ritual assistants, and dressed in the special costumes worn by the spirits who have possessed them. They also may wear white marks or designs made with a kaolin and water mixture, so that they look ghostly, clownlike, dramatic, or like walking sculptures. This ritual whiteness, a sign of the sacred, is a constant in Vodu and spirit possession in West Africa. In the present case it is curiously an inscription of wildness and ultrarefinement at the same time, or, perhaps, a transcendence of that dichotomy.

In this context ambiguities concerning authority, power, control, and identity are dazzling, both to anthropologists and to the people performing the rituals.[10] Questions arise regarding who created whom in the relationships between these "exotic" gods and their "domestic" worshipers, regarding who possesses whom during trance (and who possessed whom during the period of domestic slavery). Wonderments multiply over the seemingly ironic scenario, descendants of masters divinizing the spirits of their forebears' slaves. We also ask ourselves just which "north" is flowing into the generalized south, taking with it cultural objects, music, and fragments of religious forms which are adopted into southern ceremonies and pantheons. Is there a northern or southern hegemony spreading its tentacles, or a nonhegemonic exchange between regional and national cultures? What are the political translations, if such exist, of these cultural flows? How does gender play itself out in these religious, economic, and political exchanges? What does it mean to say that a man is the wife of a *vodu*, or that a goddess is a husband? How is it that Ewe now worship the spirits of northern slaves, "bought people" (*amefefle*) their forebears acquired in trade or sometimes captured in skirmishes? Were the northern slaves not unwilling sojourners in the south? If so, how can the Gorovodu people speak of southern hospitality to northerners, caring for strangers, taking them in, marrying them, and raising children together?

DOMESTIC SLAVERY ON THE SLAVE COAST: THE NORTH IN THE SOUTH

Clearly not all northerners present in the south were slaves, or "bought people." Some of them were just travelers, traders, strangers, or foreign guests (*amedzrowo*), who were taken in or given quarters in the *zongo*,[11] sometimes entertained, on occasion loved. Certain priests say that the Gorovodus are in the general category of spirits from the north, including such free strangers (and at times their unfree children, as the introductory quotations indicate). Other priests say they are specifically spirits of northern slaves. Mama Tchamba gods, however, are by definition spirits of slaves, usually women from the north, who married into the families of the southern Ewe and Guin-Mina worshipers.

Ewe in the Volta region (now part of Ghana) were neighbors of Asante, who, according to Rattray, might speak of anyone from the northern grasslands as a slave, because they were in a category that Asante considered to be enslavable (Rattray 1929:35). Ewe might do the same, but even if they were just as quick to believe in the potential slavehood of northerners, they were faster to normalize, almost equalize the status of their slaves, according to many informants.[12] Ewe had never had a grand empire such as that of Asante or a kingdom such as that of Dahomey, where during certain periods slaves were sacrificed to deities. Today in Togo many Ewe are likely to express contempt for such centralizing political systems and admiration for what they believe to be the more egalitarian nature of their own coastal Ewe society. While the reportedly humane Ewe treatment of slaves is not precisely documented, it is significant that many Ewe claim their forebears loved their slaves in ways that other peoples did not, and thus integrated them fully into Ewe society.

Sandra Greene (1996), who writes the history of the Anlo Ewe state a bit farther west, says that the Anlo polity was far from statehood like that of the Asante empire. Most attempts at hierarchy and centralization were linked with clan formation, which in turn was of a piece with religious orders, and never produced a significant distinction between royal families and commoners. However, Greene does provide a somewhat different picture regarding the treatment of domestic slaves in Anlo, where it seems there was not so much difference between Ewe and Asante attitudes and practices. On the other hand, to protect those with slave forebears, it is to this day forbidden by law in Anlo to speak of the slave origins of a person or a family, and there are many such slave descendants in the Volta region.

Only a few miles away in Togo, the Mama Tchamba order has inscribed a certain pride in descendants of slaves, thereby taking away any discomfort that might have otherwise existed in regard to slave ancestors. In 1990 I recorded limited genealogies of a number of middle-aged and older women in a Togolese village founded in the 1880s, where there was a sizeable Gorovodu community. All the women who were descendants of the founding brothers of the village spoke freely about their great-grandmother, who was a slave from the north, the wife of one of the brothers, who came from the Anlo area. I asked them how they felt about having descended from a slave woman, and they answered that this was "a good thing" (*enyo*). Several women told me that their slave ancestry was what gave them the right to join in Mama Tchamba celebrations and to go into trance. Most of these women also attended Gorovodu ceremonies. Mama Tchamba priestly activities are passed on matrilaterally. The very name of the order bespeaks its female nature (*mama* means "grandmother" in Ewe). To be sure, of all the marriages contracted between northerners and southerners there were more northern wives than husbands. (Yet in Gorovodu the northern spirits are husbands rather than wives.) These slave wives had rights and sometimes were closer to their husbands than their free co-wives who might have independent market activities and travel often.

Even Asante (who also had Abrewa and Kunde deities) accorded rights to slave wives and their descendants. As late as 1930 the son of a Nago (Yoruba) slave wife inherited his Asante father's estate over the protests of his half-brothers from a free wife, for the Asante are matrilineal, so the sons of the free wife could not inherit from their father, but had to wait for their inheritance from their maternal uncles. Matrilineal inheritance, of course, did not apply to the slave wife, so her sons could take over their father's property, to her great advantage and to the disadvantage of the free wife and her sons. And in this case the deceased Asante man had no sisters' sons who might inherit along with his sons from his slave wife, perhaps squeezing them out of most of the property (*Gold Coast Times*, 1930).

In 1913 the Committee of West African Lands answered questions concerning slavery in the Gold Coast (now Ghana) at the Colonial Office in London:

> There is no system throughout the Colony of any domestic service akin to slavery? There is no caste system the members of which could not obtain land if they wanted it?

> No. There is what is sometimes called domestic slavery, but domestic slaves are practically free people and have their farms. They are usually descendants of captured or stray Mohammedans, a people from the north, but they are free for all general purposes and they can get land from the community. (File No. 11/1/975, Accra National Archives)

It seems that the reporters are speaking about all the peoples in the relative south of the colony; but in any case, they must have been including Asante and Ewe.

Fritz Kramer writes in his remarkable book *The Red Fez* (1993:2–7) about three different categories of strangers among Asante. The *ohoho* was an Asante or Akan person from a different chiefdom, a "free stranger." The *ntafo* was a northern trader who usually lived in the *zongo*, hardly a slave, but nonetheless exempt from acquiring land. *Odonko* was the term used in former times (according to Rattray) for peoples of the north in general, but it came to mean "slave."

> [T]he specific facial scarifications for each tribe, which were customary only in the north, constituted for the Asante the personification of odonko, the personification of the barbarian's deplorable customs which legitimized enslavement. (1993:5)

Neighboring Ewe did practice facial scarification, and they too were often taken as domestic slaves by the Asante as well as slaves to be sold for the trans-Atlantic journey.

Ewe also employ the word *donko* to mean slave, and some Ewe today have Donko as their last name, evidence that their forebears were enslaved by the Asante (or another group), that at least one non-Ewe forebear was a slave. Donko as a first name indicates that as an infant a person was promised as a "slave" or attendant to a *vodu* or *tro*, a god or spirit who protected their in-utero existence and childhood from the usual pull of an *abiku* pattern; that is, a mother's repeated loss of children in infancy or early childhood, thought to be the same child dying over and over again. The fact that a child whose life and health are ardently desired by the parents can be promised as a "slave" to a deity indicates that the trope *donko* in Ewe involves a relationship between master and slave unlike anything we know about slavery in the

Americas. (It also indicates that "master" and "slave" are not correct translations.)[13] Even so, according to some informants, naming a child Donko is like naming it "Trash" or "Throw-Away," indicating on the face of it that no value is given to the little person. This tricks the forces responsible for "calling the child back" after each birth into leaving the child alone, for it is worthless.

It is almost as though the slaves from the north were just "called" slaves too; in legend, according to the aesthetics of ideal reciprocity, they were lovers, wives, adored children. This ideal no doubt differs from a certain reality in much of Eweland, by which northern "bought people" were in fact unfree but could not be called slaves. This is the pattern that is reversed by naming free children Donko. To be sure, a person promised to the Vodu from childhood is not precisely free, for she or he has much service to perform. Nor are Gorovoduviwo (Gorovodu "children," including adults) entirely free. They must carry out work for their slave spirits if they want the gods to continue to work for them.

In Togolese Gorovodu communities, children are often given non-Ewe names from the "north," such as Seydou, Musani, Alimata, Asana, Salamatu, and Fusena for the same reasons that children elsewhere are called Donko, and this practice is marked by the same fascinating ambiguity, the same paradox that runs through other aspects of slave spirit worship. It is rare for Togolese or Ghanaians who are not Gorovodu worshippers to give their children such names. It is said that northern names protect these Ewe children from an early death brought by witchcraft, evil magic, or jealousy, because the names camouflage their Ewe identity; and northern identity either is not valuable enough to be envied (at least not for Ewe witchcraft) or is not vulnerable to such wicked domestic forces. (Ewe destructive magic usually seeks out Ewe victims, seldom foreigners.) On the other hand, children receive northern names because they are brought up to worship northern spirits, and it is an honor to receive such names, linking them to powerful and beautiful divinities.[14] Gorovodu and Mama Tchamba children, especially girls, should also work well, as did the young girls who were slaves from the north, spoken of mythically as perfect workers and producers of wealth.

Decidedly, the contradiction is a strong one: Slaves are both valuable and expendable, "trash" and deity, beautiful and ugly, admirable, nevertheless non-Ewe, thus marginal, yet central to practices of the sacred. This ambiguity is exquisitely similar to that surrounding the category of femaleness, which is both less (animal) and more (divinity) than maleness, both stronger and weaker, wilder in some circumstances, more domestic in others, more desirable and beautiful, yet not as fully human a quality as maleness. The fact that in Gorovodu and Mama Tchamba slave spirits are marked as husbands while the worshiping "master" people are wifely indicates a reversal in the usual feminizing of slaves and masculinizing of "owners," including the fact that most slave spouses were wives, married to the men who had bought them. It is almost impossible to speak of slaves without an implicit reference

to gender; celebration of slaves' northern culture is also a reinscription of northern femaleness and maleness. Is it the slaves' incipient "hunterly wildness" that renders
them husbandly rather than wifely in Gorovodu and Mama Tchamba?

I have treated the ambiguity of the "wildness" of northern slaves in an earlier
interpretation of the Ewe signifying expression "The slave understands language, but
does not understand 'the wild crab'" (*Donko se gbe; mese 'adangala' o*) (Rosenthal
1995). *Adangala*, or "wild crab," is the term from which comes *adangana*, or "signifying expression"; it is akin to the "signifyin' monkey" among African Americans, a way
to "signify on" someone,[15] especially on someone's "wildness" or non-Eweness.
For Ewe wildness is both wonderful and dangerous, both less (animal) and more
(divinity) than Eweness, like femaleness in relationship to maleness. At the same time,
the "wildness" of "wild crab signifying expressions" is ultra-Ewe, a form that anyone
not born Ewe, such as northern slaves or other strangers, cannot master. Wildness, associated with the bush rather than village, the place of quintessential humanness, is
therefore female in certain circumstances and male in others.

The Ewe word employed to designate northerners makes reference to the bush:
dzogbedzitowo ("people from beyond [or on top of] the bush") may apply to members
of any number of ethnic groups.[16] Stylized elements of specific savannah cultures are
the primary models for the aesthetics of Gorovodu and Mama Tchamba; Hausa and
Mossi are mentioned by name, and there is a specific spirit called Mossi in both
Gorovodu and Mama Tchamba. But other peoples not so far north of Ewe and Mina
regions are also mentioned in both orders, the most obvious being Tchamba people.
Gorovodu songs are full of Twi words and expressions, thus indicating a close alliance
with Asante, and probably Akan origins for Gorovodu. Kumasi, the Asante capital, is
certainly north of the Ewe Volta region in Ghana. (Ironically, according to Ewe popular opinion more Ewe were taken slaves by Asante than the other way around.)

Not only Tchamba, but also Kabye people (who live north of Ewe territory but
south of the Sahel), are mentioned in Mama Tchamba ceremonies, as Ewe and Mina
spirit hosts "become" Kabye and Tchamba and speak glossolalia with fragments of
Tchamba and Kabye words. Yendi is the name of one of the Tchamba spirits, and it
also happens to be the name of a Ghanaian town crucial to the slave and salt trades.
Another Tchamba spirit is Bubluma, a name derivative of the term *blu*, which means
"stranger" or non-Anlo. It is the name of a specific Anlo Ewe "stranger" or "foreigner"
clan *(amedzrohlo)*, which was added to the original clans to accommodate refugees
and Ga-Adangbes who lived in Anlo territory. Belonging to a stranger clan was a
means for becoming Ewe-ized in spite of the fact that the *bluto* retained a portion of
foreignness. Such foreignness did not always prevent a *blu* member from acquiring
prestige or authority. Greene (1996) tells about one such *bluto*, an Adangbe trader
named Tettega, whose son, Togbui Gbodzo of Woe (born c. 1800), became the right
wing commander of the Anlo army.

Clearly, the romance of the north, even the very relative Asante north, and the exotic nature of the savannah peoples (or of Muslim culture in general) are highly charged politically, historically, spiritually, and psychically among Ewe and Mina southerners who are members of Gorovodu and Mama Tchamba orders in Ghana, Togo, and Benin. In a way northern gender is conceived of as different from southern gender, but I am not yet sure about the extent of this perceived difference. The fact that veils are employed for a certain women's dance and for spirit hosts in Gorovodu ritual bespeaks Muslim gender in general. Ewe women ordinarily do not wear veils, and even in Gorovodu communities they do so only for a single Friday morning ritual.

Having established the thoroughly contradictory and gendered status of strangers and peoples of the north (both the very relative north and the real savannah peoples from Burkina Faso, Niger, and Nigeria), including slaves, as they appear in cultures of the south, I will give attention to the sorts of narrative content these northern cultures carry in southern ceremonies.

CEREMONIAL MARKERS OF NORTHERN OR MUSLIM CULTURES

On Friday mornings one can find Gorovodu adepts dressed all in white, women with white headcoverings, carrying out a cleansing of the face and feet similar to Muslim ablutions before prayer. Prayers may be conducted with either Muslim or Catholic rosaries and a book of some sort that stands in for the Qu'ran and is held as though it were being read. A special women's dance is performed afterward; veiled participants move in a wide circle, executing steps that, according to them, come from the Sahel. All women of the Gorovodu community join this dance, not only spirit hosts. I have seen male Vodu wives join the women's dance in the Volta region. Even in Togo and Benin they are joined by a male drummer playing the Hausa *adodo*.

In several Togolese villages deities include "the Muslim God, Allah," considered female and married to Togbui (Elder or Grandfather) Kadzanka, a fierce male spirit. It is clear that a number of Vodu people in communities that worship Allah are not aware of the generally male identity of the Muslim God. In other words, it does not occur to them that Muslims ("northerners") might not worship a goddess. Or, for those who are informed of the Muslim Allah's gender, it is not sacrilegious to change Allah's gender for local aesthetics and purposes. I was told that these two Gorovodus had been "found" in Bolgatanga, in the north of Ghana.[17]

Mama Tchamba metal woven bracelets *(tchambaga)* are also "found" in fields, streets, and houses in Togo. Such an *objet trouvé* points the finder to Mama Tchamba's desire for attention from that person, to the necessity to honor the slave spirits. (We are reminded of the very different nature of the *objets trouvés* in European museums around the turn of the century, which were precisely enigmas, for Europeans did not know what they were for, whether they were "art" or not.)[18]

Finding a Tchamba bracelet is an event that demands ceremonies and divining sessions; it reinscribes rules of reciprocity and is a reminder of the ecstasy that beckons to those who respect this ethic.

Tchambaga are the remains of Tchamba slaves and their northern or savannah culture, left in the south as little fetishes of Tchamba presence and identity. They are fragments that recall an entire image of charged "contact" with the exotic north, that cannot help but impress the finder, who becomes alarmingly ill if she or he does not carry out ceremonies to honor the slave spirits. This image of contact with ultimate northern Others is like a *passio* (Kramer 1993), a ravishment that cannot be fought against. It is the desire and the mask of the Other that become one's own most overwhelming passion, a desire and an image that one also becomes or embodies, for the period of trance.

During a large Mama Tchamba celebration held in 1992 I heard watchers remark when certain people (all Ewe or Mina) fell into trance, "Oh, look, now she is becoming Kabye—listen to her speak that northern language. Now they will need to bring out all the costumes from the north to put them on the people who have been seized by the spirits." By all appearances, either ravishment or extreme pleasure seized everyone present that day, spirit hosts, priestesses, anthropologists, and even the neighborhood madman. Another Mama Tchamba ceremony I ran into quite by accident when I could not find my way in the back roads was attended exclusively by women, some forty or fifty, who, although their ceremony was hardly public, lustily enjoined the lost *yovonyaga* (old white woman) to enter into the dance.

Unlike Gorovodu, with its abstract god-objects (in the form of sculptural collages), Mama Tchamba was offered schnapps, kola nuts, and the blood of sacrificed animals in a hole in the sand. The only objects put into the hole were trade beads (*mamadzonu* or "grandmother jewels") and *tchambaga*, said to have been brought generations ago from Tchamba country, Kabye country, and Mossi country (now Burkina Faso) by slaves who became ancestors. Such beads and bracelets are an important component of women's wealth, passed on to their daughters.

In fact, Ewe and Mina traders usually buy these objects from northern traders and keep them in stock for their local clientele. Such is also the case for the metal kettles for Gorovodu ceremonies. The red fez worn by all Gorovodu priests and often by Gorovodu and Mama Tchamba spirit hosts in trance is, however, seldom found elsewhere than in the stands of Hausa traders who live in the south. These objects are absolutely necessary to trance ceremonies; without them there is no Chamba-ness or northern-ness to mime. The fact that traders from the north still bring them to the south for ceremonial consumption is a compelling detail of the north-south cultural flow.

Another highly significant object during Gorovodu ceremonies is the *adewu* or warrior/hunter shirt, decorated with cowries and pieces of metal, a sort of coat of armor and honor. The same sort of object, which was said to protect the wearer from both real and magical bullets, was at one time important to both Ewe and Asante soldiers, independent of Gorovodu practices. Similar costumes are made in the Sahel and worn by Mande hunters while hunting or during ceremonies.[19] Ewe Vodu practitioners say that the *adewu* protected its wearer from German and British bullets during the colonial period.

It is, however, the northern drum rhythms (*brekete*), played passionately and hauntingly, and the songs, correctly sung, with longing and joy, that bring about trance. Only these drumming and dancing performances seduce the Tchamba and Gorovodu spirits into the immediate vicinity of the celebration, and into the minds and bodies of the "wives." The ecstasy of the spirit hosts and the pleasure of the onlookers are gifts from the gods as well as offerings to them. Femaleness is associated with such extremes of bliss and self-abandonment. Particular forms of drumming are so important to this practice of expenditure (Bataille 1985) that the whole religious culture is called Brekete in the Volta region of Ghana. When Vodu "wives" go into trance the deities they become demand to hear certain songs and often direct the drummers. The same *brekete* dancing style may be observed during these ceremonies wherever they are held along the Bight of Benin. *Agbadza*, a well-known Ewe drumming rhythm and dance, is also performed.[20]

THE GENDERED NATURE OF POSSESSION

The *-si* ending on Gorovodu spirit host titles—*trosi*, *Kundesi*, *Albewasi*, etc.—indicates ritual wifehood (wife of the spirit, wife of Kunde, wife of Ablewa). Whether the northern spirit is male or female, it is a husband in relation to its wife/host (whether woman or man). While cross-gender possession is common, there is also much same-gender ritual marriage. Thus, one can find a woman who is a wife of Nana Ablewa, the beautiful Hausa "old lady," and a man who is a wife of Sacra, the male hunter and warrior, strong as a horse; a woman who is a wife of Banguele, the hunter god of iron, and a man who is a wife of Nana Wango or Grandmother Crocodile.

Innumerably more women than men are spirit hosts during Gorovodu and Mama Tchamba ceremonies (although in one Mama Tchamba celebration I attended, numbers of men and women were about equal). It is said that "women love the voduwo more than men do," and thus they are especially loved in turn. One priest told me that going into trance is hard work, and therefore women are more likely to be up to it than men. He also said that men are more afraid than women are of letting their minds and bodies be entered by foreign forces. One spirit host, a woman, said that being in trance was like being in love; "you want it all the time." This particular *trosi* is the wife of the fierce warrior god Banguele; she is ultra-male when possessed, and is invited to all the Gorovodu celebrations along the coast because her power is immensely attractive and satisfying to other Gorovodu participants. Likewise, a tall man who is a wife of Nana Wango, and who is thus female while in trance, "spends his entire life in service to the *vodus*," according to *his* wife. His presence is equally coveted during large festivals.

Although it is claimed that no one chooses to be a spirit host, but rather each person is chosen, there is talk about who is liable to be chosen and who is not; individual desires, conscious and unconscious, enter into the situation. Certain people pray to become spirit hosts, offering sacrifices to the deities they wish to possess them. This does not necessarily result in the person's being possessed. Both the individual social identity and the very personhood of a *trosi* (*vodusi*) or *Tchambasi* are profoundly marked by the work of going into trance, of achieving fusion with the gods. Even when not in trance such a person belongs to the spirits and thus also possesses them; her being therefore overlaps with that of the divinities at all times. In Mama Tchamba and Gorovodu this can mean that a spirit host, most often a woman, is a sort of walking intersection of foreign and familiar, wild and domestic, male and female, north and south, husband and wife, spirit and mortal, death and life, animal and human, deity and worshiper, slave and master.

This is also true of priests and priestesses—Gorovodu *sofowo* and Tchamba *wawawo* (of which there are many more men than women)—although in this case their embodiment of binary oppositions is more formal and symbolic, less stunningly "real" than is the case with spirit hosts. The priestly function contains a heavy element of managerial work, hosting obligations, and elder duties (dispute arbitration, etc.) at the social level, so that few persons continue to go into trance once they have become priests or priestesses (and some have never been spirit hosts). One priest told me this is why few women choose to become priestesses—they prefer to continue going into trance. Women who do become priestesses seldom do so until after menopause. Should a woman opt to do so at a younger age, her kinsmen, affines, or female relatives who are not menstruating must "feed" and otherwise "take care of" the god-objects when the priestess is menstruating. Human blood, whether male or female, is thought to have its own power, not to be confused with the blood of animals sacrificed as gifts to the gods. As mortals, priests and priestesses have more authority than do tronsiwo, vodusiwo, and tchambasiwo; but the latter, when in trance, fused with the "fetish," have more authority than do priests and priestesses. This means that during ceremonies there is a compelling portion of authority and outright power in the bodies and voices of beings who are by all appearances biologically female. Another portion is held by beings who are biologically male but ritually female, whether they are wives of gods or goddesses.

In both Gorovodu and Mama Tchamba we thus have a string of binary oppositions that are permutable on a north-south axis. North is to south as slave is to master, divinity to worshiper, death to life, husband to wife, foreign to family, and wild to domestic. During trance these oppositions are overcome, so that there is no longer a cleavage between male and female, spirit and mortal, *vodu* and *vodusi*, possessor and possessed, etc. Spirit and matter are fused; north and south are one for the time of trance. The "femaleness" of men in trance goes along with the maleness of the possessing deity, the husbandliness of the north and the wifeliness of the south. The gender turnarounds bespeak the nonfixity of gender as well as the mutuality in time of having Others' labor "in one's hand." If Ewe men in the past both "owned" their northern wives and appropriated their labor to the benefit of their own patrilines, descendants of such men must now be wives to the spirits of these northerners, whose turn it is to wield husbandly authority and to have Ewe minds and bodies "in their hands." The ethic of reciprocity, if not carried out within the lifetime of the slaves, must be carried out now.

There is another gendered opposition inside Gorovodu that is significant, that of "hot death" and "house death." Some of the *vodus* are hot- or violent-death deities, and some are cool- or house-death deities. The northerners who died violent deaths (also called "bush death") while serving in the south must be celebrated in the "sacred bush," a ritual copy of the wild country between villages and between the Ewe settlements and the north, the desolate places where violent death can happen (although today it often happens on the highway). Thus, it is appropriate that savannah people are called *dzogbedzitowo*, people from "beyond the wild bush." Violent "bush" death, which is said to be a man's death, participates in the same uncanniness that sticks to the foreign, northern, or Muslim Other. House death, marked female, is the domesticated death of those who "see death coming" while they lie peacefully in their beds at home. So both sides of one of the oppositions between stranger and family and male and female is repeated inside the stranger/divinity category. In this case the house-death spirits are a middle ground between foreign gods and the family of worshipers. But there is already a middle category among the Gorovodus, that of Nana Wango and Sunia Compo, *vodus* who "live in the house" rather than "in the bush," but who can also "travel to the bush to eat," unlike Papa Kunde and Nana Ablewa, who do not go to the sacred bush at all any more, even though they are "originally" from the savannah. Appropriately for the gender component, Sunia Compo is a hermaphrodite spirit, and Nana Wango comes in two forms: Grandmother Crocodile and the *piroguier* or ferryman.

MAMI WATA: WORSHIP OF YET A DIFFERENT GENDERED NORTH

Another Vodu order, often said to be "in the same family" as Gorovodu and Mama Tchamba (and who also eats kola nuts), is Mami Wata, a snake and rainbow deity including various avatars of a fair-skinned water goddess. Often depicted as a mermaid, Mami Wata is a significant figure in coastal and river areas of Ghana, Togo, Benin, Nigeria, and Cameroon. Statues and paintings associated with Mami Wata, like the costumes and paraphernalia of Gorovodu and Mama Tchamba, seem to be repositories of an "original" yet recurring uncanny impression "left by particular encounters," with a more distant north, including the ships of the first European traders which arrived on the West African coast. Paintings of the Virgin Mary and a ubiquitous lithograph of an Indian woman called "the woman snake-tamer" are central to Mami Wata cults (Kramer 1993:217–239; Jell-Bahlsen 1989).

In 1990 I visited Mamisi Kokoe of Lomé, a renowned priestess of Mami Wata who has received numerous anthropologists into her home. As the years go by, African, European, and American researchers and friends have complemented her already crowded altars and mirrors with yet other images of magical and beautiful women, mermaids, goddesses, virgins, Hindu snake-tamers, and photographs of herself with her anthropologists. Here the anthropologist enters into the *passio*, as does the worshiper, side by side on the other side of the looking glass, as it were. The Gorovodu priest who accompanied me to Mamisi Kokoe's home was so impressed by her presence that he told me later he found it necessary to neutralize her potential power over him by "changing colors," magically camouflaging himself so that she would not recognize him. The uncanny otherness of the Mami Wata image was as original as ever in the very person of the priestess, the "wife" of the goddess.

This Gorovodu priest's wife had also been an adept of Mami Wata in her natal village in Ghana, and kept a wooden carving of "Abolo" or the white man on horseback, an image of colonial inspiration associated with Mami Wata. The priest confided in me that because his wife was associated with Mami Wata she was potentially more powerful than he was, both for evil and for good.

During a Mami Wata celebration I attended on the Togolese coast, adepts preened themselves mischievously in the ceremonial yard, looking into mirrors and putting on lipstick and powder, bragging theatrically that they were so very white and beautiful, signifying on themselves and me (as well as on the "original" Mami Wata). When in trance one *mamisi* emptied an entire quart of cologne on me and several Ewe visitors, and would have emptied a huge can of talcum powder on us if she had not been restrained. Thus, the *passio* of the vain and painted white woman with hand mirror and perfume mixes with that of ancient water spirits in the worship of Mami Wata. (The Yoruba Yemoja and Cuban Yemaya partake of this same *passio*, as does Ezili Freda and Ezili Lasirene in Haiti.)

Kramer holds that in the case of Mami Wata the land is conceptualized as a place of order, whereas water is nature or wildness (1993:221), or perhaps femaleness. Obviously, the impossibly strange white women and men who alighted on the coast during the colonial period represented an utterly exotic wildness that made a lasting impression, one that could be interpreted only through mimesis. In Mami Wata worship the whiteness of European women or the relative fairness of Indian women almost replaces gender, so that whiteness is female and blackness is male. Mami Wata is about fertility, femaleness, and beauty; mostly women become *mamisis*, and men who do are particularly good-looking and often dress and plait their hair like women. But there is much irony in this theater.

Although once a pantheon of localized water spirits, Mami Wata may recently have become an image of "internationalness," a concept that "blew" West African minds as thoroughly as it did European ones, and which set them to representing the wild and natural (both savage and noble) Other in the most realistic mode possible— that of mimesis.[21] Interestingly, this representation of the "international exotic north" is completely female, given its preponderance of goddesses attended by female wives. While there are male avatars of Mami Wata, they are at a lower level of classification, and the order as a whole remains female. Market women along the lower coast of West Africa often belong to Mami Wata and attribute their commercial success to the protective and fertile care of the water goddess.

CONCLUSION

While I have chosen to limit the focus of this essay to issues of north-south cultural flows in their relation to gender, rather than to elaborate on issues of spirit possession and capitalism, I am convinced that the relationship between Vodu orders and colonialism (and, more broadly, capitalist hegemony) is heavily charged and worthy of more thorough research. For example, domestic slavery, which was for many generations at the heart of north-south exchanges, would never have taken on its historical role without the existence of the trans-Atlantic trade. Violent conflicts between Vodu orders, native authorities, and colonial administrators, as well as very recent tensions between some Vodu communities and the Togolese state, have all been struggles over political economies,[22] including their symbolic ramifications. Irreconcilable differences between systems of exchange, including conceptualizations of gender, power, and authority, remain today, straining contact between Vodu and post-independence states. These differences act as markers of a certain marginalization of Vodu, on the one hand, and of its centrality as an alternate, nonstate and noncapitalist discourse and practice of resistance, on the other hand (although it did not originate as resistance).[23] Recent interpretations of African spirit possession orders in their specific relation to colonialism, capitalism, or to a perverse "modernization" are relevant to the historical realities of Gorovodu and Mama Tchamba; for example, Hodgson's discussion in this volume about Maasai *orpeko*, Matory's work on Oyo religion (1994), Blier's research on Vodun art (1995), and Boddy's interpretations of *zar* cults (1989).

Gorovodu worship, in spite of the fact that its "fetishes" are bought and sold (but are not quite commodities), continues to perform gender and carry out exchange in ways that partially escape capitalist culture and economics. Mama Tchamba cannot be sold; it is inherited matrilaterally or miraculously "found." In a manner of speaking, both these Vodu orders are always already "postmodern," not in an ideological sense, but in the sense of a discourse and practice that admit of a continual reworking of identity, authority, and power, and a concept of charged margins and border crossings rather than full centers. I am taking the risk here of positing an Ewe ritual "postmodern" that is both precapitalist and noncapitalist, as a sort of opposite to the "modernity" that never quite arrives on much of the African continent except as anomie, unequal exchange, destruction of indigenous forms, and commodity consumption without commodity production.

The fragmentation (but not destruction) in this particular category of the "postmodern" includes a laterality of aesthetic and ethical systems, a metonymic bent that refuses the hierarchy necessary for the functioning of master metaphors. It fittingly presupposes a "hole" or a "field" of being rather than individual and collective wholeness of identity. It does not subscribe to totalizing concepts of identity or selfhood. Polysemic and heteroglossic events, states and texts abound; doctrine is rare. Colonial, capitalist, and "modern" relationships are taken into account in ritual practices and discourse. They enter into dialogue with Ewe culture, which is not merely "precolonial," "traditional," or "precapitalist." It is rather a traveling narrative and way of life that constantly rearrange certain movable parts: namely, exchange relations, gender, place, caste, and authority.

In summary, it is clear that at the heart of Gorovodu and Mama Tchamba exchange is a gendered relationship between north and south, foreigner and family, including conceptions of femaleness, maleness, slavery, and power redistribution that are unthinkable in Western culture, and therefore provide crucial elements of implicit cultural critique.[24]

Permutations of binary oppositions such as female/male, south/north, and master/slave indicate that these pairs are tropes for making sense of a world interpreted in terms of reciprocity. None of these gender, caste, and regional identities are precisely identities in the Western sense, but are almost syntactic elements in various plays of reciprocity, without essentialist applications or interpretations. The more cruelly colonial and recent history threaten the continuity of reciprocal modes of relationship in West Africa, and between West Africa and the rest of the world, the more sublimely Vodu worshipers inscribe their own aesthetics and ethics of reciprocity into the stuff of their immediate lives and vicinities.

The worship of northern slaves by Ewe and Mina southerners is a practice of sacred reciprocity, an attempt to level out unequal relations, or to reverse them in a controlled ritual text, on the part of those who once owned slaves. Gender is leveled out at the same time, permuted along other axes as a traveling sort of trope rather than a reality stuck to the bodies of real women and men.

All of these reversals or "travelings" (one is reminded of a movie camera) of gender, regional identity, and possession of/by slaves undo centralizing and essentializing identifications urged by colonial and Western hegemonies, as irruptions of a particular West African postmodern politics and aesthetics.

The political interpretations of the north-south cultural flows in Togo are especially charged today. Gorovodu and Mama Tchamba possession in Togo is increasing in popularity during a period (1985–1995) of political unrest and so-called ethnic hostility between north and south. While a government press laments the southern hatred of northerners in order to cover government practices of state terrorism, whole communities of southerners worship northern spirits and gasp in admiration at their beauty and power, "becoming" northern while in trance and speaking northern languages in glossolalia. Some of the spirit hosts actually *are* from the north, Moba or Bassari women who have married Ewe men. So they are original northern strangers who have become social southerners through affinity, and are in the process of becoming northerners again via the rapture of sacred mimesis.

I know of no cases of Hausa or Mossi people who have married into Gorovodu communities, but I have witnessed the extraordinary spectacle of an ambulatory Hausa trader making his way through a Gorovodu celebration looking for customers for the "objects from the north" he carried in an enormous headload. Ecstatically dancing on the ceremonial ground were women in trance, dressed somehow like him, being more intensely he than he was, in a religiously theatrical manner of speaking. When a *passio* meets another *passio* head-on, it is a fine day in the ritual field!

NOTES

I wish to thank the individuals, institutions, and agencies responsible for the following fellowships and grants, enabling me to engage in fieldwork and archival research, which provided data for this article: Fulbright-Hays Dissertation Research Fellowship (1989–90), Charlotte W. Newcombe Dissertation Writing Fellowship (1991–92), Sage Scholarship from Cornell University (fall 1992), Faculty Research Initiative Grant and Faculty Research Fellowship Award from the University of Michigan-Flint (1994–95). I also wish to thank Gorovodu sofowo Awudza, Dzodzi, Fo Tete, Gangube, Koliko, and Seydou; tronsiwo Adjo, Afi, Comfort, Cudjo, Koffi, Kponsi, and Pearl; kpedzigawo Kafui, Kuma, and Seydou; Edith Wood, archivist at the National Archives of Ghana; Dr. Samuel Kumodzie, Etienne Ahiako, anthropologist at the ORSTOM; Dr. Tom K. Kumekpor, University of Legon; Dr. Sandra Greene, Cornell University; and Dr. Maria Grosz-Ngaté, coeditor of this volume.

1.   The term *Vodu* is most often employed by Ewe, Adja, Oatchi, Guin, Mina, and Fon living in southeastern Togo and southwestern Benin in reference to various groups of gods or spirits, and practices of worshipping them. *Tro* (or *Etro*) refers to the same phenomena among Anlo Ewe and related groups in Ghana and Togo. Plural forms are *Voduwo* and *Trowo*. In this essay I will use the words *Vodu* and *Tro* nearly interchangeably, although a few informants insist there are subtle differences between them. I have employed the term *Vodu* (capitalized) more often in reference to the whole religious system, and *trowo* more often to mean "gods."

Rather than repeating throughout this paper the names of all of the related ethnic and linguistic groups that practice Gorovodu and Mama Tchamba, I will now simply use the word *Ewe* and trust readers to understand that immense ethnic complexity is bracketed here for purposes of brevity and simplicity.

2.   Greene 1996.

3.   De Barros 1552 and de Marees 1605 cited in Verger 1957:33–38; also Bosman 1705, Barbot 1732, Burton 1883, and Bouche 1885, all cited in Herskovits 1938 and Verger 1957. Christian evangelizing did not begin in earnest until the late eighteenth century, although there were several missionaries and priests on the Slave Coast earlier. (See Debrunner 1961.)

4. Research concerning the changing of gods' names for purposes of protecting Vodu orders from colonial bans is summarized in a separate article (Rosenthal 1996).

5. Kunde and Abrewa were sometimes two separate orders among Asante.

6. Apter (1993) recounts the large-scale accusation and punishment of women as witches in Atinga cults in Nigeria.

7. See Rosenthal 1996.

8. Matrilateral forebears are considered ancestors although Ewe are principally patrilineal. There are thus signs of nascent or previous bilineality. Close contact with Asante gave Ewe some aspects of matrilineality, such as the great importance of mothers' brothers.

9. I have carried out extensive fieldwork among Ewe and Mina, whereas my knowledge of the Ga, Fanti, and Asante versions of Kunde and Abrewa orders is mainly restricted to the archives; so this article is focused on Ewe and Mina cultures. Even so, there is much data in the National Archives regarding Asante practices, and it is important to know that virtually all the coastal peoples in this region practiced this worship of northern spirits. I visited Fanti *bosomfos* along the highway between Accra and Cape Coast during 1994 and found exactly the same god-objects ("fetishes") and drum rhythms as in Ewe and Mina Gorovodu. The Fanti names were different, but they also said that these "fetishes" came from the north. The word "fetish" in English and *fétiche* in French has been adopted by the worshipers. It is applied both to the constructed god-objects and to the spirit host in trance.

10. The first time I observed Gorovodu ceremonies, in 1985, I was not an anthropologist, but I was certainly seduced by the beauty and power of the event. Seeing that I was attracted to their *ekonuwo* (religious practices, or, literally, "clan matters"), several women who belonged to this community challenged me to write a book about them. I told them I did not have the proper anthropological training to do so. They told me I must go and get the training and then come back. I did so.

11. The area reserved for Hausa, Nago, or other "northern" or Muslim strangers (usually traders) residing in a village or town. These foreigners often brought their wives with them, for few Muslims wanted to enter into the lifetime of obligations and gift-giving with non-Muslim families required by marriage.

12. Interviews in 1990–92 with Ewe women and university professors; none of these informants had carried out formal research on the differences between Ewe and Asante treatment of slaves. Their ideas reflect Ewe popular opinion.

13. There is no word like "master" for the free person employing the services of the slave. Such a person was simply the *afeto* (father of the house) or *afeno* (mother of the house). The words employed to translate "have" indicate place, specifically, "in one's hand." Thus, "I have a slave," or *amefefle l'asinye,* means literally, "a bought person is in my hand." Possession in the Western sense does not exist in the Ewe language. And as *odonko* was employed by Asante in reference to anyone from the north, it does not always indicate slave identity.

14. I spoke very recently with an Ewe woman residing in the United States who is a Gorovodu *trosi* (spirit host). She told me her son had a name from the north, given him by the slave spirit who possesses her. She was palpably proud of this name, although she employed it only around other Gorovodu worshippers.

15. See *The Signifyin' Monkey* (Henry Louis Gates, Jr., 1988).

16. Expressions employed to speak of peoples of the north do not usually employ the Ewe word for "north" (*anyiexe*); although, speaking in French (*les gens du nord*) or English the word "north" is employed.

17. Not all of these divinities or aspects are found in every Gorovodu community; there is great variation along the coast.

18. Maria Grosz-Ngaté, personal communication.

19. Note especially Kramer's "man of the north" carving, just such an "*objet trouvé*" (1993:3).

20. In order to determine whether certain religious orders in Fanti communities along the Cape Coast road were indeed related to Ewe Gorovodu, I asked women how they danced for their gods. As soon as they performed a few steps it was clear that their dance was *brekete*. Afterward, when I was allowed to enter into their shrines, I saw that their "fetishes," or god-objects, were the same as the material Gorovodus, albeit with different names.

21. Kramer contrasts the realism of "acephalous" cult spirit possession, such as that associated with Mami Wata, Mama Tchamba, and Gorovodu, with the abstraction of ancestral mask sculptures (1993:200, 248).

22. See Rosenthal 1996.

23. This does not mean that capitalists or even dictators might not attempt to employ Gorovodu, for anyone can "buy" it. But the wealth necessary to pay for fabrication of god-objects and training in Gorovodu *ese* (law) is not sufficient to please the spirits and assure their "work." The "owner" must also abide by certain rules of reciprocity. Gorovodu law also specifically forbids killing anyone, even as an act of justice. Therefore, there is an incommensurability between the rules of the spirits and the ambitions of dictators and exploiters.

24. There are also some instances of explicit cultural critique such as that I have outlined in Rosenthal n.d.

BIBLIOGRAPHY

Apter, Andrew. 1993. "Atinga Revisited: Yoruba Witchcraft and the Cocoa Economy, 1950–1951." In *Modernity and Its Malcontents: Ritual and Power in Postcolonial Africa*, Jean Comaroff and John Comaroff, eds. Chicago: University of Chicago Press.

Bataille, Georges. 1985. *Visions of Excess: Selected Writings, 1927–1939*. Trans. Allan Stoekl with Carl R. Lovitt and Donald M. Leslie, Jr. Minneapolis: University of Minnesota Press.

Blier, Suzanne Preston. 1995. *African Vodun: Art, Psychology, Power*. Los Angeles: University of California Press.

Boddy, Janice. 1989. *Wombs and Alien Spirits: Women, Men, and the Zar Cult in Northern Sudan*. Madison: University of Wisconsin Press.

———. 1994. "Spirit Possession Revisited: Beyond Instrumentality." In *Annual Review of Anthropology*.

Debrunner, Hans Werner, 1961. *Witchcraft in Ghana: A Study on the Belief in Destructive Witches and Its Effect on the Akan Tribes*. Accra: Presbyterian Book Depot.

Fiawoo, D. K. 1971. "From Cult to 'Church': A Study of Some Aspects of Religious Change in Ghana." *Ghana Review of Sociology. Gold Coast Times*. (Accra). 1930. June 7.

Greene, Sandra. 1996. *Gender, Ethnicity and Social Change on the Upper Slave Coast: A History of the Anlo-Ewe Seventeenth to the Nineteenth Century*. Portsmouth: Heinemann.

Hodgson, Dorothy L. 1996. "Embodying the Contradictions of Modernity: Gender and Spirit Possession Among Maasai in Tanzania." In *Gendered Encounters: Challenging Cultural Boundaries and Social Hierarchies in Africa*, pp.107–124, Maria Grosz-Ngaté and Omari Kokole, eds. New York: Routledge.

Jell-Bahlsen, Sabine. 1989. *In Search of the Water Spirits*. Film.

Kramer, Fritz. 1993. *The Red Fez: Art and Spirit Possesion in Africa*. London, New York: Verso.

Matory, J. Lorand. 1993. "Government by Seduction: History and the Trope of 'Mounting' in Oyo-Yoruba Religion." In *Modernity and Its Malcontents: Ritual and Power in Postcolonial Africa*, Jean Comaroff and John Comaroff, eds. Chicago: University of Chicago Press.

———. 1994. *Sex and the Empire That Is No More: Gender and the Politics of Metaphor in Oyo Yoruba Religion*. Minneapolis: University of Minnesota Press.

National Archives of Ghana, Accra: File #11.

Rosenthal, Judy. 1995. "The Signifying Crab." *Cultural Anthropology* 10(4):581–586.

———. 1996. "Trance Against the State." *Ethnology*.

———. 1997. *Foreign Tongues and Domestic Bodies: Personhood, Possession, Gender and the Law in the Ewe Gorovodu Order*. Charlottesville: University Press of Virginia.

———. n.d. "An Afa Diviner's Message to Americans." Unpublished manuscript.

Rouch, Jean. 1954–55. *Les Maitres Fous*. Film.

Taussig, Michael. 1993. *Mimesis and Alterity: A Particular History of the Senses*. New York: Routledge.

Verger, Pierre. 1957. *Notes sur le culte des Orisa et Vodun à Bahia: la Baie de tous les saints au Bresil et à l'ancienne Côte des esclaves en Afrique*. Dakar: IFAN.

FROM STORY TO SONG:
GENDER, NATIONHOOD, AND THE MIGRATORY TEXT

HELEN NABASUTA MUGAMBI

In his untranslated collection of oral narratives, *Bukadde Magezi: Ekitabo Ky'enfumo z'Abaganda* (Age Is Wisdom: A Book of Traditional Narratives of the Baganda), Kawere (1948) aptly characterizes Kiganda prose narratives as Buganda's most precious treasure. In the process, he asserts that Kiganda traditional narratives have the intrinsic role of creating, defining, and controlling social relations as the narratives embody inherited "truths" of the Kiganda culture. He thus joins other African oral narrative scholars, such as Mudimbe (1991), who explore the various ways in which the traditional narratives function as powerful charters for the establishment of cultural and political identities. While discussing myth in central Africa, Mudimbe, for instance, characterizes mythical and historical narratives as "imbued with the sacred mission of carrying the nexus of cultural representation and being" (p. 99). Similarly, in his study of the Kiganda founding myth Ray (1980) characterizes myth as a charter for established cultural norms. He further documents that the Kiganda founding myth's interpreters ascribe the low status of women in Buganda to the actions of the primordial mother in that story. What evolves from these and other similar analyses of the function of traditional narratives is that oral narratives, myths in particular, are imbued with *unquestioned* power in the construction of collective cultural, political and gender identities. I contend that it is this unquestioned power that augments the transformative explication of the relationship between the traditional and contemporary narrative genres explored in this discussion. Moreover, the overall intricate relationship between the two genres lends credence to the various interpretations of the selected narratives.

A review of contemporary radio songs[1] reveals that these song narratives have heavily borrowed from the traditional Kiganda storytelling tradition. Traditional elements central to the function, form, style, and content of the traditional narrative (*lugero*) of the Baganda have been integrated into the radio song and placed in a new context relevant to the contemporary multiethnic Uganda nation. These borrowed elements include the narrator's explicit declaration of the function of the story, incorporation of several genres into the narrative, formulaic openings and endings, as well as the incorporation of various traditional motifs into the songs. I refer to such transferable narrative elements as "migratory texts."[2]

In this study I am concerned with exploring the significance of these migratory texts as they are transferred from traditional oral stories to contemporary radio songs.

My first aim is to demonstrate that radio songs, as urban-created narratives, are composed of aesthetically flexible, migratory elements derived from traditional preurban oral narratives. The second aim is to explore the artists' manipulation of these migratory elements and to argue that since the traditional narrative is imbued with unquestioned power to construct collective identities, by borrowing and incorporating the narrative's major structural elements, the contemporary radio song artist inherits and appropriates the narrative's unquestioned authorial and legislative power. The artist asserts, even appropriates this power in order to perpetuate or reconstruct gender and/or national identities. I focus on two sets of migratory texts, the formulaic opening and the trickster motif, to elucidate the major points in this discussion.

FROM TRADITIONAL NARRATIVE TO CONTEMPORARY RADIO SONG

Before appropriating the authority within the traditional narrative, and before incorporating traditional narrative elements into radio songs, radio artists tend self-consciously to proclaim or justify their newly acquired authorial position. In the episodic song "Nakakawa," for instance, the performer Matiya Luyima, acting as the fictional Ssepiria, recites the achievements that he claims qualify him for the position of lawmaker in his community. Part of the song dramatizes Ssepiria's journey to Bukuya, a remote village where he is not well known. While his mission is to attend the postfuneral rites for his brother-in-law, Ssepiria is mainly preoccupied with his status in this community. When he gets the opportunity to give a speech, he focuses solely on asserting his authority over the people:

> Ebitiibwa bye nimu wano abamu temummanyi
> Muntegere amatu kuba biringa musanvu
>
> . . .
>
> Ekitiibwa ekirara ndi deputy wowomuluka
>
> . . .
>
> Nkungaanya ensimbi ezisoba mu kakadde
> Ne tikiti gyenkuwa sigini maka ebaako
>
> . . .
>
> Nagula ne ku ggadi eya giya
>
> . . .
>
> Mulago gyemulaba eyo bagizimba ntunula
>
> . . .
>
> Ku kyaalo Kipuuta abaasomako tuli bana
> Wabula nga ndi omu eyayitako e Buddo
> Byebyannonza ku busigire bwomuluka

[Some of you here are unaware of my prestigious credentials
They are about seven; open your ears,

. . .

I am deputy village chief

. . .

I collect more than a million shillings in taxes

. . .

The receipts I issue bear my signature

. . .

I even once purchased a Raleigh bicycle with gears
I witnessed the building of Mulago hospital
In the village Kipuuta only four of us went to school

. . .

However, I am the only one that went to Buddo (a prestigious school)
Because of these credentials, I was selected deputy chief]

At this juncture, Ssepiria proceeds to issue laws to the assembled community. His companion, Colonali, reminds him in vain that the audience in this village falls outside his jurisdiction. Ssepiria proceeds to compose his laws, not only for his immediate audience, but also for all citizens of Uganda as a nation. This is a very important moment in the song because it signals the artist's conscious expansion of spatial boundaries beyond the village perimeters. Furthermore, the artist lays claim to superior knowledge over his audience. It is a level of knowledge comparable only to that embedded in the collective voice of the usually anonymous elders, author(s) of the traditional narrative. In "Nakakawa," Ssepiria strategically ascribes superior knowledge to education, experience, and age—for he was present at the beginning(s) of things—at the "conception" of modernity in Uganda. We could, therefore, say that this artist narrates a story of origin and, in the process, establishes new criteria for excellence within the emergent nation. It is through this process that Ssepiria, invoking his name and his individual history, appropriates the legislative authority of the anonymous collective voice of the traditional story.

Such strategies of re-creating narrative power indicate that contemporary song artists function not as passive transmitters of genres, but as astute or crafty narrators; they transfer the functions of the ethnic group's narrative to the radio song's vast national audience. As I discuss elsewhere (Mugambi 1994:48–49), Luganda is the most widely spoken language, understood by members of other ethnic groups in the various parts of Uganda. The accessibility of this vast, national audience through the radio medium amplifies the significance of issues associated with the manipulation of time, or the (re)construction of nation and gender through the migratory texts.

The migration of formulaic openings from the traditional story to the contemporary radio song provides the most obvious structural link between the traditional

narrative and its contemporary manifestation, the radio song. In the collection entitled *Engero Amakumi Abiri Mu Ebbiri* (*Twenty-Two Narratives*), the most common
openings are particularly evident in two stories, *"Awo olwatuuka mu mirembe egyedda
ennyo"* and *"Mu biro eby'edda ennyo."* The translation for both is: "It so happened in
the very remote past," that is, "Once upon a time." The stories in my 1974 collection
of narratives, by adult performers as well as by Naggalama Primary School girls, contained identical openings for the most part. In addition, the openings usually include
elements that characterize the performer directly as eyewitness to the event. Perhaps
the best example is *"Awo olwatuuka nga mbalabira,"* ("Once I witnessed for you this
one event"). The audience replies in chorus: *"Owoluganda ng' otulabira"* ("Yes, our relative, you did witness [this event] on our behalf") (Mugambi 1974:57). In this same
collection, the older performer, Magoba, usually starts his performances with the
"once upon a time" equivalent openings but ended in statements to the effect that he
left the action still in progress and returned home to narrate what he has witnessed
(Mugambi 1974:16, 23).

The radio song "Imbalu" represents songs that utilize opening formulae in all
the ways described above. In the first stanza of the song, the formulaic opening of the
oral narrative is implicit in the following lines:

> *Aboluganda, abemikwano ebyange bibino*
> *Nange nsumuludde emboozi nga ngitandika*
> *Byansanga ewaffe gye nali nsula*
> *Nali ewaffe olwegguloggulo*
> *Nkugambye kwekuwulira obugoma obwaali buvuga*
> *Nange Mbakaabya bannange kwe kukyamuka*
> *Olwonno ne mpapirira okugendayo okubulaba*

> [Relatives, friends, here is my story
> I am unwrapping the conversation as I start
> These (incidents) found me at home where I resided
> I was at home early one evening
> I am telling you—I heard the (little) drums sounding
> I myself , Mbakaabya, I got fired up
> That's when I rushed (to the scene) to see them (the drums)]

The narrator thus sufficiently roots himself in the recognizable traditional formulaic
opening as a means of establishing himself as a credible participant/eyewitness to the
very recent events he is about to narrate. Mbakaabya is, however, aware that he is a
Muganda who claims to have interviewed a Mugisu participant about the circumcision ceremony. He prefaces the story with these words:

Okutuuka ewa Wanyala eyo gye buvuga
Nga'abaana betala badda muli nga bazina
Nange Mbakaabya bannange kwekuzinamu
Wabula kwekusangamu owomukwano ye Bosco
Ne mubuuza mu lulimi awo olwawuufu
Wulira Mbakaabya bwe natandika
Mulembe . . .

[I arrived at Wanyala's residence where they [the drums] were sounding
The youths were frantically dancing
I too, Mbakaabya, joined in the dance
I bumped into a friend named Bosco
I interviewed him in the special language [Lugisu]
Listen, Mbakaabya, this is how I started . . .
Mulembe]

For his Luganda-speaking audience, the ensuing reenactment of the conversation (in Lugisu) serves to substantiate the narrator's credibility as an eyewitness. It proves his proficiency in the language through which the significance of the incidents he is about to narrate is explained to him.

The performer's credibility is further reinforced when the radio song also borrows the concept of "temporal manipulation" from the traditional story. Within the traditional narrative, the events being narrated are situated within an undefined remote past. The performer, using contemporary images, re-creates the event as she or he saw it in that remote past. Through the performance act, the artist's claim to have witnessed the events being retold in the story transfers those events across the easily remembered immediate past into the present. This is in accord with Mudimbe's statement (1991:97) that neither mythical nor historical narratives "reenact the immediate experience of the culture they claim to unveil."

Thus, the radio song, like the traditional narrative, manipulates time. Unlike the traditional story, though, the radio song, as seen in "Imbalu," witnesses not to a remote past, but to the very recent history of incidents in the Uganda nation. This exploitation of time shifts permeates the radio song narrative through the overall borrowing of stylistic elements and motifs originally attributable only to traditional narratives. It is through this kinship to the traditional narrative that the radio song indirectly sets the remote past in motion. In "Siwa Muto Lugero" (untranslated but meaning "I do not mess with the kids") Nsimbi (1948:i–v) rightly draws attention to the timelessness of meaning in traditional narratives. We can, therefore, claim that the performing of traditional narratives as embodied in radio songs functions as the channel for the transmission of the timeless meanings highlighted by Nsimbi.

The recognition of the close kinship between the traditional and the radio song should facilitate a fruitful examination of the process through which migratory elements acquire transformative meanings within the contemporary song compositions While the radio song artists re-present the past through migratory structural elements of the traditional narrative, they simultaneously propagate and interrogate received ideals. But if migratory texts contain ideals to be interrogated or propagated, they can only be meaningfully received by the audience as "interfacial texts." In his discussion of intertexts and intratexts, Doane (1991:81) describes an interfacial text as one that is

> produced in a milieu where the oral tradition is still alive and productive, one whose intended/actual audience . . . whether literate or illiterate, is conversant with the tradition and [is] capable of receiving the "oral text" as an oral audience, not just aurally, but critically, with a traditional understanding of the meaning and functions of traditional language, formulas, and themes.

In the radio song context, the audience is bound to recognize the migratory traditional elements refashioned into the song. Once the song evokes the traditional formulaic opening, it inevitably forces the audience to recall the emblematic structure and function of a traditional narrative in a manner identical to that articulated by Doane. It is this recollection that sets in motion the relationship between the listening national audience and the radio song performer in which the latter is perceived as "bearer of cultural truths." From this vantage point, the artist is able to manipulate the audience as he or she reinforces the bond between the contemporary message and that of accepted ancestral wisdom. It is no wonder that song artists utilize formulae and proverbs profusely and are fond of statements such as "as they [the ancestors] say . . ." It follows, therefore, that traditional openings are transformed into vehicles that not only link the past to the present, but also establish the artist's credibility, enabling him to validate new stories thus far not authorized by tradition.

In its migratory form, the formulaic opening can be viewed as a rhetorical device the artist utilizes to empower his song discourse. After appropriating the authority inherent in the traditional narrative, the song artist places her-or himself in a position of power and is, therefore, able to use opening formulae as a means of invoking audiences to whom she or he can legislate. In this manner, the radio song's structured opening becomes a vehicle through which the performer from the recording studio assembles an otherwise invisible national audience. The radio song "Imbalu," for instance, describes initiation rites of a group of young Gisu boys. Opening his song with *"Aboluganda, ab'emikwano ebyange bibino"* ("Relatives, friends, here are my words"), the artist constitutes a non-gender-specific target audience.

On the other hand, in the radio song "Naggayi" the artist is gender-specific. His song warns men against economic exploitation by the city woman. He addresses himself only to the male segment of his audience, who, he feels, must be protected against the cunning city woman. He opens with the words "*Basajja bannange abagalwa*" ("My dearly beloved fellow men"). By addressing "fellow men" as the primary audience, the artist simultaneously succeeds in indirectly drawing the attention of the female audience, who become interested in what might be conspiratorial male discourse. It is not surprising, then, that the singer ends his song with a direct plea to women as part of his presumed audience. The performer has, by a rhetorical strategy of exclusion, presumed the attention of the female audience. This establishes the idea of a dual audience: one intended and privileged to the direct discourse, the other expected as eavesdropper but primary target of the message in the song or narrative. This idea of a dual audience is indigenous to African oral performance as is illustrated extensively in Agovi's (1994) description of the immediate participant female audience and the wider listening male audience of the Nzima (Ghanaian) maiden songs.[3]

This type of "bifocal" audience constructed within the song's opening is best represented in the song "Nakakawa." In this radio song, the artist consciously addresses himself to two audiences. One audience is the target national audience, invisible to him in the urban recording studio. The other is one that he constitutes as his primary audience within the song to simulate the live audience of the oral narrative. He assembles the audience inside the song and re-creates the rural ambiance associated with traditional storytelling. These newly assembled members of this audience, inside the song, become participants in the story that unfolds. They do so through spoken words, running commentaries on the song's pronouncements, or through responding to the narrator in song. This is identical to instances in the Chokwe storytelling tradition when, as Fretz (1995:96–97) points out, the audience members participate to the extent that they often become "co-performers." In "Nakakawa," members of the audience become characters within the performance event, which is then broadcast to the national audience. Individual characters within this song reenact gender relationships between husbands and wives to assert or subvert accepted definitions of womanhood, as I demonstrated in my initial analysis of the song "Nakakawa" (Mugambi 1994:47–70).

Manipulation of opening formulae as a means of assembling a national audience is manifested in its most complex form within the episode "Ssepiria mu lumbe lwa Ssenfuusi" ("Ssepiria at the postfuneral rites of Ssenfuusi"). This is the final song in the song narrative "Nakakawa." Here, we witness a progressive assembling of the audience. First, Ssepiria's friends arrive at his home simply to pay him a visit, but find that he is about to set out to Bukuya to attend his in-law's postfuneral ceremony. Then Ssepiria, together with his friends, walks across the rural landscape to join the congregation already assembled from different parts of the country to participate in the rites. This opening presents an explicit manipulation of the assembling-the-audience technique to enable the artist to reconstruct national history in song for the audience gathered to participate in a traditional rite. The artist ingeniously creates a varied audience by having the story take place at a ritual in which all the relatives and friends of the recently deceased person from all over the country are bound to participate. He then appropriates an ethnic space reserved for postfuneral rites and transforms it into a site for political discourse in an attempt to create a consciousness of nation within the boundaries of this rural site.

Addressing the audience, as already discussed in the context of the song's function, he lays down the standards of conduct expected in the new nation. It is no wonder that actual key rituals associated with this function, apart from the sumptuous feasting, are not mentioned at all in the song. This clearly points to the fact that the assembling technique in this part of the song exists simply as a device to tell a story, not of remote beginnings of the Buganda, but of the Uganda nation.

Before this large audience Ssepiria initiates a discourse that first centers on him as an individual and gradually incorporates himself into the political organization of the nation. When the assembled audience, in chorus, hails Ssepiria's status and leadership, they also vow to abide by the laws of the national government. Through this act, they, like the narrator, engage in self-definition, inserting themselves into the national to facilitate the survival of the postcolonial state. In all such instances, the radio song artist transforms the traditional opening of the narrative into a site for political discourse in which she attempts to insert her people into emerging national spaces.

Furthering the idea of nation, the song "Bannange Mwenna Mbalamusa" ("I Greet You All, My Friends") represents songs that use the opening formula as a means of forging a nation, not from a homogeneous ethnic audience, but from a multiplicity of groups that constitute the Ugandan postcolonial state. In such songs, diverging from the traditional audience of their immediate community, artists use structured openings as a means of reassembling, re-creating, or reconfiguring Uganda as a multiethnic nation. The singer in "Mbalamusa" assembles his audience from a multiplicity of ethnic groups strategically selected to represent east, west, north, and south Uganda. He opens his song by symbolically greeting each group in its own language and immediately announces that the purpose of the gathering is to celebrate New Year's Day. However, as the song progresses we realize that the celebration is about surviving the massacres caused by recent political tyrannies. He uses the new year simply as a metaphor of a new beginning as he pleads for a different type of social order that accommodates peace, neighborliness, and *obuntubulamu*. Like Ssepiria, this artist uses the song to proclaim new laws that will hopefully ensure harmony in the postcolonial nation. In this case, however, the radio song's structured opening is transformed into a site for remembering the community's troubled social and political history.

Clan systems traditionally provided the structure for cementing cohesion in communities. Like the real bonds created through clan identities, recent radio songs utilize the assembling-the-audience technique as a means to recall recent shared history, not of a single ethnic group but of the whole nation. I believe this technique has the effect of forging kinship within the emergent multiethnic imagined community that constitutes the Ugandan nation.

I have focused extensively on formulaic openings because they represent features most frequently manipulated by song artists to reconstruct, reassemble, and by implication re-create new beginnings in the Ugandan nation. Similarly, manipulation of the trickster motif from the traditional narrative moves the radio song discourse into the arena of gender relations.

Woman-centered radio songs, whether performed by male or female artists, usually focus on women's power and authority. In the song "Nebundulira," performed by the female artist Sauda Batenda, for instance, the artist establishes herself as physician of society's ills and proceeds to suggest the laws that must be implemented to ensure social and gender equality as well as political harmony within the nation. Furthermore, Batenda critiques current dysfunctional laws and addresses herself to issues of gender and class at the various sociopolitical levels (Mugambi 1994). It is through such songs that we should raise questions about epistemic agency and about the construction of knowledge in the postcolonial nation. In the present discussion, however, I am not focusing on this category of song. Rather, I am concerned with songs that manipulate the trickster motif to reconfigure contemporary female power and to problematize issues of gender power within the household.

BUKALABAKALABA: RECONSTRUCTING WOMAN —WHEN MONKEY BECOMES MARY

Women performers of both traditional narratives and contemporary songs consistently reenvision womanhood. About the Chokwe female storytellers in Zaire, Fretz (1994) explains that women use ambiguity to subtly communicate their revisions of women's conventionally accepted roles. In a related manner, in the Luganda song "Nebundulira," above, the female artist utilizes her own life history to demonstrate women's acquisition of power to author stories that guide the nation. In addition, she strategically utilizes the tune of a traditional song that denigrates women to cushion her biting critique of the patriarchal system. In both of these cases, the performance becomes an empowering channel for the contemporary woman. This is not always the case with similar narratives by male performers.

Motif migration functions as the most important device in reconfiguring woman in the contemporary radio song. The well-known recurring motif in folklore conventionally labeled "trickster" is an ideal example of how male narrators utilize song as a channel for disempowering the feminized trickster figure. First, attention must be drawn to the attributes of the trickster figure. "Trickster" is a label attributed to characters that have the common trait of tricking and outsmarting others and includes such figures as Ananse (Spider) of West Africa and Wankima (Monkey) as well as Wakayima (Hare) of East Africa, among others.

As in many other traditions, a trickster character in the Kiganda oral tradition usually exhibits wisdom, ingenuity, guile, and craftiness. All these attributes, however, are not accommodated in the casual use of the term "trickster" but are contained in the more comprehensive Kiganda term *bukalabakalaba*. I use the term "trickster" in this discussion in a sense that embraces the multilayered connotations of *bukalabakalaba* as this motif gets transformed at the intersection of genre and gender. I propose that radio artists transform this motif into a rhetorical device for interrogating and reconstructing womanhood in the radio songs.

Even though one aspect implicit in *bukalabakalaba* is that of the traditional trickster character, imposing the English term "trickster" on figures in traditional orature clearly impedes access to the possibilities inherent in the more appropriate Luganda term *bukalabakalaba*. "Trickster," when applied to the traditional Kiganda folktale character Wakayima, is inadequate because it often only connotes that the trickster exploits, confuses, and sometimes misleads others into behavior that gets them into trouble. What is often overlooked is the figure's limitless expression of ingenuity in which lies the wisdom of being able to accurately and instantaneously respond to any crisis situation; to successfully evade punishment or retribution, even when caught in the most hopeless of situations; and to instantaneously invent novel solutions when facing conditions where defeat appears inevitable.

This trait is identically constructed and abounds in traditional narratives, whether it is between animal characters, animal characters versus human characters, or simply between human characters. The key lesson communicated by the trickster character's success is that one must use one's brains, not physical might, to triumph over adversaries. Two stories may serve as examples of the *bukalabakalaba* motif in two very different plots. The story of Nassange involves an innocent little girl trying to find remedies for a bad judgment call, while in the second story, a guilty trickster monkey gets the better of his adversary. Here is a brief summary of Nassange's predicament:

> Nassange is sent to fetch water all by herself. While at the well she realizes that she cannot lift the pot of water onto her head without help. She enlists the aid of the only being at the river, Ogre. But Ogre's help comes with a high price tag. As compensation for the help, Nassange is compelled to enter into a Faustian pact. At first, she offers to give Ogre a cow if he helps her. He declines. Next she offers that he eat her mother in return for the favor. He

still declines. Finally she offers herself: "Onondya" ("You can eat me [later])." He accepts. When Ogre comes to the girl's home to claim his reward, the girl ingeniously hides in various places she believes to be inaccessible to Ogre. Successively, Ogre discovers the various hiding places. Finally, Nassange takes refuge in the only place she believes no animal would reach. She jumps back into her mother's womb. Although Ogre discovers this final hiding place, he simply walks away, defeated.

Among other lessons, this story encourages the young to think of creative solutions for self-preservation. In another version of the same story, it is the mother who devises the various hiding places for her daughter. Most importantly, the plot is such that either the young girl or the girl's mother employs ingenuity to outmaneuver the physically superior figure. This plot reflects the propagation of society's esteemed virtue of *bukalabakalaba*.

The "Monkey and Leopard" story illustrates the motif in its most perfected form. Whereas the story of Nassange portrays an unaggressive ogre who will not enforce the breach of contract and gives the potential victim time to premeditate solutions, the "Monkey and Leopard" story takes place at a very fast pace, and Monkey must engineer solutions instantly during the hot pursuit that constitutes most of the action. Here is a brief summary of that story, as narrated by Kyebasuuta Jr.:

A very long time ago, Monkey and Leopard were good friends. One day, Monkey stole Leopard's delicacy snack *enswa*, flying ants. Leopard threatened to eat Monkey. Monkey outran Leopard and hid himself inside a cave. Leopard camped at the mouth of the cave and would not leave. So, Monkey advised his friend that if he wanted to eat him, he should first get him two large colocynth bolls, *entengotengo*. Leopard obliged. Next, Monkey suggested that monkey meat tasted better if roasted. Leopard brought fire and pushed it down the narrow mouth of the cave. On catching fire, the two berries exploded and flew out of the cave. Leopard was overjoyed. "These must be Monkey's roasted eyes that have popped out as he gets roasted." Leopard quickly widened the mouth of the cave to have easier access to his dinner. All the while, Monkey was watching from a dark corner in the cave. As soon as he saw the mouth widened, Monkey flew out of the cave past unsuspecting Leopard. Leopard, however, was able to chase and catch Monkey. But Monkey pleaded: "You know, Leopard, my meat will taste even better if tenderized by a heavy fall from the top of this tree. Please push me up the tree. When I fall from there you can feast on me." Leopard once again cooperated. Leopard pushed Monkey up the tree. Monkey climbed to the highest branches and never came down.

Thus, three times Monkey succeeds in extricating himself from extremely tight spots by making his pursuer unknowingly facilitate his escape. Monkey's initial temporary escape is effected through sheer physical agility. His second and third narrow escapes can only be ascribed to *bukalabakalaba,* as he ingeniously tricks Leopard into cooperating in a shrewdly engineered scheme intended only to facilitate his escape.

This archetypal plot notwithstanding, when Monkey becomes Mary in the radio songs, she instantly loses the agility to escape, and ingenuity comes to a screeching halt. In the traditional stories, the trickster figure usually got away after inflicting injury or injustice to an opponent. When the trickster attribute is transferred to woman in the radio songs, she is usually apprehended, humiliated, and admonished, while her experience is used to warn men about the "dangerous" female species.

Three typical songs into which artists have incorporated the trickster motif from the traditional narrative serve to illustrate this point. It is crucial to keep in mind that the trickster motif is employed not simply to structure the plot of the story, but as a crucial rhetorical device in the artist's attempt to invalidate the contemporary woman's claim to space conventionally reserved for men. Again, the conclusions to these stories illustrate how the traditional narrative's migration into the contemporary song becomes the code into which contemporary meanings are signified. "Eminkuduuli," "Naggayi," and "Kayanda" are three songs that reflect how various aspects of woman's interrogating of conventional norms are "framed" by the contemporary artists. As I will demonstrate, the wife in "Eminkuduuli" challenges the husband's monopoly of power in the household, while Naggayi's lifestyle interrogates men's accepted monopoly on multiple spouses in the city. The final song, "Kayanda"is a complex questioning of the totality of power relations in the household. The female figure in "Kayanda" represents woman as both wife and mother. She embodies the complications raised in the first two songs. However, her story presents the additional dimension of questioning authority over woman's choices, including her reproductive rights.

The first example, "Eminkuduuli," is the story of a wife who tries to transform the power structure in the household so that it is she, and not the husband, who wields authority and commands obedience. Even though the wife resorts to metaphysical intervention, her plan fails. Significantly, the narrator claims that her actions bring disgrace, not just to herself, but to her whole clan, and, by implication, to the community of women. At the beginning of the song, the singer first characterizes himself as one who idolizes women. This strategy is utilized to guard against alienating his female audience, an audience that he eventually chastises. He starts his song with a preamble in which he pays tribute to a mother he idolizes for giving birth to him, a birth that has resulted in his great contribution to society. He emphatically states that many in his audience have accused him of pampering women in his songs. He proceeds to say that the story he is about to narrate is meant to warn and admonish women who, instead of conducting themselves "appropriately" in marriage, put their faith in manipulating metaphysical powers to stabilize their relationships.

When the story begins, a childhood friend of the narrator is already married. In summary:

> As newlyweds, husband and wife shielded their bad habits from each other. With time, the wife's nasty character surfaced. She was jealous, condescending, and resented any criticism. Above all she was very argumentative, contesting everything she was told. The husband's patience became exhausted and he threatened to divorce her. Unwilling to end her marriage, she instantly engineered strategies that would salvage the situation.

> She set out very early one morning for the big market. She heard a man chanting the curative qualities of various medications on display. "This is for women. You want your husband to fear/obey you. Steam a chicken in a banana leaf [*luwombo*] and season it with this medicine. After he eats it, he will respond 'yes mama' to everything you say." The woman responded immediately: "I want one which will make my husband give me some respect." Little did she suspect that she was taking a *musambwa* (a nature spirit capable of disguising itself in various forms, usually that of woman). By sheer coincidence, the narrator arrived to visit his best friend, who immediately ordered that a chicken be slaughtered for a meal in his honor. When the meal was ready, the wife requested her husband's assistance in opening the *luwombo,* the dish for the guest of honor. He opened it and stared, transfixed. Instead of the expected chicken, there was a huge snake, *essalambwa,* inside the *luwombo* dish. The alarm was sounded, the neighbors congregated, the house was evacuated. Slapping her and threatening to kill her, the husband demanded an explanation. To save her life, the wife eventually confessed. The husband forced her to lead him to the man in the market from whom she had purchased the concoction. Meanwhile, the narrator says, the assembled neighbors were "dying of laughter." The final words again chastise the wife for this action.

The woman in "Eminkuduuli" is divested of the possibilities of solutions available to either Monkey or Nassange within the traditional narrative. Like Monkey, the wife has betrayed trust, but while Monkey is allowed to exploit the infinite possibilities of the intellect and to escape, the wife does not find a way out of her dilemma. When the chicken turns into a snake, the woman fails to invent a quick escape and, instead, is humiliated before all the neighbors. She also fails to avert being forced to revisit the marketplace, where she is again humiliated and obligated to expose her "benefactor."

The physical location of this song is not clearly demarcated, thus allowing it to apply equally to rural as well as urban women. In addition, this song does represent conflict between man and woman. The two male figures, the narrator and the medicine peddler, are an example in point. The narrator, as already mentioned, characterizes himself as always on the side of women, while the man who sells the medicine in the marketplace appears to subvert men's power in the household.

Since songs are constructed in response to social changes and are, by implication, commentaries on actions of individuals and social groups, the loss of *bukalaba-kalaba* in the radio songs is symptomatic of the society's construction of woman's social being. Artists are commenting on changing values and approving or sanctioning them. Artists seem to be transforming the *bukalabakalaba* into a unidimensional trickster. By feminizing the *bukalabakala-ba* figure and stripping this figure of its traditional attributes, the artist censures woman's apparent trespassing into unconventional territory, thus cautioning her against challenging dominant community values.

The song "Naggayi" moves negotiations of power and authority from the unmarked landscape to a specific urban environment. The narrator strengthens his credibility by stating that he was an eyewitness to the events in the song since he is a neighbor of Kateregga, one of the key characters in the song. The song "Naggayi" narrates the story of a city girl, Naggayi, who for a long time succeeds in tricking three men, Steven, Hadji Katende, and Kateregga, into each perceiving himself as the only boyfriend. Here is a brief summary of the rest of the plot:

> When Naggayi becomes pregnant and gives birth to a baby boy, she attributes fatherhood to each of the three men. Each father names the baby according to his clan norms. Unfortunately, malaria seizes the child, who is admitted to the hospital. Naggayi sends for each of the men. When Kateregga arrives, the child is already dead. He rushes home to organize the digging of the grave and to rent a car to fetch the dead body. Meanwhile Hadji Katende and Steven arrive at the bedside at the same time. When Kateregga returns, he finds Hadji and Steven engaged in a dispute over ownership of the dead child. He joins the fight as he too asserts his fatherhood rights. Before long, a big crowd gathers. People assemble, including doctors, to determine the nature of the disturbance. Naggayi is stuck. "Her ingenuity is entangled in a web of knots." To settle the dispute, the doctors decide to use the medical records to eliminate impostors. Naggayi had assigned fatherhood to Steven, who starts to prepare the little body for the final journey home. On close examination, however, Steven discovers that the child had already been circumcised following Islamic custom, a fact that bestows official fatherhood to the Muslim contender, Hadji Katende. Infuriated by this final discovery, Steven storms out of the hospital to avoid taking to his home

"a ghost" that does not belong to him. But by then Hadji Katende has already left. When Kateregga sees this, he too deserts mother and dead child and goes home to stop the gravedigging. The child is eventually buried by the state without the sacred rites of family and community. The story once again ends with an admonition to women.

While the above two songs re-create, then suppress, women's contestation of gendered categories and behavior by presenting definite closure to the social and moral issues raised by the story, the song "Kayanda" ends in ambiguity. Composed around 1992, "Kayanda" is a song/drama, in which Mukaabya discovers that Nakiyimba, his presumed daughter, was actually fathered by Kayanda, the migrant worker and house servant originally from Burundi. Conservative and hierarchical Buganda families usually looked down upon such workers and treated them as a marginal servant class. Mukaabya summons the village ruling council, the Resistance Council. The Resistance Council is a grassroots jury that has, in contemporary Ugandan politics, replaced the traditional council of elders that normally mediated family disputes.

At the end of the mediation, even though it is proved that the wife had deceived the husband into believing that he was the father of her child, the case is decided against the husband. He is declared guilty of wife neglect since he is always away from home on business trips, a situation that compels his wife to depend on the house servant for help in running the home. The wife gets the sympathy of the jury, as she is cast as victim of spousal neglect. Nevertheless, when it comes to announcing the moral of the story (the reason for the existence of the narrative), a male voice from the council states:

Manya bw'obeera n'abakazi
olina kuuma bukuumi
ngembwa enkambwe

[Remember when you have women
you have to keep close watch
like a ferocious dog]

This statement betrays the deep-seated sentiments of the male jury members.

The council is supposed to be the supreme authority in settling such domestic disputes. However, when it declares the woman's victory, the husband rejects the verdict, gets more enraged, and initiates a fight, intent on killing the "guilty" Kayanda. Since the concluding action is a chaotic fight, the wife is, in a sense, left with an empty victory and an uncertain future. In spite of her pronounced victory through the ruling council, the woman is, once again, portrayed as a defeated trickster, frozen in her tracks. By creating such an ambiguous ending to the song, the artist opens up spaces for multiple interpretations.

"Kayanda," like postmodern feminist discourse, does not simply reproduce gender categories but rather complicates them. By interrogating gendered power and authority within the emerging middle-class family, this song addresses the sociopolitical situation in which women are wielding more public power in the economic and political sectors of Uganda.

In summary, the husband, Mukaabya, accuses his wife of contemptuous behavior, but the Resistance Council exonerates her and in fact transfers the blame back to Mukaabya. But Mukaabya ignores their verdict and vows to impose justice in his own violent manner, determined to kill Kayanda. We also discover that the Resistance Council's decision is influenced by their attitude to Mukaabya as an emerging member of an affluent middle class. The use of the recently coined term *maayikka* betrays their sentiment. The term *maayikka*, a vernacular form of the English "my car," is a derogatory label the common man places on the affluent, who are said to always use the expression "my car" to refer to their automobiles even when they are speaking Luganda. This class of people is also known for frequently avoiding giving rides to poor pedestrians. In its wider application, the term is used to describe anyone the people consider affluent regardless of whether or not the person owns an automobile.

At the very beginning of this song/drama, Mukaabya portrays the history of his relationship with his wife. He narrates how he and his wife have risen from dire poverty to middle-class prosperity through hard work:

> *Waliwo ensonga ekwata ku mukazi wange oyo*
> *Tubadde bulungi tubadde mu ddembe*
> *Twayagalana ne mukazi wange oyo*
> *Netusula empewo netusula obukunya*
> *Alabye tuvuddeyo tutuuse mu ddembe*
>
> *Laba nze bwankola!*
>
> *Tubadde bulungi baganda bange*
> *Enyumba tuzimbye entambula weri*
> *Abakozi tubalina balima mu nnimiro . . .*

[There is a problem regarding this wife of mine
We have been living in peace and harmony
We manifested great love for each other
In dire poverty we endured the cold

She now sees us prosperous
See how she is treating me!

We have been prosperous, my kinspeople
We have built a home, we even own a car
We have workers tending the gardens . . .]

This description squarely sets Mukaabya apart from the very jury assembled to hear his case and effectively alienates him from them. Critique of the middle-class lifestyle now becomes an integral part of the voices on the stage. The husband is portrayed by this jury as placing the pursuit of economic success ahead of his wife's immediate needs within the home. The apparent consequence is the loss of power and authority over his household. This point is driven home when, at the height of this mediation, another defendant arrives. It is another woman caught having a drink in a hotel in Mukono town with her driver on their way back from a postfuneral rite, a trip actually preauthorized by the husband. This case is also decided in favor of the wife, who did not see anything wrong in her decision to stop for a drink in the absence of her husband. The council declares that the husband should have left the wife to drive herself to the postfuneral rites. Again, this is an ambiguous judgment since it does not seem to address the problem. It is important to note that the council that sits in judgment in this case, as already mentioned, has replaced the traditional village council of elders and is constituted by the laws of the postcolonial Museveni era, the laws of yet a new Ugandan nation. This song represents ambiguity and becomes a powerful interrogation of gender and class within the context of the national community. One wonders whether the council is not in effect imposing a punitive judgment on Mukaabya for his economic status by exonerating his basically guilty wife. One also wonders whether the artist appropriates the trickster motif not so much to reconfigure the contemporary middle-class woman as to demonstrate the scrambling of power relations within a middle-class family and the chaos that ensues. In this case both formulaic openings and the trickster motif as migratory elements are best characterized as tools for examining how power is conceptualized across time and space in contemporary Uganda.[4]

In conclusion, it is clear that contemporary radio artists resident in urban centers establish themselves, through their authorship of song, as legislators and re-creators of contemporary national and gender identities scrambled by recent social and political turmoil. The shift from traditional narrative to radio song represents a transformative process by which the traditional narrative is increasingly empowered as the authoritative source and nexus of new meanings transmitted through the emergent song discourses. It is the radio song as an oral form, with its accessibility to the population across ethnic, class, educational, and gender boundaries, that becomes a central channel for the flow of transformative ideas within the nation. Hence, songs that interrogate gender relations contribute significantly to the emerging culture of women's liberation in post-colonial Uganda.

NOTES

1. I use the term "radio song" as a genre that incorporates all commercially produced narrative songs (songs that tell a story) circulated through radio or audiocassette.

2. Similarly, Bukenya (1978) coined the term "interfluence of forms" to refer to the migration of genres.

3. For a comprehensive discussion of the nature of these women's discourses, see Agovi's (1994) article.

4. Byanyima (1992) explains that by successfully joining the recent political struggle, Ugandan women created for themselves a position of power in the national socio-political arena.

BIBLIOGRAPHY

Agovi, Kofi E. 1994. "Women's Discourse on Social Change in Nzema (Ghanaian) Maiden Songs." *Oral Tradition* 9(1):203–229.

Bukenya, Austin L. 1978. *Notes on East African Poetry*. Nairobi: Heinemann Educational Books.

Byanyima, Karagwa W. 1992. "Women in Political Struggle in Uganda." In *Women Transforming Politics* 129-142. Jill M. Bystydzienski, ed. Bloomington: Indiana University Press.

Doane, A.N. 1991. "Oral Texts, Intertexts, and Intratexts: Editing Old English." In *Influence and Intertextuality in Literary History*, pp. 75–113. Jay Clayton and Eric Rothstein, eds. Madison: University of Wisconsin Press.

Ekibiina Ky'Olulimi O. 1960. *Engero Amakumi Abiri Mu Ebbiri*. Kampala: Longman Uganda Limited.

Fretz, Rachel. 1994. "Through Ambiguous Tales: Women's Voices in Chokwe Storytelling." *Oral Tradition* 9(1):230–250

———. .1995. "Answering in Song: Listener Response in Yishima Performances." *Western Folklore* 54(2):95–112.

Kawere, M. B. 1948. *Siwa Muto Lugero*. Kampala: Longman Uganda.

Mudimbe, V .Y. 1991. *Parables and Fables*. Madison: University of Wisconsin Press.

Mugambi, Helen N. 1974. *Creative Expression in Kiganda Folk Narratives*. Unpublished B.A. Thesis, Makerere University (Uganda).

———. 1994. "Intersections: Gender, Orality, Text, and Female Space in Contemporary Kiganda Radio Songs." *Research in African Literatures*. Fall: 39–70.

Ray, Benjamin. 1980. "The Story of Kintu: Myth, Death, and Ontology." In *African Systems of Thought*, pp. 54–75. Ivan Karp, ed. Bloomington: Indiana University Press.

Sunkuli, L. and O. Miruka. 1990. *A Dictionary of Oral Literature*. Nairobi: Heinemann Kenya.

TRAFFIC IN MEN

Paulla Ebron

> You don't ask for sex, but the men seem to know you want it. They say
> things like, "Would you like to see the real Africa?" It's all very discreet. I had
> four different boys that holiday and the best sex I have ever had. I came back
> a new woman (Mary, English tourist quoted in Aziz 1994:12).

In July 1994, a coup in the West African country of The Gambia ended the
thirty-year reign of Sir Dawada Jawara, who had been repeatedly elected as head of
state since the end of colonial rule. The platform of the newly self-appointed state
leader, Lieutenant Yahya Jammeh, called for an end to government corruption.
Mounted alongside this plea was also a call for an end to the immorality associated
with the tourist industry. This sector had gained in notoriety in recent years as the
prevalence of European women holiday travelers seeking Gambian male friends became increasingly well known. Turning attention to all of the associated activities related to tourism in The Gambia, including prostitution and the drug trade,
Lieutenant Jammeh demanded a rigorous attack on activities perceived by some
Gambians to have gone far beyond the bounds of acceptable behavior. These feelings
were articulated by the new head of state in a press release in which he made it clear
that he would not allow women tourists to visit his country in search of sex.

> We are Africans and we have our own moral values. . . . Prostitution and
> drugs, those are all moral woes that we don't want in an African country be-
> cause those are ideas which are alien to the African people. . . . We are not
> sex machines. I want that to be clear to whoever comes here purposely for
> sex. (Reuters, August 20, 1994)

In addition to the attention paid by the Gambian state to transnational travel
and sex, the phenomenon of European women in search of male Gambian partners
has also garnered a great deal of international attention. Travel agents regularly book
flights for women visitors, some of them returnees; journalists for women's magazines
interview women travelers and write tantalizing stories of emancipated women on
holiday in The Gambia (Aziz 1994); social scientists in Europe track the migrations
of Gambians to European countries and follow their romantic connections (Wagner
and Yamba 1993; Mansson 1993); and international health agencies concerned about
the health of tourists and the potential spread of HIV study the impact of sexual encounters on holiday tourists (Pickering et al. 1992; Travel, Lifestyles and Health

Project 1994). This incessant interest in sex tourism in The Gambia has helped to codify a sociological phenomenon. Yet the significance of European women and Gambian men is not just in the new sexual partnerships—with their implications for emigration, AIDS, or local incomes—but also in the formation of allegorical narratives of personal and national mobility and morality.

This essay explores the wider significance of the sociological studies as they intersect with tales I heard about men, women, and tourism while conducting research in The Gambia in 1989–1990. During my fieldwork, the repetitious telling of a few almost stereotypic anecdotes drew my attention. These narratives, related to me by Gambian men, reiterated the sociological "facts" of tourist relationships but also gave them a wider cultural-political significance. I began to recognize a recurring set of themes in many of the narratives, and I started to hear these as more than a series of anecdotes. Their repetition, frequency, and accompanying commentary suggested that these stories could be appreciated, outside the bounds of the tourist industry, as parables that expressed national anxieties over power differences between Africa and Europe, and between men and women.

The stories were regularly marked by ambivalence about tourism as well as a sense of the excitement created by anticipated possibilities. In villages and urban neighborhoods near the tourist areas, I repeatedly heard comments that echoed Lieutenant Jammeh's fear of national moral decay. Stories that centered around sex and the transgressive behavior of Gambian male youth and *toubob* (European) women friends became a regular part of public discussion. My Gambian male associates frequently entertained me with the adventures of their friends and acquaintances who had traveled to Europe. Initially, these men appeared as successful winners in a game of chance, but soon enough—inevitably—they fell into the less appealing circumstances that seem intertwined with these kinds of African travel adventures. Even for those who had themselves never traveled beyond urban areas, such tales took on the aura of a national trajectory.

There were, however, striking gender differences in the ways travel was understood by Gambians. Women's travels, and this includes Gambian women as well as European women, were never described in a complimentary way, for women can never carry national hopes and dreams in their travels. The Gambian men I knew often portrayed European women as engaged in a morally distasteful, single-minded search for attractive Gambian men. The Northern women in these stories were uncontrolled sex zealots. In contrast, the Southern men were adroit businessmen ready to design their success by capturing raw European passions. The stories told, then, of Gambian men crafting a masculine national trajectory in which political and cultural agency depended upon African male abilities to fashion themselves as entrepreneurs who could shape themselves to suit Europeans desires. In this nexus of dreams, the power and charisma of Europe was imagined as that of sexually promiscuous women, while Gambian men were desperate catchers of an opportunity.

Gambian "traffic-in-men" narratives disrupt our taken-for granted axioms about the gendered locations of sexual agency. In these stories, women are not merely targets of male sexual opportunities. The European women, empowered by national status, comparative wealth, and racially defined mobility, are imagined as the controllers of sexual opportunity. Furthermore, Gambian men's stories seem plausible and "true" because they overlap just enough with the stories European women tourists tell about themselves. In one magazine article, English tourist women pronounce themselves enchanted by the prospect of having their pick of "beautiful men" (Aziz 1994: 12). Still, the women appear unable to completely invert European hierarchies of gender dominance; their sexual vacations are empowering precisely because they tell their narratives as temporary emancipation from the male dominance of their ordinary lives. There are other ways, too, in which their stories are no simple inversion of European men travelers' tales. The women do not imagine Gambian men as easy victims. And Gambian men's stories are certainly not tales of their victimization. Men imagine these connections as the means to wealth, status, and transnational mobility. Thus, the sets of stories woven around romantic travel between The Gambia and Europe upset conventional parables about male sexual subjects and female sexual objects—though not in any simple ways. They refuse universal assumptions to demand specification of the transnational content of these erotic fantasies as well as the erotic charge of these transnational interconnections.

This essay focuses on the construction of gender, desire, and social location across geographic boundaries and the ways these figure into Gambian commentaries about tourism. Integral to the discussion are the continual refigurings of gender and power differences at the intersection of North-South relations. I begin with a discussion of the development of tourism in The Gambia to offer some background to the allegorical aspects of the stories people tell about tourism. The inclusion of this section is more than just an orientation point, however, for this contextualization points to the vulnerability of The Gambia as a tiny Southern nation in the global economy. Another section of the essay engages feminist theories that draw attention to the significance of political status in the negotiation of gender. Writing against many of the formations that assume gender as a universalized category of women's subordination, I argue that theorists who ignore the specificity through which gender is figured and reconfigured overlook a critical transnational aspect of the social construction of gender categories. This section is followed by a focus on the fashioning of charismatic style by Gambian male participants in transnational tourist adventures and the development of what I call the "personalistic economy." I then turn to address specifically a few genre pieces that typify the narratives I heard during my fieldwork, analyzing the ways these stories rhetorically help refigure theories of gender and the nation. Finally, I revisit the literature on transnational sexuality as I position my work within these debates and attempt a reformulation of the relation between gender and transnational travel.

WOMEN TOURISTS AND THEIR HOSTS

Relations between Western women visitors and Gambian men fit into an emerging body of literature on the sexual encounters of "Third World" men and Northern women tourists. Bowman (1989) describes Arab shopkeepers' use of sexual stories as a means of challenging the political and economic discrepancies between their lives as tourist merchants and the privilege and economic power of tourists. The stories are vehicles for expressing what Bowman refers to as a vengeance towards the tourists; the stories are also a means of creating status distinctions between themselves and their fellow merchants as they try to one-up their friends. As Bowman suggests, the currency of the stories is created in the telling of successful seductions; through the telling of sexual conquest of Northern women this becomes a means for redressing power imbalances.

A similar discussion of Northern women and Southern men in an earlier article by Cohen (1971) describes the vulnerabilities of Palestinian men who long for the favors of Israeli women tourists. Their pursuit of these women becomes a means of escaping the conditions of local life. Palestinian men, according to Cohen, construct a "mythology of emigration" that will transport them beyond the strains and moral confines of everyday life. Both of these essays begin the process of specifying local interpretations of travel and lives caught in complex power imbalances between Northern visitors and Southern hosts. Yet much is left to be explored: How is the construction of men's agency, as sexual and national subjects, always refigured in transnational interactions? How does the formation of sexual national Others offer insight for understanding gender in these global exchanges? What is the articulation of the narratives of Southern men with Northern women in complicated interactions?

A set of issues converges in the case of The Gambia. The historical conjunction between the development of tourism in The Gambia and the allegorical thread present in contemporary commentary are intimately intertwined. Former president Jawara joined with international development agencies and set the course for the country's economic future with tourism as the cornerstone of that development. In a vulnerable position to suggest alternatives for economic growth, he hoped that as a nation The Gambia would find its ability to move forward through enticing European visitors. Yet it was precisely this strategy of national enticement that many found distasteful. This would lead, almost thirty years after the end of the British colonial presence, to current efforts to reclaim the nation. According to Jawara's critics, placing the nation in the position of catering to European guests reinscribed The Gambia's peripheral status.

Indeed, from the start, Gambians controlled few of the terms of the tourism business. Furthermore, tourism produced the kind of social relations that lieutenant Jammeh and others consider immoral. As he stated in his press release, echoing the rumblings of leaders in other countries concerned about the presence of sex tourism, "Africans are not sex machines." The "Africans" he refers to are almost certainly not women; it is the objectification of the nation's men, and their reduction to mechanical parts without agency, that brings the lieutenant so close to abjection. Once again, gender becomes the terrain for an imagined rearticulation of "traditional" values. When powerful Northern women are thought to be stalking junior Southern men, a disturbing gender inversion has occurred. Gambian men are feminized. National honor and masculinity are jeopardized.

The historical specificity of this Gambian allegory of national revitalization intersects with specific changes in Europe as well. In the 1970s European and North American women began to discover travel as a form of self-making. The travel industry created a niche for women travelers, as women were promised the freedom and power they could not experience at home. If they could travel, perhaps they might find themselves abroad. Women's travel memoirs became particularly popular and travel advertising increasingly targeted women.[1] Women's magazines featured articles not only about female travel, but about its erotic and romantic possibilities (see, for example, *Marie Claire*, May 1994). The Gambia became one site within the new female travel trajectory for Europeans. Women travelers rushed to see "the Africa" of Jawara's tourism plans. They also found the possibility of more-informal encounters with local men.

Most literature on culture and travel assumes that travel traffic is a disruption of ordinary life. Here, however, I begin with the assumption that global traffic is one aspect of culture making. It offers a way of understanding the spatial intermeshing of relationships. Culture is a dynamic process; there is no "once upon a time" when places were enclosed and bounded systems. Rosaldo's (1989) image of culture as a busy intersection is suggestive of the kinds of overlapping, crosscutting connections and agendas that help frame the discussion found in this paper. The notion of intersection allows an appreciation of the fluidity in which "culture" is formed and the ways a diverse set of discussions—in this instance, conversations that surround global traffic and the configuration of transnational zones of desire—get formed and reformed.

TRAJECTORIES IN FEMINIST THEORY: TRAVEL, STATUS, AND DESIRE

The title of this paper is intended to recall Rubin's now-classic essay "The Traffic in Women" (1976). Rubin refers to an earlier essay in which Emma Goldman expresses concern about white slavery and the trafficking of white women in prostitution. Many feminist theorists have pursued an interest in the traffic in women, but it is Rubin's contribution that is most significant to this essay, for she moves from the existence of transnational sexual procurement to a theory of gender and desire. Rubin takes the concept of traffic in women and *localizes* it to illustrate a crucial point: Where common morality condemns the long-distance circulation of prostitutes as unfortunate for women, Rubin argues instead that objectionable power asymmetries are crucial to every local context—in marriage as well as prostitution.

Rubin's work inspired a generation of feminist scholarship analyzing the gender asymmetries of the local (e.g., Ortner and Whitehead 1981; MacCormack and Strathern 1981). We can now move beyond this work to the wider import of the original meaning of the "traffic in women." The key to this analysis must be simultaneous attention to local contexts of power and meaning and to the translocal interchanges that both reaffirm and challenge locality. In this paper, I argue that this double focus can be achieved by specifying travel trajectories. This specification involves attention to their possibilities as well as their constraints; it highlights how power is shaped in relation to travel. I examine both the institutional and symbolic features of travel. In this we are able to see that the world is always localized at the same time as never closed. Using the specificity of travel agendas we can engage in an analysis of gender and power.

Cultural theorist Wolff (1995) suggests that travel is the key trope of many current theories of culture making. Travel creates cosmopolitan subjects, subjects whose agency takes cultural difference in stride. This is the kind of agency intended to inhabit a culturally diverse world—that is, a world of divergent cultural positions as well as social locations. Cultural and social boundaries—and their crossings—are at the heart of the psychic formation of traveling subjects. These subjects cannot be imagined coming into being in a closed cultural enclave—whether "Europe" or its Other, imagined as parallel universes. Any desires and fantasies that the traveling subject has are fundamentally patterned by social and cultural difference.

As Wolff further argues, traveling is imagined through a gendered history, in which traveling and masculine agency are intertwined. In this formation, cultural stability is the imagined female to the traveling male. And even as this history is twisted and transformed to allow us to imagine women finding themselves through travel, these traveling women, like traveling men, must deal with the gendered history of travel. Wolff does not point out that our imagination of travel assumes the mobility of a European passport. Yet the point is similar. African and European travelers alike must measure their different kinds of mobility against that historical standard. If agency and the ability to be a subject of desire are understood through mobility, then Africans and Europeans and women and men are each shaped within the forms of agency and desire developed in relationship to the kinds of mobility to which they can socially aspire. If desire involves traveling, it is always asymmetrical and social in relation to the social construction of travel.

Rubin's article continues to offer useful clues about how to approach this analysis. In an insightful reading within and across theoretical frameworks, the work of Lévi-Strauss, Engels, and Lacan becomes central to her engagement with two major strands of feminist theory in the 1970s: structural Marxism and psychoanalysis. Lévi-Strauss maintains that the exchange of women is central in the formation of culture. However, where he naturalizes this exchange, Rubin pushes his ideas to show that the exchange of women is at the heart of inequality. Rubin argues that in order to understand male dominance it is necessary to understand the ways women are traded as pawns in sex and marriages.

Drawing on Engels's emphasis on social location, and on Lacan's emphasis on the centrality of a psychoanalytic approach to notions of psychic formation, Rubin's analysis moves in two important directions: first, to show that the inequality involved in the exchange of women is linked to all other kinds of inequality, including class and rank; and second, that this inequality helps to constitute the psyche in relationship to desire, through the asymmetrical creation of men and women in relationship to desire, such that men become the subjects of desire and women the object of men's desire. Thus, in Rubin's formulation, the traffic in women is at the heart of both social inequalities and the bodies and psyches through which we participate in them.

Although she links the social and the psychoanalytical in her analysis, Rubin stands at a bifurcation of positions within feminist theory that persisted into the 1980s. I frame these positions as those in which female agency is defined through status and social location, on the one hand, and through fantasy and desire, on the other. Theorists of these two directions often appear not to communicate with each other. Feminists interested in social location have rarely paid adequate attention to either sexuality or fantasy, while theorists of desire, in their allegiance to psychoanalytic theory, have often had a limited appreciation of social difference beyond gender. I argue here for an analysis of how social categories of locational differences, once taken seriously, are constitutive of a different formulation than one where social categories are just lined up and acknowledged for their existence. In short, how does an appreciation of difference reshape our theoretical insights around social positioning and psychoanalysis?

Each of the trajectories of feminist thought holds useful possibilities for the argument of this paper in understanding Northern women and their Gambian male friends. Rubin's methodological approach is suggestive of how theoretical borders must be traversed. The power relations between Africa and the West can be understood as an eroticized asymmetry and it is necessary that theories of desire take account of the relation between real men and women having relationships and the discourses and institutions that shape attractiveness and availability. Theories of the intersection of race, class, and gender are notably weak in showing how sexuality is constructed and how sexual agency is created. Status is the male feature of desire. Yet theories of desire have tended to ignore the specificites of culture, race, and class in favor of a universalized notion of the subject. In this formulation fantasy is marked primarily through universalized notions of gender. The sexual adventures of Western women in Africa are linked in part with the power asymmetries between Africa and the West as these reformulate male and female in significant distortions of European and American myths.

Efforts at joining psychoanalytic perspectives with materialist theories of identity have, in recent years, revitalized social theory. Two examples are worth noting: McClintock's (1995) study of colonial Africa points to the centrality of the intersection of multiple social categories—race, class, gender, and sexuality—in making colonial culture. Her analysis refuses the privileging of a single category of social location that can be read in any other way than complicated. She proposes the notion of situated psychoanalysis (1995:72), which can address what many perceive as the ahistoricity of psychoanalysis. Mercer (1994) considers the meaning of sexual representation and the fetishization of the black male body in the photographic work of Robert Mapplethorpe. The presence of black men as the object of the gaze revises many of the early theories that naturalized a binary between men as gazers and women as objects of the gaze. Both of these works illustrate the ways in which our early theoretical propositions can now be understood as more than mere parallel categories that can be added in any simple manner. Rather, they shake the fundamental principles embedded in our social theories.

FASHIONING CHARISMATIC STYLE

The development of tourism in The Gambia is intimately linked to the end of a particular form of colonial presence. In the mid-1960s, Scandinavian charter companies began marketing The Gambia as an ideal vacation spot for Europeans during the winter months. Hotels were soon built to accommodate tourists, and by the early 1970s holiday visitors began arriving, particularly during the peak months of December to April (Wagner 1977; Brown 1992). Initially, much of the control of the tourist industry was in the hands of foreign companies. Lacking the resources and the infrastructure to control nationally the industry placed The Gambia in a vulnerable position, and charter tours organized and facilitated by European countries continue to jeopardize Gambian control of much of the financial revenue and employment opportunities. Upper-level management positions are usually reserved for expatriates while Gambians, primarily men, work in restaurants and hotels as service staff, as hotel security guards, and as taxi drivers. Perhaps a more inclusive sector for women is the tourist markets adjacent to villages such as Bakau, where textiles and garden vegetables produced by women's cooperatives are marketed to tourists (Wagner 1982).

Tourism, however, provides a measure of employment in a job market that is otherwise tenuous. Even as the largest employer, the Gambian government cannot support the burden of the population needing jobs. Most people are relegated to the non-self-sustaining agriculture-based economy since few regularized employment opportunities exist. Increasingly, youth migrate to urban areas in search of alternatives to farming. An outgrowth of the service industry is the presence of what Wagner refers to as "professional friends," who move alongside tourism yet outside many of the formal aspects of the system. These "friends" are not paid a wage; their services are multiple and they can be compensated in a number of ways.

Many male youths, generally between the ages of sixteen and twenty-five, are part of a "professional friend" circuit. (The sociological literature also refers to them as "bumpsters" (Brown 1992).) These young men comb the beaches and hang around hotels in search of potential "friends." They are often prohibited from entering hotels. Thus, they stand outside hotel entrances waiting for tourists who, upon exiting, encounter a number of boys and men approaching with such welcoming phrases as "Hello, I want to be your friend; I want to show you around The Gambia. I can make your stay very nice." Relationships formed between tourists and bumpsters can include a number of activities—they act as tour guides to both men and women, as interpreters and negotiators between local people and tourists, as facilitators of sexual liaisons for male travelers who seek female companions, and as escorts for tourist women to the nightlife in The Gambia.

Some bumpsters also seek involvement in romantic affairs with women tourists who potentially have the resources to help them travel. Indeed, with the arrival of each tour group, the scene is scanned for prospective patrons. Two brothers interviewed in one magazine article spoke of surveying the possibilities in a recently arrived group of tourists. With a sense of confidence, they walked up and down the beach and commented on two middle-aged women guests. One said, "She's a new arrival —she's still white—and she's ready for it. . . . She's been here before. I bet she hasn't unpacked yet, she's so eager to be picked up by one of us." The second commented, "She's a first timer, but she's up to it. You can tell by looking at her. I'll know more when I speak to her. You always know if they want sex when you look into their eyes—there's an invitation" (Simon and John, quoted in Aziz 1994:12). From the perspective of these professional friends, all tourist women are potential sexual partners.[2]

Gambian response to bumpster activity is one of ambivalence. Male elders are often urged to enforce sanctions against them and they are disparaged by the state as well as the Ministry of Tourism. In 1989, after increasing reports by tourists of being harassed, bumpsters were targeted and a few were detained for hours by the police. The gendarmes were soon deployed to patrol the beaches. In addition, the ministry of Tourism attempted a registry of guides to make the status of bumpsters official by providing identity badges and uniforms. But bumpsters soon rejected the ministry's efforts. After all, such policies could not accommodate their crafted efforts of individual style and the appeal of both pleasure and danger. The threat bumpsters pose appears formidable to Gambian officials. The 1989 conflict mobilized some of the bumpsters' mothers, who supported their sons' activities by staging a protest at a major hotel.[3] In a recent sweep that was part of one of the governmental cleanup campaigns, prostitutes and cannabis smokers—men with long dreadlocks—were targeted and their heads were shaved (Reuters, August 16, 1994). These men became a visible sign of what was partially responsible for the crisis in the national consciousness.[4]

Bumpster men are symbols in another sense as well. The Gambian men I knew were not bumpsters; however, they identified deeply with the dilemmas of bumpsters. Like bumpsters, they saw available forms of employment as unstable and inadequate. They hoped for a lucky break, usually imagined as a tie with a foreign acquaintance that would make it possible for them to either gather some capital or, better yet, leave the country for employment in the North. They told stories of possible romances or marriages with Northern women as a way to make a new life. And at the same time they also laughed and scoffed at Northern women, whom they considered dissolute and morally decadent. The stories of these men—not bumpsters themselves but those who shared the bumpster dilemmas—are the subject of my analysis.

The men themselves pointed me toward the national significance of their stories. One friend joked about the long line of Gambians that formed early in the morning outside the American embassy as people hoped for the miraculous charisma to convince embassy officials to offer them a trip to the United States. Romantic hope in The Gambia, he argued, was caught up in leaving—or forming ties with powerful foreigners.

CROSSING CONVERSATIONS OF DESIRING SUBJECTS

The inclusion of stories as a critical point of negotiation between the social science "fact" and an allegorical rendering of "the real" owes a great deal to the work of Tsing (1993), whose use of stories effectively illustrates the importance of cross talk and overlapping agendas in the ways social worlds are constructed by those we interview, as well as by the anthropologists themselves. Within the space of structural figurings, Tsing urges us to appreciate the ways subjects actively contest, talk back, refigure, or just comment on the social worlds they inhabit. In the following sections I present four stories, each representative of a genre of which I heard different versions a number of times. I recount them here in parable form to protect the identity of my informants. More important than details of identity is how the narratives become allegories that express much larger concerns than the dilemmas confronting individuals. As I mentioned previously, there are deep distinctions between the stories Gambian men told me about men and those told about women. The storytellers recount men's travels as stories of masculine agency and national dilemmas. Men's liaisons were presented as entrepreneurial strategies and career moves, with contradictory aspects and feminizing qualities. (This feminization is created in the unequal relations between the North and South.) Despite nationalist claims, like those of Lieutenant Jammeh, that men should not be a part of these encounters, young men were pulled into this activity. In contrast, the stories of women travelers were commonly relayed by Gambian men and women as if the women were moral transgressors. The stories emphasized the inappropriateness of female travelers and the problem of their lack of containability, understood simply as promiscuity.

Significantly, these stories crosscut or reinterpret stories that Northern women travelers tell of the search for self-fulfillment, knowledge, and power. They are parables, then, of a persistent misunderstanding with consequences for scholarship as well as all forms of knowledge and discovery. The tourist gaze becomes the medium for creating contradictory stories of national agency. For men, the crucial skill is the ability to fashion oneself as the bearer of natural charisma.

Intimate stories of the adventures of women travelers to The Gambia were somewhat more difficult for me to come by than those of Gambian men. My research required close work with Gambian men, which was disturbed by my occasional attempt to interview tourist women. Indeed, it became essential to my research rapport to separate myself from tourist women. And yet I too, as an anthropologist traveling without the guardianship of a male protector, was implicated in many of the same ways as other women travelers. One particularly useful source in constructing the story of women as travelers presented itself in an article in *Marie Claire* (May 1994), a monthly women's magazine marketed as being about "real fashions, real stories, real women." The article, "Seeking Sex in The Gambia," offers possibilities for understanding these transnational connections from the point of view of women travelers. The "reportage," as *Marie Claire* calls it, fits into a genre of popular-magazine storytelling much like that of *Cosmopolitan* and other women's magazines sold at supermarket checkout lines, where the agency of women is supported and encouraged through a certain bravery, badness, and more-blatant eroticism than what is allowed in "conventional" ideals of femininity.

The women tourists interviewed in *Marie Claire* appear as allegorical figures of female travel, nomadic subjects who challenge the confining boundaries of marriage and home. The article is surrounded by a number of photos of European women informants and their Gambian friends. The women speak frankly about their sexual desires. The quotation that opened this essay is that of Mary, a fifty-eight-year-old art dealer who travels to The Gambia twice a year in search of Gambian men. Initially traveling with her husband, Mary and her spouse once accepted an offer to be escorted by a young Gambian man. After her husband grew tired of sightseeing, Mary desired to travel with their guide on her own:

> Towards the end of our holiday my husband just wanted to lie on the beach, so I went out with Mace on my own. He offered to take me to less touristy beaches and I agreed. Once we were alone it all happened quickly, on the beach, under the palm trees. Afterwards I was shocked but I wanted more.

> My husband lost interest in sex a long time ago, and after my encounter
> with Mace I realized how much I missed it and how important it was to me.
> (Aziz 1994:12)

Initially, Mary was reluctant to tell friends about her adventures, but once she confided in a few friends, they cheered her on. One of her friends expressed a desire to join her on a future trip to The Gambia. She too found the prospect of having a Gambian friend inviting, for her husband too had long since tired of sex. Mary insists that she is committed to her marriage and in fact her travels to The Gambia strengthen their marriage (Mary, quoted in *Marie Claire* 1994: 12).

However, other stories suggest that there is more to women's travel than new sexual encounters. "I didn't come with the intention of picking up someone," one woman tries to explain (Aziz 1994:16), but the reporter is mainly interested in their sexual bravery. Their vulnerabilities and dreams of romance and self-fulfillment must slip through the lines of the "reportage." Women speak, for example, of being left by husbands, after several years of marriage, for younger women. The Gambian men, at least initially, seemed devoted to them. So captivated by the attention are they that some of the women go to great lengths to keep their connections alive. They speak of working three jobs—even five—in order to bring their Gambian friends to Europe. They mention public disapproval, the rejection of their families, and their hopes for an alternative to the loneliness of their ordinary lives. Unlike male sex tourists, at least in stereotype, many are hoping that their Gambian lovers will really turn out to be the loves of their lives. They are willing to work hard to fulfill their boyfriends' desires to return with them to Europe—even though they know the men might leave them for someone younger and more desirable once there.

STRATEGIES OF ENTREPRENEURIAL ROMANCE

Let me return to Gambian men's stories. One of the narratives I heard during my fieldwork was of a man I will refer to as Lamin Sane,[5] who was eager to go to Sweden to find a wife, that is, a patron. Unlike many men of his age, he could afford the trip with his own financial resources because he had recently inherited control of the family assets. As with an investment, he tried to increase his possibilities through finding a wealthy donor. This story was whispered about since, in order for Lamin Sane to pursue his marriage dreams and schemes in Sweden, he had to divorce his Gambian wife. He did divorce and every account suggested that his wife was unaware of his action. (Yet one wonders how much a story can circulate before it comes back to haunt. I had heard the story a number of times, from more than a few people.) Should he need to present divorce papers to prove he was able to marry while in Sweden, he could do so. His wife, thinking this was a business trip—and perhaps in a way it was—went to the airport with all of his well-wishers. Like those who went by invitation to Europe, Lamin Sane had the same dreams of catching a woman and marrying. He was at a disadvantage, however, because he did not come with the necessary contacts to provide him with an entree into the society. An important facilitator of many of the travelers is a host, and without this Lamin Sane's journey was made more difficult. He traveled on a three-month tourist visa to Sweden, where he stayed with friends and distant relatives. But he was unsuccessful in his marriage attempts, and at the end of the three months he returned to The Gambia to resume his regular routine—and his marriage.

In stories such as this one, men are smart enough to outmaneuver Gambian wives but not always successful in netting Swedish patrons. Stories of men and their dreams of travel and attachment tell us about the ways men are vulnerable as well as tricky in these encounters. Subordination is created in part through the marginal and dependent status of the Gambian economy. The Gambia remains a neocolonial outpost with no industry and no sustaining means of support other than a personalistic economy. Catching women is one option within a niche of desperate strategies to make ends meet. Yet I would caution one not to reduce these relationships to mere utility. Worth considering is the integral part a fashioned identity plays; men imaginatively create themselves as cultural ambassadors crafting Africa as well as their own Africanness. Complicated constructions of masculinity are operating, as a global masculine identity is often constituted through travel. Again, however, we are reminded of the difference between these travelers and the relative ease we have come to associate with European men's ability to travel.

DILEMMAS OF A KEPT MAN

"It is really tragic," Malimin Keita, one of my associates, said to me one day as he told me of a friend who had traveled to Denmark to be with a woman he had met while she was vacationing in The Gambia. "He has to stay at home all day while his wife goes out to work. And she expects him to sweep the floors and do the housework and watch television all day. And when the lady comes home, he says, all she wants to do is have sex. She won't stop even if he tells her he is tired. The only time he is let out of the house is to go to language class twice a week."

I tried to express my sympathy for Malimin's friend's predicament as a "kept man," while at the same time I kept probing further the meaning of this gender-inverted image of domestic constraint. Over the next few months, I heard this story frequently. Curious, I asked about the experiences of others and how such encounters were made. Malimin explained, "Often white ladies come on holiday and meet up with men here. While a lady is in The Gambia, before she leaves for home, the man will try to get her address and he will write to her. He may write many letters and they will correspond for a time and then hopefully he will be invited to come to where she is. Then if he is really lucky he can stay long enough to get a residence permit and then he can stay. Sometimes people get married."

Other accounts of Gambian men traveling to Europe and the difficult life they lead there are offered by Wagner and Yamba (1986). They confirm the vulnerability of Gambian emigrants, who often lack access to social services, suffer from discrimination, and have few legal rights and recourses. Men often express a sense of loneliness and isolation, as many of their women hosts work much of the time. Often arriving without appropriate language skills, they find that life is difficult. One woman, aged fifty-six, regularly sent her twenty-five-year-old Gambian partner out on Sunday afternoons when her adult sons came to visit. Thus, her circles of friends and family members were not a source for integrating her Gambian partner.

The clubs frequented by Africans provide a way for Gambians to meet fellow countrymen. Wagner and Yamba explain this as one option to isolation. While this may appear to be the solution to the sense of isolation many men experience, these clubs can also become threatening to one's ability to stay in Europe. As one meets other Gambians, often in the same vulnerable position of seeking a residence permit, one is also meeting men who might compete and vie for the same position with a woman. For example, while one man was at work, someone called his partner to say he had been seen with another woman. This led to his being kicked out by his partner and eventually being deported (Wagner and Yamba 1986: 213). Other men find the company of younger women in the clubs appealing and seek the friendship of these women over that of their older companions. This, too, jeopardizes the relationship and the critical probationary period before a man receives a residence permit.

The story of Malimin's friend suggests a reversal of sorts: His friend was relegated to doing housework. Malimin commented, "Can you imagine, he's treated like a woman. He was locked in all day with nothing to do but watch television, and upon her return all she wants is sex." Read as an allegory of power and difference and not simply as an account of fact, the powerlessness of the Gambian émigré is expressed in what are familiar categories generally associated with women in both The Gambia and the West. Indeed, while travel affords men agency, as the story is told, this mobility also places them in the position of women.

In considering the allegorical nature of such tales, it is useful to remember that the European women may have other stories to tell. A tour organizer quoted in the *Marie Claire* article reports, "The British embassy here has loads of letters from women in the UK complaining that the boys have stayed in bed all the time, or disappeared—mostly with someone younger" (Aziz 1994:16). Domestic imprisonment from the perspective of the men may look like laziness to the women. But these differences are even clearer in relation to the stories Gambian men tell about women.

"TRUE-LIFE ADVENTURES" OF LOVELY LAURA

As women seek to pursue their goal of self-fulfillment through travel, they are often drawn into stories that are not always of their own choosing. I heard a number of stories that spoke past each other on the subject of *toubobs*. One example of cross talk in these narratives is the story of a woman commonly referred to as Lovely Laura. Her name used in conversation suggested that she was not considered very lovely. Indeed, she became an exemplar of all of the aspects associated with Western women. New installments were regularly added to the "Lovely Laura stories" but the most consistent set of "facts" suggested that she was a comparatively well-off Englishwoman who had been married and divorced. In the settlement her husband had given her enough money to travel. My friends said, with dripping sarcasm, that Lovely Laura came to The Gambia every three months or so to find a new boyfriend. Each time she came she would invite them to visit her in England. "When she tires of them she throws them out and then soon returns to The Gambia to find another friend."

One person telling this story, a man just turning twenty, projected many of his fears onto this symbol of Northern promiscuity. He spoke of his own hesitation in entertaining a Laura fantasy. In his words, "Any woman who has slept with that many men could be passing on disease." With repugnance, he said, "I wouldn't have anything to do with her." Still, while the gossips talked and people found her behavior distasteful, while in her presence they all treated Lovely Laura like a queen. As soon as she left, mouths flew fast about her latest conquest. In this narrative she represents the double edge of power and danger.

Lovely Laura raised a number of questions about what it means for women to travel, particularly alone. Both as a woman of means and a decidedly unruly woman—that is, one whose movements are not confined by the sanction of marriage—she was a woman out of place, though she could play at the margins unavailable to most local women and still, at least to her face, be treated as a respectable woman, —her national status offering a momentary reprieve. Yet by local standards, any woman unattached to a man was suspect; for respectable local women, having multiple male partners was out of the question. Fortunately for Lovely Laura's schemes, however, there was never a lack of male companionship, and her money continued to allow her to appear to rise above the stories.

These stories, however, also spoke of the disdain toward her among the elders and women without the same privilege and of "the rudeness of foreign women who flaunt their naked bodies and love affairs in the face of the people." Though her journey was always described in sexual terms, she, like many women, did not see her travels as simply sexual. Sex was only one part of a larger project of self-discovery in Africa.[6] Women like Lovely Laura are drawn to Africa in part because of their desire to learn about the "real Africa." Thus, Lovely Laura was not easy to classify as "culturally insensitive." She occupied the more contradictory position of a "woman out of place."

White women traveling in Africa feel empowered in searching for male lovers because they can expect these men to accompany them on their own terms. These women do not have to feel constrained in the ways they might at home. Similarly, Gambian men find their agency from accessing their situation as dependent entrepreneurs. As allegorical figures, unruly Western women and African trickster men come together to negotiate their attraction. Although these singular constructions of men as tricksters and unruly women are somewhat reductive, they do challenge the common presumption that power structures allow us to easily separate oppressor and oppressed. Scholars and activists are often better at pointing to victims than at seeing complex negotiations. This is true of both the feminist literature and the growing body of literature focused on non-Western men and Western women.

Yet, in these transnational relationships Gambian men and Western women each have a different notion of what is going on. Each imagines him or herself evading or escaping the worst aspects of domination. It is in the misunderstandings and overlaps between these two forms of agency that both the pleasure and the danger of the relationship develop. Women believe they are escaping the patriarchy of their homeland as men believe they are escaping national inequality. While Northern women describe themselves as strong in their beliefs and determination, African men speak of these women as a means to a national, entrepreneurial end.

HOPES, DREAMS, AND ASPIRATIONS

The situation becomes even more complicated once we take into account the fact that not all women from the North in The Gambia are white. One significant group of women travelers in The Gambia are African Americans. Since the publication of *Roots* (Haley 1976) and the airing of its television version, African Americans have visited The Gambia as a site in which to envision an African home. In many cases African American women travel without male escorts; indeed, many hope that this site of "home" will also be a site for kinds of female empowerment not always available in their other, more mundane, home across the Atlantic. Yet the travels of these African American women are subject to the same reinterpretations as are those of white women, in the stories of Gambian men. To many Gambians, African American women are just another kind of promiscuous *toubob*, for the mark of difference is wealth and mobility.

Furaha Salim traveled as an assistant to a Gambian artist-entrepreneur on one of his brief trips home to The Gambia. Like many African Americans who visit Africa in search of an ancestral home and a sense of connection, she too thought this would be an opportunity to reconnect with Africa. Even her Africanized name suggested her efforts to redraw family ties with Africa and pan-Africanist dreams. Yet her dreams were not those of her hosts.

I first met Furaha Salim during a debate she was having with an older, distinguished Gambian man while she was trying to convince him of her thoughts on women's agency. She thought that it was unfair that women could not have as many husbands as men could have wives. Unlike European missionaries, she was uninterested in forcing African men into monogamy. Instead, she endorsed what she thought of as an egalitarian but "African" alternative: multiple spouses all around. She pressed her point that every woman has the right to her own "hopes, dreams, and aspirations." Meanwhile, I sat uncomfortably, caught between her opinion—a version of a womanist perspective—and the Mandinka views with which I had become familiar. Familiar as I was with her position and the intervention she was trying to make, I also sensed that she was quickly beginning to represent what some Gambians perceive as the arrogance of feminist Northern women. Though the older man remained polite, it was obvious that he was not at ease with the conversation.

Furaha Salim was intent on exploring Africa and her own "hopes, dreams, and aspirations" during her brief stay in The Gambia. She had decided to accompany the Gambian artist after meeting him in the United States earlier in the year. Their friendship, at least in her understanding, was platonic. For her this was a trip home with a distant relative, so to speak. The gap in understanding became clear, however, as I heard of what was seen as her unruly behavior from Boubacar, the artist-entrepreneur. He approached me about the problem of her staying out all night, "sleeping with any man she could find." These were not important men, he suggested, but bus drivers and the like. He asked if I couldn't speak to her and tell her to stop. "She is a mother with a husband at home; her husband entrusted her care to me." It was not clear to me that she was the loose woman that he indicated, and when she told me her version I learned, as I had suspected, that she had not been running about, dating man after man, as had been repeatedly suggested. Rather she said she had been "talking" to a man from a different ethnic group—which infuriated her host. Furaha was aware of the tension this caused both for her host and for his family. She insisted, however, that Boubacar was not going to control her. "Every woman," she said, "has a right to her own hopes, dreams, and aspirations."

Boubacar was humiliated by a woman he obviously could not control. The public display of her independence, even more than her actual behavior, threatened his stature as the head of a house. As he told his friend of her offensive behavior, thinking that I did not understand, he again repeated that she was nothing but a whore, the mother of children with a husband at home, someone who was acting like a prostitute. His speech helped me to understand some of the contradictions of the situation. On the one hand, he had used the lure of family and home to get her to come to Africa and had assumed that she understood what her obligations and his expectations were. Her behavior, however, soon came to resemble *toubob* behavior—just another sign of the West. For him, she showed that sense of European privilege that appears to put individual desire over obligations to the collectivity and assumes mobility when others are bound by many constraints.

Lovely Laura and Furaha Salim, as women travelers, carried parallel imaginings of Africa—an imagined Africa as a place of free expression and sensuality. Africa is that primordial place where one can transcend the confines of a constricted life in the North. Though they came with different agendas, they were quickly joined in a set of tales that spoke of their blatant disregard of appropriate feminine behavior. Although aware of the constraints placed on local women, they saw themselves as liberated and even as opening up possibilities for other women through their behavior. Yet, neither woman could become the friend of other women, for their presence and actions made even more apparent the restrictions on many Gambian women's lives.

Anthropologist Tsing asks a series of questions that illustrates some of the overlapping and contradictory aspects of women travelers and women anthropologists. Where does the woman anthropologist stand in this story as she listens to the construction of Western women since she herself is "out-of-place"? Lovely Laura was more than a passing visitor; she returned many times and tried to incorporate herself—at considerable expense—into the same compound. She, not unlike myself, was trying to develop an understanding of Africa through processes familiar to anthropologists—through social immersion. While I listened to the stories of her transgressive behavior there was no way I could stand outside of this commentary about North-South relations; rather I was deeply implicated as well. While a man's status and reputation could be made through travel and adventure, and to a certain extent through heroic tales of conquest, a woman's reputation would be drawn through a series of derogatory characterizations and exaggerated tales of bad behavior. Lovely Laura served as a reminder of what happens to the reputation of unruly women. Again, the gendered power dynamics, once shifted, do not simply reverse the effects of the story.

The dilemmas here for the woman anthropologist—and particularly an African American woman anthropologist—appear even more stark. African American women tourists in The Gambia are engaged in a search for African culture, a culture that will help them alter their own U.S. predicament. How different is the task of anthropology, the discipline that inevitably describes cultures by illuminating their differences against a European standard? And what of the African American feminist anthropologist who intervenes in the discipline to show the power and plurality of transnational spaces? These are questions that cannot be avoided as I describe the way African American women's attempts to reach out to build a bridge of cultural knowledge in The Gambia are insistently and repetitively reinterpreted as promiscuity. These reinterpretations are ones I too must negotiate.

RETHINKING TRANSNATIONAL SEX AND DESIRE

Transnational sexual encounters have been considered more frequently in the context of Northern male travelers and Southeast Asian women than in the context of Africa, and this Southeast Asian discussion serves as the basis for much of the literature on international sexual relations. The images of Southeast Asian women traded and claimed by Western as well as Japanese men have become almost cliché: sex tourism, prostitution, and mail-order brides dominate the global representation of international sexual liaisons. In this global imaginary, Asian women become objects of the Western male gaze; they are fashioned as sexual commodities for "white" male desires (Lee 1991; Enloe 1990; Hall 1994; Odzer 1995). In many instances, attention to women as sexual objects in the global economy remind us of the intertwined relationship between travel, national development schemes, and the sexual services of "local" women in easing national debt.

Yet in most of the studies of the international sex industry, many of the authors take as a starting point the parallelism of power differences between men and women, on the one hand, and the West and Asia, on the other; Asian women are vulnerable in the same ways as Western women but even more so. The politics of representation is key, as women are seen as desirable especially *because* they are imagined as docile and obedient as a result of their Asianness. In this imagined geography, men are imagined as active agents and women as passive victims.

Theories of international sexuality and national and class differences have tended to assume that internationalization brings an increasing homogenization of the sexual (Barry 1984). This assumption parallels in many ways how many have come to think about the penetration of the market in relationship to capitalism; the market is a homogenizing force, creating a singular global culture (Jameson 1991). Indeed, the market and sexuality come together in the discussion of international sexuality because most discussions focus on the tourist industry and prostitution, that is, on commercialized sexualities. The international prostitute appears as the sign of a global circulation of sexuality in which local cultural markers seem increasingly archaic. Just as scholars have tended not to look at the localization of capitalism but instead assumed the unified nature of capitalism as a homogeneous cultural and political economy (Gibson-Graham 1996), discussions of the international commodification of sexuality also assume a homogeneous logic. This assumption, however, creates a single and monolithic standard of the sexual. Sexual meanings, forms, and identities are assumed to be constructed through an imagined single logic. My argument, in contrast, calls attention to the specificity of sexualities across national boundaries. Rather than thinking of a homogeneous global sphere of circulation, it is critical to attend to the localizing processes in which particular male and female sexualities are discursively and institutionally created. In The Gambia, international sexualities are not merely commodified reinforcements of Western contrasts between male sexual subjectivity and female sexual objectification.

As Southeast Asian prostitutes and mail-order brides begin to organize, they insist on their own agency. As long as they are considered victims, they can only bemoan their situations, not improve them. Yet despite the attempts of feminist scholars to participate in this rethinking, our scholarly tools have not been very helpful. We can think only of "agency" as erasing "oppression"; where there is a clear power imbalance, we reasonably want to show cohesion and vulnerability, not self-fashioning. The Gambian "traffic" I describe is perhaps different enough to be illuminating. It is difficult to imagine any of the participants as victims, for none will let themselves be described that way. Power differences, instead, are inscribed in different configurations of mobility. And agency involves the storytelling events in which all participants negotiate contact despite differences in power and perspective.

Rather than beginning with "women" and "men" as universal categories, I have argued that we need to think through different kinds of travel and their possibilities and limitations. Travel trajectories are trajectories of desire in transnational space, yet they are not constituted homogeneously. The narratives people tell of their own and others' travels are key to our understandings of these trajectories—because narratives help us see the flow of hope, dreams, and aspirations that can make power asymmetries both livable and intolerable—reminding us of both our constraints and our chances for freedom. The contradictory and unequal narratives I have described here chart out the space worth fighting over—in coups, love affairs, and, indeed, cultural analysis.

NOTES

Earlier versions of this paper were presented at the Stanford Feminist Faculty Seminar, spring 1994, and the Five College Women's Research Seminar, autumn 1994. This paper has benefited from a number of additional conversations. In particular I thank Diane Bell, Brenda Bright, Kathryn Chetkovich, Karen Gaul, Frank Holmquist, Mary Hoyer, Saba Mahmood, Rachel Roth, Mitziko Sawada, Anna Tsing, and E. Frances White. I am also grateful to the editors of this volume, Maria Grosz-Ngaté and Omari Kokole. And to Purnima Mankekar, a special thanks for kindly introducing me to the article in *Marie Claire*.

1. Marilyn Ivy (1995) analyzes a parallel development in Japanese travel advertising, as women became the model travelers of the industry; her insights are also relevant to changes in North American and European images and ideals of travel.

2. On the surface, bumpsters fashion themselves after Rastafarians, adopting a cosmopolitan style of dreadlocks and urban sophistication. The international image of Rastas as oppositional men thus becomes a model of masculinity in transnational configurations of race and desire. Yet scholarly models have ignored the importance of emergent local versions of this transnational masculinity.

3. The demonstration of the mothers and not fathers, in contrast with the lobbying of state officials by male elders, who urged the officials to control their sons, suggests that male elders are more likely to feel threatened and displaced by the young male independence that comes with bumpster activities. Male elders are less involved in the family strategies of which bumpster activity plays a part.

4.   Worth noting here is the overlap with other transnational sex literatures. Analogous to what many have suggested about female prostitution in Southeast Asia, bumpsters' behavior can be seen as part of a family strategy for gathering resources. As bumpster "John" recounts his initial involvement in bumpsterlike activity, he reports that he and his brother started going to the beach in search of tourists when his mother could not provide for all of her children. Their father was too old to provide adequate support to the family through farming. John and his brother Simon began neglecting   school to follow tourists. This became one way to funnel back money and resources to the family (Aziz 1994:12).

5.   The names used here are pseudonyms to protect the identities of the tellers.

6.   *Polite Society* (Summer 1995) is one fictional white woman's account of a voyage of self-discovery in Africa, which includes sex with local men. The novel shows some of the elements most central to the allegorical white female journey, the inability to feel self-respect, beauty, or power at home, and its frustrating search elsewhere amongst what seems to white people as native anarchy.

BIBLIOGRAPHY

Aziz, Christine. 1994. "Seeking Sex in The Gambia." *Marie Claire*, May: 12–18.

Barry, Kathleen. 1984 [1979]. *Female Sexual Slavery*. New York: New York University Press.

Bowman, Glenn. 1989. "Fucking Tourists: Sexual Relations and Tourism in Jerusalem's Old City." *Critique of Anthropology* 9(2):77–93.

Brown, Naomi. 1992. "Beach Boys as Cultural Brokers in Bakau Town, The Gambia." *Community Development Journal* 27(4):361–370.

Cohen, Erik. 1971. "Arab Boys and Tourist Girls in a Mixed Jewish-Arab Community." *International Journal of Comparative Sociology* XII(4):217–233.

Enloe, Cynthia. 1990. *Bananas, Beaches and Bases: Making Feminist Sense of International Politics*. Berkeley: University of California Press.

Graham, Julie. 1996. "Economic Difference and the problem of Capitalist Representation." In *The End of Capitalism*. J. K. Gibson-Graham, ed. Oxford: Basil Blackwell.

Haley, Alex. 1976. *Roots* . Garden City, NY: Doubleday.

Hall, C. Michael. 1994. "Gender and Economic Interests in Tourism Prostitution: The Nature, Development and Implications of Sex Tourism in South-east Asia." In *Tourism: A Gender Analysis*, pp. 142–163, Vivian Kinnaird and Derek Hall, eds. New York: John Wiley.

Ivy, Marilyn. 1995. *Discourses of the Vanishing*. Princeton, NJ: Princeton University Press.

Jameson, Fredric. 1991. *Postmodernism, or the Cultural Logic of Late Capitalism*. Durham: Duke University Press.

Kinnaird, Vivian and Derek Hall. 1994. "Introduction." In *Tourism: A Gender Analysis*, pp. 1–33, Vivian Kinnaird and Derek Hall, eds. New York: John Wiley.

Lee, Wendy. 1991. "Prostitution and Tourism in South-east Asia." In *Working Women: International Perspectives on Labor and Gender Ideology*, pp. 79–103, Nanneke Redclift and M. Thea Sinclaire, eds. New York: Routledge.

MacCormack, Carol and Marilyn Strathern. 1980. *Nature, Culture, and Gender*. Cambridge: Cambridge University Press.

Mansson, Sven-Axel. 1993. *Cultural Conflict and the Swedish Sexual Myth: The Male Immigrant's Encounter with Swedish Sexual and Cohabitation Culture*. New York: Hanover House.

McClintock, Anne. 1995. *Imperial Leather*. New York: Routledge.

Mercer, Kobena. 1994. *Welcome to the Jungle*. New York: Routledge.

Odzer, Cleo. 1994. *Patpong Sisters: An American Woman's View of the Bangkok Sex World*. New York: Blue Moon Books.

Ortner, Sherry and Harriet Whitehead, eds. 1981. *Sexual Meanings: The Cultural Construction of Gender and Sexuality*. Cambridge: Cambridge University Press.

Pickering, H. J., D. Todd, J. Dunn, J. Pepin, and A. Wilkins. 1992. "Prostitutes and Their Clients: A Gambian Survey." *Social Science and Medicine* 34(1):75–88.

Reuters News Service: August 16, 1994; August 20, 1994.

Rosaldo, Renato. 1989. *Culture and Truth*. Boston: Beacon.

Rubin, Gayle. 1975. "Traffic in Women: Notes on the Political Economy of Sex." In *Toward an Anthropology of Women*, Rayna Reiter, ed. New York: Monthly Review Press.

Sumner, Melanie. 1995. *Polite Society*. Boston: Houghton Mifflin.

Tsing, Anna Lowenhaupt. 1993. *In the Realm of the Diamond Queen*. Princeton, NJ: Princeton University Press.

Wagner, Ulla. 1982. *Catching the Tourists: Woman Handicraft Traders in the Gambia*. Stockholm, University of Stockholm.

———. 1987. "Out of Time and Space: Mass Tourism and Charter Trips." *Ethnos* 42(1–2):38–52.

———. 1981. "Tourism and the Gambia: Dependency." *Ethnos* 46(3–4):190–206.

Wagner and Bawa Yamba. 1986. "Going North and Getting Attached: The Case of the Gambia." *Ethnos* 51(III–IV):199–222.

Wolff, Janet. 1995. "On the Road Again: Metaphors of Travel in Cultural Criticism." In *Resident Alien: Feminist Cultural Criticism*, pp. 115–134, Janet Wolff, ed. New Haven, CT: Yale University Press.

POSTLUDE

Omari H. Kokole

Ten women (including the main editor, Maria Grosz-Ngaté) and two men (Ch. Didier Gondola and myself) comprise the contributors to this volume, entitled *Gendered Encounters: Challenging Cultural Boundaries and Social Hierarchies in Africa*. All twelve writers have been students of Africana and gender studies for many years. They bring stimulating and extremely challenging interpretations and insights into complex, changing gender relations in Global Africa from precolonial times, through the colonial interlude, right up to the postcolonial period. The three temporal categories—precolonial, colonial, and postcolonial—remain fundamental and most useful in analyses of things African. This anthology traverses all three, and to good effect.

The writers have touched on virtually all the major parts of the continent: West Africa (both Greene and Lake on Ghana, Rosenthal on Togo, and Ebron on the Gambia); East Africa (Hodgson on Tanzania, Mugambi on Uganda, and Feeley-Harnik on Madagascar); Arab Africa (Bernal on Arab-ruled Sudan); Central Africa (Gondola on Zaire), and southern Africa (Moss on Zimbabwe). Clearly, then, this volume has been geographically representative of the continent that is its focus—Africa—almost in the same manner in which it is temporally wide-ranging, as already indicated.

In a sense it is fitting that ten of the twelve writers involved in this volume are women. This is partly because in utterly false, albeit equally insulting terms to both Africa and women, this oldest of all continents has for long been perceived and portrayed as the "female continent" *par excellence*. As such, it has been deemed eligible for "penetration," "domination," even "conquest" (if not worse) by others.

The essays assembled in this collection go to substantial lengths to expose and debunk these myths and stereotypes about women, and about Africa. Needless to say, Africa, like any other part of the world, is not an island unto itself. But it would be erroneous to conclude that for all its powerlessness and underdevelopment the continent has invariably been a passive recipient of alien influences, or for that matter a mere pawn in global change and seldom a transmitter of influences or a player in its own right. The truth is more complex and more multidirectional than widely assumed. Sandra Greene's contribution, for example, demonstrates that even female slaves in precolonial Ghana helped to determine collective thought and behavior. These women slaves also participated in the trans-Atlantic slave trade—an event of monumental historical significance which, *inter alia*, helped to broaden the international horizons of all involved in it and much more.

The trans-Atlantic slave trade helped to create Africa's oldest and largest diaspora—namely, Africa's diaspora of slavery. As a result, today millions of Africa's descendants are domiciled in the so-called New World. Africa's second diaspora is of course its diaspora of colonialism. Both diasporas feature in this collection in the explorations undertaken by Obiagele Lake and Victoria Bernal.

Lake investigated how female diaspora Africans relocated and resettled in postcolonial Ghana. This experience is reminiscent of the precedent set by leading diaspora figures like Dr. W.E.B. Du Bois, the towering African American intellectual of the late nineteenth and early twentieth centuries, and his fellow pan-Africanist, Trinidadian George Padmore, among others. Both Du Bois and Padmore became citizens of independent Ghana upon the liberation of the former Gold Coast from British imperial rule in 1957. Both died Ghanaians—Padmore in 1959, and Du Bois in 1963. Both were buried in Ghana's capital city, Accra.

If Du Bois preceded his African American sisters in relocating to independent Ghana, Padmore led the way for his Caribbean compatriots. Neither man lived long enough in Ghana to share with us his experiences as citizen of a newly independent African country. But in this volume, Lake helps to fill in the void by telling us about the increasing liberation, the centering, and to some extent the empowering of the diaspora women who have "returned" to Ghana since the early 1960s. Future analysts may want to explore the intergenerational and gender ramifications of all this for Global Africa as well as for the descendants of these "returnees" in particular. These women have helped to interpret Africa to their relations in the diaspora of slavery just as they must be interpreting the Western world to their newly found Ghanaian compatriots. At the same time these diasporic women's own understanding of Africa has been deepened by living there and by sharing their lives with the native Africans on the continent itself.

The diaspora of colonialism investigated in this volume is precisely that which Victoria Bernal examined in her piece, entitled "Islam, Transnational Culture, and Modernity in Rural Sudan." Focusing on the rural northern Sudanese village of Wad al Abbas, Bernal demonstrated how indigenous Africa, Islam, and the West have been meeting and interacting in contemporary Africa.

Like all contemporary African nation-states, the Sudan is indeed a recent and artificial political community that resulted from the colonial intrusion upon Africa (mainly in the nineteenth century). One of the significant consequences of the colonial partitioning of Africa has been the emigration of hundreds of thousands of Africans fleeing from the political, economic, and ecological ravages and difficulties that have ensued from colonial rule.

As Bernal demonstrated, not all African emigrés end up in the industrial and affluent North. In other words, the direction of Africa's exilic traffic has not been unidirectional from the South to the North. Sometimes Africans have moved to other Southern countries, in this case an oil-rich country, the kingdom of Saudi Arabia.

Islam must be counted as one of the global forces that have helped to broaden the horizons of many Africans, even as it continues to inform and color their gender relations. It is convincingly demonstrated here that the Sudanese men who seek employment opportunities in Saudi Arabia return home with not just Western goods and gadgets purchased in the Arabian peninsula, but also with a more learned understanding of Islam, if not necessarily with greater piety. And how have gender relations been affected? The traveled men of Wad al Abbas have become *de facto* accomplices in the growing liberation, centering, and even creeping empowerment of their women folk even as their wider society is increasingly absorbed into a global community, described by an eminent Palestinian scholar as one "which has shrunk so small and has become so impressively interconnected" (Said 1994:300).

It would be unnecessarily repetitive to summarize and reiterate here the major points individually made by all our contributors. Suffice it to note that the volume deals with what some have called "Global Africa"—that is, the African continent and its two diasporas (diasporas of slavery and of colonialism).

It is abundantly evident from these multiple analyses that Global Africa is dynamic, complex, and everchanging. To some extent, and at least toward the conclusion of this second millenium, Global Africa impressively vindicates and even transcends the following observations made by the first president of independent Ghana, the late Osagyefo Kwame Nkrumah (1964:78): "Our society [i.e., Africa] is not the old society, but a new society enlarged by Islamic and Euro-Christian influences."

To be sure, Global Africa has been inextricably and irreversibly incorporated into a wider global international society which continues to impact on it even as Global Africa itself also helps to shape and determine the wider world. These multifaceted and reciprocal relations are likely to continue into the next millenium. If many Africans have increasingly thought globally but acted mainly locally, it is equally true that the global community has been relentlessly intruding upon the local. In this incessant flux nothing is fixed or permanent, nor purely indigenous or purely exogenous, nothing simply local or totally alien.

The essays in this anthology have focused on gender, especially changing gender relations across Global Africa. These relations are determined by a vast and wide-ranging array of social forces that have varied across both geography as well as history. A rather full future research agenda exists and cries out for further work in this field since not all aspects of these rich and mutating relations have been adequately explored and written about.

BIBLIOGRAPHY

Nkrumah, Kwame. 1964. *Consciencism*. London: Heinemann.

Said, Edward W. 1994. *Culture and Imperialism*. New York: Vintage Books.

INDEX